SAVAGE

Don flipped the wall switch, flooding the kitchen with light, and his world exploded! His mind reeled as the orderly room seemed to swirl about and a shriek of horror lodged silently in his throat. *This couldn't be . . . !*

His wife lay on the floor as still as a statue. She faced him, her eyes closed, her lips slightly parted. Her arms were extended from her sides, each motionless hand lying about six inches from her hips. Her white sweater gapped open revealing her blouse. The thin shoulder strap of her purse was still looped over her upper arm.

Bright crimson blood pooled around her gray-blond hair and seeped in a stream reaching eighteen inches away. A gaping red wound in her throat had drained her life away.

The room was rapidly closing in on him. He desperately needed to gulp some clean night air, and try to clear his head. The scene didn't seem real. It had to be a horrible nightmare.

But he knew it wasn't . . .

Savage Vengeance

GARY C. KING
and DON LASSETER

P

PINNACLE BOOKS
KENSINGTON PUBLISHING CORP.

PINNACLE BOOKS are published by

Kensington Publishing Corp.
850 Third Avenue
New York, NY 10022

First Pinnacle Books Printing: April, 1996

Printed in the United States of America
10 9 8 7 6 5 4 3 2 1

Foreword

April 14, 1982

Speeding across the Snohomish River bridge, Detective Rick Bart felt grateful for the light traffic on Washington State Highway 9, a narrow, two-lane road twenty miles northeast of Seattle. He knew every curve and dip of the old highway, but in the deepening darkness, anything could happen. There had been enough tragedy already. He didn't need to add to it with a foolish accident.

The words he'd heard over the telephone just a few minutes earlier still seemed incredible. A triple homicide in the quiet countryside outside tiny Clearview? Three female victims found in one house, all of them nearly decapitated? A thousand questions ran through his mind. In five years as a homicide detective, Bart had seen his share of murders, but this report ranged far off the scale of everything he'd previously investigated.

Of course, Snohomish County had the usual killings. A drunken barroom brawl might explode into a shooting, or a domestic dispute could escalate into a strangling. Now and then, a gas station robber would go nuts and start pulling the trigger, or a wino might stab another homeless soul in a shadowy culvert by the Puget Sound waterfront. Most of the killings occurred close to Everett, the county seat. Such incidents had increased in recent years, causing the sheriff to double the size of the homicide team from two to four detectives.

Down Interstate 5, in the city, multiple murders or serial killings were not quite so rare. At Lake Sammamish and Issaquah, a law student named Ted Bundy had probably killed several young women. Confined on Florida's death row for sneaking into a sorority house and bludgeoning two young women to death, then ravaging and slitting the throat of a twelve-year-old girl, Bundy would never face a jury for the slayings in Washington. Seattle residents had endured more than one reign of terror while waiting for serial rapists and killers to be captured. At this very moment, the festering mind of another predator approached flash point, and in a few weeks the mutilated body of a young woman, the first in a long series, would be discovered south of Seattle in the Green River.

But Snohomish County hadn't experienced such savagery. The lush valleys, rolling, evergreen-covered hills, meandering river, and pristine towns seemed more suited to the ideal life painted by Norman Rockwell. Murder didn't fit. Most of the bad people sat in prison cells over in Monroe, a few miles to the east. The killers were confined two hundred miles away, behind the cold stone walls of Washington State Penitentiary at Walla Walla, some of them waiting for the hangman's rope.

Nevertheless, Rick Bart found himself speeding through the night toward a grisly triple homicide. One of the victims had been discovered lying in a pool of blood in the hallway, with a gaping throat wound. Two more lay in a bedroom, one of them nude, also with throats slashed.

Slowing at Clearview, nothing more than a crossroads containing a few stores and repair shops, Bart swung left and began a slow ascent between walls of dark evergreens lining both sides of 180th Street, S.E. Even on high beam, his headlights seemed inadequate. After dipping into a quarter-mile valley, Bart climbed one last hill, and pulled into a driveway easily identifiable by flashing blue and red lights and parked emergency vehicles.

Even with his experience in viewing gory crime scenes, he still wasn't prepared for what he was about to see.

One

November, 1973

Small caliber bullets whined past Rosalie Campbell's ankles and pinged off the gravel behind her. She knew in her heart that she was going to die. Rosalie cringed at the muzzle blasts belching orange flame each time the gaunt, wild-eyed man squeezed the pistol trigger. His towering frame, topped by a frizzy moon of wiry hair, stood silhouetted against the afternoon sun. He squinted down the barrel of the weapon, aimed it carefully in her direction, and grinned. Explosions echoed across the gravel pit, sounding like the thunder of hell to the trembling young woman.

As worried as she was about her own life, Rosalie anguished even more about the five-month-old fetus in her rounding belly. Five shots, then six, raised miniature dust clouds around her shoes. He'd ordered her to stand near a row of bottles lined up among millions of sparkling shards where men drank beer and proved their prowess with guns. Rusty cans on the slope behind her leaked light through countless ragged, round holes. She visualized a bullet entering her body and wondered if it would kill her immediately or cause a slow, agonizing death.

How could he be so heartless? Rosalie knew it was the booze. He always grew cold, violent and mean when he drank. Even so, how could he keep shooting? Seven shots, eight, then nine. Didn't he care that he was risking the lives of his bride of only four months and his own unborn child? Somewhere in the world of nice people, men were already shopping for gifts to place under

Christmas trees in a few weeks. But not Charles Rodman Campbell. He stood there, fifteen feet away, with a Budweiser in one hand, and his pistol in the other, firing deadly missiles that threatened to snuff out two lives, simultaneously. And laughing in that hideous, arrogant shriek of his. En route to the gravel pit, in his battered old pickup, he'd told her he was going to kill her. Now, Rosalie felt sure that he meant it.

Her life didn't exactly flash before her eyes, but she did catch herself reflecting back over the past few months, and wondered just what she'd seen in Charlie Campbell. For a while, he'd seemed so nice, sexy, and mature for his age. At eighteen, he was four years younger than Rosalie, but she thought her petite stature next to his lanky height compensated for the age difference. Rosalie, and the tiny daughter she'd had from a previous relationship, had been living with her parents, and she had wanted desperately to move out and start over. Charlie seemed different from the father of her first child, who had deserted her as soon as she became pregnant. She convinced herself that Campbell would make a fine husband, even though he sometimes drank a little too much. She chose to ignore his warning that it would be an "awful hard marriage." Nonsense, she thought, as they snuggled into bed. Their courtship, if it could be called that, had lasted a little over six months, and they were married on August 24, 1973. Shortly after the wedding, performed by a judge in Snohomish County, Washington, they'd moved to a rural hamlet called Brewster, on the eastern slope of the towering Cascades, nestled above a loop in the Columbia River. It should have been a utopian existence.

Rosalie had hoped for a cozy cottage, but found herself in a rotting tent smack in the middle of a shabby mobile home park, landscaped with battered old cars and trash. Few of the residents held jobs. Surrounded by natural beauty and clean air, it was an enclave of pain and sorrow.

The beatings began almost immediately.

At first, Rosalie's drunken husband pummeled her primarily in the abdomen. The bruises weren't noticeable that way. But the more he drank, the more careless his aim. Her face became his target, and the accumulating injuries reflected his anger. New bruises in black and blue replaced older ones that yellowed as they healed. With his knees pinning her shoulders down, Charlie used his fists on every part of her body. His flailing blows split her upper lip, leaving a scar that not only marred her appearance, but caused her to speak with a lisp thereafter.

Maybe he felt guilty about his broken marriage vows. She knew of his frequent dalliances with other women, but felt helpless to even protest.

Once, Rosalie worked up enough courage to actually make an attempt to escape the daily battering. After packing her few miserable rags, she walked out, found a cop, and described what Charlie had been doing. To her, the officer seemed apathetic. She didn't stop to think that if the small police department in Brewster made an arrest every time they received a complaint in the mobile home park, the place would have been emptied, and the jail crammed full. She later lamented, "So I ended up going back to him, and he beat me again when I came back."

Frustrated, frightened, and confused, Rosalie sought relief in the very source of Charlie's meanness. A few drinks eased the pain, and a few more anaesthetized the sorrow.

Rosalie prayed that a change of towns might give them a chance to start over. Leaving the tattered tent behind after just one week, Charlie and Rosalie moved to Wenatchee, thirty miles down the winding Columbia. But Charlie couldn't leave behind the virulent animosity raging inside him. Following a particularly painful beating, Rosalie once again tried to sneak off to beg for help from the police. She wandered along a country road, hoping that a patrol car would pass, but none came along. Overcome with a feeling of complete futility, she turned around to head home. As a child might do, she stopped to watch some tiny frogs in a pond. Bending over, she cupped her hand over one, scooped it up, and carried it home. When she stepped in the door, she had no explanation for her absence. Instead, she extended her hand, and showed her furious husband the captive frog. He slapped it away. She later told a friend, "He beat me for catching the frog. Once, he even beat me up for killing a fly."

After another move, this time to Edmonds, north of Seattle, where the ferry docks after crossing the Puget Sound, Rosalie felt marginally safer living close to his relatives. "We had a meeting with the parents to decide whether we should get a divorce, but they refused to help me leave him."

The ferocity of Charlie's blows to her head and stomach became unbearable. "He told me he wanted to kill my unborn child."

So Rosalie stood in the gravel pit, waiting expectantly for the mortal wound, the bullet that would end her misery and prevent the child from being born. Charles Campbell pulled the trigger until the firing pin slammed repeatedly on an empty chamber, gurgled his raucous laugh, grabbed Rosalie's wrist, and pulled her back to the pickup. She didn't know if she was relieved or disappointed.

On Christmas Eve, when other families gathered around trees to open gifts and celebrate in the warm spirit of harmony, Charlie celebrated by beating up his wife. Rosalie often felt sick during the first few months of her pregnancy, and not in the mood for sex. That didn't bother Charlie. Whenever he wanted it, he just grinned and took it anyway.

Charles Campbell continued to threaten the life of the unborn baby. He had unusual ideas about how to kill a fetus. "He raped me, forced me to have sex close to my delivery date. It caused my water bag to break which put me in labor."

In the brief respite of a hospital, on March 30, 1974, Rosalie delivered a baby girl by cesarean section. "When I came home," she bitterly recalled, "Charlie asked to see my stitches. I showed them to him. He pulled them out and caused me to hemorrhage."

While visiting her parents' home, which had a redwood deck built over a steep slope, Charlie found new amusement with the infant. To terrorize Rosalie, he held the tiny child out over the deck railing and threatened to drop her to the rocky ground twenty feet below. Screams of terror from his wife seemed to satisfy some sick hunger inside Campbell. He handed the baby back to her, unharmed. He was "possessed" she whispered to herself. The realization came to her that Charlie Campbell was actually turned on by violence.

Rosalie later recalled, "When the baby was about two or three months old, Charlie took us to an area near 212th Street in Edmonds. At the time, he drove a pickup truck with the passenger-side door handles off so I couldn't run or escape when we went places. I was usually weak from a beating. He had a syringe with one hundred hits of speed in it. He injected speed regularly and could take eighty hits at once. He pointed to a place off the road and told me he was going to bury my body there after I died from an overdose of speed he injected into me." Perhaps dissuaded by Rosalie asking what he planned to do with the baby, he didn't carry out the threat. "Instead, he injected the speed (into himself) and we left."

To reinforce his threats, Campbell often pulled a large hunting knife from beneath the pickup seat, where he kept it hidden. He had a fascination with big, sharp knives. "On one occasion," Rosalie remembered, "I found him throwing a butcher knife at the baby while she was in her play pen. She was about two months old, and he laughed when it would barely miss her."

That weird laugh of his frayed Rosalie's nerves. "When he used to beat me, he would laugh out loud. I remember screaming one time, 'Oh, God,' as he was beating me."

Campbell's reply sickened her. "God is not going to help you now."

She decided once and for all that her husband was "evil" or "possessed." "My marriage," she said, "could be summed up in one word: hell."

Early in Rosalie's relationship with Charles Campbell, she made the mistake of calling him a name that sent him into frenzied violence. In a moment of recklessness, she called him "punk." It triggered something deep inside him that reacted like a dropped vial of nitroglycerine. He told her that he hated that word, and to emphasize it, he slammed her to the floor and administered a new array of bruises over her aching body.

Eventually, Rosalie grew bold enough to call Campbell a punk just to aggravate him, especially if he was sloppy drunk and incapable of beating her. "It was my only way of getting even," she explained.

Many battered women never find the exit from their doomed relationships, but Rosalie Campbell finally had enough. On August 22, 1974, after several weeks of separation and just two days before the first anniversary of the marriage, she divorced Charles Rodman Campbell.

Even though the ties of marriage were finally broken, and she no longer lived with her brutal husband, he still insisted on seeing his child periodically. The violence hadn't ended.

Two

Vinny Garafolo, manager of the Pizza Palace restaurant in Renton, near the southern tip of Lake Washington, needed a new cook. On Saturday, November 9, 1974, he interviewed three men. The third and final man seemed like he would work out okay, so Garafolo glanced down at the application form, read the name, and told Dan Leslie Kyle that he was hired. He explained the dress code policy to Kyle, pointing out that male employees must wear either a solid red shirt, or a white one, along with trousers other than blue jeans.

A few days later, Garafolo frowned when Kyle walked in wearing a red plaid shirt and jeans. But the new employee was young, only twenty, so maybe he didn't really understand the necessity of a good business image. Once more, the patient manager, with a touch of strain in his voice, pulled Kyle aside and reminded him of the requirement. Kyle shrugged and nodded agreement.

In spite of Kyle's variance from the dress code, and humorless attitude, Garafolo thought the new cook reasonably competent and reliable. In his written application for the job, Kyle had expressed an interest in becoming a manager. Garafolo decided to teach Kyle how to close out the cash register at night, count the money, and either secure it in the safe or make a night deposit at People's bank nearby. The youth readily accepted the additional responsibility.

Another employee, Terry Ortlip, twenty-two, who drove a small van to deliver the pizzas, waited a couple of weeks before befriending Kyle. When he felt comfortable with the tall, rangy cook, Ortlip learned that Kyle lived with his mother. If they could find a house with cheap rent, close to the Pizza Palace, Ortlip suggested, he and Kyle could split the rent, walk to work, and save a bundle of money. Kyle agreed. Within a few days, they located the perfect place, and signed an agreement with the land-lady on December 8. The house wouldn't be ready for occupancy for a few more days, so Kyle invited his new buddy to spend a night with him at his mother's place. They moved in together on December 12.

The following afternoon, both men were scheduled to start work at five P.M. They walked to work together, stopping en route at a liquor store for a bottle of tequila they planned to share when the shift ended.

Ortlip made his final delivery at one-forty-five A.M. and re-turned to the restaurant. He later recalled, "As near as I could tell, there was about one hundred and twenty dollars that I had taken in that night. Then I began to help clean up the restaurant." He completed his work at three-thirty A.M. "I told Dan, who was the only one still there, that I was going home. When I left, he was still accounting for that day's money."

After just a few hours' sleep, Ortlip felt his roommate jostle him awake. Kyle explained that he wanted to go up to Bothell, near the north tip of the lake (which forms the eastern border of Seattle) to visit a girlfriend. "He wanted to borrow my guitar to play it for her. I told him he could. The guitar was a Lyle, six-string acoustical." Kyle picked up the instrument, left, and Ortlip went back to sleep.

Upon Vinny Garafolo's arrival at the Pizza Palace at ten-forty-five that morning, he opened the safe to retrieve money for the cash register, and couldn't believe what he saw. There should have been at least $500 to "start the till and provide change and petty cash." Someone had completely cleaned it out. Immediately suspicious of Kyle, he raced to the bank, and found that Dan had dutifully filled out a receipt for the night deposit for $1,196.07. Unfortunately, he hadn't bothered to put the cash with it.

When Garafolo managed to wake Kyle's roommate, Ortlip, he

e Institute of Geological Sciences
s formed by the
orporation of the Geological Survey of Great Britain
d the Museum of Practical Geology
th Overseas Geological Surveys
d is a constituent body of the
atural Environment Research Council

irst published 1935

econd edition 1948

hird edition 1971

SBN 11 880152 X

Front Cover

The Eildon Hills near Melrose, from Scott's View. The hills are the denuded remains of a composite laccolith of trachytic rocks intruded into the Upper Old Red Sandstone in Carboniferous times.

Plate I—*Frontispiece* (*overleaf*)

Siccar Point, Berwickshire. The south-eastern side of the headland is formed of Silurian greywackes and shales capped by red sandstones and breccias of the Upper Old Red Sandstone. The older rocks are strongly folded on east-north-eastward axes, the beds on the headland dipping very steeply towards the camera. The red sandstones rest on a highly irregular surface of the greywackes which has a general northward slope parallel to the relatively gentle dip of the sandstones themselves. The gully left of centre follows a fault which throws the sandstones down towards the south-east. (Geol. Surv. Photo. No D.1228).

NATURAL ENVIRONMENT RESEARCH COUNCIL

Institute of Geological Sciences

British Regional Geology

The South of Scotlan

(THIR

By D. C. Greig,

with

G. A. Goodlet, MA, G. I. Lumsden, BSc,

W. Tu

EDINBURGH

HER MAJESTY'S STATIONERY OFFICE

1971

FOREWORD TO THE THIRD EDITION

Few alterations had been made to 'The South of Scotland' since the first edition by the late Dr J. Pringle was published in 1935. The chapters concerned with the Lower Palaeozoic systems have now been completely revised to take account of the revolution of ideas concerning the stratigraphy and structure of these systems and also the large volume of other research which has been undertaken in recent years. Furthermore important contributions to the understanding of the Carboniferous and post-Tertiary geology of the region had rendered obsolete most of the original descriptions of these systems. Recent developments in structural geology, sedimentology, and geochronology which have a relevance to the rocks of the South of Scotland have been incorporated in the appropriate sections of this edition, and the opportunity has also been taken to bring up-to-date the bibliography of the regional geology. The lists given are by no means exhaustive, but are designed as an introduction and to guide the reader to further relevant literature.

Mr Greig has revised the chapters dealing with the Lower Palaeozoic, New Red Sandstone, Tertiary and the economic geology and has also compiled the whole account. The chapter on the Old Red Sandstone has been prepared by Mr W. Tulloch, those on the Carboniferous and on the Volcanic Rocks of Carboniferous Age by Mr G. I. Lumsden, and the late Mr G. A. Goodlet contributed the account of the Pleistocene and Post-Glacial periods.

INSTITUTE OF GEOLOGICAL SCIENCES,   K. C. DUNHAM
EXHIBITION ROAD,   *Director*
SOUTH KENSINGTON,
LONDON, S.W.7
20th May, 1971

An EXHIBIT illustrating the Geology and Scenery of the district described in this volume is set out in the Geological Museum, Exhibition Road, South Kensington, London SW7

CONTENTS

ILLUSTRATIONS
Figures in Text

Plates

I. INTRODUCTION

Summary of Geology

The South of Scotland is the region lying between the English border and the Southern Upland Fault, which crosses the country from Loch Ryan to Dunbar. For convenience of description an area of Lower Palaeozoic rocks north of the Fault near Girvan is also included in this account. (Plate XIII).

The geological formations present are:

RECENT and PLEISTOCENE	{	Soils, blown sand, peat, river and lake alluvia. Raised beach deposits. Solifluxion deposits. Fluvio-glacial sand and gravel. Glacial moraines and boulder clay.
TERTIARY		Tholeiite dykes.
NEW RED SANDSTONE	{	Trias. Annan Series: red sandstones, shales, and marls. 'Permian'. Red desert-sandstones and breccias. Lavas and agglomerates.

Unconformity

CARBONIFEROUS	Coal Measures	Sandstones, shales, mudstones, coal seams, and seat-earths. Some thin marine mudstones in Canonbie area. Late quartz-dolerite dykes.

Non-sequence or unconformity

	Millstone Grit Series	Upper beds mainly sandstones with many seat-earths and thin coals, bauxitic clays at Thornhill. Some thin marine shales and limestones. Lower beds of Yoredale facies, sandstones, mudstones, limestones, coal seams and seat-earths. Thin basaltic lava at Loch Ryan.
	Carboniferous Limestone Series	Upper beds of Yoredale facies, sandstones, mudstones, limestones, coal seams, and seat-earths. Lower beds mainly sandstones, with mudstones and thin cementstones. Basaltic lavas and tuffs, volcanic vents and acid and basic intrusions, especially near base.
OLD RED SANDSTONE	Upper Old Red Sandstone	Conglomerates, sandstones, marls, cornstones.

Unconformity

	Lower Old Red Sandstone	Conglomerates, sandstones, cornstones, lavas, agglomerates, acid intrusions.

1

Unconformity

SILURIAN	Wenlock	Riccarton and Raeberry Castle beds; grey-wackes, shales and fossiliferous grits. Upper part of Dailly Series near Girvan; shales and fossiliferous grits.
	Llandovery	Birkhill Shales in Moffat area. Gala Group; greywackes, flags, and shales, with bands of conglomerate and grit. Dailly Series (lower part) and Newlands Series in Girvan area; greywackes, flags, shales, limestones, and conglomerates.
ORDOVICIAN	Ashgill	Upper Hartfell Shales in Moffat area. Shales and greywackes with limestones and con-glomerates elsewhere, e.g. upper part of Portpatrick Group. Upper part of Ard-millan Series of Girvan; sandstones and shales, with limestones and conglomerate.
	Caradoc	Lower Hartfell Shales and Glenkiln Shales in Moffat area. Shales, greywackes, and con-glomerates elsewhere, e.g. lower part of Portpatrick Group and Kirkcolm and Corsewall groups. Lower part of Ardmillan Series and Barr Series of Girvan; conglom-erates, sandstones, shales, limestones, and greywackes. Lavas, tuffs, and intrusions.
	?Llandeilo	Lavas, cherts, and mudstones.
	Unconformity	
	Arenig	Lavas, pyroclastic rocks, cherts, and mud-stones; basic and acid intrusions.

The geological map (Plate XIII) shows clearly that by far the greater part of the region is occupied by Ordovician and Silurian sediments, which form the broad zone of dissected high land known as the Southern Uplands. The oldest, Arenig, rocks occur principally between the Southern Upland Fault and Girvan, and elsewhere form only small isolated outcrops. The map also shows that these Lower Palaeozoic rocks lie in zones which become progres-sively younger towards the south-east, but, as will be seen in Chapter 2, the disposition of the strata is much more complicated than this broad pattern suggests. In general terms the Old Red Sandstone and younger rocks form a low-lying fringe on the south-east side of the Uplands, but in places they occur in valleys and broad depressions within the Uplands themselves. The Lower Old Red Sandstone lavas along the border south of Kelso occupy high ground which is part of the Cheviot Hills. In the north-east the small area of Lower Carboniferous rocks south-east of Dunbar constitutes an extension of the adjacent large area of similar rocks to the west of that town.

The absence of sediments younger than those of the New Red Sandstone does not imply that no such rocks were ever deposited in the area, but any which were have been removed by subsequent erosion.

Physical Features

The geological diversity introduced into the Lower Palaeozoic by the granitic intrusions of the south-west is reflected by a more rugged topography in Wigtownshire and Kirkcudbrightshire, where rock-ridges, corries, and hill-lochs participate in a landscape of almost Highland aspect. Here are the highest hills of the region, the Merrick, 842 m, and the Rhinns of Kells, 813 m, composed of metamorphosed sediments close to the Loch Doon Granite. Cairnsmore of Carsphairn, east of Loch Doon, and Cairnsmore of Fleet, to the south, are granite hills over 700 m in height. The highest hills of unaltered Lower Palaeozoic rock lie near the headwaters of Tweed and Annan, where Broad Law, White Coomb, Hart Fell, and other summits all exceed 800 m. The summit-levels decline towards the north-east, the highest hills of the Moorfoot and Lammermuir hills, south and south-east of Edinburgh, being Blackhope Scar, 651 m, and Meikle Says Law, 533 m. North-east of Nithsdale the characteristic smoothly rounded form of the Upland landscape results from the general uniformity of rock-type in the Lower Palaeozoic sediments. In the low ground adjacent to the Solway and in the lower reaches of the Tweed the scenery is locally diversified by geological variations. The granite of Criffell (Plate VIB), the intrusive trachytes of the Eildon Hills (Front cover and Plate XIB), and various intrusive rocks of the Jedburgh area all form isolated hills of varying extent.

The principal drainage of the region is southwards towards the Solway and eastwards, by the Tweed, to the North Sea. In the south-west the rivers Stinchar, Girvan, and Doon flow northwards and westwards into the Firth of Clyde. The Clyde itself rises well within the region, whereas the headwaters of the Tweed system lie in part in the Midland Valley. In general the main watershed between the Midland Valley drainage and that of the Solway–Tweed lies close to the north-western limit of the Southern Uplands, and the highest ground of the Uplands is in the same area. Recognition of these facts has led to the view that the main south-eastward-flowing rivers are but the beheaded remnants of greater ancestors which had their sources far to the north-west. Moreover it has long been realized that the main directions of drainage are unrelated to the outcrop pattern of the rocks, that the streams appear to have been superimposed from an overlying surface of a different geological nature, now completely eroded away, and that in places, for example near Biggar, the main watershed lies in a wide flat valley which clearly at one time carried through-drainage. The drainage pattern is believed by George to have been initiated in late Tertiary times on a benched surface formed possibly during a prolonged period of intermittently falling sea-level. A view expressed earlier by Linton is that the initial surface was an eastward slope of Cretaceous rocks extending from the Grampians to northern England and dating from the later stages of the Cretaceous period.

There is considerable evidence of river-capture in the upper reaches of the Nith, Annan, Clyde, and Tweed. The upper part of the Nith follows an anomalous course, leaving and then re-entering the Southern Uplands in a broad U-turn past New Cumnock towards the Carboniferous outlier of Sanquhar. George describes the Nith as a composite stream, the upper section of which originally flowed northwards towards Cumnock, and the Sanquhar section north-westwards as part of the Upper Clyde, which itself at that time probably joined the Tweed by way of the Biggar Gap. The antiquity of the present course of the upper Nith is shown by the recognition of the buried channel of its pre-Glacial or inter-Glacial ancestor flowing south-eastwards through the New Cumnock Gap.

The Lyne flows south-eastwards from its source in the Pentlands across the lower land beyond West Linton, before entering the Ordovician uplands to join the Tweed above Peebles. Prior to their capture by the Clyde the streams near Carstairs may have followed a similar course towards the Tweed. The rivers of the Tweed basin may be guided by Caledonian tectonic trends, either on east-north-easterly lines or at right angles to them, and in parts of its lower reaches the system appears to follow the axial region of a broad down-warp which also probably originated in Caledonian times.

History of Research

Interest in the geology of the South of Scotland goes back to the very begin-nings of the science, notably to the examination by James Hutton in the late 18th century of the unconformities near Jedburgh, and at Siccar Point (Plate I) on the Berwickshire coast. His interpretation of the phenomena displayed at these localities was embodied in his *Theory of the Earth*, pub-lished in 1795, and incorporates principles fundamental to scientific geology. The earliest laboratory experiments in the production of folds were carried out by his friend and collaborator, Sir James Hall, inspired by the impressive folding of the Silurian rocks of the Berwickshire coast (Plate IIB). Sir James also recorded his views that the granite of Loch Doon had been emplaced from below, as a liquid, into the Silurian rocks, and that some of the con-volutions of these rocks were due to the dynamic effects of this process. Early discoveries of graptolites in the Lower Palaeozoic shales were described by Carrick Moore and Nicol in 1840 and 1841, and both these authors made significant subsequent contributions to the geology of the Lower Palaeozoic rocks, which included stratigraphical correlation with Wales and structural interpretation. Further advances in this field were made by Harkness and Salter, and in 1850 their work was complemented by investigations by Murchison and Sedgwick, with their knowledge of the Lower Palaeozoic systems of Wales and the Welsh Border.

The early work of the Geological Survey in Scotland led to the publication in the 1860's of accounts of areas of Ayrshire, East Lothian, and Berwickshire, prepared by Sir Archibald Geikie and his staff. During this period the Survey was also engaged in the Leadhills area and between Moffat and the south-west coast.

These researches had raised numerous problems of succession, correlation, and structure within the Lower Palaeozoic rocks to many of which the extended and detailed work of Charles Lapworth was to offer a solution. Between his account in 1870 of the Galashiels area and that of Ballantrae published in 1889 Lapworth built up a structural hypothesis concerning the Southern Uplands based largely on field observation and the study of graptolite faunas, which was explained in detail in the second part of the latter paper. His hypothesis was generally accepted until the recent phase of research began in the 1950's. Lapworth's investigations were succeeded from 1888 by a re-examination of the Southern Uplands by Peach and Horne of the Geological Survey. This work culminated in the publication in 1899 of a comprehensive memoir on the Silurian rocks of Scotland, from which the progress of research so far described has been condensed. As a work of reference to geological localities and to earlier literature this publication is of unparalleled value.

Lower Palaeozoic research in the first half of the present century was confined largely to the Girvan and Ballantrae areas. Brachiopods and trilobites were described by Reed in a number of papers and Balsillie studied the Ballantrae Igneous Complex. Other important contributions were made by Dewey and Flett, Begg, Lamont and Bulman. The Ballantrae rocks were most recently described in two papers by Bailey and McCallien. The Geological Survey memoir of 1949 on Central Ayrshire includes a discussion of the general classification of the Ordovician and an account of the stratigraphy of the Craighead Inlier.

Since 1950 there have been several local investigations using modern techniques in sedimentology, petrology, palaeontology, and structural geology, from which has evolved a view of Lower Palaeozoic structure and stratigraphy different in essence from that of Lapworth. Details of this continuing work are given in Chapter 2.

Prior to the 1920's studies of the Old Red Sandstone in the region were in the main of a general type, either forming but part of the descriptions of large areas, as in Geikie's publications on ancient volcanoes and on the Old Red Sandstone of Western Europe, or dealing in a general way with the rocks of the system in a part of the region. Between 1887 and 1890, however, appeared three detailed accounts of metamorphic and igneous phenomena in Kirkcudbrightshire and Berwickshire. A comprehensive account of the Galloway granites, with some details of other intrusive masses, is given by Teall in the Geological Survey memoir of 1899 on the Silurian rocks of Scotland. Arid conditions during the deposition of the Upper Old Red Sandstone were suggested by Goodchild in a paper of 1903. In the same year a lithological account of the Upper Old Red Sandstone near Canonbie was given by Peach and Horne, and the same rocks as they occur in East Lothian were described in the 1910 memoir on that area by Clough and his collaborators.

In subsequent years research work has been directed much more towards the igneous rocks of the Lower Old Red Sandstone than to any other parts of the system. In the late 1920's a number of papers dealt with the smaller intrusions, and in the 1930's the large granite masses of the south-west were described in a series of papers by Gardiner and Reynolds, Deer, and Malcolm MacGregor. Studies of smaller intrusions were published during the succeeding decade. In the years prior to 1939 members of the Geological Survey were engaged in the eastern Borders, and published several reports on the Upper Old Red Sandstone sediments and associated igneous rocks. Since 1950 a number of specialized investigations have been carried out in such fields as geochemistry, geophysics, radiometric dating, metamorphism and sedimentology. The large intrusions of the south-west have continued to attract the major part of the research, but important new palaeontological finds have been reported from Duns, and the Geological Survey has published a comprehensive account of the Upper Old Red Sandstone in the Langholm area.

Much of the early work on the Carboniferous system was done by officers of the Geological Survey. The Canonbie Coalfield was described in 1903 by Peach and Horne in the paper already mentioned, and in 1910 the coastal area south-east of Dunbar was described in the East Lothian memoir by Clough and his colleagues. The first detailed account of the outliers at Sanquhar and Thornhill was given by Simpson and Richey in 1936, and the report of a wartime resurvey of the Canonbie Coalfield by Barrett and Richey was published in 1945.

Since the war there has been detailed study by Craig and Nairn of the outcrops on the Solway coast, and resurveys of the Langholm area and of the Sanquhar outlier by the Geological Survey. Knowledge of the Carboniferous geology of the Canonbie area was greatly increased by the Geological Survey's deep borehole at Archerbeck, described in 1961 by Lumsden and Wilson. Little has been published on the Carboniferous rocks of Berwickshire apart from a recent description of the sandstone sedimentation. The relevant results of the Geological Survey's recent resurvey of East Lothian are incorporated in this account. A valuable description of the region as a whole was given by George in his 1958 account of the Lower Carboniferous palaeogeography of the British Isles

A general description of the volcanic rocks of Carboniferous age was given in 1897 by Geikie in his account of the ancient volcanoes of Britain. In two papers published in 1914 and 1920 Lady McRobert described the igneous rocks around Melrose and in the country south-westwards to Langholm and Canonbie. An account of the Kelso Traps by Eckford and Ritchie was published in 1939, and detailed accounts of the Birrenswark Lavas by Pallister and by Elliott appeared in 1952 and 1960. Additional descriptions of igneous rocks in Roxburghshire were given by Tomkeieff in the 1950's. The igneous rocks of the Langholm district are fully described in the Geological Survey memoir on that area, published in 1967.

The distinctive nature of the New Red Sandstone sediments was noted by Binney in 1856, but the principal stratigraphical accounts are those of Simpson and Richey in 1936 on the Sanquhar and Thornhill basins, and of Horne and Gregory in 1916 and Barrett in 1942 on the Annan basin. Studies of igneous intrusions by Scott and by Walker were published in 1915 and 1925. In recent years there have been gravity surveys of the Dumfries and Stranraer areas, published in 1960 and 1963.

Research into the problems of the Tertiary igneous rocks has in most cases dealt with the South of Scotland only as part of the Tertiary Volcanic province of Scotland and Northern Ireland. In 1880 Geikie published petrographic details of the Eskdalemuir dyke and presented a general hypothesis concerning the genesis of the Tertiary igneous rocks. Elliott's account of the same dyke, published in 1956, is in some ways complementary to Geikie's, with additional and more specialized petrological discussion. The Geological Survey memoir on Central Ayrshire, published in 1949, includes details of intrusions in a small area between the Southern Upland Fault and the Cairnsmore of Carsphairn Granite.

The first account on modern lines of the glaciation of the South of Scotland was given in 1926 by Charlesworth, and in 1956 George described the development of the drainage pattern of the central part of the Southern Uplands. Otherwise research in the last few decades has been more specialized in terms of the geographical area studied or of the scope of the subject. The main fields of study have been phenomena of glacial retreat by Sissons and Price, palaeobotany and radio-carbon age determination by Erdtman, Mitchell, and Jardine, and post-glacial changes in sea-level by Sissons and Donner. Sand and gravel deposits have been studied from both a philosophical and an economic point of view by Bailey and Eckford and by Goodlet. In its recent and current work in Ayrshire, the Langholm area, East Lothian, and Berwickshire the Geological Survey has paid considerable attention to the distribution of Glacial and Post-Glacial deposits and to their historical interpretation.

Research in the field of economic geology has been carried out principally by officers of the Geological Survey and by individuals engaged by them for the purpose. It is published in two main phases, the Special Reports on the Mineral Resources, which were initiated during the period of the Great War, and the Wartime Pamphlets which arose from the exigencies of the Second World War. In more recent years the Geological Survey has published a complete record of sources of underground water in the region, and reports on sources of road aggregate and on sand and gravel. In addition to the work of the Geological Survey the Leadhills–Wanlockhead district was studied in the 1950's by Temple and by Mackay and his colleagues, and research into the resources and uses of peat was promoted by the Department of Agriculture and Fisheries for Scotland.

2. LOWER PALAEOZOIC ROCKS

Lower Palaeozoic rocks of the Ordovician and Silurian systems form the Southern Uplands, the principal physical feature of the South of Scotland. In contrast to the younger formations the beds are strongly folded, the predominant trend of the structures being between north-east and east-north-east. These rocks are mainly greywackes, a form of sandstone with a variety of mineral and rock fragments and a paste-like matrix of the same material, and finer-grained siltstones and shales. They were deposited on the floor of an elongate marine trough, which was at the time evolving in response to the deep-seated stresses of the Caledonian earth-movements and to the weight of the sediments themselves. The early Ordovician rocks exposed in places between north-west Scotland and North Wales give no clear indication of the form of the area of deposition at that time, but in late Ordovician time and in the Silurian, when the rocks of the Southern Uplands were being laid down, the trough, or geosyncline, appears to have extended from south-west to north-east between fluctuating shore-lines which lay in the Scottish Highlands and the English Midlands. The greywackes and shales are of deep-water origin. The shales are most persistently developed along a north-eastward 'axis' passing through Moffat, which has been interpreted as the central deep of the geosyncline, remote from sources of sediment, but may represent the line of a submarine ridge too high to receive the greywacke material.

In recent years it has become recognized that the distribution and deposition of the greywackes was effected by submarine turbidity currents which carried large quantities of rock material, and were able to persist, and to preserve their individual identity, over considerable distances. They are believed to have originated on the steep margin of the continental shelf, perhaps under the influence of earthquakes, climatic variations, or as a consequence of gradually increasing instability. As a current gradually lost momentum it began to deposit sediment and quickly built up a bed of sand which, in the general case, became progressively finer in grain from the base to the top. The currents and the material carried by them in many cases eroded the soft material on the sea-floor so that the sand was in time deposited on a channelled or grooved surface. As a result the under-surface of many a bed of greywacke is now seen to be intricately patterned by the projecting casts of such channels (Plate V), most commonly flute-casts and groove-casts, the latter caused by the dragging of rock-fragments along the sub-stratum. The direction of current is parallel to the elongation of the casts, and the bulbous ends of the flute-casts mark the upstream direction. The most common direction of flow in the Southern Uplands is either north-eastward or south-westward, parallel to the elongation of the basin. Load-casts are random-oriented bulbous features developed at the base of a greywacke by the downward and sideways squeezing of the underlying mud under the weight of the material above. Transverse current ripple-marks often occur on the

8

upper surface of a greywacke, in the comparatively fine-grained material (Plate IVв). Organic tracks may occur on the upper surfaces of greywacke units. All these structures, which have been described in detail by Kuenen, Walton and others, are of prime value in determining the tops and bottoms of the beds, which are seldom self-evident.

The stratigraphy of the Lower Palaeozoic rocks of the region was first described by Lapworth in the 1870's and '80's, and his principles were adopted, and extended over the whole region, by Peach and Horne in the comprehensive Geological Survey memoir of 1899. Lapworth's stratigraphical interpretation was based primarily on the succession of graptolites which he found in shales at certain localities, but, recognizing that the main mass of the rock was unfossiliferous, he formed the opinion that the recurrence of shales with similar faunas must represent repetition of the same bands of rock, brought about by folding. In the Southern Uplands these shales were thought to crop out in elongate boat-shaped anticlinal inliers. Tight folding is often conspicuous in the fossiliferous shales to which Lapworth devoted much of his attention, and the rocks in general were thus considered to be affected by such folds, so that relatively thin series of steeply dipping, oft-repeated beds were regarded as forming the broad formational outcrops of the Southern Uplands. Open folding superimposed on these tight structures was thought to be responsible for the present disposition of the major formations, the Ordovician rocks in the north-west being exposed in the axial region of an anticlinorium, the Leadhills Endocline, and the Silurian rocks being preserved to the southeast in the complementary synclinorium, the Hawick Exocline (Fig. 1). The three parallel outcrops of Ordovician, Llandovery, and Wenlock rocks were described respectively as the Northern, Central, and Southern belts.

Research carried out in different parts of the region during the last 20 years has prompted the widely held opinion that Lapworth's general interpretation of the structure, and in consequence his views on formational thicknesses and some of his stratigraphical conclusions, are incorrect. The new interpretation owes much to the advances in sedimentology and the study of sedimentation structures referred to above, in correctly determining the order of succession of strata. The broad structural pattern now envisaged for the whole of the Southern Uplands is one of alternate zones of steeply dipping beds, becoming younger to the north-west, and of closely folded beds, involving no great thickness of rock, in which the *faltenspiegel*[1] is horizontal or dips at a low angle to the south-east. The effect (Fig. 1) is thus of a series of monoclines or grossly asymmetrical anticlines, facing towards the northwest, which, if uninterrupted, would lead to successively younger rocks coming to outcrop in that direction. The fact that, in broad terms, the opposite is the case is explained by the occurrence, often at the boundaries between the structural zones just described, of large faults with downthrow to the southeast, which outweigh the effect of the folding. Several of these faults are visible and have been described in detail.

With much of the area still to be re-examined in the light of the new techniques it is not yet possible to present a comprehensive revised description of the Lower Palaeozoic and indeed it is clear that there remain major

---

[1] *faltenspiegel*—In tightly folded beds, a surface tangential to any one stratum across the crests or troughs of individual folds. A 'generalized' bedding-plane.

B

South of Scotland

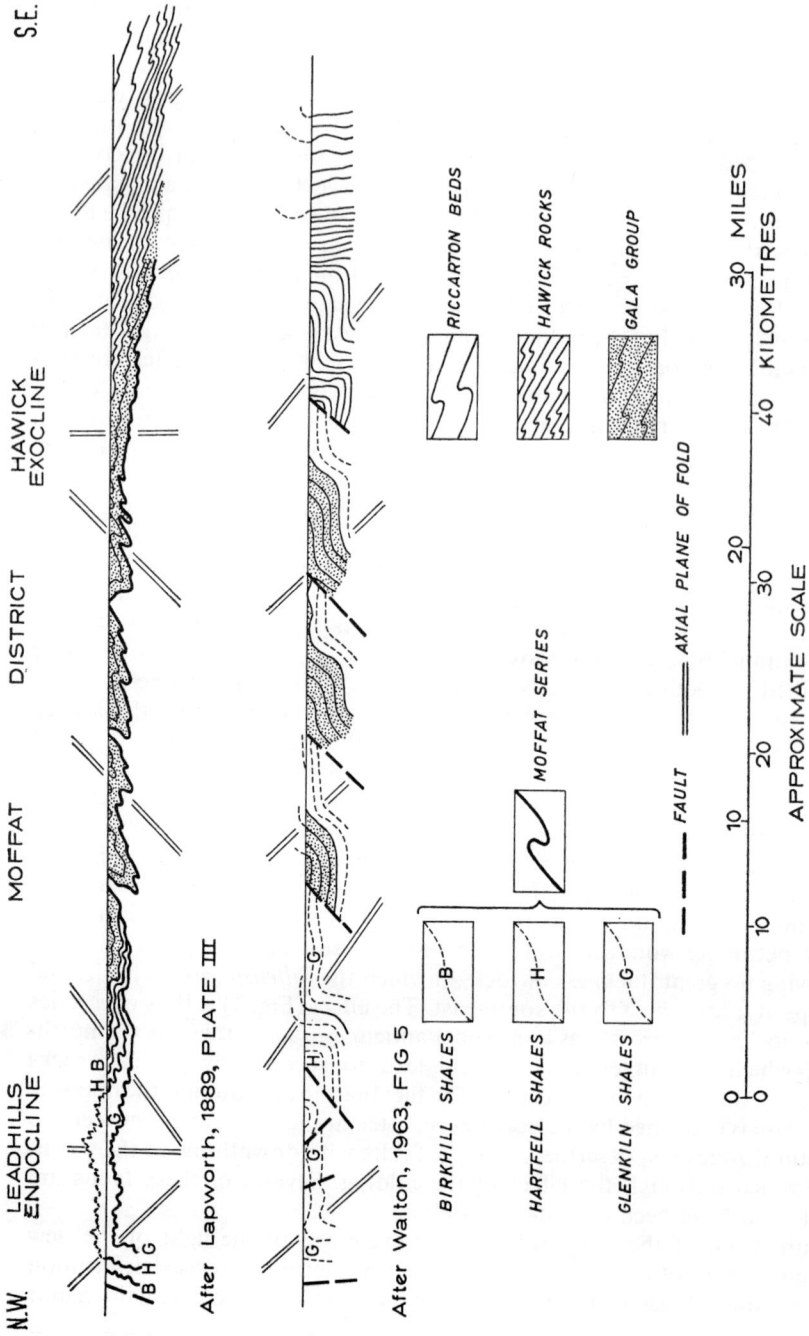

Fig. 1. *Schematic cross-sections from the Southern Upland Fault to the Solway Firth showing alternative interpretations of the structure of the Lower Palaeozoic rocks*

problems of correlation upon which considerable differences of opinion exist. The stratigraphical position of the unfossiliferous Hawick Rocks (p. 35) is an important example of current controversy. Much of the difficulty in the solution of these problems arises from the generally sparse exposure of rock in the Uplands. It is often very difficult, too, to assess the importance, or even to recognize the occurrence, of strike-faults, which collectively play a major part in the structural pattern.

The broad structural pattern in the Southern Uplands is clearly due to horizontal compression in a north-north-westerly to south-south-easterly direction, resulting in folding along east-north-easterly axes and the development of strike-faults. This compression is a late expression of the Caledonian orogeny, which was responsible in several Lower Palaeozoic phases for much of the deformation of the rocks of the Highlands and for the development of the geosyncline in which the sediments of the Southern Uplands were deposited. In recent years detailed structural studies in a number of areas have shown that several tectonic phases are represented.

In each case the main folding, and usually the earliest that can be readily studied, has arisen from a near-horizontal compression in a direction between south-east and south. In some areas this force has tightened up or contorted pre-existing folds formed under broadly similar stress systems and possibly not significantly different in age. Later Caledonian phases are recognized locally, as in Wigtownshire where folds resulting from a north–south compression lie in zones parallel to the prevailing east-north-easterly strike. Near Girvan early folding and thrusting is thought to have led to resistance to continuing vertical relief of pressure and to the development of wrench-faults and horizontal fold-faults. The latest Caledonian movements are responsible for the unconformity between the Lower and Upper Old Red Sandstone.

Reversed strike-faults and subsequent wrench-faults are widely developed in association with the main folding and there is widespread evidence of the later re-activation of many faults under different stress conditions. The Southern Upland Fault, which however may not have originated until the Lower–Upper Old Red Sandstone interval, presents a notable example of re-activation. In the Galloway peninsula it is mapped as a normal fault but there are also indications of later strike-slip movement. In upper Nithsdale there is evidence of normal displacement in the Pleistocene. There is some controversy as to the tectonic processes responsible for the many oblique-slip faults and for many of the complexities of folding, and in consequence as to the detailed tectonic history of the region.

Although they lie within the Midland Valley the Lower Palaeozoic rocks of the Ballantrae and Girvan area (Figs. 2 and 3) are described here since they were originally studied by Lapworth in relation to those of the Southern Uplands, to which they are physically adjacent. Whereas the late Ordovician and Silurian rocks of the Southern Uplands are rarely of shallow-water origin those of Girvan are predominantly so, having apparently been deposited in an archipelago of islands of Arenig rock. Extensive outcrops of the Arenig are restricted to this area. For clarity the contrasting rocks of the two areas are described separately.

3. ORDOVICIAN

The Ordovician System in Britain is divided into a number of series which take their names from localities in Wales, Shropshire, and the Lake District. Graptolite studies begun by Lapworth at Moffat in the 1870's have led to the further subdivision of the system into thirteen zones, each with a characteristic assemblage of graptolites, and on this basis the rocks of the South of Scotland can be fitted into the classification, as shown in the table opposite. Peach and Horne recognized the stratigraphical break between the Arenig and Caradoc rocks only in the Girvan area, but it is now widely, though not universally, accepted that the break exists throughout the Southern Uplands. It has been suggested however that it is more apparent than real, the Llanvirn and Llandeilo rocks being unfossiliferous, and Llandeilo rocks have recently been reported to occur at several localities.

An outstanding feature of the Caradoc Series, first pointed out by Lapworth, is the change which takes place in the rocks as they are followed from Girvan to Moffat. At Girvan there are at least 2400 m of neritic rocks, conglomerates, sandstones, shales, and shelly limestones, which are abruptly replaced beyond the River Stinchar, some 8 km to south-east, by an equally thick series of greywackes, with conglomerates, spilitic lavas, and cherts. Greywackes with black graptolitic shales pass, across the width of the Northern Belt, into a thinner and predominantly shaly succession which reaches its ultimate expression in the Moffat area, where the whole series is represented by 18 m of shales and cherts. The same type of change is seen in the Ashgill Series and in the lower part of the succeeding Llandovery Series, but in these formations equivalent stages in the transition from a greywacke to a shale succession occur progressively farther to the south. Less conclusive evidence is seen of a complementary reversal of this change as the beds are followed south-eastwards from Moffat.

Arenig Rocks: Ballantrae Igneous Complex

The Ballantrae Igneous Complex comprises a group of spilitic lavas and pyroclastic rocks, with associated cherts and fossiliferous shales, and a number of major and minor intrusions. These rocks crop out on the Ayrshire coast between Ballantrae and Kennedy's Pass and extend inland for some 5 to 10 km to the north-east (Fig. 3). The Middle Arenig age of some of the lavas is proved by the occurrence in associated black shales of several species of the genus *Tetragraptus* and of *Didymograptus extensus,* all characteristic of the Zone of *D. extensus.*

The lavas and pyroclastics are intensely folded and are typically exposed at Bennane Head where the succession is:

Series	Zones	Moffat Area	Girvan Area	Northern Belt	Geological Survey (Peach and Horne) 1899
Ashgill	*Dicellograptus anceps* / *Dicellograptus complanatus*	Upper Hartfell Shales	Ardmillan Series	Lowther Shales with conglomerates and greywackes. Black shales passing laterally into greywackes, shales, and conglomerates. Some limestones. Volcanic rocks in middle zone	Caradoc
	Pleurograptus linearis / *Dicranograptus clingani* / *Climacograptus wilsoni*	Lower Hartfell Shales			
Caradoc	*Climacograptus peltifer* / *Nemagraptus gracilis*	Glenkiln Shales	Barr Series	Black shales passing north and west into grits, greywackes, and shales. Volcanic rocks at Bail Hill, etc. ?	Upper Llandeilo
Llandeilo	*Glyptograptus teretiusculus*	?	Unconformity		
Llanvirn	*Didymograptus murchisoni* / *Didymograptus bifidus*				Lower Llandeilo and Middle Arenig
Arenig	*Didymograptus hirundo* / *Didymograptus extensus*		Ballantrae Igneous Complex ?		

Classification of the Ordovician System in the South of Scotland

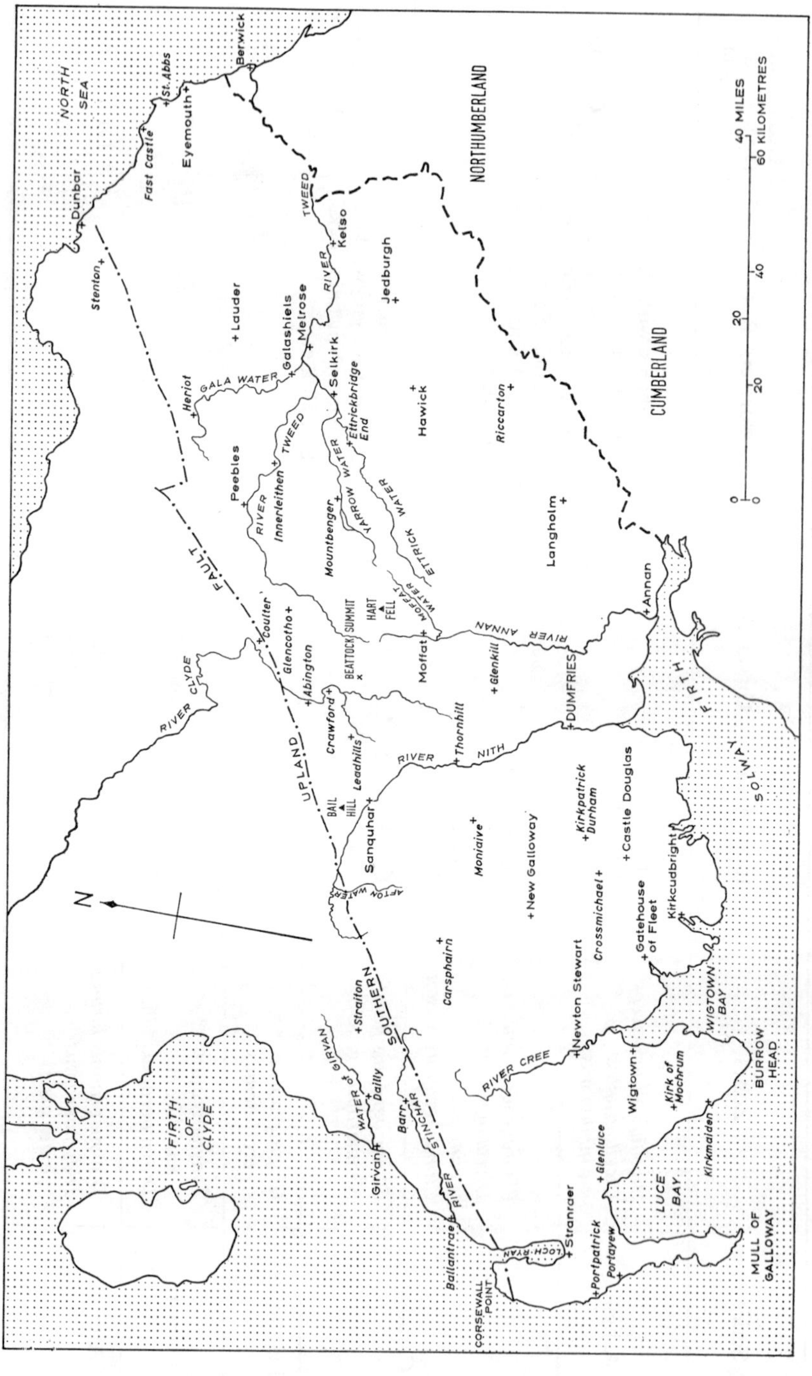

FIG. 2. *Map showing localities referred to in Chapters 3 and 4*

	metres
Red, green, and grey radiolarian cherts interstratified with tuffs and volcanic breccias	20
Bedded coarse-grained agglomerates and tuffs, with a thin bed of fossiliferous black shale within 6 m of the top . . about	200
Spilitic lavas, occasionally associated with agglomerates and tuffs, and including two thin bands of fossiliferous tuffaceous mudstone at least	200

The base of the lavas is not exposed. In addition to the graptolites the fossiliferous beds contain small horny brachiopods, such as *Acrotreta* and *Lingula*, and a crustacean *Caryocaris wrighti*.

Bailey and McCallien recognized two distinct groups of spilites, the Knockdolian and Downan Point groups, lying respectively below and above the widely occurring serpentinite. The main outcrops of all these rocks are shown in Fig. 3, their southern limit lying near Downan Point, some 7 km south of Bennane Head. The separation of the two groups was not related to any petrographic difference, although earlier work by Teall had described two types of lava, diabase and diabase-porphyrite, the latter distinguished by the presence of large phenocrysts of plagioclase. The rocks have a deeply weathered appearance, the feldspars are altered in varying degree to albite, which is itself replaced by other minerals, and the olivines are in some cases replaced by serpentine. Small vesicles are generally abundant.

A characteristic feature of the spilites is the development of 'pillows' from 0·15 to 0·6 m high and exceptionally 3 m long. They are very well displayed on the shore at Downan Point (Plate IIA), and indicate that the lavas were extruded under water. The pillow-lavas are generally fine-grained, the pillows being typically compact in the centre with layers of vesicles towards, and parallel to, the outer surface. The order of deposition of these highly folded beds may be indicated by a greater abundance of vesicles in the original upper part of a pillow, or by the moulding of pillows against those over which they were formed. The spaces between the pillows are occupied by silica and, near the tops of lava-flows, by limestone.

The agglomerates and tuffs which are associated with the lavas, and may in places comprise the infilling of volcanic necks, are made up of a variety of rock and crystal fragments. Large fragments in a number of areas suggest the proximity of a centre of eruption. An agglomerate at Stockenray Bay, north of Lendalfoot, includes blocks of glassy lava with unaltered feldspar. This has been taken to show that the agglomerate formed prior to the albitization of the lavas, a process from which the blocks in the agglomerate were in some way protected. Alternative views are that the glassy matrix of the lava protected the feldspar, or that the cooling lavas were permeated by volcanic water which prevented the soda-rich sea-water from altering them. Macadam-like agglomerates, composed of angular fragments with very little matrix, occur on Knockdolian and on Prieston Hill near Colmonell. At the latter locality, where the fragments are of albite-granite, the rock has been alternatively described as a concussion-breccia formed in place, or as a volcanic agglomerate derived possibly from a concealed extension of the Byne Hill granite. Certain andesites, basalts, and trachytes are known only as fragments in the agglomerates. Various altered rocks considered to be younger than the serpentinite occur in agglomerates at one locality.

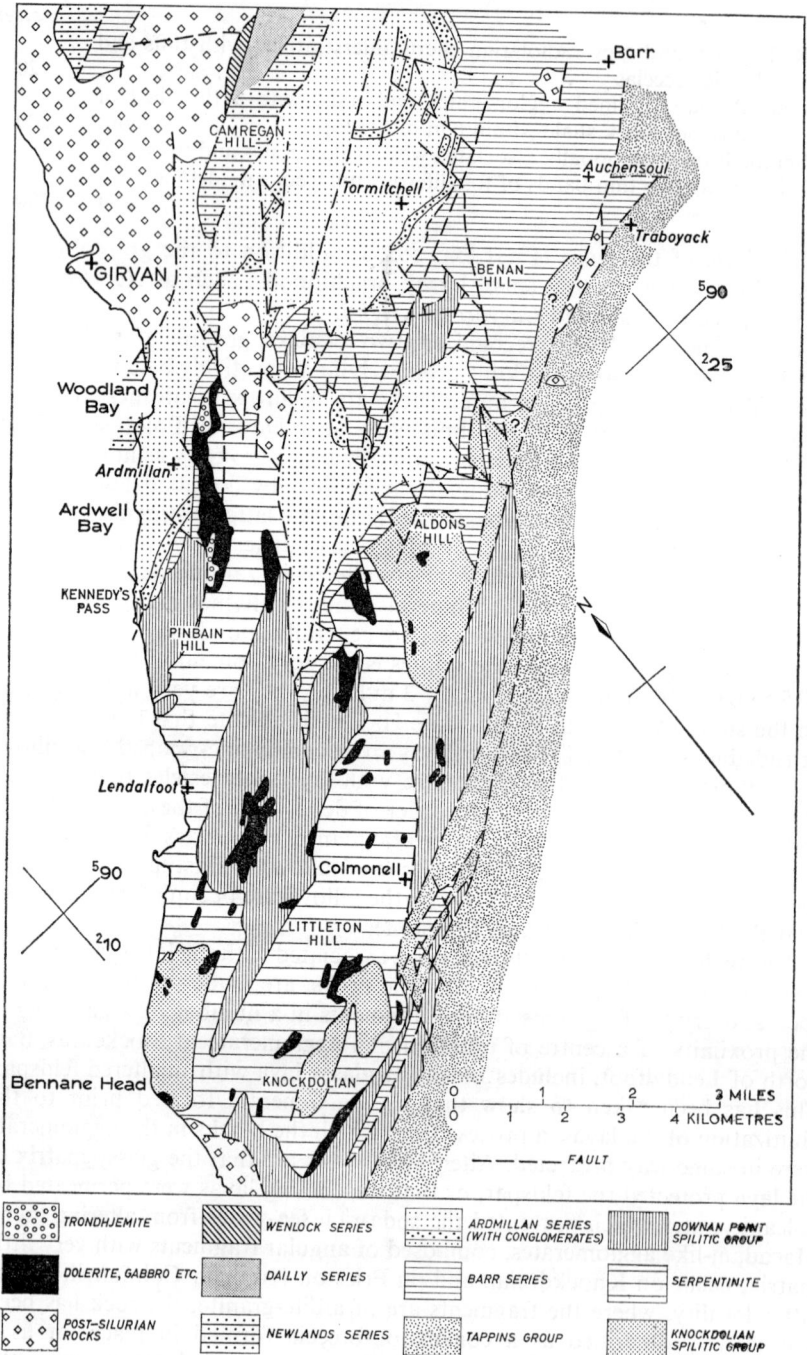

FIG. 3. *Geological map of the Girvan area*

(Based on work of the Institute of Geological Sciences, Bailey and McCallien
1957 and Williams 1962)

The many-coloured shales and mudstones, in some cases tuffaceous, which are intimately associated with the volcanic rocks, have locally yielded valuable faunas of graptolites and inarticulate brachiopods. Chert occurs amongst the lavas and in a series of beds, associated with tuffs and agglomerates, which overlies the graptolitic Middle Arenig shales. Radiolaria can be seen in hand-specimens of the rock but no detailed study of them has yet been made in this area. In places the chert appears to be devoid of radiolaria, and it is probable that the silica was predominantly precipitated by inorganic processes.

Serpentinite crops out in two broad zones extending inland from Bennane Head and Lendalfoot (Fig. 3), bounded to north-west and south-east by Arenig lavas. Several varieties are present, the most common being bastite-serpentinite, of which an example is described as a dark green or black rock with large, lustrous crystals of bronzite. Other varieties are serpentinized dunite, a dark green rock with pale yellow crystals of largely unaltered olivine, and tremolite-serpentinite. Other ultrabasic rocks associated with the serpentinite include picrite, pyroxenite, and bronzitite, the whole assemblage often having a banded appearance. At several localities adjacent to the central spilite zone a schistosity parallel to the boundary is developed in the serpentinite. This has been ascribed to the dynamic effect of intrusion or faulting. In one area the rock is described as a hornblende-schist, derived possibly from both serpentinite and spilite.

Gabbro and dolerite, albitized, granulitized, and foliated in varying degree, occur in many small areas within the serpentinite. They have been interpreted as intrusions into the latter or, in some cases, as xenoliths of older rock caught up and metamorphosed by it. Some authors have regarded them as altered spilitic lavas. Dynamic and thermal metamorphism have been alternatively invoked to explain the wide variety of rocks which is present, and the possible existence of a concealed mass of acid rock below the southern serpentinite has also been postulated. The largest outcrop of these rocks forms the ridge between Grey Hill and Byne Hill, east of Ardwell Bay, and consists of a series grading from gabbro to trondhjemite, a series generally regarded as the product of differentiation of a basic magma.

Many different opinions have been expressed as to the sequence of events in the development of the igneous complex. It is universally agreed that the lavas and associated sediments are of Arenig age and that many of the basic rocks are intrusive into the serpentinite. Peach and Horne held, and most later workers have agreed with them, that the serpentinite was itself intrusive into the spilites, in the form of two thick dykes. The lack of positive evidence for this theory, the lack of contact alteration attributable to the serpentinite, the degree of metamorphism in some of the rocks within the serpentinite, the development of a foliation in the serpentinite which is absent in the spilites, and the occurrence of fragments of the metamorphic rocks in the Arenig agglomerates led Pringle and Balsillie to adopt the view that the serpentinite and the rocks associated with it were pre-Arenig in age, probably Pre-Cambrian. More recently Bailey and McCallien have suggested that the serpentinite may be an ultra-basic submarine lava intermediate in age between a lower and an upper spilite formation. This hypothesis is based primarily on a study of the sequence of rocks at a number of localities, and is supported by the general disposition of the serpentinite outcrops in relation to the spilites, modified slightly from that shown on the Geological Survey map, and the presence of metamorphic fragments in (upper) agglomerates, as noted by Balsillie. The possibility that the gabbro-granite series of Byne Hill may be part of the pre-Arenig basement has been entertained, even by some workers who have assigned an Arenig age to the other basic rocks within the serpentinite, but differences between the trondhjemite of Byne Hill and the granite fragments in the adjacent Benan Conglomerate led Pringle to suggest that the former might be a post-Benan intrusion.

The albitization of the spilites and of the basic intrusive rocks is considered to be a hydrothermal process active during the consolidation of the rocks. The serpentinite is derived from an original peridotite, modified by hydro-thermal solutions at a time shortly after its consolidation, possibly at the time of the emplacement of the basic intrusions. The expansion involved in this process may have been partly responsible for the metamorphism of the crystallizing basic rocks.

Arenig and Llandeilo Rocks: Southern Uplands

Decomposed basic lavas at Raven Gill, near Crawford, are overlain by mudstone containing Arenig graptolites, brachiopods, and conodonts. At some other localities similar lavas were recognized by Peach and Horne to be of Glenkiln or Hartfell age, but in general the occurrence of cherts and mudstones, whether or not associated with volcanic rocks, was taken by these authors to indicate the development by sharp folding of an inlier of Middle Arenig to Llandeilo age. Recent work by Lamont and Lindström has shown that in some instances these sediments yield a conodont fauna of Llandeilian type. The opinion, expressed by Pringle in earlier editions of this publication, that no rocks of Llanvirn or Llandeilo age are present, is thus refuted, although it may still be maintained that there was a hiatus in sedi-mentation at some time between the Arenig volcanics and the Glenkiln Shales. Spilites associated with the Llandeilian cherts at some localities in Wigtownshire, South Ayrshire, and Peeblesshire, may be said to be of the same age, but at other localities the relationship between the lava and the chert is uncertain and the age of the former cannot be positively stated.

The occurrence together, in many different areas of the world, of pillow-lavas and radiolarian cherts was commented on by Teall in 1894 and it is now accepted that the ultimate source of the silica of the cherts is to be found in the submarine effusion of the lavas. This essential link between the two rocks is emphasized by the frequent occurrence of chert between the pillows of lava, and by the fact that chert may succeed lava but never underlies it. The siliceous environment and conditions favourable to the deposition of the chert can be expected to persist for only a short period after the effusion of the lava, and it may therefore be asserted that lavas and cherts occurring together will be of essentially the same age.

Raven Gill is the only locality at which lavas lying close below Glenkiln Shales have been proved to be of Arenig age. The succession of rocks below the Llandeilian lavas of other localities is quite unknown and their relation-ship to the Arenig is conjectural.

On Bail Hill, near Sanquhar, cherts which underlie Glenkiln Shales with interbedded lavas are possibly of Llandeilo or even Caradoc age, rather than Arenig as was formerly believed.

Caradoc and Ashgill Rocks: Southern Uplands

The **Glenkiln Shales** in the Central Belt are exposed only in scattered lenticular inliers which were formerly thought to represent the culminations of sharp anticlinal folds. Recent research indicates the importance of strike-faults in determining the occurrence of these inliers, and it is probable that many of them are fault-bounded on their south-eastern margins. The rocks, which are about 6 m thick in the Moffat area, are in general black shales with thin cherty ribs, and grey and orange tuffaceous mudstones with bands of grey radiolarian chert. In the type-section of Glenkill Burn, between Dumfries and Moffat, they consist of black shales yielding, amongst many other species, the following graptolites characteristic of the Caradoc zones of *Nemagraptus gracilis* and *Climacograptus peltifer*—*Climacograptus bicornis*, *C. peltifer*, *Dicellograptus intortus*, *D. patulosus*, *Didymograptus superstes*, and *N. gracilis*. To the north-east the shales are seen again in several localities, notably at Dobb's Linn, Hartfell Spa, and Ettrickbridge End, between Moffat and Selkirk, but farther to the north-east the general plunge of the fold-axes in that direction carries them below the level of exposure. They occur also in a number of outcrops to the south-west, most notably between Crossmichael and Kirkpatrick Durham, and near the Water of Malzie, some 13 km west-south-west of Wigtown.

More numerous inliers of Glenkiln Shales occur in the Northern Belt. The south-eastern outcrops are like those farther south, but to the north-west the shales are variably interspersed with grey mudstones, sandy shales, and greywackes. This change is accompanied by an increase in overall thickness, to a figure estimated by Peach and Horne to be about 350 m but by Kelling, working in the Galloway peninsula, to be about 1850 m. Kelling also observed that at Portayew, close to the southern margin of the Northern Belt, Glenkiln shales and cherts are only about 9 m thick. At Leadhills shales of Glenkiln and Hartfell age are seen to be bounded to the south-east by reverse-faults which hade north-westwards. The younger Ordovician greywackes beyond the faults are traversed by important veins of galena and zinc blende.

Farther to the north-west, between the Southern Upland Fault and the River Stinchar, rocks of Glenkiln age, and possibly somewhat older, constitute the Glen App and Tappins groups which include graptolitic shales, but consist mainly of greywackes and siltstones, with thick conglomerates in the older Glen App Group. Spilites and cherts are present in the basal subdivision of the Tappins Group, and higher beds have yielded a trilobite fauna closely similar to that of the *Didymograptus superstes* Mudstones of the Barr Series. Williams has estimated the thickness of the Tappins Group to be about 2450 m in contrast to the 150 m of isoclinally folded beds described by Peach and Horne.

In the Rhins of Galloway Kelling divided the Glenkiln rocks into the Corsewall and Kirkcolm groups, approximately correlative with the Glen App and Tappins groups. The Corsewall Group, which crops out north of the Southern Upland Fault, contains chaotic slide-conglomerates derived from the north-west, interspersed with laminated and current-bedded greywackes and siltstones laid down in shallow water. The greywackes and siltstones of the Kirkcolm and Portpatrick (p. 23) groups are predominantly deep-water turbidites. The upward succession shows a progressive variation in source-

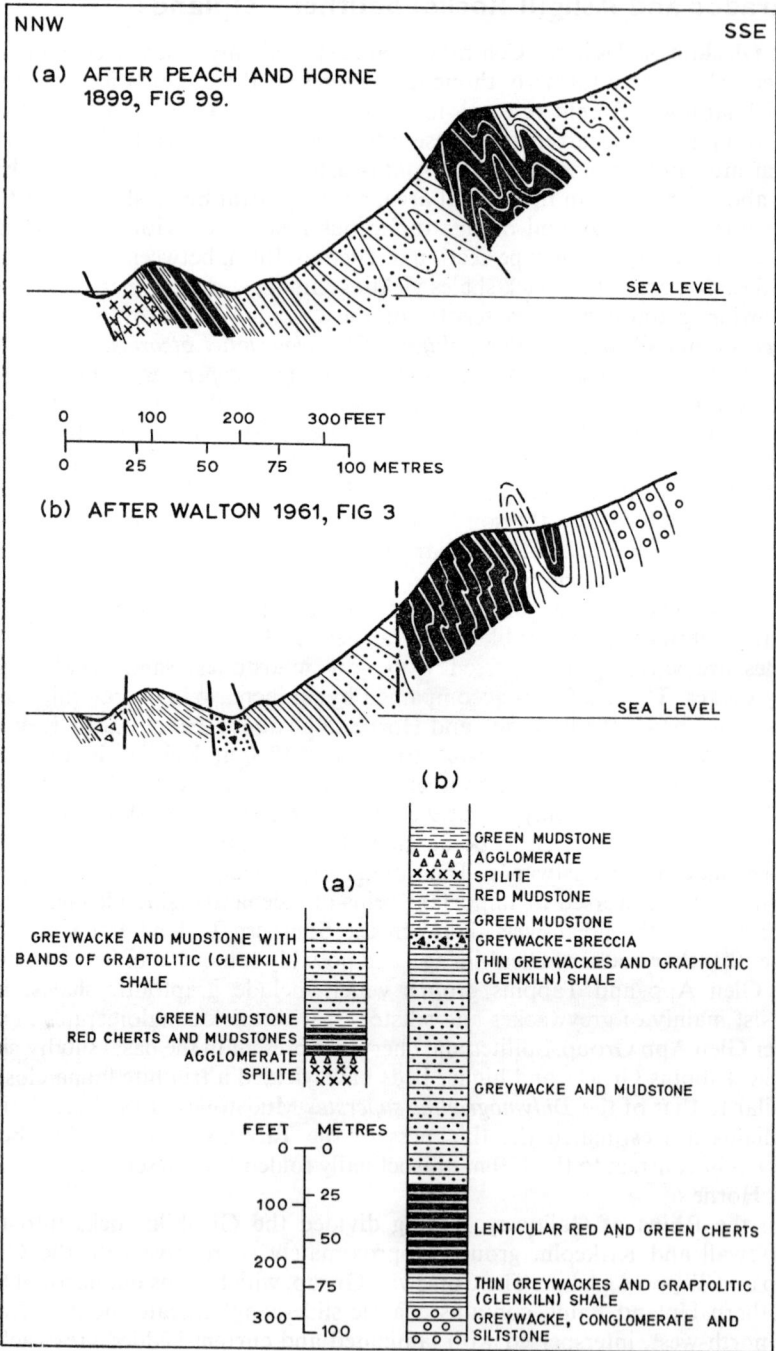

FIG. 4. *Alternative interpretations of structure and stratigraphy in Ordovician rocks at Portandea, south of Ballantrae*

rock, from igneous rocks of local type to metamorphic rocks from farther north.

Kelling and Walton have shown that several lithologically distinctive bands of shale with Glenkiln graptolites can be recognized (for example in the Glen App and Tappins groups and throughout the Kirkcolm Group)

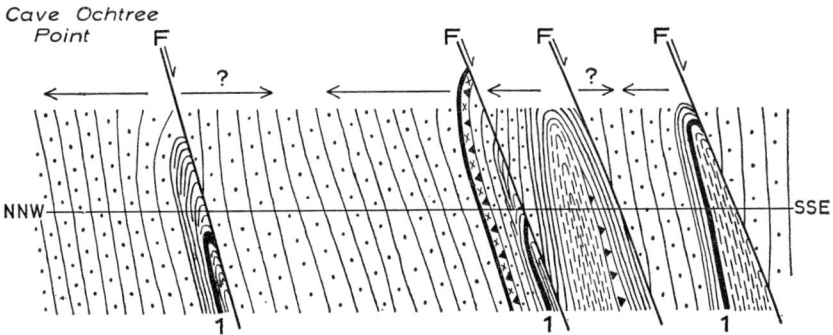

(a) Horizontal cross-section based on the work of Peach and Horne 1899, pp. 413-5, and on their unpublished six-inch map. One band of Glenkiln shale, repeated by folding.

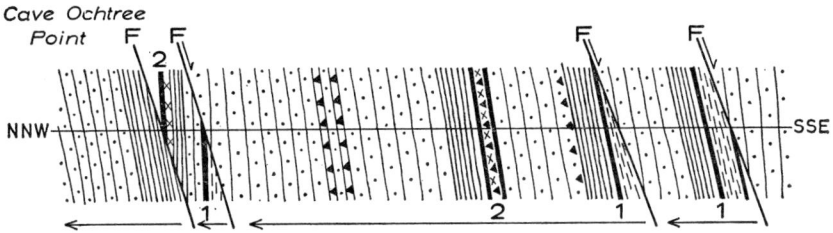

(b) Horizontal cross-section based on the work of Kelling 1961, pp. 45-7. Two bands of Glenkiln shale, repeated by faulting.

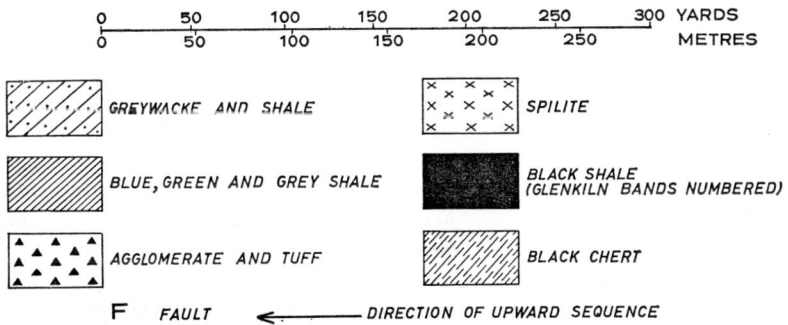

| 0 | 50 | 100 | 150 | 200 | 250 | 300 | YARDS |
| 0 | 50 | 100 | 150 | 200 | 250 | | METRES |

GREYWACKE AND SHALE

SPILITE

BLUE, GREEN AND GREY SHALE

BLACK SHALE (GLENKILN BANDS NUMBERED)

AGGLOMERATE AND TUFF

BLACK CHERT

F FAULT ◄———— DIRECTION OF UPWARD SEQUENCE

Fig. 5. *Alternative interpretations in Glenkiln Shales and associated rocks near Portslogan in the Rhins of Galloway*

interbedded with greywackes, as are the volcanic rocks with which they are in many cases associated. In general the rocks young towards the north-west and there is no doubt that such repetition as may occur is due mainly to strike-faulting and not to folding, of which there is apparently no important development (Figs. 4 and 5). It is reasonable to suppose that this is the general pattern of sequence and structure throughout the north-western part of the Northern Belt, and that the facies change from graptolitic shale to greywacke was of a more oscillatory nature than Peach and Horne seem to have thought. A corollary of the newer interpretation is that the total thickness of the Glenkiln rocks must be considerably greater than was inferred from the hypothesis of tight-folding and continued repetition of horizons.

The **Hartfell Shales** are typically developed on the 'Score' at Hartfell Spa, 7 km north of Moffat, and form the middle member of the graptolitic shales of that district, the Moffat Series. They are about 30 m thick and typically comprise a lower group of graptolitic black shales with thin partings of pale mudstones, and an upper group, the Barren Mudstones, of mudstones with beds of black shale. They are in general lithology similar to the Glenkiln Shales, which they follow with no apparent stratigraphical break. At Ettrick-bridge End, near Selkirk, the most south-easterly outcrop of the Moffat Series, there is however an important change in the lithology of the Barren Mudstones which here comprise about 55 m of greywackes with thin bands of green shale and fossiliferous black shale. Some of the shales include bands and nodules of limestone similar to the Wrae Limestone of Peeblesshire (p. 24).

The Lower Hartfell is richly fossiliferous, with many species of graptolites and an abundance of the horny brachiopods *Acrotreta* and *Siphonotreta* and of the sponge *Hyalostelia*. The great abundance of certain species of graptolite on individual bedding-planes has been taken to indicate frequent interruption of the deposition of sediment. By contrast the fauna of the Upper Hartfell is rather sparse, graptolites occurring only in thin dark beds interbedded with the barren mudstones. Lapworth drew attention to the fact that most of the graptolite genera of the Hartfell Shales die out before the highest beds are reached. There is thus a marked faunal break between the Ordovician and Silurian members of the Moffat Series, as there is between the corresponding formations in the Girvan area.

The uppermost five zones of the Caradoc and Ashgill series (p. 13) are recognized in the Hartfell Shales of the Central Belt. The zones are character-ized by the species shown below, in addition to the zone-fossil itself:

Dicellograptus anceps:	*Climacograptus supernus, Orthograptus truncatus abbreviatus.*
Dicellograptus complanatus:	*C. miserabilis, O. truncatus socialis.*
Pleurograptus linearis:	*Amphigraptus divergens, C. styloideus, C. tubuliferus, Dicellograptus elegans, Leptograptus capillaris, L. flaccidus, Neurograptus fibratus, O. quadrimucro-natus.*
Dicranograptus clingani:	*A. radiatus, C. caudatus, Corynoides calycularis, D. morrisi, D. caduceus, D. forchhammeri, Dicrano-graptus ramosus, L. flaccidus, N. margaritatus, O. calcaratus, O. truncatus truncatus, Hyalostelia fasciculus.*

Climacograptus wilsoni: '*Buthograptus laxus*', *Climacograptus bicornis, D. nicholsoni, D. ramosus. Glossograptus hincksi, O. vulgatus.*

Sections similar to that at Hartfell Spa, in which the Hartfell Shales occur between the Glenkiln and Birkhill shales, occur in most of the outcrops to the north-east, as, for example, at Dobb's Linn, Craigmichan Scaurs, and Mountbenger. In the Selkirk–Melrose area the Hartfell Shales are the oldest rocks exposed, but their base must be nearly reached at Lindean, between these towns, where the problematical '*Buthograptus laxus*,' confined to the Zone of *C. wilsoni*, has been recorded. The Zone of *P. linearis* is recognized at Leaderfoot Bridge, near Melrose, and Lower Hartfell graptolites are present in the most north-easterly exposure, near Lauder.

South-westwards from Moffat the Hartfell Shales occur wherever the Glenkiln Shales are found. Peach and Horne described several localities rich in graptolites in streams between Dumfries, New Galloway, and Kirkcudbright. Farther west good sections in fossiliferous black shales occur in the Cree north of Newton Stewart, some 11 km south-east of Glenluce, and at Clanyard Bay near the Mull of Galloway.

Towards the north-west, along the southern edge of the Northern Belt, the outcrops of the Lower Hartfell Shales are in many cases similar to those of the Moffat area. For example at Morroch Bay, south of Portpatrick, some 18 m of shales at the top of the Kirkcolm Group yield an abundant graptolite fauna of Upper Glenkiln or Lower Hartfell age, but higher beds of the Lower Hartfell consist of thick greywackes with graptolite shales. When the outcrops are traced farther to the north-west, however, the change to a greywacke succession, in which the graptolites are confined to interbedded thin bands of black shale, is seen to affect the lower beds as well. The temporary development in the Northern Belt of neritic conditions, which prevailed in the Girvan area, is indicated by the occurrence of impure limestones and conglomerates with a shelly fauna including trilobites. The lateral change in lithology is similar to that described above in the Glenkiln Shales, the rocks becoming coarser-grained and thicker towards the north-west, but it takes place farther south in the Hartfell rocks than in the Glenkiln. Largely because of the coarser nature of the sediment not all the graptolite zones of the typical Hartfell Shales have been recognized in the Northern Belt. The transitional fauna at the base of the formation at Morroch Bay implies the presence of the Zone of *C. wilsoni* but this zone has not been proved elsewhere. Younger rocks in this area form the Portpatrick Group of Kelling, extending from the Lower Hartfell possibly to the Silurian. The group is some 1200 m thick and consists of greywackes with thick bands of bluish black shale. The topmost Zone of *D. anceps* may however be completely absent in the Northern Belt, the youngest rocks present belonging to the underlying Zone of *D. complanatus*, which is rare in north-eastern districts but has been recorded on the northern slope of the Lammermuir Hills south of Stenton. Near Abington the Lowther Shales are regarded as being of Upper Hartfell age. They are grey and blue shales associated with greywackes and pebbly grits, estimated by Peach and Horne to be about 250 m thick. There are also a few thin ribs of limestone associated with calcareous grits yielding traces of fossils.

Between the Nith and the Clyde a coarse conglomerate has been taken as the base of the Hartfell and a similar bed, probably on the same horizon, occurs in the Shinnel and Chanlock waters, north of Moniaive, in the hills near Carsphairn, and in the Afton Water. The pebbles consist of gabbro, granite, felsite, lava, chert, greywacke, black shale and quartzite. In the Glenaylmer Burn, north of Sanquhar, the conglomerate rests unconformably on radiolarian chert, and includes blocks of lava up to 0·6 m across. Correlation with the Benan Conglomerate of the Girvan area is suggested by the similarity of the constituent pebbles. A pebbly grit known as Haggis Rock may locally occupy this stratigraphical position. It consists of small fragments of coloured chert and igneous rocks, in a matrix of igneous material, but the name has been applied to a number of different bands and no single stratigraphical connotation can be associated with it.

Fossiliferous conglomerates are associated with shales and grits at Duntercleuch, Snar, Wallace's Cast, and Kilbucho, in the ground between Sanquhar and Peebles. Fossils from these localities include *Christiania tenuicincta, Rafinesquina deltoidea, Strophomena kilbuchoensis*, and species of *calymenid, cheirurid, homalonotid, phacopid, remopleuridid,* and *trinucleid* genera. It is not known whether or not the conglomerates lie on one stratigraphical level.

The Wrae Limestone and its associated conglomerates and contemporaneous volcanic rocks were formerly regarded as being of Upper Hartfell age. The limestone occurs as a volcanic breccia within a band of tuff, and at Wrae, Glencotho, Drumelzier, and Winkston, to the west and north of Peebles, has yielded a fauna which includes corals, crinoids, brachiopods, and trilobites. Graptolites from a higher horizon in the tuff, and those just above, in the Stobo Slates, are indicative of a position high in the Lower Hartfell Zone of *D. clingani*, but conodonts from the Limestone have recently been said to be of pre-Caradoc aspect.

In the Rhins of Galloway Kelling divided the Hartfell rocks into two groups, of which the more northerly and more generally arenaceous Galdenoch Group is regarded as correlative with the lower part of the Portpatrick Group. This correlation is supported by consideration of the rock fragments in the greywackes. Greywackes and shales of the Portpatrick Group extend southward to the boundary with the Silurian rocks of the Centra lBelt. They include occasional inliers of Hartfell and Glenkiln shales, generally seen to be faulted on their southern sides, and young fairly consistently towards the north, as do the adjacent Silurian rocks. This evidence requires that the Ordovician–Silurian boundary is a fault with large downthrow to the south. North of Portpatrick a similar parallel fault is thought to separate the Portpatrick and Kirkcolm groups. Visible shearing suggests that both are reverse-faults with a rather low dip towards the north.

Volcanic Rocks of Glenkiln and Hartfell Age

The work of Walton and Kelling on the coast between Ballantrae and the Mull of Galloway has shown that spilitic lavas are developed at several horizons in the Glenkiln rocks, where they were formerly regarded as fold-repeated occurrences of one volcanic episode. It is probable that many of the other occurrences of lava in the Northern Belt previously assigned to this one Glenkiln episode, or to another in the Zone of *D. clingani*, were in fact extruded during a larger number of separate episodes. Reference has been made (p. 18) to the indications that many of the lavas formerly thought to be of Arenig age are now considered to be Llandeilian, and in general terms the Glenkiln Shales are seen to be much more closely linked to underlying lavas and cherts than was formerly supposed. In the Central Belt fine tuffs are interbedded with the Glenkiln Shales at several localities, for instance at Dobb's Linn, and at Trowdale, near Castle Douglas, and probably represent wind-blown volcanic dust.

The Glenkiln volcanic rocks are present in many localities in the Northern Belt, extending from the Rhins of Galloway to beyond Gala Water, and are best displayed in the neighbourhood of Bail Hill, near Sanquhar. Mrs. Eyles[1] showed that they are there younger than shales with Upper Glenkiln graptolites. The lavas and minor intrusions commonly have dioritic affinities and among the pyroclastic rocks, which are more abundant, is the unusual augite-tuff first described by Teall. This rock, with large crystals of augite, often unbroken, was thought by Mrs. Eyles to be an auto-brecciated basalt. The whole complex was regarded as a denuded volcanic pile, the vent being marked by a central area of coarse agglomerate containing a variety of rocks not known at outcrop in the vicinity, such as a soda-syenite. Mrs. Eyles confirmed Teall's observation of the similarity of the tuffs to those in other areas, particularly to the augite-andesite-tuff of Mains Hill, near Ballantrae, later examined by Pringle and thought to be possibly of Glenkiln age. To the same period may be referred the tuffs and breccias which are found in the area between the Euchan and Kells waters, near Sanquhar, and said by Eckford to be closely associated in the Poltallen Burn with shales yielding Glenkiln graptolites. In the Rhins of Galloway agglomerate and spilite at Broadsea Bay were described by Peach and Horne as of Upper Glenkiln age, and Pringle suggested they be correlated with the Bail Hill volcanics. Kelling however thinks that they lie in the basal Glenkiln Zone of *Nemagraptus gracilis*.

Biotite-hornblende-andesite is exposed at several points between Bail Hill and Coulter, in the Clyde Valley. A short distance south of Coulter there are one or two beds of augitic ash which closely resemble the tuffs of Bail Hill. The pyroclastic rocks are perhaps not more than 15 m thick and are associated with shales which have yielded a Glenkiln fauna. Lavas in the Hope Burn, near Heriot, are now believed to be of Glenkiln age, rather than Arenigian.

The Hartfell volcanic rocks are restricted to the valley of the Tweed in Peeblesshire. They were originally assigned to the Upper Hartfell, but Eckford and Ritchie proved that they lie in the Lower Hartfell Zone of *D. clingani*. The lavas are exposed at many localities between Winkston Hill, 3 km north of Peebles, and Glencotho, some 23 km to the south-west, and are associated with tuff, limestone-breccias, grits, cherts, and shales. At Winkston Hill they are at least 30 m thick but thin rapidly towards the south-west. At Wrae Hill, 16 km south-west of Peebles, the lower lava, 5 m thick, is succeeded by some 20 m of greenish calcareous tuff and tuffaceous grit. This is full of blocks of trachytic lava and contains two flows of similar rock as well as, at a higher level, the Wrae Limestone (p. 24). Lower Hartfell graptolites occur some 2 m below the top of the tuffaceous grit at Stobo. The overlying Stobo Slates are about 90 or 120 m thick. The lavas are described as quartz-keratophyre and soda-trachyte, banded and perlitic forms

---

[1] More detailed notes by Mrs. Eyles are quoted in earlier editions of this publication.

C

occurring near Peebles, and are regarded as local varieties of the same spilitic suite as the Arenig and other earlier Ordovician lavas of southern Scotland.

Caradoc and Ashgill Rocks: Girvan Area

In the Girvan area the rocks coeval with the Glenkiln and Hartfell shales form respectively the Barr and Ardmillan series. The **Barr Series** is of variable constitution and thickness. A characteristic section, given below, is exposed in the Benan Burn, about 2 km west of Traboyack (Fig. 3). The stratigraphy of the Series, and of the lower part of the Ardmillan Series, has recently been studied by Williams, to whom much of the detail in this account is due.

	metres
Benan Conglomerate	over 30
Didymograptus superstes Mudstones: grits and conglomerates; siltstones, pebbly mudstones, and greywackes; calcareous siltstones and mudstones	40
Stinchar Limestone: thickly bedded limestones, platy above; rubbly fine-grained limestones	60
Valcourea confinis Flags: fine-grained calcareous platy sandstones, coarser-grained and more massive downwards	45
Gap	34
Kirkland Conglomerate: current-bedded calcareous pebbly grits .	6
massive conglomerate	12
(seen nearby to be at least 240 m thick)	

The Series was laid down upon an irregular surface composed mainly of members of the Ballantrae Igneous Complex and the age of the earliest rocks differs widely over the area. For example, the Kirkland Conglomerate occurs only on the south-eastern side of Benan Hill, whereas on the eastern slopes of Aldons Hill the oldest rocks are conglomerates of Stinchar Limestone age. There is also considerable evidence of lateral change of facies and of local erosion during the period of deposition. Thus the Stinchar Limestone thins from 60 m to 18 m between the Benan Burn and Auchensoul, less than 2·5 km to the north-east. The upper part of the limestone of Benan Burn is represented near Auchensoul by conglomerate, with brachiopod and crinoid fragments, and the *D. superstes* Mudstones by a more calcareous rock attenuated by erosion prior to the deposition of the Benan Conglomerate. An additional limestone, formerly thought to be the Stinchar Limestone, is developed at Auchensoul below the *V. confinis* Flags. It is of variable thickness up to 18 m. Some 3 km to the north, near Brockloch, the Stinchar Limestone lithology extends upwards into the Benan Conglomerate and downwards into the *V. confinis* Flags.

The most notable examples of contemporaneous erosion are afforded by the Benan Conglomerate which cuts down into the Stinchar Limestone in a channel less than 1·5 km wide south-west of Benan Hill, and cuts rapidly across the whole of the Barr Series east of Aldons Hill to rest directly on the igneous basement.

The Kirkland and Benan conglomerates are similar in their content of pebbles and boulders, which are mainly of local rocks but include some of unknown origin such as a red granite. The sandy matrix is characteristically

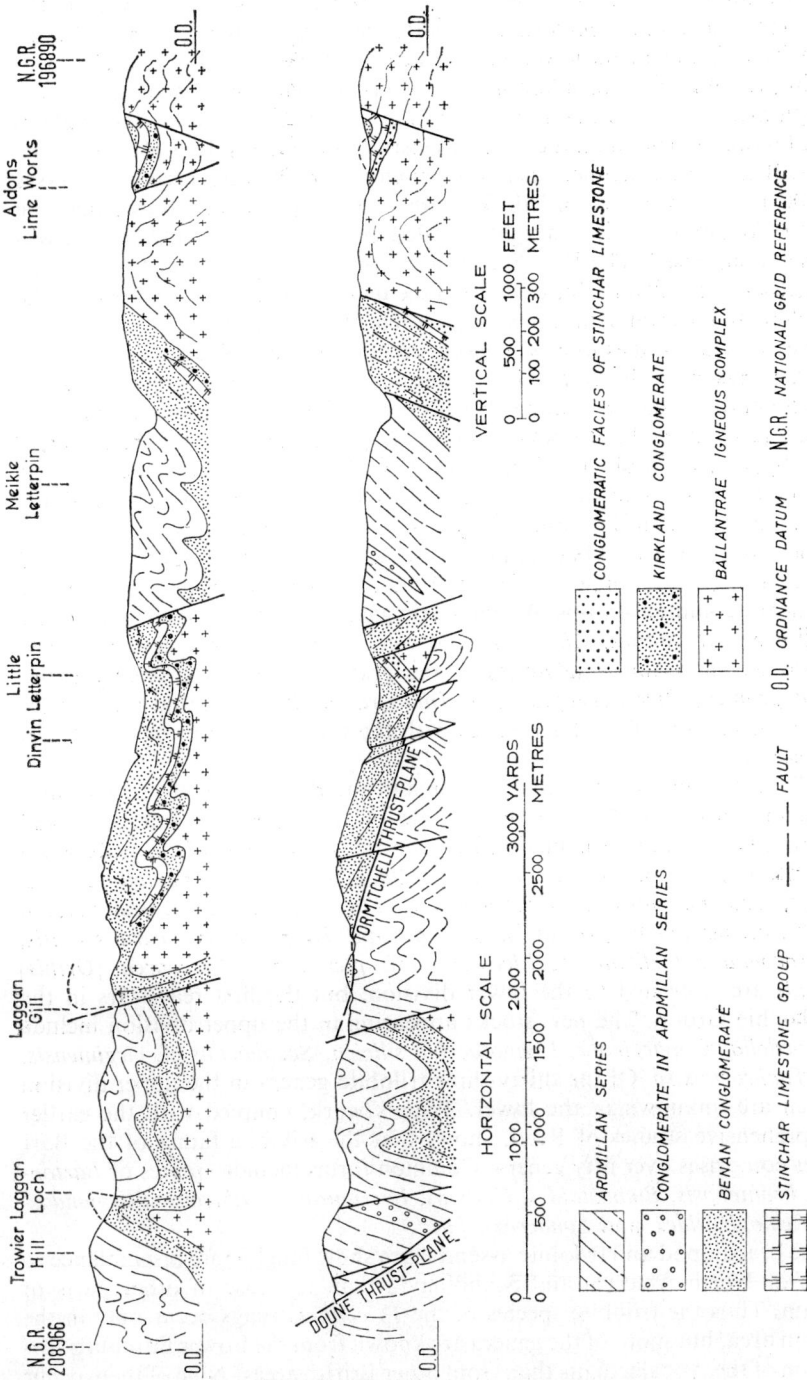

FIG. 6. *Alternative interpretations of Ordovician structure and stratigraphy in the Girvan area* (Based on the work of Peach and Horne 1899 (above) and Williams 1962 (below).)

purple in the Kirkland Conglomerate and dark grey or green in the Benan. The Benan Conglomerate includes thin mudstones and siltstones in the Stinchar valley, and *Leptellina semilunata* and crinoid stems, its only fossils, have been found in its lower beds. Facies changes and differential down-cutting account for considerable variations in the thickness of the Benan Conglomerate, from a maximum of 640 m in the Stinchar and Assel valleys to not more than 90 m on the north-western limb of the Aldons Hill anticline. In the Benan Hill syncline, where no younger rocks are preserved, thicknesses of 500 to 600 m are recorded. Williams' recent work has shown that the Benan Conglomerate is less tightly folded and accordingly thicker than was formerly supposed. The Barr Series was thought by Peach and Horne to be altogether about 250 m thick, whereas the incomplete succession between the Stinchar and Benan Hill appears to reach about 900 m.

The Stinchar Limestone is worked in extensive quarries at Tormitchell, where it has been thrust from the south-east over Ardwell greywackes. At least 50 m thick, the Limestone occurs in several lithological types ranging in grain-size from muddy to pebbly, oolitic in some bands, elsewhere crinoidal or shelly, and variously massive, nodular, or platy. The underlying calcareous grit and breccia of igneous rocks are probably to be correlated partly with the Limestone of Benan Burn and partly with the *V. confinis* Flags.

The three formations between the conglomerates contain an abundant and varied fauna, largely of neritic forms. Brachiopods and trilobites are the more significant common groups. A diagnostic gastropod is *Maclurea logani*, and the limestones contain *Girvanella* and *Saccamminopsis* in abundance. The occurrence in certain mudstones of the graptolite genera *Climacograptus*, *Cryptograptus*, *Dicranograptus*, and *Diplograptus* is of essential importance in the correlation of the Barr Series with the Glenkiln Shales of the Moffat succession.

Williams divides the brachiopod fauna of the Barr Series into two groups, occurring below and above the middle of the Stinchar Limestone, and Tripp draws a similar distinction between the trilobites of these beds. Over half the brachiopod species, including *Bimuria* cf. *buttsi*, *Leptellina semilunata*, *Orthambonites parvicrassicostatus*, *Phragmorthis buttsi*, and *Ptychoglyptus* cf. *virginiensis*, occur in both groups. *Hesperorthis australis exitis*, *Macrocoelia macallumi*, *Multicostella* aff. *plena*, and *Valcourea* [*Orthis*] *confinis* are restricted to the lower division, but the first reappears in the Balclatchie Group. The new stocks appearing in the upper division include *Craspedelia* cf. *marginata*, *Eremotoechia silicica*, *Scaphorthis* cf. *virginiensis*, and *Taphrorthis sp.* Of the thirty-three trilobite genera in the upper division sixteen are unknown in the lower. Tripp's work, coupled with the earlier comprehensive studies of Reed, shows that the trilobite fauna of the Barr Series comprises over fifty genera. Common forms include species of *Bartoninus*, *Bronteopsis*, *Bumastoides*, *Calliops*, *Encrinuroides*, *Illaenus*, *Raymondaspis*, *Remopleurides*, and *Sphaerexochus*.

The brachiopod and trilobite assemblages show much more resemblance to those of North America and Scandinavia than to those of other parts of Britain. Thus the trilobite species of the *V. confinis* Flags occur only in the Girvan area, but more of the genera are known from the Lower Edinburg formation of the Appalachians than from other British areas. Nine of them occur also in older American rocks but there is no link with older rocks in Britain.

The Ordovician conglomerates of the Girvan area have been described by Kuenen and Williams as slide-conglomerates, deposited against steep submarine slopes which were probably fault-planes, in such a way as to tend to remove the topographic irregularity arising from repeated movement of the faults. The northern limits of the Kirkland and Kilranny (p. 30) conglomerates, for example, are formed by such faults, trending eastward or east-north-eastward and with southward downthrow, and the variable thickness of the Benan Conglomerate is also in part due to them. By this hypothesis the detrital rocks of the Stinchar and Craighead (p. 31) groups were laid down in the shallower water to the north of the faults, and the greywacke associations of the Tappins (p. 19), Balclatchie, and Ardwell groups in the deeper water beyond the reach of the sliding conglomerates.

Hubert, on the other hand, regards the Kilranny Conglomerate as having been laid down gradually by strong bottom-currents, probably in quite shallow water. The younger Ardmillan rocks are thought to have been similarly formed, the bottom-currents having flowed south-eastwards, in contrast to the south-westward flow of Kilranny times. The upper beds of the Whitehouse Group (p. 31) are interpreted as the sediments of a delta spreading out from the north-west.

The rocks of the **Ardmillan Series** are not markedly different from the Hartfell rocks of the Northern Belt, but their thickness, which is probably considerably in excess of 2000 m, is much greater. The five groups which constitute the Series were recognized by Lapworth.

		metres
Drummuck Group	Mudstones, calcareous sandstones	120
	Sandstones and grits	
Shalloch (Barren) Flagstone Group	Flagstones, shales, mudstones	240
Whitehouse Group	Soft green mudstones and grey flagstones with ribs of limestone. Thin band of conglomerate at base.	90
	Grey and green shales.	
Ardwell Group	Grits, greywackes, siltstones, and mudstones, with bands of conglomerate and lenticular pebbly grit.	1200
Balclatchie Group	Calcareous conglomerates, grits, and sandstones.	300
	Calcareous mudstones.	
	Conglomerates and grits.	
	Grits, greywackes, siltstones, and mudstones.	

The thicknesses of the Balclatchie and Ardwell groups are based on the recent work of Williams and are altogether nearly four times the figure given by Lapworth, whose estimates for the other three groups are given above. No later independent figures for these higher groups have been published.

The Balclatchie Group is typically exposed in Penwhapple Burn, some 3 km north-west of Barr. The base is not seen, the lowest rock being the Doon Hill Conglomerate, formerly regarded as part of the Benan but now considered to lie at least 9 m above it. The succeeding Balclatchie Mudstones, dark green and calcareous, and at least 25 m thick, have yielded over 100 species of fossils from a roadside exposure near 'Balclatchie Bridge', south

of Green Hill. These include the sponge *Nidulites favus,* the graptolites
Dicranograptus tardiusculus and *Orthograptus apiculatus,* and the brachiopods
Glyptomena girvanensis, Glyptorthis balclatchiensis, and *Leptellina llandeilo-
ensis.* Trilobites are remarkably abundant and include several species of
Amphilichas, Ampyx, Diacanthaspis, Illaenus, Proetus, and *Remopleurides.*
At the top of the Group is the Balclatchie Conglomerate, a calcareous
fossiliferous rock about 30 m thick. Farther to the south-west the Group
includes several conglomerates, some now correlated with that of Doon Hill,
but locally it consists mainly of massive greywackes and mudstones.

In the Laggan Burn, south-east of Girvan, Balclatchie mudstones contain
limestone nodules with an abundance of well-preserved graptolites. The
fauna, described by Bulman, includes *Climacograptus brevis, C. scharenbergi,
Cryptograptus tricornis, Dicranograptus nicholsoni, Diplograptus lepthotheca,*
and *Orthograptus apiculatus,* and is indicative of a horizon close to the
Glenkiln–Hartfell boundary.

The well-known occurrence of 'Benan Conglomerate' on the shore at
Kennedy's Pass (Fig. 3) is believed by Williams to be of a Balclatchie formation
which he has called the Kilranny Conglomerate. This rock is about 150 m
thick and its base is thought to lie some 90 to 150 m above the top of the
Benan. It is seen in places as far north as the latitude of Woodland Bay.
The beds above it belong by original definition to the Ardwell Group, but
near Ardwell and on Ardmillan Braes they contain a rich fauna like that of
the Balclatchie Mudstones.

Greywackes of the Ardwell Group are typically exposed on the shore north
of Kennedy's Pass, but the succession here is incomplete and complicated
by folds and faults. Williams has recorded a succession through the Group
in the ground north-east of Tormitchell, which may be abbreviated as
follows:

		metres
Cascade Grits and Conglomerates	at least	120
Grits, greywackes, and mudstones	about	600
Assel Conglomerate		70
Grits, greywackes, and mudstones, fossiliferous near base . .		135
Tormitchell Conglomerate (Barbae Grits of Lapworth) . . .		90
Sandstones, siltstones, and mudstones, with lenses of fossiliferous grit in lower beds		195

Of the named conglomerates the Assel band is of much more restricted
development than the other two. The conglomerates and grits are variably
fossiliferous, the fauna including algal and bryozoan nodules and corals in
addition to the abundant brachiopods and trilobites. The most valuable
fossiliferous horizon is just above the Tormitchell Conglomerate.

The Group occurs also in a number of areas between Camregan Hill and
Aldons Hill, and in a narrow inlier running north-east to Delamford, 5·5 km
north-north-east of Barr. The thickness does not reach the 1200 m recorded
near Tormitchell but many of the local successions are incomplete. Brachiopods and graptolites permit stratigraphical comparison between several of the
outcrops. Secondary cementstone nodules occur locally, especially in the
lower rocks, but conglomerates are in general poorly developed, or ill exposed,
except in Penwhapple Burn.

On Ardwell shore the Ardwell Group consists of greywackes, siltstones, and mudstones, with some massive pebbly grits and nodules and thin bands of cementstone. About 500 m of rock is exposed, but the section is fault-bounded above and below and the full thickness in this area is estimated to be of the order of 1100 m.

Graptolites from the Ardwell Group include *Climaccgraptus bicornis, C. caudatus, C. scharenbergi, Corynoides calycularis, Dicellograptus forchhammeri, Dicranograptus ramosus, Neurograptus margaritatus,* and *Orthograptus apiculatus,* indicative of horizons low in the Hartfell Shales. Many of the brachiopod species are the same as in the Balclatchie Group but an important new form is *Reuschella* cf. *americana.* The Balclatchie–Ardwell brachiopods, like those of the Barr Series, are more readily compared with those of the Appalachians than with those of other parts of Britain, and a correlation has been established between these Girvan groups and the middle and upper parts of the American Edinburg (Porterfield–Wilderness) formation.

The Craighead Limestone is the oldest member of the Caradoc Series in the Craighead Inlier, which lies on the northern side of the Girvan Valley to the west of Dailly. In the Craighead quarries it is seen to consist of a variable succession, up to about 90 m thick, of sandy limestones and calcareous mudstones overlapping across an uneven floor of Llandeilian cherts and spilites. The basal deposit is often seen to be a dark green spilitic conglomerate. Algae of the genus *Girvanella* and corals form the framework of the sediment, and the rich fauna also includes several forms of graptolites, crinoids, annelids, brachiopods, molluscs, and trilobites. Lapworth and Peach and Horne correlated the Limestone with the Stinchar but subsequent work placed it in the Balclatchie Group, although retaining it and the succeeding Plantinhead Flagstones in the Barr Series.

Recent research work by Tripp on the trilobites has shown however that the fauna, which includes such species as *Achatella consobrina, Encrinurus praecursor, Flexicalymene shirleyi,* and *Otarion beggi,* is more like that of the Drummuck Group than that of the Balclatchie. Williams' study of the brachiopods points to a correlation with a horizon slightly below that of the Cascade Grits. The Craighead Limestone is thus considered to be post-Balclatchie, probably high in the Ardwell Group, or even higher within the Ordovician.

The boundary between the divisions of the Whitehouse Group established by Lapworth (p. 29) is taken as the boundary between the Caradoc and Ashgill series. The highly inclined beds of the lower division occupy the shore northwards from Ardwell Bay and have yielded *Dicellograptus forchhammeri* and several species of brachiopod. Members of the upper division are visible at low tide to the west of Ardmillan House, their lowest beds distinguished by the occurrence of a band of bright purple mudstone. Highly fossiliferous calcareous grits and shales lie above. This division can be followed northeastwards to Woodland Bay, but the inter-relationships of the strata are complicated by inversion and folding. Further subdivision was however made in Woodland Bay by Lapworth. At the base is a band 1·5 m thick, predominantly of black shale, yielding amongst others the zone fossil *Dicellograptus complanatus,* and this is succeeded by 3 m of hard flaggy shales with grey calcareous ribs and in some bands an abundance of specimens of

Dictyonema. About 2 m of highly calcareous sandstones form the topmost member, the *Dionide* Beds. Other characteristic fossils from this locality include *Nematolites, Halysites catenularia, Leptellina albida, Strophomena shallochensis, Tentaculites anglicus*, and many gastropods and cephalopods. The trilobites include *Corrugatagnostus sp., Dionide lapworthi, Illaenus shallochensis, Stygina latifrons, Symphysops subarmatus*, and *Telephina reedi*.

Lapworth recorded nearby the presence of graptolites of the highest Caradoc Zone of *Pleurograptus linearis*. These include *Climacograptus tubuliferus, Dicellograptus morrisi, Leptograptus flaccidus, Orthograptus quadrimucronatus*, and *P. linearis*. In the Barr area a similar fauna was obtained by him from the lower division in Penwhapple Burn.

The Whitehouse Group is succeeded by the Shalloch (or Barren) Flagstone Group, a series of almost unfossiliferous flagstones and shales with bands of greywacke. They are best exposed in Woodland Bay, and are also seen in Penwhapple Burn in a section 1200 m in length. In this section the beds have an inverted dip to the south-east, apparently running under the Whitehouse Group, and are faulted to the north-west against Silurian rocks. Green mudstones near the base of the Group have yielded, in Penwhapple Burn, the characteristic trace-fossil *Nematolites*.

In the Craighead Inlier the Craighead Limestone and Plantinhead Flag-stones, of upper Ardwell age, are succeeded by rapidly alternating sandy and shaly rocks typical of the Ardwell, Whitehouse, and Shalloch Flagstone groups. The only fossils seen, however, are forms such as *Nematolites*, characteristic of the Shalloch Flagstones, and there is no evidence of the presence here of the Whitehouse Group. The inlier has an anticlinal form with north-eastward plunge.

The Drummuck Group occurs only in the Craighead Inlier. It consists mainly of mudstones, with sandy beds and, in places, a basal conglomerate or grit. Lamont has divided the Group into two parts distinguished by their brachiopod and trilobite faunas. On Quarrel Hill olive-green mudstones low in the Group have yielded many trilobites, including *Cryptolithus portlockii girvanensis, Flexicalymene* cf. *meeki, Lonchodomas drummuckensis, Pterygometopus*? *quarrelensis*, and a variety of *Tretaspis seticornis*. Brachiopods are more abundant in the succeeding 'Crinoid Bed', a shelly sandstone, the most common species being *Brachyprion matutinum* and *Fardenia scotica*, both unknown in the upper division. Other forms confined to the lower division are *Leangella discuneata, Nicolella actoniae* var., and *Sowerbyella subcorrugata*. Gastropods and bivalves are also common.

PLATE II
A. Pillow-lavas of Arenig age near Downan Point, Ayrshire, showing vesicular margins. The interstices are filled with limestone and chert, and the pillows are smoothed by modern wave action. (Geol. Surv. Photo. No. C706).
B. Folded Silurian rocks at Pettico Wick, near St. Abbs, Berwickshire. A broad horizontal syncline in greywackes and shales. The complex axial region of the fold forms the low rocks near water-level. The crag in the right fore-ground is of Lower Old Red Sandstone lava which forms the peninsula of St. Abb's Head, separated from the Silurian rocks by a fault in the bay. (Geol. Surv. Photo. No. D1230).

PLATE II

A

B

PLATE III

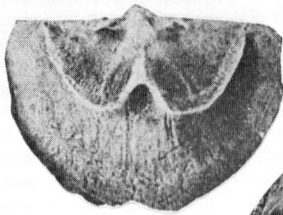

1   x 4

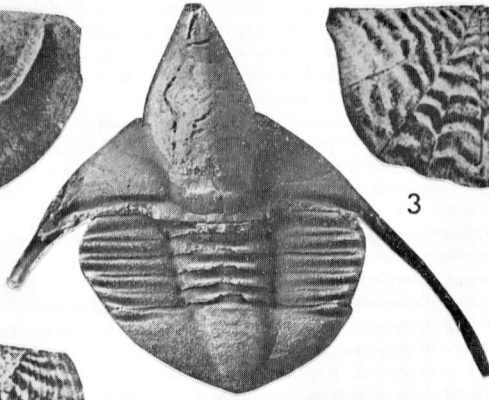

2   x 2

3   x 3·5

4   x 4

5   x 4

6   x 4

7   x 2

8   x 1

9   x 1

10   x 3

11   x 3·5

The higher division is well exposed in the Lady Burn near South Threave. The highly fossiliferous 'Starfish Bed' is a hard greenish grey calcareous sandstone rich in cystoids, asteroids, brachiopods, molluscs, and tribolites. Over thirty genera of trilobites have been recorded. They are grouped in the Zone of *Phillipsinella parabola*, which has been equated to that of *Dicellograptus complanatus*, and include *Bartoninus keisleyensis, Diacalymene drummuckensis,* and *Sphaerocoryphe thomsoni,* as well as *P. parabola. Dicellograptus anceps,* of the highest Ordovician zone, has been recorded in mudstones above the 'Starfish Bed' in the Lady Burn. The highest beds are sandy mudstones rich in trilobites, brachiopods, and molluscs, and are also referred to the Zone of *D. anceps.* Higher Ashgill beds may be cut out by an unconformity at the base of the Silurian, but may be represented by the High Mains sandstone (p. 45).

The Drummuck trilobite fauna, like those of older Ordovician formations, includes a high proportion of forms peculiar to the Girvan area.

PLATE III

LOWER PALAEOZOIC FOSSILS

1. *Leptellina semilunata* Williams. Ordovician, Stinchar Limestone.
2. *Lonchodomas drummuckensis* Reed. Ordovician, Drummuck Group, Starfish Bed.
3. *Ptychoglyptus* cf. *virginiensis* Willard. Ordovician, Albany Division, Tappins Group.
4. *Glyptorthis balclatchiensis* (Davidson). Ordovician, Craighead Limestone.
5. *Scaphorthis* cf. *virginiensis* Cooper. Ordovician, Stinchar Limestone.
6. Starfish. Ordovician, Drummuck Group, Starfish Bed.
7. *Orthograptus rugosus* (Emmons) *apiculatus* Elles and Wood. Ordovician, Ardwell Group.
8. *Monograptus communis* (Lapworth) *rostratus* Elles and Wood. Silurian, Birkhill Shales.
9. *Chasmops bisseti* (Reed). Ordovician, Drummuck Group.
10. *Orthambonites parvicrassicostatus* Cooper. Ordovician, Stinchar Limestone.
11. *Hesperorthis australis* Cooper *exitis* Williams. Ordovician, *Valcourea confinis* Flags.

Nos. 1, 3, 4, 5, 10 and 11 are reproduced by permission of the Geological Society of London from:

Williams A. 1962. The Barr and Lower Ardmillan Series (Caradoc) of the Girvan district, south-west Ayrshire. *Mem. geol. Soc. Lond.,* **3.**

4. SILURIAN

More than half of the area of the South of Scotland is occupied by Silurian rocks, which crop out in a belt up to about 50 km wide to the south-east of the Ordovician. The belt extends from the Mull of Galloway to the North Sea, but in the east the outcrop is much interrupted by areas of Upper Palaeozoic rocks. There are also small areas of Silurian to the north of the Ordovician of Girvan.

Llandovery rocks, the oldest of the Silurian system, form the 'Central Belt' of Peach and Horne, by far the greater part of the main outcrop, lying between Ordovician rocks to the north-west and younger Silurian, of the Wenlock Series, to the south-east. These last constitute the narrow 'Southern Belt', which extends from Burrow Head to near Hawick, east of which rocks of the same age occur in a number of large inliers surrounded by Upper Palaeozoic strata. As pointed out in Chapter 2 the Silurian rocks are highly folded and their outcrop is modified in many places by the presence of Ordovician inliers.

			Graptolite Zones
Wenlock Series	Raeberry Castle Beds		*Cyrtograptus lundgreni* *C. ellesi* *C. linnarssoni* *C. rigidus*
	Riccarton Beds		*Monograptus riccartonensis* *C. murchisoni*
Llandovery Series	Gala Group	Hawick Rocks (unfossiliferous) Queensberry Grits Abbotsford Flags	*M. crenulatus* *M. griestoniensis* *M. crispus* *M. turriculatus*
	Birkhill Shales	Upper	*Rastrites maximus* *M. sedgwickii* *M. convolutus*
		Lower	*M. gregarius* *M. cyphus* *Cystograptus vesiculosus* *Akidograptus acuminatus* *Glyptograptus persculptus*

The subdivision and order of succession of the Silurian rocks of the Southern Uplands are controversial subjects. The classification shown opposite is based on the work of Lapworth and Peach and Horne, and also takes into account subsequent published research and changes in taxonomy.

The recognition of the lowest zone, which is about 1 m thick at the base of the Birkhill Shales at Dobb's Linn, is due to Jones and Pugh. The classification of the Wenlock Series requires complete revision as a result of recent research by Mrs. C. Clarkson, Craig, and Walton, which has confirmed the earlier view of the latter authors that the Raeberry Castle Beds in the type-area in Kirkcudbrightshire are of Llandovery age, and that the Hawick Rocks there are younger than the Riccarton Beds. The name 'Riccarton Group', used by Warren for all the Wenlock rocks of the Riccarton area in Roxburghshire, might appropriately be adopted for the Southern Uplands as a whole, and the term 'Raeberry Castle Beds' used only as a local name for Llandovery rocks near Raeberry Castle. It seems that the term 'Hawick Rocks' has been used in the past on a primarily lithological basis and may now be seen to be devoid of any precise age significance. In Kirkcudbrightshire and Roxburghshire evidence favours a Wenlockian age, but similar rocks in Wigtownshire have yielded Llandoverian graptolites (p. 41).

The subdivision of the Silurian rocks of the Girvan district, and their correlation with those of the Southern Uplands, were worked out by Lapworth and later slightly modified by Peach and Horne and by Pringle.

	Southern Uplands	Girvan District	
Wenlock Series	Raeberry Castle Beds		Dailly Series
	Riccarton Beds	Straiton Group	
Llandovery Series	Gala Group	Drumyork Group Bargany Group Penkill Group	
	Birkhill Shales	Camregan Group Saugh Hill Group Mulloch Hill Group	Newlands Series

The Newlands Series consists largely of shallow-water rocks with a fauna characterized by corals, brachiopods, molluscs, and trilobites. Graptolites occur in widely separated thin beds. The Series thus contrasts with the much thinner graptolitic Birkhill Shales in the same way as the varied Ordovician rocks of Girvan contrast with the Glenkiln and Hartfell shales of Moffat. Such differences are absent in the younger rocks, which in both areas include conglomerates, grits, greywackes, flaggy sandstones, shales, and mudstones, and are indeed more finely grained in the lower part of the Dailly Series than in the Gala Group. In this account the two areas are described separately.

Llandovery Rocks: Southern Uplands

The type-locality of the **Birkhill Shales** is Dobb's Linn, near Birkhill
Cottage, at the head of Moffat Water (Fig. 7). Details of the rocks and of the
graptolite sequence were first published by Lapworth in 1878, but those given
here are based largely on the recent account by Toghill, which modifies only
slightly Lapworth's original conclusions by the application of modern
palaeontological and petrological knowledge.

The Lower Birkhill Shales, 20 m thick, consist largely of black graptolitic
mudstone in bands between about 0·1 and 0·3 m thick. These bands are
separated by partings of pale soft claystone, generally less than 0·1 m thick,
which include occasional bands of grey calcareous nodules. The claystone is
possibly of volcanic origin and is common also in the Upper Birkhill Shales,
some 23 m thick, which are made up mainly of alternations of grey and black
mudstone ranging from very thin layers up to beds about 0·3 m thick.
Graptolites are abundant throughout and, although there is no apparent
discontinuity at the base, there is a striking difference between the fauna
and that of the underlying Upper Hartfell Shales. Lapworth observed that
none of the many genera of many-branched graptolites of the Glenkiln and
Hartfell shales survived in the Birkhill Shales. In contrast, except in the two
lowest zones, there is in the Birkhill Shales a profusion of individuals and
species of *Monograptus*, and, to a less extent, *Rastrites*, genera unknown in
older rocks. The following list indicates the fossils characteristic of each
graptolite zone at Dobb's Linn and neighbouring localities.

Rastrites maximus:	*Monograptus halli, M. nudus, M. turriculatus minor Petalograptus altissimus, R. maximus.*
Monograptus sedgwickii:	*Climacograptus scalaris, Glyptograptus tamariscus, M. decipiens, M. involutus, M. nudus, M. regularis, M. sedgwickii, M. tenuis, Discinocaris browniana.*
Monograptus convolutus:	*Cephalograptus cometa, Climacograptus scalaris. G. tamariscus, M. clingani, M. convolutus, M. denticulatus, M. jaculum, M. leptotheca, M. limatulus, M. lobiferus, Orthograptus bellulus, P. folium, R. hybridus, R. peregrinus.*
Monograptus gregarius:	*M. argutus, M. fimbriatus, M. gregarius, M. leptotheca, M. triangulatus, O. cyperoides, P. folium, R. peregrinus, D. browniana.*
Monograptus cyphus:	*Climacograptus innotatus, M. atavus, M. cyphus, M. revolutus, M. sandersoni, O. mutabilis, Rhaphidograptus toernquisti.*
Cystograptus vesiculosus:	*Climacograptus medius, C. rectangularis, Cystograptus vesiculosus, Dimorphograptus confertus, D. decussatus, D. elongatus, D. erectus, M. atavus.*
Akidograptus acuminatus:	*A. acuminatus, A. ascensus, Climacograptus normalis, Diplograptus modestus.*
Glyptograptus persculptus:	*C. medius, C. normalis, G. persculptus.*

The Llandovery outcrop was interpreted by Peach and Horne as being
formed mainly by rocks of the Gala Group in which the Birkhill Shales were
frequently exposed in narrow, tightly compressed anticlines. The recent re-

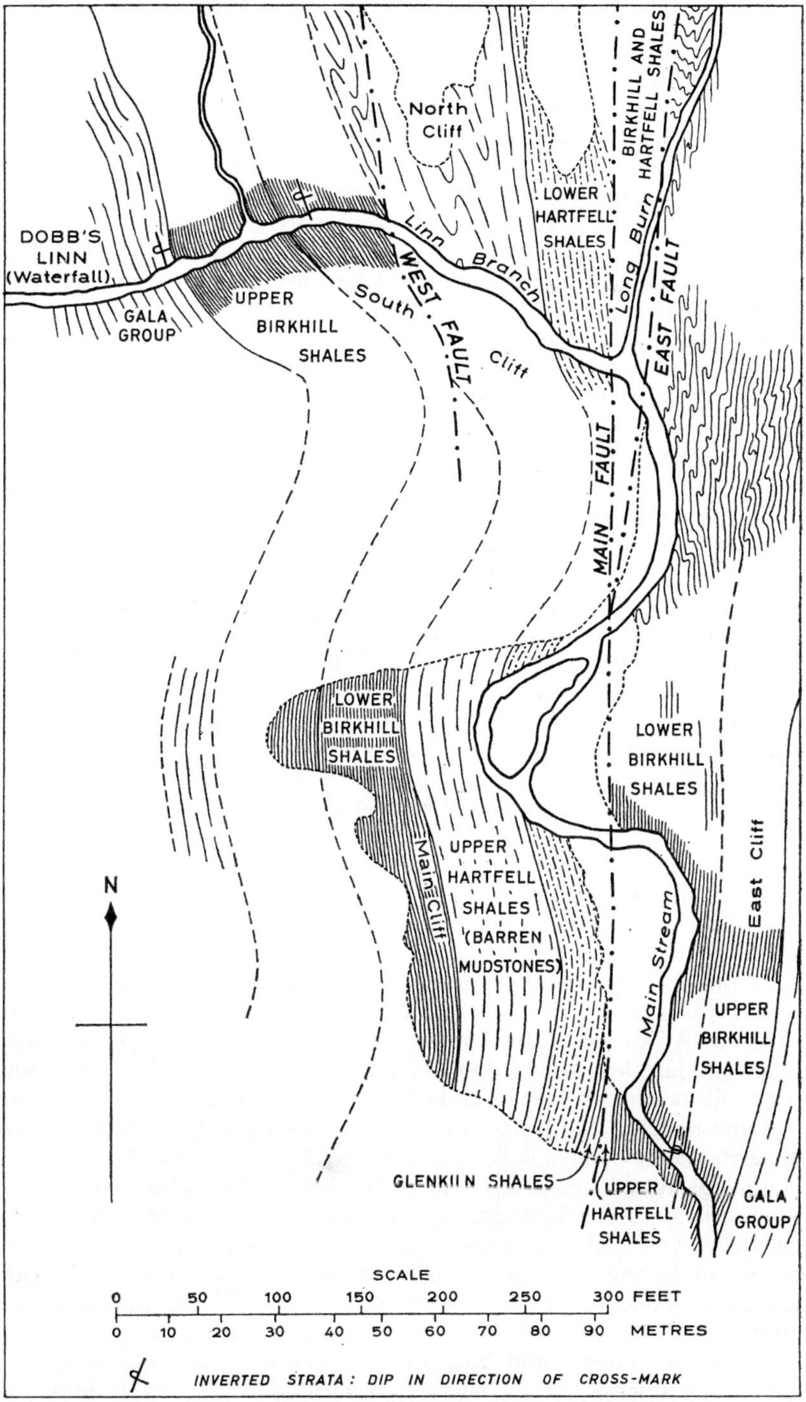

FIG. 7. *The Moffat Series at Dobb's Linn, Moffatdale*
(After Lapworth.)

interpretation of occurrences of the Glenkiln Shales in south-west Scotland (Figs. 4, 5) inspires doubt as to the fold-repeated nature of outcrops of the Birkhill Shales, such as those described by Peach and Horne at Clanyard Bay, near the Mull of Galloway, and in Selcoth Burn in Moffatdale. It may be that at these localities a number of bands of graptolitic shale are developed within a shale-greywacke sequence, as these authors themselves recognized elsewhere, for example near Slunkrainy, some 11 km north of Clanyard Bay. Positive evidence for this is given by recent work south of Glenluce in Wigtownshire. Such an interpretation is not necessarily inconsistent with the apparent facies change in the Shales as they are followed north-westwards from the Clanyard Bay–Moffat line (see below).

Little change is seen in the Birkhill Shales, even in minute details, as they are followed to north-east or south-west from Dobb's Linn, the characteristics of the type-section being maintained from the Mull of Galloway to Melrose. When they are followed across the strike, however, either to north-west or to south-east, changes in lithology and thickness occur within a very short distance. The onset of the greywacke facies, which characterizes the Gala Group, occurs generally earlier than along the 'Moffat Line' through Dobb's Linn. Black grits and greywackes appear in the Upper Birkhill Shales in the Entertrona Burn, in the upper Ettrick. At Ettrickbridge End, some 7 or 8 km south-east of the 'Moffat Line', greywackes and black shales make up the Lower Birkhill Shales, and the Upper consist of greywackes, flags, and shales, like those of the succeeding Abbotsford Flags. A similar change takes place to the north-west, for example in Peeblesshire and southern Midlothian. Near Fountainhall, some 16 km north-west of Galashiels, all the zones of the Birkhill Shales except the highest are represented by thin beds of graptolitic shale interstratified with conglomerates, grits, greywackes and sandy shales. Toghill points out that the highest graptolite shales are exposed at localities, such as Craigmichan Scaurs, a short distance south-east of the line through Dobb's Linn. These beds, higher in the Zone of *R. maximus*, yield specimens of *R. maximus* and *M. halli* in an abundance unknown at Dobb's Linn.

At Hartfell only the Zone of *R. maximus* is formed of massive grits, but at Newton Stewart the whole of the Birkhill Shales appears to consist of greywacke and shale. In the intervening ground the change in lithology is seen to be developed to a variable extent. The change is well displayed in the Galloway peninsula. At Clanyard Bay, as described above, the whole formation resembles equivalent beds at Dobb's Linn, but at Dumbreddan Bay, some 6 km to the north, the Zone of *M. sedgwickii* is represented by grey shales and limestone nodules, and farther to the north the change to coarser-grained sediments is developed in lower beds also.

Lithological variation of this type is not observed in the **Gala Group** which includes, in both the Southern Uplands and the Girvan area, flags, grits, greywackes and shales. Coarse-grained greywackes and conglomerates are common in the central region of the Central Belt. Peach and Horne estimated the maximum thickness of the Group to be between 900 and 1200 m whereas recent work in Wigtownshire and near Hawick suggests that in these areas the Hawick Rocks alone are at least 3000 m thick and the lower beds of the Gala Group at least 750 m. The difference is due to the realization that the beds are less tightly folded than was formerly thought, and is in accord with similar recent studies in the Ordovician rocks.

In the Moffat district the Gala Group is divided into three lithological formations:

Hawick Rocks	Grey, green, and red shales with brown flags and micaceous greywacke bands.
Queensberry Grits	Greywackes and shales with massive grits and bands of conglomerate.
Abbotsford Flags	Purple and grey flags and shales.

Three graptolite zones have been recognized, indicating the equivalence of the Group to part of the Upper Llandovery Series.

Monograptus griestoniensis	*M. griestoniensis*, *M. marri*, *Retiolites geinitzianus*, etc.
Monograptus crispus	*M. crispus*, *M. discus*, *M. exiguus*, *M. spiralis*, etc.
Monograptus turriculatus	*M. exiguus*, *M. galaensis*, *M. halli*, *M. turriculatus*, etc.

Grey shales at the base of the Group, and their junction with the Birkhill Shales, are well displayed at the waterfall at Dobb's Linn (Fig. 7). As the beds are followed towards the north the grey shale facies occurs progressively earlier, within the Birkhill Shales (p. 38). The main development of the Abbotsford Flags is in the ground between Moffat and Melrose, and the graptolites of the Zone of *M.turriculatus* have been found at several localities near Abbotsford.

In the Moffat area the Queensberry Grits are repeated by a series of over-folds inclined towards the north-west, the intensity of folding being sufficient to induce in places a schistose structure. The grit, which is locally conglomeratic, forms beds between 0·6 and 6 m thick. On Pin Stane hill, north-east of Beattock Summit, a bed which can be followed from the Clyde to the Tweed contains boulders up to 0·25 m across and rounded pebbles. They include Ordovician volcanic rocks, and metamorphic rocks like some from the Eastern Highlands. Shales between the grits yield the trace-fossils *Crossopodia scotica* and *Myrianites tenuis*.

In Wigtownshire and Kirkcudbrightshire, north-west of a line through Mochrum, Gatehouse of Fleet, and the northern edge of the Criffell Granite, the Llandovery outcrop is largely made up of Queensberry Grits, with local developments of Abbotsford Flags as on Culcaigrie Hill, east of Gatehouse, and in Trowdale Glen, north-east of Crossmichael. On Craigenputtock Hill, south of Moniaive, the Queensberry Grits include a conglomerate like that of Pin Stane, in that it contains pebbles of metamorphic Highland rocks second in abundance only to those of greywacke, which are up to 0·25 m across. The broad outcrop of the Grits is interrupted in places by narrow zones of Birkhill Shales, in some cases with Ordovician members of the Moffat Series, universally interpreted until recently as anticlinal inliers. Hawick Rocks lie to the south-east and are well exposed on the coast between the Mull of Galloway and Kirkcudbright.

The Queensberry Grits in the Glenluce area, studied recently by Gordon, may be represented by the Garheugh Formation, a group of greywackes with current-bedded siltstones and shales. No fossils have been found in these

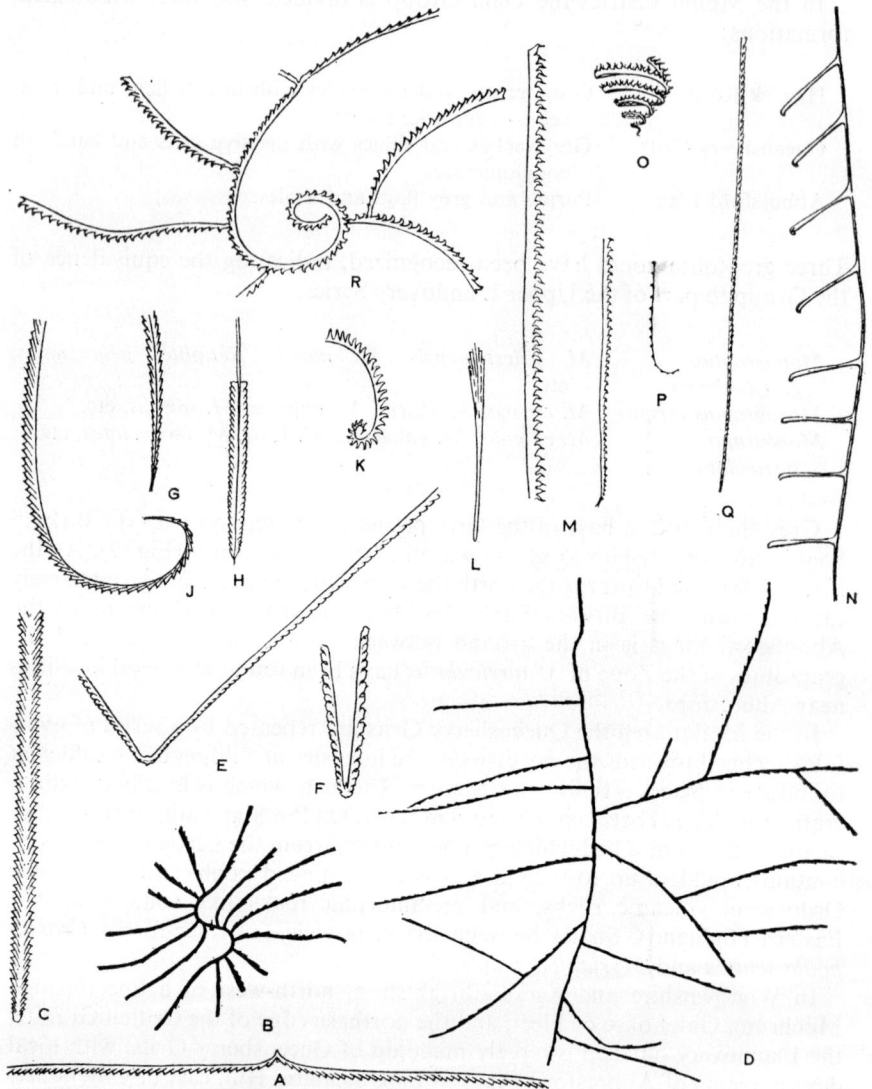

FIG. 8. *Ordovician and Silurian Graptolites*

(All drawings natural size after Elles and Wood.)

Ordovician, Arenig Series, **A,** *Didymograptus extensus* (Hall). Glenkiln Shales, **B,** *Nemagraptus gracilis* (Hall). Hartfell Shales, **C,** *Orthograptus truncatus* (Lapworth), **D,** *Pleurograptus linearis* (Carruthers), **E,** *Dicellograptus complanatus* Lapworth, **F,** *Dicellograptus anceps* (Nicholson). Silurian, Lower Birkhill Shales, **G,** *Akidograptus acuminatus* (Nicholson), **H,** *Diplograptus modestus* Lapworth, **J,** *Monograptus cyphus* Lapworth, **K,** *M. fimbriatus* (Nicholson). Upper Birkhill Shales, **L,** *Cephalograptus cometa* (Geinitz), **M,** *M. sedgwickii* (Portlock), **N,** *Rastrites maximus* Carruthers, **O,** *M. turriculatus* (Barrande), **P,** *M. crispus* Lapworth, **Q,** *M. griestoniensis* (Nicol). Wenlock Series, **R,** *Cyrtograptus murchisoni* Carruthers.

rocks, which include red and green shales and a boulder conglomerate, as seen elsewhere in the Queensberry Grits. The outcrop of the formation includes an inlier of graptolitic Birkhill Shales and is bounded to the north-west and south-east by, respectively, a group of greywackes of Birkhill Shales age, the Kilfillan Formation, and the Hawick Rocks, which crop out between Kirkmaiden and Burrow Head. The nature of the inter-formational boundaries is not clear.

These Hawick Rocks have been divided by Rust into the older Carghidown beds, characterized by the occurrence of primary red beds, and the younger Kirkmaiden beds, which have yielded graptolites characteristic of the zones of *M. griestoniensis* and *M. crenulatus*, the highest of the Llandovery Series. From the Carghidown beds through the Kirkmaiden beds into the older Garheugh Formation the direction of upward sequence is universally north-westward, and it is therefore concluded that the boundary between the last two groups is a strike-fault with a large down-throw towards the south-east.

Between Wigtown Bay and Kirkcudbright the Hawick Rocks consist of thin greywackes with siltstones and unfossiliferous shales, in some cases red in colour. Craig and Walton demonstrated that here too the direction of upward succession is nearly always north-westwards. They recognized a transition in this direction from the Wenlockian Riccarton Beds, with graptolitic shales, to the Hawick Rocks, and concluded that the latter formation is the younger, and of Wenlock or Ludlow age. They suggested also that the Queensberry Grits too might be partly Wenlockian. Rust contends that the Riccarton–Hawick boundary is a fault, and that the apparent interbedding of graptolitic (Riccarton) shales with red (Hawick) shales is the result of fault-slicing. The northern boundary of the Hawick Rocks is a strike-fault, as in the Kirkmaiden district. Structurally the Hawick Rocks may be divided into three broad zones. The central zone consists of closely folded beds in which the *faltenspiegel* (p. 9) is almost horizontal, whereas to north and south the steeply dipping strata are little folded, and young consistently towards the north-west. Subsequent research by Craig and Walton has reinforced their belief in the unbroken upward passage from the Riccarton Beds to the Hawick Rocks. It has also shown that the Raeberry Castle Beds, formerly considered to be Wenlockian, include graptolites of the Llandoverian zones of *Monograptus gregarius*, *M. sedgwickii*, and *M. crispus*, and lie in normal succession below the Riccarton Beds. They are typically developed, to a thickness of at least 400 m, on the coast eastwards from Kirkcudbright Bay, and consist of thin greywackes, olive-green shales with limestone nodules, and occasional bands of fossiliferous grit and conglomerate, the 'Balmae Grits'. The shales have yielded gastropods, bivalves, and cephalopods such as '*Orthoceras*' *etheridgei*. The fauna of the 'Balmae Grits' includes corals, crinoids, bryozoans, brachiopods, molluscs, and trilobites. A fossiliferous grit with a similar fauna occurs in the Wenlockian Zone of *Cyrtograptus linnarssoni* at Wrae Hill, north of Langholm (p. 44).

To the east and north-east of the Moffat area the rocks of the Gala Group are less massive and coarse-grained, and are often fossiliferous. Graptolitic shales occur at Deloraine in the upper Ettrick, some 16 km south-west of Selkirk, and in the Tima Water and Rankle Burn, large right-bank tributaries. The old Grieston slate quarry, west of Howford, is one of several graptolite localities near Innerleithen, and was one of the first to be recorded in the

D

south of Scotland. Blue and grey shales with limestones and calcareous ribs yield *Monograptus griestoniensis, M. priodon,* and other graptolites. The Queensberry (Buckholm) Grits are well exposed on Buckholm Hill, at Clovenfords, and in the Caddon Water, to the north and west of Galashiels. The shales locally yield graptolites of the zones of *M. turriculatus* and *M. crispus,* and the bedding-planes are locally covered with trace-fossils such as *Crossopodia* and *Nereites.* These last are particularly common in old quarries at Thornylee, west of Clovenfords, and Greenhill, south of Selkirk. Graptolites have been recorded from many sections near Lauder, but in the Easter Burn, some 8 km to the north-east, a fine-grained conglomerate has yielded poorly preserved corals, crinoid stems, and brachiopods, which have suggested a correlation with the Blackwood Beds of the Girvan area (p. 48).

Between Selkirk and Hawick lies the type-area of the Hawick Rocks. They consist of shales and thin greywackes, and, apart from trace-fossils, and fragments of the crustacean *Ceratiocaris* found near Hawick, they have yielded no fossils. In the Jed Water just south of Jedburgh vertical Hawick Rocks are overlain by horizontal beds of the Old Red Sandstone in a striking unconformity first recorded by Hutton.

Warren has recently postulated that the Hawick Rocks of Hawick belong to the Wenlock Series (see below). Their boundary with the Wenlockian Stobs Castle Beds appears to exhibit a transitional lithology which includes the red shales of the Hawick Rocks and the graptolitic shales of the Stobs Castle Beds. Warren sees no evidence at the boundary of the strike-fault, with a throw of at least 3500 m, which would have to be present if the Hawick Rocks were the older formation, but Rust dismisses this difficulty and interprets the evidence here in the same way as in the Kirkcudbright area (p. 41).

In Berwickshire there are two general areas of Llandovery rocks separated from each other and from the main outcrop by strips of Upper Old Red Sandstone rocks. On the coast for more than 9 km west of St. Abb's Head the Queensberry Grits are almost continuously exposed (Plate IIB). They consist of greywackes, siltstones and shales, which are locally graptolitic, many of the bands of greywacke attaining a thickness of 6 m or more. The spectacular unconformity of the Upper Old Red Sandstone on the Llandovery at Siccar Point (Plate I) near the western end of the outcrop, is of considerable historical importance because of its inspiring influence on the developing ideas of Hutton as a result of his visit to the locality in 1788. The impressive folding of the Queensberry Grits in this area prompted Hall to conduct the earliest laboratory studies of tectonics, by which he showed how rocks might be folded under horizontal compression. Many of the folds are markedly asymmetrical, and strike-faults, usually of small throw, are commonly developed in the axial regions. From west to east the direction of dip of the axial planes changes from north-north-westward to south-south-eastward, the broad inverted-fan structure being similar to, and perhaps corresponding with, Lapworth's 'Hawick Exocline' or synclinorium (Fig. 1). However, if the incalculable effects of strike-faults are discounted, the beds which are exposed in the middle of the structure appear to be older than those on the flanks, and not younger as the name would suggest. In addition to minor intrusions of basic composition the rocks east of Fast Castle are in places cut by volcanic breccia, made up largely of fragments of greywacke and shale.

An isolated area of 'Silurian' rocks north of Eyemouth includes two formations, described and named by Shiells and Dearman. The same authors have recently suggested on structural grounds that the more northerly formation, the intensely folded Coldingham Beds, may be of Dalradian age. The Linkim Beds, lying to the south, are tectonically less complex, but the generally broad folds face downwards. The general structure of the two groups is interpreted as a pre-Devonian recumbent anticline, facing south-eastwards, with a horizontal axial plane. The outcrop of the Linkim Beds lies in the lower inverted limb and that of the Coldingham Beds in the upper uninverted limb, the boundary between the two formations being a reverse-fault with south-eastward hade. The first folding of the Coldingham Beds is not developed in the Linkim Beds and is thus inferred to be of pre-Gala Group age. The Linkim Beds are known to be of Silurian age by the recent discovery in them of monograptid material, during the resurvey of the area by the Geological Survey.

The Silurian rocks extending southwards from Eyemouth have many of the characteristics of the Hawick Rocks, including a marked absence of fossils. Their structure is locally complex and sharp flexures of fold axes have been described by Dearman and his collaborators.

Wenlock Rocks: Southern Uplands

The most westerly occurrence of Wenlock rocks is on Burrow Head in Wigtownshire, where a small area of Riccarton Beds (p. 41) is shown by Rust to be faulted against Hawick Rocks to the north, with some tectonic interjacency of the two formations. The graptolite fauna is that of the basal Wenlock Zone of *Cyrtograptus murchisoni* and includes excellent specimens of the zone-species. The formation is similar in fauna to the Stobs Castle Beds (p. 44), but its lithology of greywackes and shales lacks the red beds of that group.

On Meikle Ross, the headland east of Wigtown Bay, the Riccarton Beds are estimated by Craig and Walton to be at least 550 m thick. They consist of grey greywackes, about 0·6 m in average thickness, flaggy siltstones, shales, and slates, with thin bands of bluish grey graptolitic shales. Recent study of the graptolites has demonstrated the presence of the zones of *Cyrtograptus murchisoni, Monograptus riccartonensis*, and *C. ellesi*. Sedimentary structures occur on many bedding-planes and indicate a general flow of turbidity currents from the north-east. The adjacent Raeberry Castle Beds, deposited by currents from the south-west, and at times from the north-west, are described on p. 41.

The Riccarton Beds appear to be present in a narrow strip of altered Wenlock rocks south of the Criffell Granite. North-east of the River Nith they include the characteristic graptolites *C. murchisoni* and *Monograptus riccartonensis*, but the Raeberry Castle Beds are not recorded until the area of Langholm and Riccarton is reached.

South of Hawick, and in the Riccarton inlier to the south-east, the term 'Riccarton Group' has been applied by Warren to all the Wenlock rocks, which span the full range of Wenlockian time. He has subdivided the Group thus:

Caddroun Burn Beds 1500 m	Upper	*Cyrtograptus lundgreni*
	Lower	*C. rigidus*
Penchrise Burn Beds 450 m		*Monograptus riccartonensis*
Shankend Beds 600 m		
Stobs Castle Beds 1350 m		*C. murchisoni*

The zones of *C. ellesi* and *C. linnarssoni* are thought to be present between those of *C. lundgreni* and *C. rigidus*, but the zone-fossils themselves are generally rare in northern England and southern Scotland. The Zone of *C. linnarssoni* is, however, recognized in the Langholm area, adjacent to the west. The graptolite fauna resembles in some respects that of Bohemia, for example in the occurrence of *C. insectus* and *C. centrifugus* in the Zone of *C. murchisoni*.

The Stobs Castle Beds, which occur only in the main outcrop, consist of thin fine-grained greywackes, siltstones, greyish green and red mudstones, graptolitic shales, and carbonaceous, non-graptolitic shales. The higher formations are distinguished from each other mainly on a palaeontological basis. The Shankend Beds include massive greywackes, often coarse-grained, but lack red mudstones. A 3-metre band of coarse-grained greywacke, the 'Berryfell Grit', is the basal member of the Penchrise Burn Beds. Above, the greywackes become in general progressively finer-grained. Graptolite shales become more common in the Upper Caddroun Burn Beds, in which olive-green mudstones are characteristic.

In the Hawick–Riccarton area as a whole the structural pattern conforms with the modern hypothesis for the Southern Uplands, namely a succession of open asymmetrical north-west-facing folds, often with much close folding on the gently dipping limbs, the rocks becoming generally younger to the north-west. Large strike-faults with downthrow to the south-east outweigh the effect of the folds, so that the units between them are successively older towards the north-west.

Warren's interpretation of the 'Riccarton Group' in the Hawick area is confirmed by the recent revision by the Geological Survey of the ground adjacent to the west, near Langholm. The zones of *Cyrtograptus murchisoni*, *Monograptus riccartonensis*, and *C. linnarssoni* are recognized, the older rocks lying to the north-west although this is also the general direction of upward succession in individual exposures. Major shatter-belts, trending north-north-eastwards, are seen in two cases to mark wrench-faults with a sinistral displacement of about 800 m. One large strike-fault, with a southward downthrow, lies in the crestal region of a major north-facing anticline. Unusual lithological features are the development of ironstone nodules in mudstone at two places, and of thin tuffs in three places, apparently in the Zone of *C. linnarssoni*.

North-east of the Riccarton inlier, between the Cheviot Hills and Jedburgh, there are several small inliers of Wenlock rocks within the Old Red Sandstone. The largest are in the valley of the Jed Water some 10 km above Jedburgh, in the uplands of the Leithope Forest to the east, and around Oxnam, about 6 km east of Jedburgh. Small patches of Silurian rocks occur here and there in this general area, usually with graptolites of the Zone of *M. riccartonensis* and clearly overlain unconformably by the Old Red Sandstone.

Llandovery Rocks: Girvan Area

The facies change seen in the Central Belt as the Birkhill Shales are followed north-westwards from the 'Moffat Line' (p. 38) is continued into the Girvan district, where rocks of this age constitute the **Newlands Series.** The Series occurs in three separate areas, in the Craighead Inlier north-west of Dailly, at Woodland Bay, and in a narrow outcrop extending north-eastwards and south-westwards for some 5 km through Camregan Hill. The sub-division shown below was established by Lapworth, and the correlation with the succession at Llandovery by Freshney. The Zone of *M. convolutus* includes at the top a band with *Cephalograptus cometa,* the zone-fossil of Lapworth's Birkhill classification. Except for the *R. maximus* Shales all these beds have been recognized in the Craighead Inlier, but south of the Girvan Valley *Pentamerus* Grits are the lowest Silurian rocks exposed.

The Mulloch Hill Group is well seen in the Craighead Inlier. Lamont suggested that the High Mains sandstone, unconformable on Ordovician rocks, should be taken as the basal member of the Group. It has, however, yielded the brachiopod *Hirnantia* ['*Orthis*'] *sagittifera,* a form characteristic of the topmost part of the Ashgill Series. The overlying conglomerate is mainly composed of pebbles of Ordovician volcanic and associated plutonic rocks, chert, and quartzite, embedded in a sandy matrix of a dull purple colour. Fossils obtained from the conglomerate at Quarrel Hill are mainly forms of brachiopods not seen in lower beds, thus emphasizing, as in the

Stage	Graptolite Zone	Local Classification	
Upper Llandovery	*Rastrites maximus*	Upper Camregan Grits *Rastrites maximus* Shales Camregan Grit and Limestone *Rhynchonella* Grits	Camregan Group 60 m
	Monograptus sedgwickii	*Monograptus sedgwickii* Shales	
Middle Llandovery	*M. convolutus* *M. gregarius* *M. cyphus*	Saugh Hill Sandstones and Grits Glenshalloch Shales Newlands *Pentamerus* Grits	Saugh Hill Group 150 m
Lower Llandovery	*Orthograptus vesiculosus* *Akidograptus acuminatus*	Glenwells Shales Mulloch Hill Sandstone Mulloch Hill Conglomerate	Mulloch Hill Group 110 m

Moffat Series, the palaeontological break between the Ordovician and Silurian rocks. The Mulloch Hill Sandstone consists of green and yellow sandstones and mudstones which are calcareous and highly fossiliferous. Typical Lower Llandovery brachiopods are common, such as *Cryptothyrella angustifrons*, *Dalmanella biconvexa*, and *Leptostrophia mullochensis*. Other characteristic fossils are *Heliolites interstinctus*, *Pinacopora grayi*, *Clorinda undata*, '*Camarotoechia*' *llandoveriana*, *Leangella scissa*, *Schizophorella mullochensis*, *Stricklandia lens*, *Conularia sowerbyi* and species of *Calymene*, *Encrinurus*, and *Illaenus*. The green and blue concretionary mudstones of the Glenwells Shales include striped shales from which Lapworth recorded *Akidograptus acuminatus*, *Climacograptus normalis*, and *Monograptus atavus*. A thin green conglomerate marks the top of the Shales.

In the Craighead Inlier the *Pentamerus* Grits appear to have an unconformable and overstepping relationship to the underlying Glenwells Shales and Mulloch Hill Sandstone. They are fine-grained calcareous sandstones and grits, weathering yellow or brown, with an abundant fauna characterized by *Clorinda undata*, with *Encrinurus* and other trilobites. Other fossils from the Grits are *Halysites catenularia*, *Coolinia* [*Fardenia*] *applanata*, *Craniops implicata*, *Resserella sp.*, *Stricklandia lens*, *Cyrtolites*, *Platyceras*, *Orthoceras*, *Acidaspis*, *Calymene*, *Cheirurus*, *Illaenus*, *Lichas*, *Phacops*, and *Staurocephalus*. The overlying grey and black flaggy shales are named alternatively from Glenshalloch, in the Craighead Inlier, or from the graptolites *Diplograptus modestus* and *Monograptus gregarius* which are found in them. The fauna includes also *Climacograptus normalis*, *Glyptograptus tamariscus*, *Monograptus argutus*, *M. atavus*, *M. crenularis*, *M. fimbriatus*, *M. leptotheca*, *Petalograptus palmeus*, and *Rastrites peregrinus*. Some pebbly beds occur in the upper part of the formation. The succeeding thick pebbly sandstones, until recently regarded as being of Old Red Sandstone age, resemble the Saugh Hill Grits and have yielded unidentifiable brachiopods.

The succession is continued in the Craighead Inlier by greyish brown shales and mudstones, formerly mapped as Old Red Sandstone but now assigned by Freshney to the *M. sedgwickii* Shales. They contain *Monograptus variabilis*, *Petalograptus palmeus*, and *Trematis sp.*, and pass upwards into purple sandstones and conglomerates with a brachiopod-trilobite fauna which includes such forms as *Pentamerus oblongus*, *Pholidostrophia sefinensis*, and *Eocoelia sp.*, all indicative of the Upper Llandovery. These sandy beds appear to be correlative with part of the Camregan Group and are unconformably succeeded to the north by the Old Red Sandstone.

The Llandovery outcrop of Camregan Hill is fault-bounded to the south and along most of its northern edge, the beds in many places seeming to dip beneath the Ordovician. In Penwhapple Glen, east of Camregan Hill, the oldest Silurian rocks are green and grey calcareous flags and shales which have yielded specimens of *Clorinda* and are probably equivalent to part of the Woodland Limestone (see below). They are succeeded by the Glenshalloch Shales, black mudstones and shales with a rich graptolite fauna, including *Climacograptus hughesi*, *C. normalis*, *Dimorphograptus swanstoni*, *Glyptograptus tamariscus*, *Diplograptus modestus*, *Monograptus crenularis*, *M. gregarius*, *M. leptotheca*, and *Petalograptus palmeus*. The Shales are followed by the Saugh Hill Grits, which form a prominent feature at the type-locality, south-west of Camregan Hill, where they contain bands of conglomerate and a breccia with angular fragments of grit and shale. The *M. sedgwickii* Shales are well exposed in Penwhapple Glen. They consist of greyish green and black mudstones and shales, with graptolites especially abundant in the upper beds. The assemblage includes *Monograptus convolutus, M. intermedius, M. nudus, M. sedgwickii,* and *Rastrites peregrinus.*

The basal beds of the Camregan Group succeed the *M. sedgwickii* Shales in Penwhapple Glen. The massive basal grits and flags, with rhynchonellid casts, are inverted and are succeeded to north-west by flags and limestones, and beyond by fossiliferous calcareous shales and mudstones. The fauna includes brachiopods and trilobites, such as *Cyrtia exporrecta, Dicoelosia biloba, Dolerorthis rustica, Eospirifer plicatellus, Pentamerus oblongus, Protomegastrophia walmstedti,* '*Rhynchospira*' *camreganensis, Acidaspis bispinosus, Calymene blumenbachi, Encrinurus mullochensis, Eophacops elegans, Illaenus sp, Scutellum andersoni* and *Youngia trispinosa.* These beds are overlain by purple and green mudstones with a band of dark shale yielding *Monograptus nudus, M. runcinatus, M. turriculatus, Petalograptus palmeus,* and *Rastrites maximus,* characteristic of the highest Birkhill Zone of *R. maximus.* The massive unfossiliferous Upper Camregan Grits which succeed these shales may be more correctly assigned to the base of the Dailly Series. Fossiliferous grits and shelly mudstones of the Camregan Group, and the *R. maximus* Shales at the top, are exposed in Lauchlan Burn, about 2 km to the east.

The Newlands Series is also exposed in the area of Woodland Bay. At the northern end the basal conglomerate of the Saugh Hill Group forms the prominent Horse Rock. It is 15 m thick and rests unconformably on Ordovician rocks. Beds with pebbles of chert, greywacke, and gneissose rocks, are interbedded with thick bands of green grit. They are approximately coeval with the oldest Silurian rocks of Penwhapple Glen, but in appearance and pebble-content have been closely compared with the Ordovician conglomerates of the Corsewall Group in Galloway. Nearby on the islet of Craigskelly, which has locally given its name to the bed, the grits contain *Atrypa reticularis, Eocoelia hemisphaerica,* and *Strophomena.* The impure flaggy limestone above is known as the Woodland Limestone and contains *Alveolites labechei, Favosites gothlandicus,* and such brachiopods as *Stricklandia lens.* At Woodland Point, at the southern end of the bay, the limestone is about 9 m thick. The long list of fossils collected from it includes sponges, corals, brachiopods, gastropods, cephalopods, and trilobites. Here and at Craigskelly it is succeeded by the Glenshalloch Shales which have yielded, from thin dark beds, *Climacograptus normalis, Dictyonema sp., Diplograptus modestus, Monograptus atavus,* and *M. cyphus.* The highest beds are conglomerates and sandstones, which at Woodland Point are correlated with the Saugh Hill Sandstones and Grits and are divided into a basal quartz-conglomerate and the Scart grits and conglomeratic sandstones above.

The Gala Group is represented in the Girvan area by the lower part of the **Dailly Series.** The rocks are divided as follows:

| Drumyork Group and Bargany Group 330 m | Green flagstones and shales, unfossiliferous
Yellow, blue, and grey flagstones, with shales (Blackwood Beds)
Pale blue thick-bedded flagstones and shales (Glenfoot Beds) |

	Crytograptus grayi mudstones and shales
Penkill Group	*Protovirgularia* grits
300 m	Penkill flags and shales
	Purple shales and mudstones with *Crossopodia*, etc.

They occupy a narrow area between Penwhapple Glen and Knockgardner, some 8 km east-north-east of Dailly. North-eastwards from Hadyard Hill, south of Dailly, the outcrop is for much of its length a very narrow strip upfaulted between Old Red Sandstone and Carboniferous rocks. Normal stratigraphical junctions with the Wenlock Series and with the unconformable Old Red Sandstone occur beyond, respectively, the north-eastern and south-western ends of this strip.

The *Crossopodia* Shales resemble in lithology and fauna the 'slates' of Thornylee Quarry, near Clovenfords (p. 42), and are covered with annelid tracks, such as *Crossopodia scotica*, *Myrianites tenuis*, *Nereites sedgwicki*, and *N. cambrensis*. The dark shales yield many graptolites, including *Monograptus becki*, *M. exiguus*, *M. galaensis*, *Rastrites equidistans*, and *Retiolites obesus*, indicative of the basal Gala Zone of *M. turriculatus*. In Penwhapple Glen the grits and flaggy greywackes which succeed the *Crossopodia* Shales are perhaps equivalent to part of the Queensberry Grits, and are equally poor in fossils. In the succeeding *Cyrtograptus* Mudstones there is an interesting mixture of graptolitic and shelly faunas. Well displayed in the Glen the rocks include the following fossils: *Cyrtograptus grayi*, *M. galaensis*, *M. marri*, *M. nudus*, *Rastrites equidistans*, *Atrypa reticularis*, *Cyrtia exporrecta*, *Dolerorthis rustica*, *Glassia obovata*, *Leptaena rhomboidalis*, *Eoplectodonta penkillensis*, *Triplesia insularis*, *Lunulicardium elegans*, and *Dawsonoceras annulatum*.

The Glenfoot Beds are well exposed near the foot of Penwhapple Glen and in another burn some 2·6 km to the north-east. In the latter locality they are succeeded to the north-west by the Blackwood Beds, which include thin beds containing *Monograptus acus* and *M. priodon*. In this burn also, about 100 m south of the fault which truncates the Lower Palaeozoic succession, shales with limestone ribs have yielded fossil plants and a fauna which includes *Heliolites interstinctus*, *Palaeocyclus sp.*, '*Orthis*' *polygramma*, *Pentamerus oblongus*, *Poleumita discors* and *Discinocaris gigas*.

The Drumyork Group forms a narrow outcrop, steeply inverted towards the south-east, near Drumyork, about 6 km east-north-east of Dailly. From its lithology and unfossiliferous character, and its position immediately below the Wenlock rocks to the north-west, the Group was tentatively

---

PLATE IV

A. Bedding and axial-plane cleavage in Silurian rocks, about 8 km north of Langholm, Dumfriesshire. Greywacke, siltstone, and mudstone, with a marked cleavage in the mudstone beds. The gentler dip of the cleavage indicates that the beds are inverted, the original upper surface being to the right. (Geol. Surv. Photo. No. D617).

B. Ripple-marked Silurian greywacke, Berwickshire. Transverse current ripple-marks on upper surfaces of thinly bedded greywackes and siltstones. Haud Yauds, about 7 km north-west of Coldingham. (Geol. Surv. Photo. No. D1226).

correlated by Peach and Horne with the Hawick Rocks. Lapworth however had grouped them with the Straiton beds and Walton has pointed out that they may be of Wenlock age, together with the Bargany Group and at least part of the Penkill Group.

Wenlock Rocks: Girvan Area

Rocks of the **Straiton Group,** the upper part of the Dailly Series, form a narrow outcrop, some 8 km long, which extends south-westward from Straiton to beyond Drumyork. Except in the Drumyork area, where they rest conformably on the flags of the Drumyork Group, the south-eastern boundary of these Wenlock rocks is a fault. To the north-west they are succeeded unconformably by the Upper Old Red Sandstone, and immediately north-east of Straiton they are faulted against Lower Carboniferous rocks. The lower beds, the Blair Shales, contain an abundance of graptolites in thin layers of dark shale, and from a quarry near Blair, just west of Drumyork, the following forms have been recorded: *Cyrtograptus sp., Monograptus flemingi, M. priodon, M. riccartonensis, M. vomerinus,* and *Retiolites geinitzianus.* In associated strata there is a varied fauna including corals, brachiopods, cephalopods, and arthropods. The higher beds, the Straiton Grits and Conglomerates, include some fossiliferous bands of grit in the ground east of Knockgardner. The fauna includes *Atrypa reticularis, Eoplectodonta transversalis, Resserella* cf. *elegantula, Acaste downingiae, Calymene blumenbachi, Encrinurus punctatus,* and *Warburgella stokesi.*

PLATE V

A. Linear groove-casts in Silurian greywacke, Berwickshire. The casts, on the under surface of a bed of greywacke, are the infilling of grooves eroded in the sea-floor by the passage of solid objects, such as rock fragments, at the base of the material suspended in a turbidity current. Shore 5·5 km north-west of St. Abbs. (Geol. Surv. Photo. No. D1227).

B. Longitudinal ripple-casts on the under surface of a bed of Silurian greywacke. The dendritic pattern shows mutual interference between casts. Windy Cleuch, about 3 km west-north-west of Riccarton Junction, Roxburghshire. (Geol. Surv. Photo. No. D658).

5. OLD RED SANDSTONE

Prior to the deposition of the Old Red Sandstone the older rocks underwent severe earth-movements and were subjected to great erosion. Part of the area became a basin of deposition, the floor of which was occupied by one or more lakes. The deposits fall into two distinct subdivisions—the Lower Old Red Sandstone and the Upper Old Red Sandstone. The earliest sediments were laid down on the upturned edges of the older rocks, and consist of sandstones and conglomerates, the latter being deposited as torrential gravels. Great thicknesses of lava were poured out of volcanoes situated along the flanks of the high ground bordering the depressed area, and some of the lavas appear to have flowed into the lakes where they were later covered by sediments which were partly lacustrine and partly fluviatile in origin.

Further upheaval and very extensive denudation of the area is indicated by the marked unconformity at the base of the Upper Old Red Sandstone, and during the subsidence which followed sediments consisting mainly of conglomerates, sandstones and marls were spread over the Lower Palaeozoic rocks far beyond the boundary of the earlier basin. Cornstones, nodular or lenticular masses of fine-grained limestone and sandy limestone, are numerous in the upper part of the succession, and, as pointed out by Burgess, may possibly represent soil replacement deposits formed in semi-arid conditions.

The problems concerning the junction between the Upper Old Red Sandstone and the Carboniferous are discussed on p. 63. It is very probable that in this region the Upper Old Red Sandstone facies persisted into Carboniferous times, and that at least some of the strata here described as Upper Old Red Sandstone are in fact of Carboniferous age.

Lower Old Red Sandstone

As a result of pre-Upper Old Red Sandstone denudation, the Lower Old Red Sandstone occupies relatively small areas in the Girvan district and in the counties of Roxburgh and Berwick. In the latter area the rocks are exposed near Eyemouth, Reston, and St. Abbs. They include red feldspathic sandstones and conglomerates, with a few thin cornstones and partings of red marl, which were laid down in a freshwater lake, and associated beds of coarse tuff and flows of andesitic lava (Plate VIA). The volcanic rocks are estimated to be at least 600 m thick. In the neighbourhood of Eyemouth and St. Abbs several vents filled with agglomerate largely composed of andesitic fragments are well exposed on the shore. The age of the sediments and lavas is determined by the occurrence of *Pterygotus*, and also by the fact that the beds are unconformably overlain by the Upper Old Red Sandstone.

In Roxburghshire the Lower Old Red Sandstone is mainly represented by a great thickness of lavas which form part of the Cheviot Volcanic Series. The lava-flows are predominantly andesitic and include basaltic andesites and

PLATE V

A

B

PLATE IV

A

B

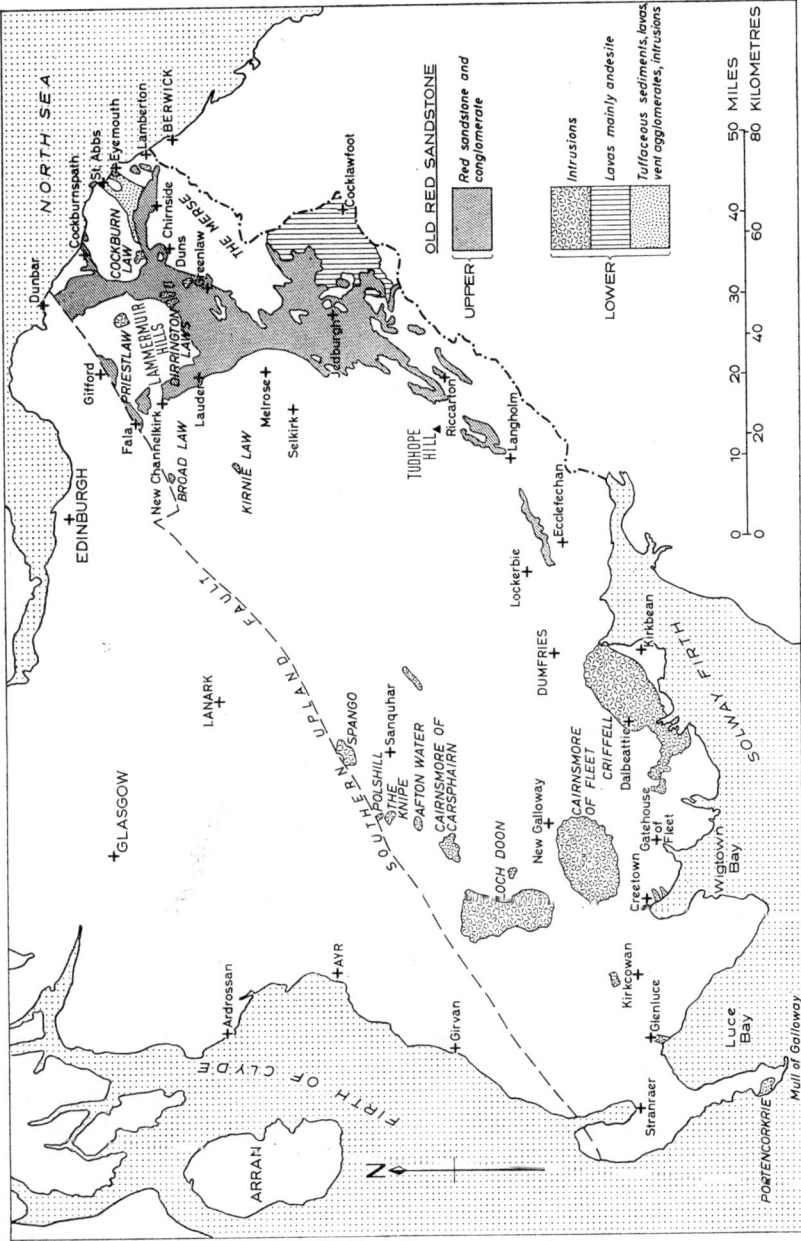

FIG. 9. *Outcrops of the Old Red Sandstone in the South of Scotland*

felsic glassy pyroxene-andesites; rare mica-felsites have also been recorded. In places the rocks are vesicular and agates have been found in the vesicles. While the flows are locally separated by beds of tuff, there are few intercalations of sediment. Isolated patches of coarse breccia probably indicate the sites of volcanic vents; such a patch has been mapped near Cocklawfoot at the head of Bowmont Water.

In addition to the lavas, numerous intrusions of Lower Old Red Sandstone age occur in the region, and the most striking feature of this igneous activity is the prevalence of a granodioritic or tonalitic magma over a wide area. In the eastern part of the Uplands the intrusions occupy small areas at Priestlaw in the Lammermuirs, and at Cockburn Law and Stoneshiel Hill, near Duns. Smaller masses also occur on Broad Law in the Moorfoot Hills and Kirnie Law, near Innerleithen. Near Lamberton Beach, 2·5 km south-south-east of Burnmouth, there is a small knob of granodiorite or quartz-diorite, but the commonest type is basic hornblende-biotite-granodiorite. At one time the intrusive masses of Dirrington Laws, Blacksmill Hill and Kyles Hill near Duns were regarded as being of Lower Old Red Sandstone age, but evidence was brought forward by Irving that they may be Carboniferous. The field-evidence, although not conclusive, is considered by A. G. MacGregor to favour the older view (see also p. 89).

The more important intrusions, however, are the Loch Doon, Cairnsmore of Fleet, and Criffell granitic masses in Galloway. The first is intruded into Ordovician rocks, along with smaller intrusions such as Cairnsmore of Carsphairn, The Knipe, Afton Water and the granodiorite of Spango Water (Fig. 9). The rocks surrounding the Cairnsmore of Fleet mass are mainly Silurian, but also include some of Ordovician age, while the Criffell complex is intrusive in Silurian strata.

The Loch Doon mass occupies an area extending from Loch Doon to Loch Dee, a distance of over 18 km (Fig. 10). It has a maximum width of 10·5 km and is surrounded by a girdle of altered sediments which form the Kells Range to the east and Merrick to the west. Gardiner and Reynolds subdivided the plutonic rocks into three main types, a basic rock (norite), an intermediate rock (tonalite) and an acid rock (granite), while more recent work by Higazy indicates that the chief plutonic rocks of the complex are norite, diorite, granodiorite and adamellite. The description given below is based on the work of Gardiner and Reynolds. The granite forms a central ridge of hills, the highest of which is Mullwharchar. The rock is a biotite-granite, nearly white in colour, and consists of quartz, biotite and orthoclase with microcline and oligoclase. Occasional crystals of orthoclase and microcline occur as phenocrysts, and muscovite and hornblende are sometimes present. The tonalite and other closely allied rocks occupy the country on either side of the central ridge, and are generally grey in colour. The commonest variety consists of oligoclase, biotite and quartz, with or without subordinate orthoclase and hornblende. In many places the tonalite contains xenoliths of highly altered sediments, and over much of the contact between the tonalitic mass and the surrounding sediments a distinctive type of rock is formed, dark in colour, fine-grained and highly biotitic.

There are two principal masses of norite in the Loch Doon complex, at the southern and north-western ends, and along the greater part of their outer boundaries they are in contact with Ordovician sediments. The norite is a dark-coloured medium- to coarse-grained rock composed of plagioclase, rhombic pyroxene (hypersthene and enstatite) and augite, and in the more granitoid types quartz and orthoclase occur as interstitial matter. The marginal mingling of norite and tonalite magma has produced rocks of hybrid character.

The granitic mass of Cairnsmore of Fleet occupies an oval-shaped area

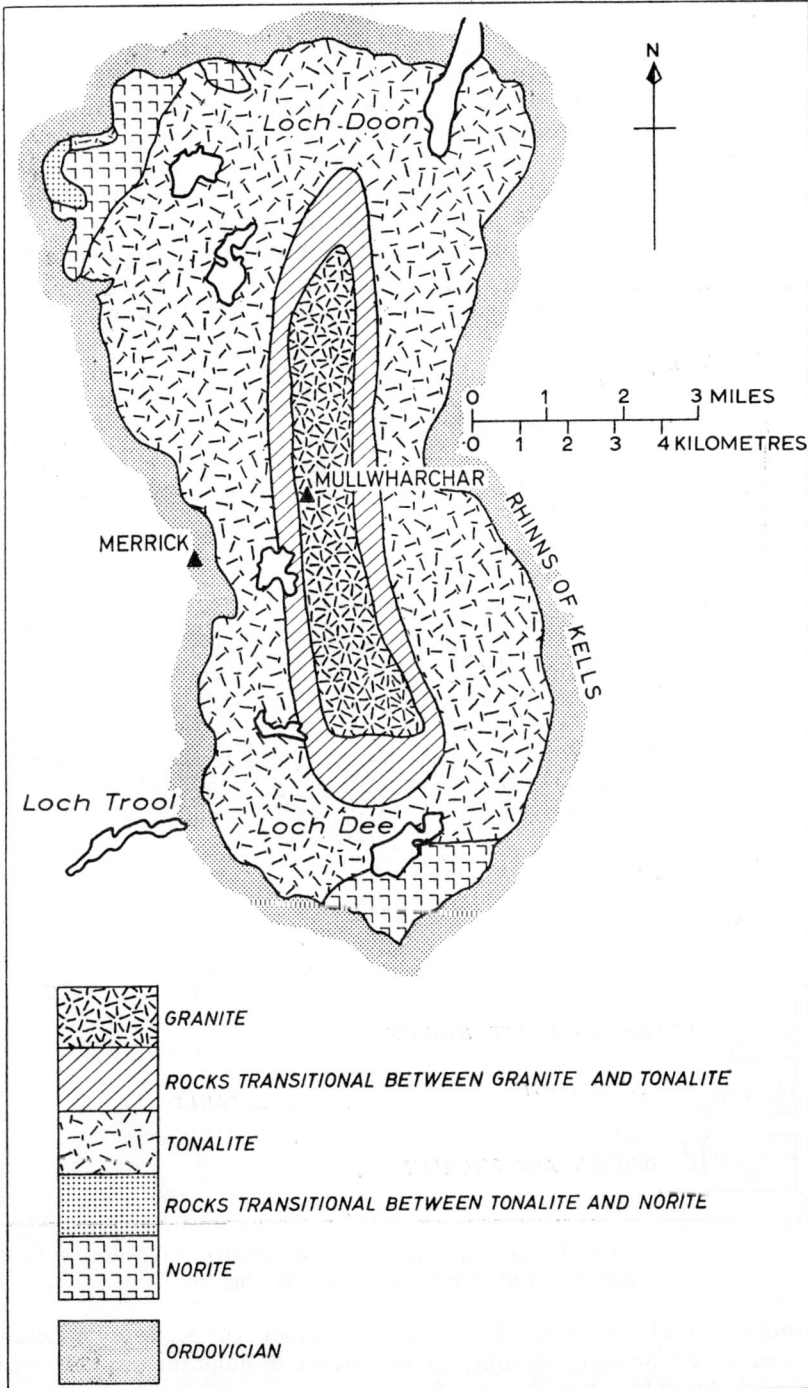

FIG. 10. *The Loch Doon Granite and associated rocks*
(Based on Gardiner and Reynolds 1932, pl. IV.)

17 km long and 11 km wide lying between the Loch Doon mass and the Criffell complex. The longer axis of the pluton, trending north-east, is parallel to the regional strike of the country rocks. The outcrop of the mass is described by Gardiner and Reynolds as being composed of two related rock-types, an almost continuous marginal area of biotite-granite and a central muscovite-biotite-granite (Fig. 11); both are more acid in composition than the rocks of the two large adjacent complexes. The muscovite-biotite-granite forms the greater part of the outcrop, the principal constituents being muscovite, biotite, quartz, and microcline with oligoclase and orthoclase;

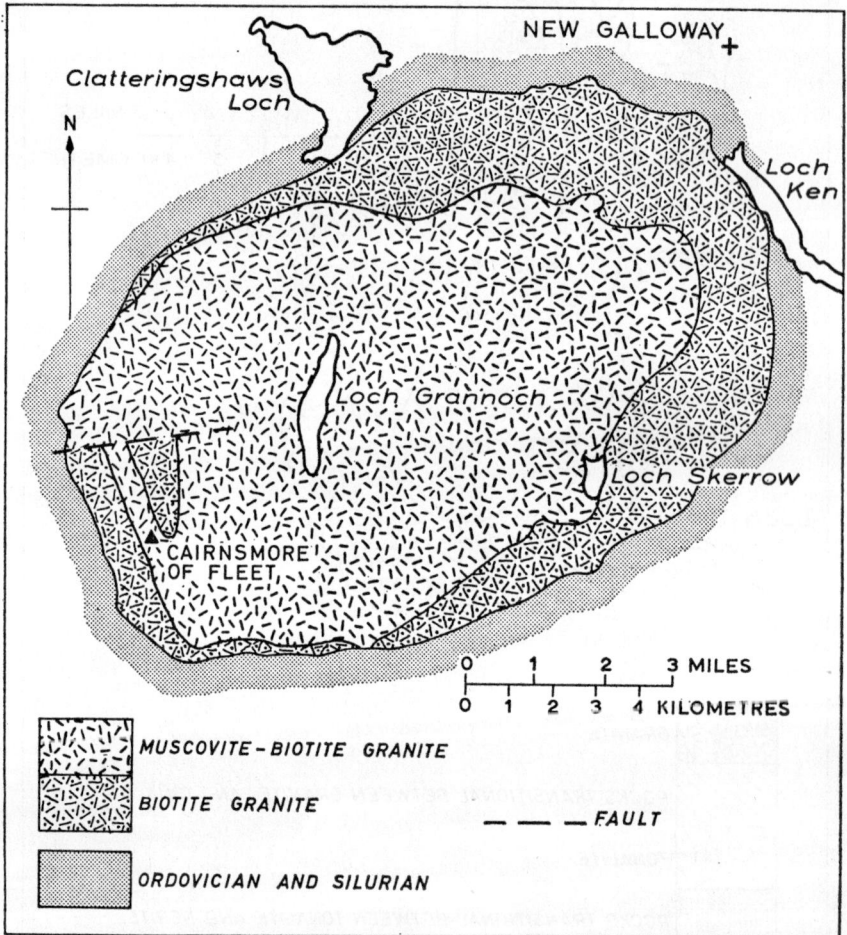

FIG. 11. *The Cairnsmore of Fleet Granite*
(Based on Gardiner and Reynolds 1937, fig. 1.)

hornblende has been noted only in one or two cases. The accessory minerals are apatite, zircon and iron-ores; the occurrence of monazite has also been recorded. Apart from the absence of muscovite, the composition of the outer granite is almost identical with that of the inner. The width of the outcrop of the outer granite is variable and reaches a maximum of about 3 km in the north-eastern part. A distinctive foliation has been observed in the outer granite near Clatteringshaws Loch on the north-western margin of the mass.

The Criffell igneous complex forms an elevated tract of land, extending from the River Nith to Bengairn, a distance of 27 km (Fig. 12) (Plate VIB). East of the Urr Water the average breadth is 11 km. The longer axis of the mass has a north-easterly trend, coinciding with the regional strike of the Silurian rocks. The emplacement of the plutonic rocks has resulted in a pronounced deflection of the strike of the adjacent country rocks at the ends of the complex. The mass, described by Malcolm MacGregor and Phillips, includes three granodiorites with associated quartz-diorite rocks. The outcrop of the main granodiorite, which forms the greater part of the complex, extends from the north-eastern extremity of the mass to Torr Point in Auchencairn Bay, and is composed of a medium-grained rock which becomes porphyritic towards the centre of the outcrop. The medium-grained variety contains hornblende, plagioclase ranging from oligoclase to andesine, microperthite and quartz; sphene is prominent among the accessory minerals. Basic segregations are locally abundant along the margin of the intrusion. In the porphyritic granodiorite microperthite forms phenocrysts, hornblende is usually lacking, and the plagioclase is oligoclase. Two smaller areas of granodiorite are found at the south-west of the complex; both are finer-grained and more acid in composition than the rocks of the main mass. The most acid and most finely grained variety crops out in an ill-defined area on the west side of Auchencairn Bay; it contains more quartz and potash-feldspar and less plagioclase than the main granodiorite, and is flanked to the north, west and south by a granodiorite intermediate in composition and grain-size between the other two. On the north and west margins of the intermediate granodiorite lies the Bengairn quartz-diorite, typically grey in colour and composed essentially of quartz, potash feldspar, plagioclase, biotite and hornblende, with sphene, apatite and pyroxene as accessory minerals. Along the south-eastern margin of the main granodiorite, from Bainloch Hill to the eastern slopes of Criffell, and again along the northern margin, the rock has a marked foliated character, a secondary structure which may have been developed by dynamic action connected with earth-movements. A gravity survey by Bott and Masson-Smith suggests that the complex has a batholithic shape, probably reaching a depth of over 11 km. The contacts appear to slope outwards with depth at moderately steep angles.

Several smaller intrusions of similar composition occur outside the area occupied by the large masses just described. The outcrop of the Cairnsmore of Carsphairn igneous complex is roughly triangular, being about 6 km from west to east and about 4 km from north to south. A central area of granite is surrounded by a granite-tonalite hybrid, which is in turn encircled by a tonalite. On its northern margin the latter is in contact with the country rocks. The southern and eastern parts of the complex are composed of a group of basic hybrid rocks. There are no chilled margins between the four principal rock types in the complex, the contacts being transitional. The rocks of the two relatively small intrusions in the upper reaches of Afton Water, about 7 km north-east of the Cairnsmore of Carsphairn mass, include granodiorite and microdiorite.

The composition of the intrusion at The Knipe was shown by Walker to be almost identical with that at Polshill just to the north, where the centre of the

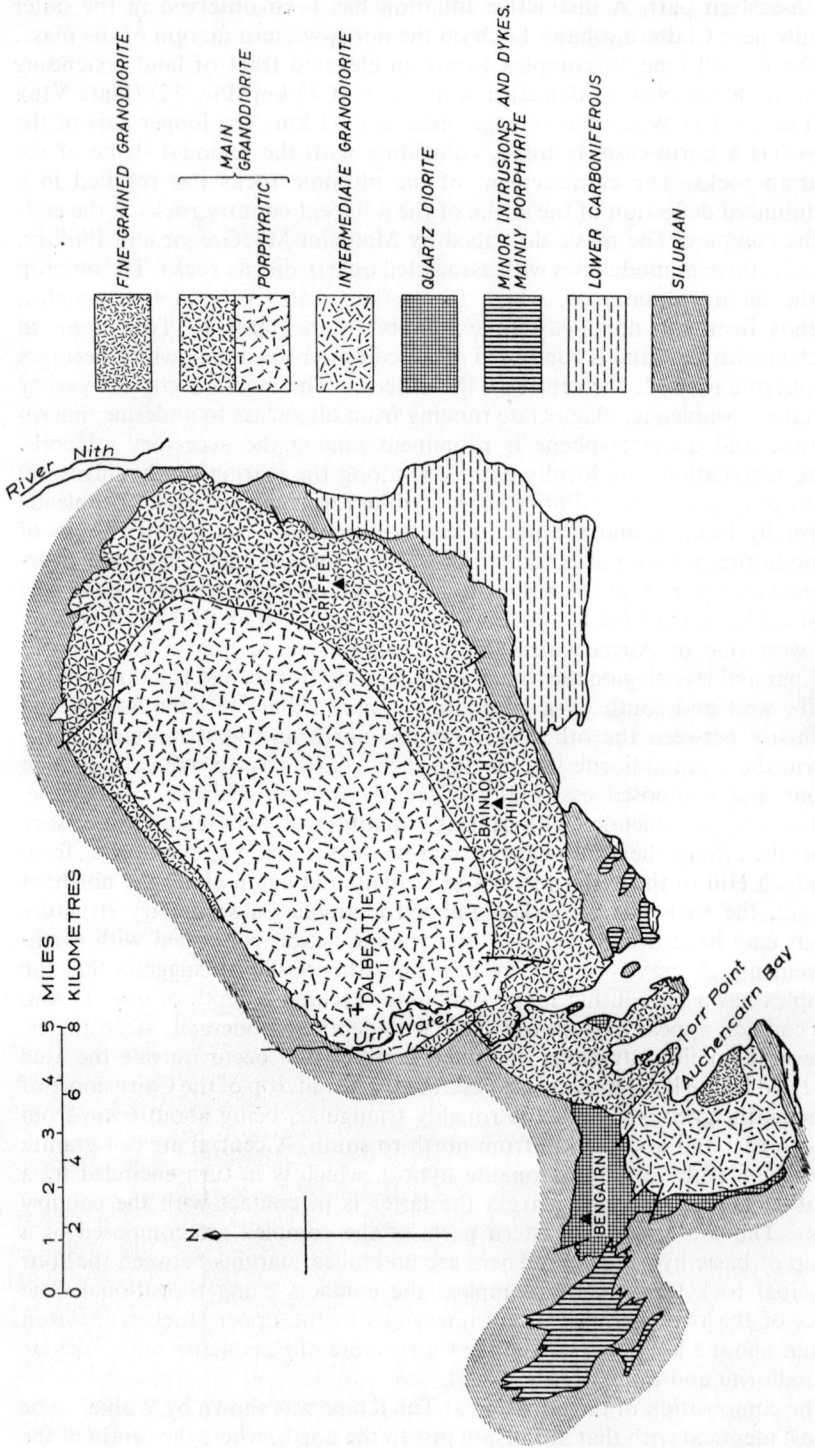

FIG. 12. *The Criffell Granite and associated rocks*
(Based on Phillips 1956a, pl. VII.)

mass is a basic hornblende-biotite-granodiorite or quartz-diorite which passes outwards into pyroxene-bearing modifications.

The Spango intrusion is a biotite-hornblende-granodiorite, containing numerous inclusions of greyish dioritic rocks which probably represent fragments of a relatively basic earlier intrusion caught up in the granodiorite.

The Portencorkrie complex, about 7 km north-west of the Mull of Galloway, is composed of an outer zone of pyroxene-mica-diorite and hornblende-mica-diorite, intruded by an inner mass of adamellite. The Glenluce intrusion and the mass north of Kirkcowan (Fig. 9) include quartz-diorite, augite-diorite with hornblende, and augite-diorite with enstatite.

On the east side of the estuary of the Cree, about 2·5 km south of Creetown, a dyke-like mass of granodiorite trends east-north-east. Quarries in this intrusion show a prominent series of north-north-westerly joints resembling a large-scale fracture-cleavage, which may have been caused, according to Blyth, by relative movement of the walls of the intrusion.

Radiometric age-determinations carried out on specimens from a large granite dyke at Creetown gave the following results: K/A method 390 ± 12 m.y.; Rb/Sr 388 ± 19 and 410 ± 20 m.y. These ages are close to that assigned to the Siluro–Devonian boundary.

As already mentioned, one of the characteristic features of Lower Old Red Sandstone igneous activity is the prevalence of a similar magma over a wide area. In the south-west, as in the north-east, all the plutonic rocks are intimately related, and the occurrence of the same types in widely separated localities suggests that they belong to the same petrographical province. While the various rocks of the plutonic masses probably originated by differentiation of the same magma, it is believed by some authors, for example Gardiner, Reynolds and Deer, that, in complexes like those at Loch Doon and Cairnsmore of Carsphairn, each of the constituent rock-types represents a separate intrusion, the emplacement taking place in order of increasing acidity. Others, however, such as Higazy, favour a metasomatic mode of origin for the rocks of the Loch Doon complex. Malcolm MacGregor, as a result of his work on the western part of the Criffell complex, came to the conclusion that the Bengairn quartz-diorite was the result of a transformation of hornfelses by a process of granitization.

Dykes are extremely abundant in the Galloway district and especially so in the neighbourhood of the Criffell and Loch Doon masses, where they cut both the plutonic rocks and the surrounding sediments. The western end of the Criffell complex is cut by numerous dykes with a north-westerly trend, which are mainly porphyrites with a few lamprophyric types. The minor intrusive rocks associated with the Loch Doon pluton fall into three groups: (1) acid rocks, such as aplites, granite-porphyries, granophyres, micro-granites and orthophyres; (2) porphyrites, and (3) diorites and lamprophyres. Thermally metamorphosed dykes have been recorded in the aureoles of the Loch Doon, Cairnsmore of Fleet and Portencorkrie masses.

The Ordovician and Silurian rocks of Wigtownshire are cut by many dykes, described by Read, which range in composition from feldspathic varieties to lamprophyres. A group of sheared dykes, mainly porphyrites, trending east-north-east, is found in the area between Creetown and Gatehouse-of-Fleet, but in Galloway as a whole the dominant trend of the dykes is north-easterly,

E

and the majority consist of rocks to which the term porphyrite has been applied. In typical rocks of the group phenocrysts of plagioclase, hornblende and biotite are found in a compact groundmass of the same minerals, associated with quartz and alkali feldspar. The rocks vary in colour from grey to red, the latter tint being characteristic of the most highly altered varieties. The diorite dykes are usually dark-coloured crystalline rocks essentially composed of hornblende and plagioclase feldspar. The lampro-phyre dykes of Galloway include malchites, spessartites and kersantites.

Dykes similar to those described above occur scattered throughout the eastern part of the district. Quartz-porphyry and lamprophyre dykes trending north-eastwards occur in association with the Cockburn Law intrusion. The Priestlaw mass is cut by several dykes of decomposed porphyrite and the Lamberton Beach intrusion is intersected by a lamprophyre dyke.

The metamorphism resulting from the emplacement of granitic material into the surrounding sedimentary rocks varies widely in amount and intensity. Thus, narrow dykes have generally effected little or no alteration in the adja-cent strata, but around the margins of such large masses as those of Criffell, Loch Doon and Cairnsmore of Fleet great alteration has been produced; a broad ring of metamorphosed sediments surrounds the intrusions. In Gallo-way the altered rocks comprise greywackes, grey and black shales, cherts, Ordovician igneous rocks, and dykes of Old Red Sandstone age. Character-istic minerals resulting from the metamorphism are biotite and garnet, while cordierite is also plentiful in the inner parts of the metamorphic aureoles of the Loch Doon and Cairnsmore of Carsphairn masses. The greywackes are characterized by the development of abundant brown biotite, while flaggy beds sometimes pass into a dark hornfels containing cordierite. Highly metamorphosed sediments occur at Knocknairling Hill, about 2 km west of New Galloway, where argillaceous rocks pass into andalusite-mica-schists, and gritty beds become quartz-mica-schists. Corundum, sometimes with the dark blue colour of sapphire, has been noted in highly metamorphosed sediments at Buchan Hill, Loch Trool, in the aureole of the Loch Doon mass, at Bennan Hill near the north-east end of the Cairnsmore of Fleet intrusion, and at Broad Law.

Upper Old Red Sandstone

The extent of the denudation which took place in the interval between the deposition of the Lower and the Upper Old Red Sandstone is indicated by the disconnected nature of the remnants of the earlier formation. In Upper Old Red Sandstone times according to Wills the south-western part of the region probably continued to project as a land-mass, while much of the remainder formed part of the North British Cuvette. In the Eyemouth district the depo-sits of the Upper Old Red Sandstone rest with marked discordance on the Lower Old Red Sandstone, and in parts of Roxburghshire they lie on the Cheviot lavas, but elsewhere these beds repose on an uneven floor of folded Ordovician and Silurian rocks.

From the vicinity of Greenlaw to the Jedburgh area the Upper Old Red Sandstone occupies a tract of undulating country. Near the former locality the succession appears to be divisible into two groups, a lower formed largely of conglomerates and an upper composed of interbedded red sandstones and marls. In the Jedburgh district the greater part of the formation is composed of soft and crumbly dark red and brown arenaceous and marly beds with sandstone ribs. Thicker beds of red and white sandstone occur throughout the succession, with conglomerates and conglomeratic sandstones in the basal part. The conglomerates are composed mainly of greywacke pebbles, with scattered fragments of porphyrites and other igneous rocks derived from minor intrusions in the Lower Palaeozoic. Wind-rounded sand grains in the sandstones seem to indicate a semi-arid continental climate. Sun-cracked surfaces are a common feature and indicate periodic desiccation.

To the south-west of Jedburgh the outcrop narrows and the formation continues as a faulted strip towards Riccarton and Langholm. In the last-mentioned district the rocks are predominantly red sandstones, in part pebbly, and a coarse conglomerate of Silurian fragments is normally present at the base; the thickness of the formation ranges from 15 to 180 m. Five kilometres west-south-west of Langholm another narrow belt of Upper Old Red Sandstone crops out from beneath the Birrenswark Lavas and extends south-westwards to the railway midway between Lockerbie and Ecclefechan, where it passes beneath a small patch of 'Permian'. On the west side of the Nith the formation is represented in the Kirkbean district by a thin development of conglomerate, siltstone, shale and sandstone.

At the northern end of the outcrop, near Lauder, conglomerates and sandstone extend as a narrow tongue up the Leader Valley to New Channel-kirk. The main outcrop, however, swings to the north-east towards Duns and then eastwards towards Berwick, forming the western and northern boundaries of the Merse of Berwickshire. From the vicinity of Duns a branch of the outcrop passes northwards through the Lammermuir Hills to join the Upper Old Red Sandstone outcrop which borders the Carboniferous basin south of Dunbar on its western and southern sides. On the south-east side of the Lammermuir Fault near Fala and Gifford there are two patches of Upper Old Red Sandstone. The lowest member of the succession in both areas is a conglomerate consisting of rolled fragments of greywacke. It is followed in the Gifford valley by red sandstones and red micaceous marls, while south-east of Fala a more variegated set of sandstones occurs, and the coarser grits include small fragments of chert.

There is evidence that the Upper Old Red Sandstone originally covered a greater area than it at present occupies. It is probable, for instance, that much of the eastern part of the Lammermuir Hills was at one time overlain by Upper Old Red Sandstone conglomerates and sandstones, since the conglomerate ascends to a height of over 410 m on Monynut Edge, and several outliers occur between St. Abb's Head and Berwick. The formation crops out on the lower slopes of the Eildon Hills, near Melrose, and several other outlying patches are found in the area between Melrose and Selkirk, while on Tudhope Hill, east of Mosspaul, a large block of Upper Old Red Sandstone is preserved in the agglomerate infilling a volcanic neck.

The sections in the Jed Water, near Jedburgh, and at Siccar Point, about 4 km east of Cockburnspath, are of historical interest. They were visited and described by Hutton, and his studies of the highly inclined Silurian rocks overlain by nearly horizontal sandstones and marls of the Upper Old Red Sandstone were the means of establishing some of the fundamental principles of geology.

The upper part of the formation, in which the colour is generally less red, is characterized by the occurrence of irregular masses of cornstone. Bands and lenses of chert have been noted in this part of the succession near Cockburnspath and in the Riccarton area. The fact that similar calcareous rocks are found in the Upper Old Red Sandstone and in the lower beds of the overlying Carboniferous makes it difficult to separate the two formations where fossil evidence is lacking.

Two rich fish-beds recently found in the grounds of Duns Castle have yielded *Bothriolepis* and *Holoptychius*. Scales of *Holoptychius* have been collected at several other localities within the region, and plates of *Bothriolepis obesa* have been recorded from the Jedburgh and Chirnside areas.

A number of isolated exposures of igneous rocks to the west and south-west of Greenlaw have in the past been mapped as lavas intercalated in the Upper Old Red Sandstone, but the investigations of A. G. MacGregor and Eckford have shown them to be intrusions.

Two lavas, interbedded with red marls and cornstones, recorded in a boring for water at Stonefold, near Greenlaw, have been referred by Manson and Phemister to the Upper Old Red Sandstone. These are olivine-basalts of Dalmeny type, similar to those of the Kelso volcanic series at the base of the Carboniferous. It is possible that they represent an early effusion of the same series, but in view of the difficulties in separating the Upper Old Red Sandstone from the Carboniferous the question of age cannot be regarded as settled.

PLATE VI

A. Lower Old Red Sandstone volcanic rocks at Horsecastle Bay, St. Abbs, Berwickshire. Two andesitic lava flows separated by water-laid tuffaceous grits and sandstones. The irregular base of the upper flow is clearly displayed. (Geol. Surv. Photo. No. D1229).
B. Criffell Granite, Kirkcudbrightshire. Southwards view of Criffell (569 m) from north of New Abbey. The porphyritic division of the main granodiorite forms the wooded ridges on the right (Fig. 12); the non-porphyritic division crops out over the remainder of the area in the photograph. (Geol. Surv. Photo. No. C3583).

PLATE VI

A

B

6. CARBONIFEROUS

The Carboniferous System is well developed in the South of Scotland but strata representing the whole sequence are present only in one small area near Langholm, where there are some 3500 m of beds. They include rocks greatly varied in character, ranging from thick beds of sandstone, mudstone and limestone to thinner developments of coal, seatclay, ironstone and cement-stone, together with basalts and tuffs of volcanic origin. Elsewhere in various disconnected outcrops throughout the district only parts of the sequence are present. Nevertheless the evidence is sufficiently complete for most of the history of deposition and erosion, earth-movement and volcanic action to be understood.

Throughout Britain a threefold classification of the Carboniferous System, based mainly on lithology, has been adopted. The Carboniferous Limestone Series at the bottom is succeeded by the Millstone Grit Series which, in turn, passes up into the Coal Measures. Although the lithological differences are less marked in the South of Scotland the three divisions have been recognized because broad correlations can readily be made with other districts from studies of the varied fossil assemblages found in the rocks.

The most westerly outcrop is a narrow strip of strata of Millstone Grit Series age along the western margin of the outlier of New Red Sandstone rocks around Loch Ryan (Fig. 13). Two prominent outliers occupy much of the valley of the River Nith. In the more northerly, around Sanquhar and Kirkconnel, the beds are mostly of Coal Measures age. Small thicknesses of both Carboniferous Limestone Series and Millstone Grit Series are present below an unconformity. In a small outlier a few kilometres to the north-east in the valley of the Duneaton Water adjacent to the Southern Upland Fault much of the Carboniferous sequence is represented in a thin development. Around Thornhill the strata are mostly red and are concealed in places below basaltic lavas and sandstones of New Red Sandstone age. Nevertheless rocks of both Carboniferous Limestone Series and Coal Measures age have been recognized with certainty. No evidence has been found as yet that Carboniferous rocks are present below the New Red Sandstone around Dumfries, Lochmaben and Moffat.

The largest outcrop of Carboniferous strata extends north-eastwards for about 130 km from Kirkcudbright to the Cheviot Hills. It fringes the great areas of Carboniferous outcrop in the northern counties of England to the south. The beds are mostly of Carboniferous Limestone Series age but the Millstone Grit Series and Coal Measures are well represented in a small area around Canonbie on the River Esk. There is no doubt that Carboniferous rocks are present below the New Red Sandstone outcrop around Kirkpatrick but the age of these beds is unknown. Around Kelso and north-eastwards to the coast south of Eyemouth basaltic rocks and sediments of Carboniferous Limestone Series age crop out but they are not well seen because of lack of

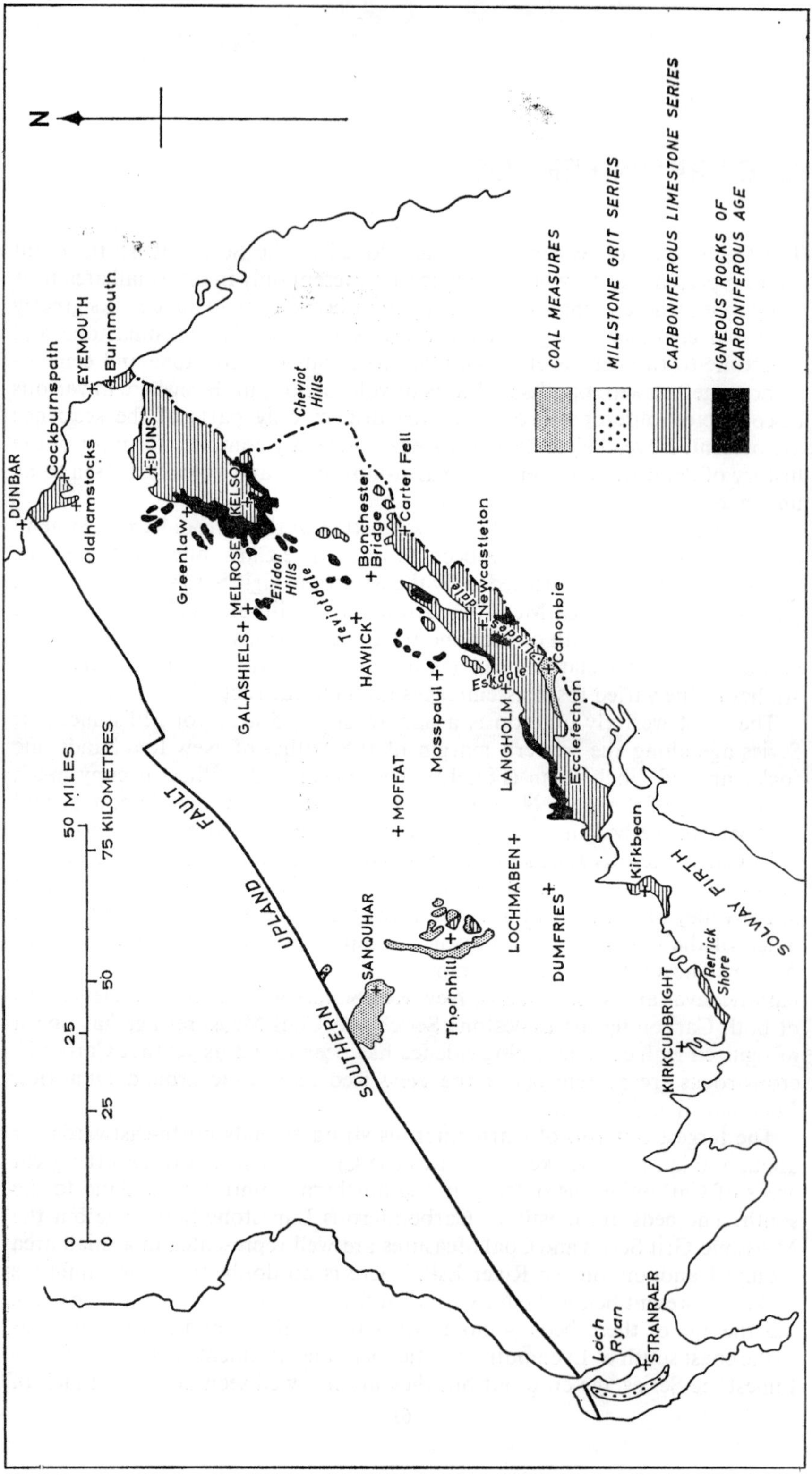

FIG. 13. *Outcrops of Carboniferous rocks in the South of Scotland*

exposure. A further small outcrop of strata of similar age occurs along the coast from Dunbar south-eastwards to Cockburnspath.

Outside the principal areas of outcrop there are numerous remnants of ancient volcanoes which are thought to have been active during Carboniferous times. These small outcrops of igneous rock intruded into strata of Silurian and Upper Old Red Sandstone age are mostly scattered over the district between Langholm and Duns.

Apart from strata of various lithologies which have been quarried for building-stone and roadstone the Carboniferous rocks which have so far proved to be of economic value in the South of Scotland are coal and limestone. In the sequence coals occur mainly in the Coal Measures with the result that the coal industry has developed round Sanquhar and Canonbie. No coal has been worked at Thornhill because such coal seams as were in the sequence there have been chemically altered during a secondary process of oxidation. Limestones of workable thickness are developed mainly in the upper part of the Carboniferous Limestone Series. Consequently, although many beds have been quarried over much of the outcrop for local agricultural purposes, limestones are at present being worked only near Canonbie and, on a larger scale, south-east of Dunbar (Plate X).

History of Deposition

The true base of the Carboniferous System has not been established anywhere in the south of Scotland. An arbitrary base has been chosen in each district at a convenient and mappable horizon below the lowest beds which are known from their fossil content to be undoubtedly Carboniferous in age. The base is therefore at a lithological boundary and, since lithology is seldom a criterion of age, the chosen base is not necessarily at the same horizon from district to district. It may be also that some or all of the underlying Upper Old Red Sandstone strata should be included in the Carboniferous. There is doubt about the age of these beds but, because they do not contain a diagnostic fauna and because their lithology differs in detail from that of younger strata, they have not hitherto been regarded as part of the Carboniferous.

Along the southern flank of the Southern Uplands a great outburst of volcanic activity is taken to mark the beginning of the Carboniferous period. Whether the beginning of the volcanic episode was everywhere contemporaneous has not been established but numerous flows of basaltic lavas of similar nature were deposited over the whole area from the Solway Firth to Berwickshire at about the same time. In the south-west they are called the Birrenswark Lavas and farther to the north-east the local name is the Kelso Traps. In the Cockburnspath area there is a transition from sediments assigned to the Upper Old Red Sandstone to Carboniferous sediments with no evidence of volcanic activity at that time. Elsewhere the Carboniferous rests unconformably on Silurian and Ordovician strata and because of successive overlap the beds immediately above the unconformity are of different ages from place to place.

Following the volcanic activity in the southern districts great thicknesses of sediments were laid down in the slowly subsiding Northumbrian Trough. Sandstones and mudstones constitute the bulk of the sequence. These are of deltaic and fluvial origin and were deposited in shallow water between the principal land mass to the north and the open sea to the south. Thin bands of cementstone are common in the lower beds of the Carboniferous Limestone Series. They suggest the frequent recurrence of lagoonal conditions with wide estuarine flats submerged in shallow water undisturbed by violent movement. The presence of sun-cracks and rain-pits in associated beds make it clear that there was periodic emergence of the top of the sediments above water-level. Higher in the sequence, although sandstones and mudstones are still predominant, the cementstones give way to highly fossiliferous calcareous mudstones and limestones resulting from recurring marine incursions. At the same time thin coals and beds containing roots appear in the sequence showing that there were periods of emergence sufficiently prolonged to allow the establishment of vegetation. The marine beds, coals and rooty beds are more prominent in the upper part of the Carboniferous Limestone Series, where the succession is distinctly of cyclic Yoredale type. The strata were clearly laid down during rapid alternations between terrestrial and deltaic conditions and truly shallow marine conditions.

During the first half of the time during which the sediments were deposited volcanic activity was sporadic and apparently confined to south-east Scotland. The volcanic province was roughly triangular, lying to the south of a line from Dumfries to Dunbar. The evidence of volcanic activity which has been preserved is diverse and includes extensive flows of basaltic lava and beds of tuff interbedded with the sediments, remnants of many old volcanoes from which the lavas and tuffs were extruded, and various intrusive bodies of acid and basic igneous rocks. The first outburst at the beginning of Carboniferous Limestone Series times appears to have been the most extensive. Almost the whole province was covered at about the same time by the Birrenswark Lavas and Kelso Traps, interdigitating flows of basalt with a cumulative thickness seldom less than 15 m and reaching up to 120 m. Some time later there was renewed but local activity over a small area just to the east of Langholm during which the Kershopefoot Basalt was laid down. The latest extrusive activity was over a somewhat greater area mainly in Eskdale and Liddesdale. At this time the tuffs and tuffaceous sediments with minor lava flows, collectively known as the Glencartholm Volcanic Beds, were deposited while the area was covered by a shallow sea. Far to the east, at Oldhamstocks in the Dunbar outcrop, lavas with subsidiary beds of tuff are present amongst Carboniferous sediments. They are thought to be limited in extent and their age is uncertain although they may be associated with the Garleton Hills Volcanic Rocks of East Lothian. The ages of the scattered volcanic vents and intrusions can be implied only from the knowledge that none of them has been intruded into beds later than early Carboniferous Limestone Series. It seems likely, therefore, that the emplacement of the intrusions was contemporaneous with the extrusion of the lavas and that activity in the province became extinct in early Carboniferous times.

The Millstone Grit Series is the part of the Carboniferous sequence which is least well known. Strata of this age are known only near Loch Ryan, around Sanquhar and Thornhill and to the south of Langholm in Dumfriesshire. They are so poorly exposed near Loch Ryan that neither the sequence nor the precise age has been established. Around Sanquhar and Thornhill the beds are less than 30 m thick. Although the age of some of the strata is in doubt there is evidence of unconformities and non-sequences amongst the beds suggesting that they were deposited during a period of instability when there were several episodes of earth-movement. The only volcanic activity known at this time was around Loch Ryan where a thin basaltic lava was deposited. The most complete sequence of sediments is south of Langholm where the total thickness is thought to be about 430 m. Even in this area the details of the higher beds are not well known. The lowest strata are a continuation of the rhythmic Yoredale facies of the underlying Carboniferous Limestone Series. At this time the environment was predominantly marine with the area covered almost continuously by a shallow sea. There are few coals or rooty beds in the sequence suggesting that emergence was infrequent and short-lived. This was followed by a period of deltaic deposition during which a sequence composed predominantly of sandstones accumulated. There were frequent periods of vegetation as shown by the numerous rooty seatearths and thin coals. Thin marine bands show that marine incursions were common but relatively short-lived. Similar conditions continued until the end of Millstone Grit Series times. A greater development of thin coals and rooty beds indicates that the depositional surface was about or above water level much of the time. No shells have been found in these strata suggesting that the sea did not invade the district at any time during this period. Near the top of the sequence some secondary reddening of the strata has taken place. This is attributed to oxidation of grey strata below a land surface and is probably related to a period of uplift and erosion which took place before the younger Coal Measures rocks were deposited unconformably.

Beds of Coal Measures age have been preserved only in the Sanquhar and Thornhill outliers and in a small area south of Langholm. Although similar ranges of strata are present in all three areas thicknesses range from 180 m at Thornhill to 600 m at Sanquhar and over 900 m south of Langholm. The basal beds of the Coal Measures appear to be absent everywhere. In places around Sanquhar and Thornhill strata of the lowest non-marine bivalve zone, the *Anthraconaia lenisulcata* Zone, have been deposited disconformably or after a non-sequence on beds of the Millstone Grit Series. Widespread deposition did not take place, however, until much later during *Carbonicola communis* Zone times. In the area south of Langholm the earliest known Coal Measures strata, containing a fauna indicative of the lower part of the *Anthraconaia modiolaris* Zone, rest with angular discordance on older beds. The sediments were laid down in cyclic sequences of variable thickness. A typical lithological sequence in ascending order is: coal, carbonaceous shale with plant remains and fish debris, mudstone with non-marine bivalves (mussels), siltstone, sandstone, seatearth with roots, coal. These beds are freshwater or brackish in origin and the environment was one of shallow water except during the numerous periods when vegetation was established on sediments at or above water-level giving rise to the many coal seams and rooty beds in the sequence. A number of the coals, from 0·6 to 4·6 m thick, have proved to be workable and have been mined extensively underground and at outcrop in the Sanquhar outlier and to a lesser extent in the Canonbie Coalfield south of Langholm. In the latter area considerable reserves remain intact at depths up to 600 m in a concealed coalfield. In common with most other areas in Britain there are several thin beds of mudstone with marine faunas in the lower part of the sequence, evidence of widespread but short-lived marine transgressions.

At Sanquhar and south of Langholm the lower beds of the Coal Measures are grey, but the upper beds in these areas and all the strata of this age at Thornhill are red and purple as a result of the oxidation of their iron content. The reddening is thought to have taken place in a semi-arid climate during an interval between Carboniferous and New Red Sandstone sedimentation. The depth to which beds have been reddened completely and partially is considered to have been controlled by the level of the pre-New Red Sandstone water-table. The process of oxidation has altered the character of some of the fine-grained sediments. The bedding in shales and mudstones has, in places, completely disappeared and has been replaced by pseudobrecciation which is accentuated by variations in colour. In seatearths all the carbonaceous material has been altered, leaving only vestiges of roots here and there. Coal seams have been destroyed leaving only thin bands of deep-brown irony rubble. This is particularly important at Thornhill where the whole of the attenuated sequence has been oxidised and, as a result, no coal has been recorded although coal-positions are clearly seen in a normal cyclic development. In association with the reddening some coals in the area south of Langholm have been replaced totally or to some degree by dolomitic limestone.

Towards the end of Carboniferous times and before the deposition of the earliest New Red Sandstone strata there was a period of non-deposition while the Carboniferous and older rocks of the South of Scotland were folded and faulted by the earth-movements of the Armorican orogeny. The only evidence of the last phase, the Borcovician movements, are a few quartz-dolerite dykes intruded into the sediments with east–west orientation.

Fossil Record and Age of Strata

Many of the strata, particularly the shales and limestones, contain plant and animal fossils. They are so abundant in some beds that much of the rock is composed of their remains. Some research has been carried out on the plant fossils of this area but it is from the identification of individual marine shells and the correlation of faunal assemblages that ages of the sedimentary strata have been worked out.

The oldest fossiliferous beds occur in Liddesdale to the east of Langholm where the fauna is predominantly composed of the calcareous-tubed worm *Serpula*, the bivalve *Modiolus latus* and ostracods. In some beds these fossils occur in great profusion. This type of assemblage represents the so-called 'Modiola-phase' of the Carboniferous in Britain, which seems to be associated with the first invasions of the sea over an area when conditions were such that only a few organisms could tolerate them. The beds and their faunas became more marine upwards and the earliest occurrence of a typical Carboniferous shelly fauna is a rich marine assemblage including corals, bryozoa, *Cleiothyridina glabristria*, orthotetoids, productoids, *Syringothyris* and marine molluscs. Locally, in the Langholm area, great developments of rock-forming algae are associated with these faunas. Only one marine band, that containing specimens of the brachiopod *Syringothyris* cf. *cuspidata* and locally called the Harden Beds, has been recognized over a widespread area. Occurrences have been recorded on the Rerrick shore, in the Kirkbean outcrop, near Ecclefechan, in Liddesdale and in the Bewcastle district of the north of England.

The age of the early Carboniferous strata is difficult to establish. The species which are diagnostic of the Tournaisian coral-brachiopod zones of the South-West Province of England are absent and, as a result, the shelly faunas present suggest only an approximate age of upper Tournaisian or early Viséan. Recent work on ostracods has suggested a Tournaisain age for strata in the north of England which can clearly be correlated with beds near the bottom of the succession in the south of Scotland.

Along the Solway Firth and eastwards to the Cheviot Hills the upper half of the Carboniferous Limestone Series has an abundant rich marine fauna consisting mainly of corals, brachiopods and bivalves. In the lower beds several species of *Lithostrotion*, trepostomatous bryozoa and Gigantoproductids are particularly prominent. Somewhat higher in the sequence, in strata locally called the Dinwoodie Beds, a large number of new forms appear for the first time in the fauna. They include *Lithostrotion junceum*, *Gigantoproductus* cf. *latissimus*, *Leptagonia* [*Leptaena*] cf. *analoga*, *Plicochonetes*, *Tornquistia* and *Actinopteria persulcata*. In the uppermost beds the limestones contain a rich fauna mainly of corals and brachiopods and the associated roof-shales contain mainly brachiopods and molluscs. The corals include *Aulophyllum*, *Dibunophyllum* and several species of *Lithostrotion*. Productoids are common, particularly *Eomarginifera* and Gigantoproductids of both latissimoid and giganteid form. There is no doubt that all these faunas are of Viséan age and there are sufficient diagnostic forms present to show that the coral-brachiopod zones C_2S_1, S_2, D_1 and D_2 are represented. No significant goniatite evidence has been found but the presence of the bivalve *Posidonia becheri* in strata near the top of the sequence shows that these beds at least are of P_1 age.

In the Sanquhar and Thornhill outliers only a few fossiliferous bands have been found. These have yielded poor faunas consisting mainly of brachiopods and bivalves which indicate that the strata are upper Viséan in age.

In the Berwickshire and Dunbar to Cockburnspath outcrops most of the Carboniferous Limestone Series is poorly fossiliferous and contains no marine bands. The correlation of these beds is based on lithology and, while they are thought to be mainly Viséan in age, some Tournaisian strata may be present by analogy with neighbouring sequences in the north of England. The earliest marine bands, present on the coast at Cove and in neighbouring streams, contain mainly brachiopods and bivalves. These bands are thought to be of the same age as the Dun and Woodend limestones of Berwickshire and the Redesdale Ironstone and Limestone of Northumberland. The coral-brachiopod assemblage suggests a D_1 age and the presence of *Beyrichoceratoides redesdalensis* suggests that the goniatite zone B is represented. The topmost beds of the Carboniferous Limestone Series, outcropping on the shore south of Dunbar, are much more fossiliferous with assemblages very similar to those of beds of the same age around Langholm. Corals are particularly abundant, *Saccamminopsis fusulinaformis* is strikingly developed in bands and numerous weathered surfaces are crowded with 'cauda-galli' markings. There is no doubt about the upper Viséan age of these beds.

During Millstone Grit Series times the environment became progressively less marine. Consequently the most abundant marine faunas are found only in the lowest beds and these are essentially an impoverished continuation of those found in the underlying Carboniferous Limestone Series. In the

Langholm area the bulk of the fauna is brachiopods and bivalves including *Eomarginifera*, Gigantoproductids of latissimoid form and *Streblopteria ornata*. In the higher beds plant remains are more common and, apart from a few thin limestones with shelly faunas, animal fossils are restricted to thin shale bands containing mainly *Lingula* and *Orbiculoidea*. The precise age of all the strata is uncertain. No diagnostic goniatites have been found and so the Namurian goniatite stages have not been established. Nevertheless, by comparison with other areas, there is no doubt that at least the two lowest stages, E_1 and E_2, are represented. In the Stranraer outcrop the only fossils recorded are plants and no precise age is known for the strata. At Thornhill the fauna is mostly poorly preserved brachiopods and bivalves from which it has been suggested that the strata are probably of E_2 age. In the Sanquhar outlier two marine bands have yielded mainly brachiopods from which an E_2 age has been deduced for all the strata. Recent work on plant spores, however, has suggested that beds of E_1 age are present and that the uppermost strata included in the Millstone Grit Series may rather be of Westphalian A age.

In the Coal Measures many bands carry fossils which are mainly non-marine bivalves or mussels of the genera *Anthraconaia*, *Anthraconauta*, *Anthracosia*, *Anthracosphaerium*, *Carbonicola*, *Curvirimula* and *Naiadites*. The non-marine bivalve zones known to be present are (in ascending order): *Anthraconaia lenisulcata* Zone, *Carbonicola communis* Zone, *Anthraconaia modiolaris* Zone, Lower *Anthracosia similis–Anthraconaia pulchra* Zone, Upper *A. similis–A. pulchra* Zone, *Anthraconauta phillipsii* Zone and *Anthraconauta tenuis* Zone. All the zones except the topmost have been recognized with certainty in the Sanquhar outlier but in the neighbouring outcrop around Thornhill only the *C. communis*, *A. modiolaris* and Lower *A. similis–A. pulchra* zones are known to be present. At Canonbie all the upper zones are well represented but the first Coal Measures deposits resting unconformably on older strata are of late *A. modiolaris* age. Ostracods and *Spirorbis* are associated with the mussels in some bands and the latter occurs in freshwater limestones in the upper part of the sequence. Fragmentary fish remains are common, particularly in beds immediately overlying the coals. Specimens of '*Estheria*' are abundant in beds which are mostly associated with the marine bands of the sequence. Marine faunas are restricted to a few bands which occur mainly near the bottom of the sequence and in the Lower and Upper *A. similis–A. pulchra* zones. The forms present are mostly foraminifera, *Lingula*, *Orbiculoidea* and the trace-fossil *Planolites ophthalmoides*, but brachiopods and bivalves are abundant in Skipsey's Marine Band of Sanquhar and a distinguishing feature of the Skelton Marine Band of Canonbie is the presence of conodonts.

Extent of Deposits

In the South of Scotland the area of deposition became more and more extensive during Carboniferous times. The earliest known deposits, the Birrenswark Lavas and Kelso Traps, were laid down over an area probably little more extensive than that of the present outcrops from Kirkbean on the Solway Firth eastwards to the Cheviot Hills and around Kelso (Fig. 13). They do not extend far south into England and are not present in the sequence at Loch Ryan, in the most westerly outcrops on the Solway Firth, at Sanquhar and Thornhill and on the coast southwards from Dunbar. The earliest sediments fringe the southern and eastern margins of the Southern Uplands and in places there are local indications of proximity to the edge of the depositional basin. The coarse-grained strata along the Kirkcudbrightshire coast appear to be marginal facies. From Dumfries north-eastwards to the Cheviot Hills there are bodies of sandstone which appear to represent the deposition in local deltas along the northern margin of the slowly subsiding Northumbrian Trough. It is less easy to define the margin of deposition farther to the east. The earliest deposits in Berwickshire and south of Dunbar were clearly in shallow water. Nevertheless this type of environment may have been extensive. The presence of debris of Carboniferous lithology in some vents shows that the original deposition extended some way beyond the limits of the present outcrops. It would appear, therefore, that in Tournaisian or early Viséan times deposition was confined to areas south and east of a line from Kirkcudbright to Hawick and northwards through Galashiels.

Deposition extended farther northwards only in late Viséan times as is shown by the Carboniferous Limestone Series strata at Thornhill and Sanquhar. It seems likely that at the same time the Midland Valley basin of deposition extended southwards to encroach upon the Southern Uplands because the strata at Sanquhar and the north end of the Thornhill outlier are similar in lithology and fauna to the development in neighbouring areas to the north. The extent of these deposits is uncertain since nowhere has a marginal facies been preserved. The extremely thin developments at Sanquhar and Thornhill, however, suggest that in the eastern part of the Southern Uplands the overlap of these younger beds beyond the limits of deposition of the earliest Carboniferous strata may have been patchy. There is no evidence of deposition at this time over the western part of the Southern Uplands.

The presence of beds of Millstone Grit Series age near Loch Ryan shows that there was a further extension of the depositional area during that period. The thin developments there and at Sanquhar and Thornhill suggest again that the main depositional areas lay along the southern and eastern flanks of the Southern Uplands and that elsewhere in the region deposition was slight and patchy.

Most of the evidence of deposition during Coal Measures times has been removed by subsequent erosion. It is assumed that there was widespread deposition in fairly stable conditions in common with much of Europe. Nevertheless it is clear that there was no deposition at the beginning of this period in the area to the south of Langholm where the earliest Coal Measures recorded are of *A. modiolaris* Zone age. Although early Coal Measures are thin in both the Sanquhar and Thornhill outliers, the upper parts of the Coal Measures sequence are fully represented there and at Canonbie. The strata at Sanquhar are closely related to those farther north in adjacent areas of the Midland Valley and there is a great thinning south-eastwards to Thornhill. It may be, therefore, that in the south of Scotland the Coal Measures were deposited in at least two separate basins, one in the north associated with the Midland Valley and one in the south linked with the north of England, and that some parts at least of the Southern Uplands remained free of deposition.

Loch Ryan

A narrow outcrop of strata thought to be of Upper Carboniferous age extends southwards for about 16 km from Jamieson's Point. The rocks are poorly exposed but it is clear that they rest unconformably on Ordovician strata and are in turn overlain unconformably by breccias of New Red Sandstone age. They consist of grey, red and mottled sandstones with beds of purplish grey shale and seatclay. One thin flow of basaltic lava has been noted in the sequence. The strata probably represent part of the Millstone Grit Series. The only fossils recorded so far are plants from shales cropping out in the Craigoch Burn. A thin bed of kaolinitic rooty clay crops out near Low Knockglass to the south-west of Stranraer.

Sanquhar

The Sanquhar outlier in the valley of the River Nith comprises a rectangular outcrop of about 45 square kilometres in which the rocks at the surface are mainly Upper Carboniferous, together with several smaller detached outcrops in which strata mainly of Lower Carboniferous age have been preserved. To the north-west the outlier lies adjacent to the Southern Upland Fault and the north-eastern margin is clearly marked by an abrupt change of slope across a fault intrusion separating Carboniferous and Ordovician strata. Elsewhere the margin is the outcrop of the unconformable junction between Carboniferous and older strata. The towns of Sanquhar and Kirkconnel have grown up around the mines in which several coals in the sequence have been worked, an industry which is now dying rapidly.

Structurally the outlier comprises two adjacent faulted basins. The western part is a shallow syncline plunging gently to the north-east while the eastern part is a much-faulted basin parallel to the elongation of the outlier. In Coal Measures times the main depositional basin appears to have been orientated north-westwards and probably lay near the line of the present north-eastern boundary fault. The strata are heavily faulted, the dominant trend being north-west. Many of the fractures have throws of only a few metres, several have throws of over a hundred metres and the calculated displacement across the boundary fault is at least 550 m in places. The strata have been further disrupted by the intrusion of numerous thin dykes of doleritic rock during the Tertiary period.

The Carboniferous Limestone Series is represented by about 10 m of mudstones, siltstones, sandstones, seatclays and thin argillaceous limestones, which rest unconformably on Ordovician strata and are in turn overlain unconformably by younger Carboniferous strata. These beds are restricted to the eastern part of the outlier where they are best seen in Howat's Burn. Marine fossils are common in most of the strata with assemblages consisting mainly of brachiopods and bivalves of upper Viséan age. Some of the strata have yielded plant spores which have been compared with those from strata of the P_2 goniatite zone elsewhere.

Strata referred to the Millstone Grit Series have a maximum thickness of just under 30 m. They occur in a number of disconnected outcrops on the western and southern margins of the outlier where they rest unconformably on Ordovician strata. The most extensive sections are exposed in the Polhote and Polneul burns. Much of the sequence is composed of sandstones, many of which are coarse-grained with irregular bases suggesting several periods of erosion and subsequent non-sequence in the deposition. Near the base there is a widespread occurrence of an unusual development of kaolinitic sandstone about 2 m thick. Interbedded with the sandstones are a few thin beds of mudstone, siltstone and rooty seatclay. The fauna is restricted to two marine bands. The lower, the Polhote Marine Band, is up to 1·2 m in thickness and contains predominantly bivalves together with brachiopods and gastropods. The macrofaunal assemblage is not diagnostic but it seems to indicate an E_2 age in terms of the Namurian goniatite zones. The upper band, Tait's Marine Band, is a bed of dark grey mudstone up to 1·8 m thick which was first described from a good exposure at the junction between Macan's Burn and the Polneul Burn. In the southern part of the outlier it yields a rich marine fauna mainly of brachiopods. Farther north and west the fauna is restricted to *Lingula* and *Orbiculoidea*. The evidence as to the age of the marine band is conflicting in that the shelly brachiopod assemblage suggests an E_2 age whereas spores collected from associated strata indicate that they may be of Westphalian A age and should be more properly included in the Lower Coal Measures.

A marked faunal change occurs above Tait's Marine Band. It is associated with a plane of angular discordance in places and there is a marked eastward overlap by the earliest beds of the Coal Measures. In common with the Midland Valley the Coal Measures, which are about 600 m thick, have been divided into Lower, Middle and Upper Coal Measures (Fig. 15). The lower limit of the Middle Coal Measures is taken at the base of the Queenslie Marine Band and the upper limit at the top of Skipsey's Marine Band.

The Lower Coal Measures, totalling some 120 m of strata, are mainly sandstones with a few thin coals in the lower part while the upper part is typical Coal Measures cyclic development of sandstones, siltstones, mudstones, coals and seatclays. No diagnostic non-marine bivalve faunas have been recorded from the lower beds but the presence of two marine bands yielding *Lingula mytilloides* suggests that some of these beds at least belong to the *A. lenisulcata* Zone. Numerous boreholes have shown that the upper beds are characterized by a group of coals, the Swallowcraig Coals, which have proved to be of little value because of their great variation in number and thickness. Shortly below them occurs a persistent mussel band containing abundant specimens of *Carbonicola communis*, *C. pseudorobusta* and *C. robusta* which, together with the associated fauna, represent a typical assemblage of the *C. communis* Zone. A prominent mussel band just above the coals contains numerous forms of *Anthracosia* typical of the lower part of the *A. modiolaris* Zone. The only coal which has been mined extensively is the Kirkconnel Splint which occurs near the top of the group. Mussels, including specimens of *Anthraconaia modiolaris*, are commonly found in the roof-beds.

The Middle Coal Measures, some 120 m thick, are typically cyclic in their development throughout. They contain two persistent thick coals, the Creepie and the Calmstone, together with a number of thinner seams. Mussels occur in many of the mudstone beds overlying the coals. Assemblages indicative of the *A. modiolaris* Zone have been found in the lower part of the sequence while the upper part contains faunas of Lower *A. similis–A. pulchra* Zone age. Two distinctive bands have been noted. The lower including *Anthraconaia salteri* in its assemblage lies just above the Parrot Coal, and

South of Scotland

Anthraconaia pulchella is found in the upper band, above the Twenty Inch Coal. Four marine bands have been found so far. The Queenslie Marine Band at the bottom of the group is represented by a thin bed of mudstone containing *Lingula mytilloides* and foraminifera. In the Lower *A. similis–A. pulchra* Zone the Bankhead and Eastside marine bands contain *Lingula* and the trace-fossil *Planolites ophthalmoides*. Skipsey's Marine Band at the top of the group is distinctive in its lithology of black, carbonaceous, calcareous siltstone. Although it is only a thin bed it carries a varied fauna of brachiopods, bivalves, foraminifera and conodonts.

Just over 300 m of Upper Coal Measures are present. Much of the sequence has been subjected to secondary reddening by oxidation but in the lower beds cyclic sequences similar to those of the Middle Coal Measures can be recognized. The upper beds are predominantly red sandstone with subordinate bands of purple mudstone and siltstone. The strata are poorly fossiliferous with only a few bands containing *Spirorbis*, *Anthraconauta*, *Naiadites* and *Euestheria*. The occurrence of *Anthraconauta phillipsii* suggests that the *A. phillipsii* Zone is represented and the presence of the Lagrae Marine Band in lower strata indicates that the Upper *A. similis–A. pulchra* Zone is also represented, although none of its diagnostic mussel fauna has been found.

Thornhill

An outlier of Carboniferous strata, only slightly larger than that of Sanquhar, occupies the valley of the River Nith a few kilometres downstream around the village of Thornhill. The Carboniferous beds crop out in a fringe around outcrops of basaltic lava and sandstones of New Red Sandstone age. Much of the boundary of the outlier is the outcrop of the unconformity between the Carboniferous and underlying Ordovician and Silurian strata, and the Carboniferous is in turn overlain unconformably by the New Red Sandstone strata. Most of the Carboniferous outcrop is of beds of Coal Measures age but older strata occur in narrow outcrops along parts of the western and southern margins of the outlier.

Little is known in detail about the outlier because there has been no mining of coal and only a few exploratory boreholes have been sunk. From surface observations the structure can be seen to be an elongate basin with a north–south axis lying towards the eastern side of the outlier. The more important faults appear to have a northerly orientation.

At the northern end of the outlier the Carboniferous Limestone Series is represented by some 15 m of mottled grey and purple sandstones, siltstones and mudstones best seen in the Enterkine Burn. Two marine bands have been recorded. The upper contains only a poor fauna but the lower yields a rich assemblage of brachiopods and bivalves similar to those found near Sanquhar. In the southern part of the outlier about 45 m of strata have been recorded. The beds are similar in lithology and include at least four marine bands, two of which are limestones of sufficient thickness to have been worked in several quarries. One of these is a red dolomite at least 3·5 m thick which has been quarried and mined at Barjarg. Some of the bands contain a fairly rich fauna of brachiopods and bivalves together with a few corals. These assemblages suggest comparison with those from similar strata in areas to the south of Thornhill. All the Carboniferous Limestone Series of Thornhill is thought to be of upper Viséan age.

The Millstone Grit Series consists of about 20 m of mainly white sandstones with beds of mottled shale and seatclay. Some of the sandstones are coarse-grained and pebbly and their bases clearly mark planes of erosion, suggesting that the beds were accumulated during intermittent periods of deposition. One or two beds of bauxitic clay have been reported as up to 2·5 m in thickness. Poor faunas of brachiopods and bivalves have been found in two thin marine bands which may represent the Polhote and Tait's marine bands of Sanquhar. In places the whole sequence passes laterally into sandstones which are indistinguishable from those of the overlying Coal Measures. The base of the Coal Measures is therefore difficult to establish although there may be a substantial break in sequence, since the poor faunas suggest that the strata of the Millstone Grit Series represent only the lower part of the Namurian.

The Coal Measures (Fig. 15) are about 150 m thick. They are mainly grey, red and purple in colour and consist of cyclic developments of sandstone, siltstone, mudstone and seatclay. Coals which may have been in the sequence originally appear to have been removed by oxidation which also gave rise to the secondary reddening of the associated strata. Non-marine bivalves or mussels are commonly present in the roof-beds of the coal-positions. The sequence has been divided at the base of the Queenslie Marine Band into Lower and Middle Coal Measures. The topmost strata may include a thin development of Upper Coal Measures but the presence of Skipsey's Marine Band, normally at their base, has not been definitely established.

The Lower Coal Measures are 73 m in thickness. The lowest beds are coarse-grained sandstones which locally form a prominent topographic feature. In the overlying cyclic deposits four coal-positions have been recognized and mussels occur at several horizons. The *C. communis* Zone is well represented in the lower bands and at least one band near the top contains an assemblage typical of the lower part of the *A. modiolaris* Zone.

The Middle Coal Measures show a cyclic development throughout their 76 m. Except for their red colour and the lack of coal they are very similar to Middle Coal Measures strata in other areas. Several coal-positions have been recorded and mussels are found in the overlying beds of mudstone. Although the faunas are poor they clearly represent both the upper part of the *A. modiolaris* Zone and the Lower *A. similis–A. pulchra* Zone. The sequence contains three marine bands including the Queenslie Marine Band at the base. It has been recognized in only one borehole where the fauna comprised *Lingula mytilloides* with specimens of *Lioestheria vinti* in closely associated strata. Of the two younger marine bands, the lower has yielded only *Lingula* while the upper contains in addition several forms of foraminifera and the trace-fossil *Planolites ophthalmoides*.

Solway Firth

Five small areas of Carboniferous outcrop are well exposed on the shore of the Solway Firth between Kirkcudbright and Dumfries. In each of these outcrops only beds of the Carboniferous Limestone Series are known to be present. The Carboniferous strata are faulted against the Silurian rocks of the Southern Uplands to the north but there are also several good sections showing the unconformable relationship of the Carboniferous to the underlying Silurian strata.

F

The most westerly outcrop extends along the Rerrick shore for 12 km from White Port to Door of the Heugh. The sequence includes some 750 m of strata which consist mostly of pink, red and brown sandstones and conglomerates with subordinate bands of shale and mudstone and a few thin limestones. The following succession has been established:

		metres
Rascarrel Sandstones and Conglomerates		400
Barlocco Conglomerate . . . . over		60
Orroland Limestone Beds		25
Wall Hill Sandstones		275

Apart from plants fossils are restricted to the Orroland Limestone Beds in which a poor marine fauna, including specimens of *Antiquatonia teres* and *Syringothyris cuspidata,* has been recorded.

Farther east on the Colvend shore three small patches of Carboniferous strata are exposed. From Castlehill Point to Gutcher's Isle the beds total less than 30 m and consist mainly of a basal breccia overlain by sandstones and conglomerates in which two fossiliferous bands have yielded a fauna comprising mostly brachiopods and bivalves. At Portowarren the succession is just over 45 m of sandstones and conglomerates with thin beds of shale and sandy limestone. Algal fragments have been recorded together with a poorly preserved marine fauna in which nautiloids are the most abundant forms. The smallest outcrop is at Southwick Merse where only patches of conglomerate are seen.

In the Kirkbean outcrop due south of Dumfries Carboniferous strata are at the surface over an area of about 25 square kilometres and are best seen on the shore from Southerness to Carsethorn. The strata are folded into anticlines and synclines most of which plunge towards the north-east. Numerous faults are orientated in a west-north-westerly direction. About 750 m of beds are present and they are classified locally as follows (Fig. 14):

		metres
Arbigland Group . . . . at least		300
Thirlstane Sandstone		25
Powillimount Beds		135
Gillfoot Beds		120–180
Southerness Beds		135
Basal Cementstones . . . . . possibly hundreds of metres		
Basaltic lavas		15

The basaltic lavas are not exposed in the shore section but there are several outcrops in Kirkbean Glen. Some doubt has been expressed as to their age but they are thought to represent the Birrenswark Lavas which in other areas are taken to be of Carboniferous age. The Basal Cementstones are poorly exposed and their relationship to the underlying strata is obscure. They consist of thinly bedded mudstones, shales, siltstones and sandstones with thin bands and lenses of fine-grained limestone or cementstone. The few fossiliferous beds yield poorly-preserved molluscs. The Southerness Beds consist of thinly bedded limestones, sandy limestones, calcareous shales and flaggy sandstones. Some beds are highly fossiliferous with a faunal assemblage mainly of brachiopods and molluscs. Prominent algae have been recorded at two horizons. In one limestone specimens of *Antiquatonia teres* and *Syringothyris*

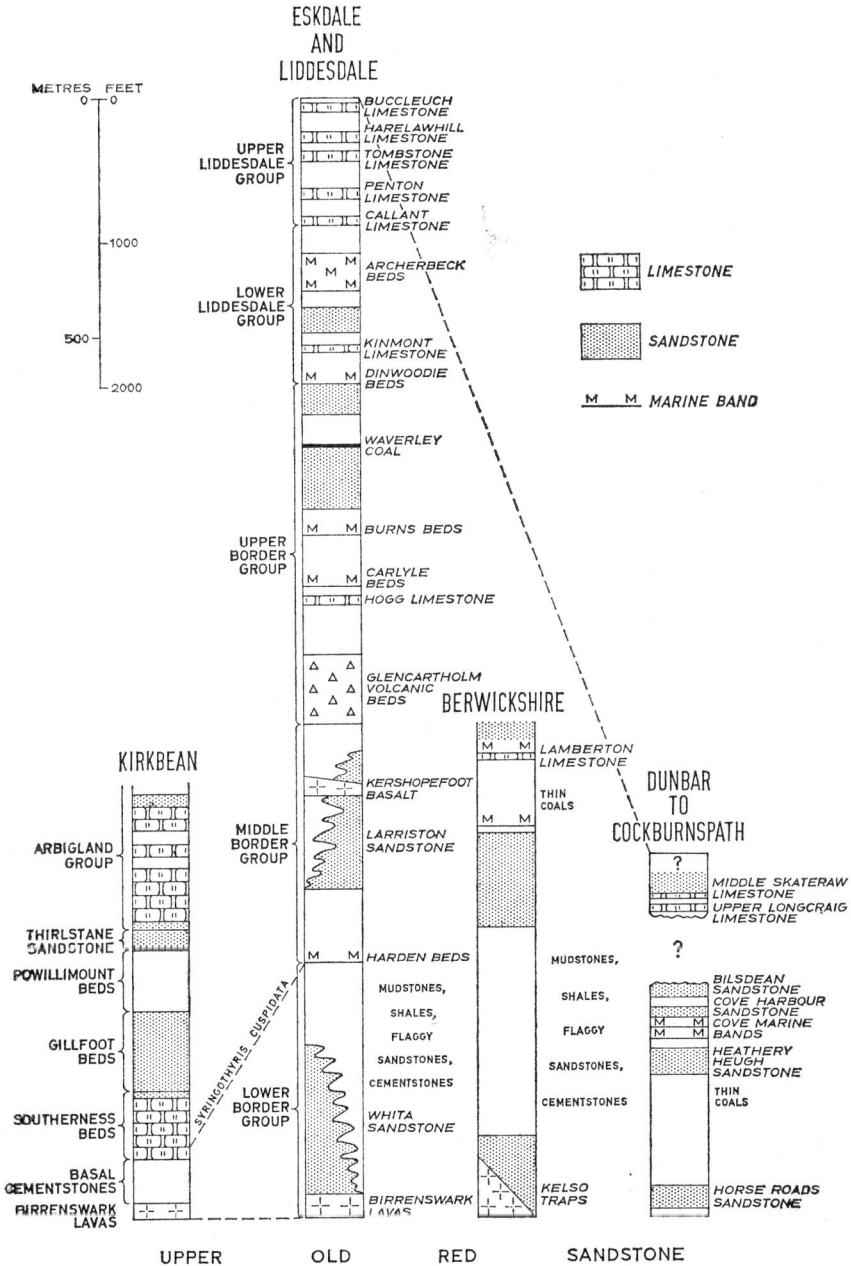

FIG. 14. *Comparative vertical sections of the Carboniferous Limestone Series*

cuspidata are closely associated, suggesting that the strata may approximate in age to the Orroland Limestone Beds farther west and the Harden Beds to the east. The dominant lithologies of the Gillfoot Beds are reddish brown sandstones, conglomerates and breccias. Subsidiary beds of shale, calcareous sandstone and limestone occur and some of these yield a poor marine fauna comprising mainly brachiopods and bivalves together with a few specimens of the coral *Lithostrotion*. Although they consist mainly of sandstones and shales the Powillimount Beds are notable for the oolitic nature of some of their limestones together with the associated prominent development of algae. They pass up abruptly into the Thirlstane Sandstone which is pink and red, mostly medium-grained and prominently current-bedded. This sandstone is faulted against the highest beds in the local sequence, the Arbigland Group, and the throw of the fault is unknown. In the Arbigland Group the lowest beds are sandstones, in places calcareous and argillaceous, with thin bands of gritty and oolitic limestones containing algal debris. They pass up into massive coarse-grained carbonaceous and calcareous sandstones interbedded with limestones and shales which yield an abundant marine fauna. The assemblages include corals, brachiopods, bryozoa and molluscs and are notable for the abundance and fine preservation of compound corals. These topmost strata are clearly of Viséan age and may be somewhat later in the Carboniferous sequence than any of the other strata present along the shore oʝ the Solway Firth.

Solway Firth to Cheviot Hills

This most extensive of Carboniferous outcrops extends over about 470 square kilometres for a distance of some 75 km along the border between Scotland and England from Cummertrees on the Solway Firth by way of Ecclefechan, Langholm, Canonbie and Newcastleton to the Cheviot Hills. It contains the thickest development, totalling some 3500 m, and most complete sequence of Carboniferous strata in the south of Scotland. The outcrop is the northern fringe of the great area of Carboniferous outcrop in the north of England. In most places along its northern margin the strata rest conformably on beds which have been referred to the Upper Old Red Sandstone, but here and there the Carboniferous appears to overlap on to the Silurian. The Carboniferous in turn is overlain unconformably by New Red Sandstone, which oversteps westwards from the youngest Carboniferous beds near Canonbie on to strata low in the Carboniferous sequence in the Eaglesfield area. Coals in the sequence gave rise to the now abandoned mining industry near Canonbie and

---

PLATE VII
LOWER CARBONIFEROUS FOSSILS

1. *Sphenopteris affinis* Lindley and Hutton
2. *Woodocrinus liddesdalensis* Wright
3. *Edmondia sulcata* (Fleming)
4. *Polidevcia attenuata* (Fleming)
5. *Nuculopsis gibbosa* (Fleming)
6. *Composita* cf. *ambigua* (J. Sowerby)
7. *Eomarginifera setosa* (Phillips)
8. *Lithostrotion junceum* (Fleming)
9. *Limipecten dissimilis* (Fleming)
10. *Spirifer trigonalis* (Martin)
11. *Productus concinnus* (J. Sowerby)
12. *Syringothyris* cf. *cuspidata* (J. Sowerby)
    All figures approximately natural size.

PLATE VII

1

2

3

4

5

6

7

8

9

10

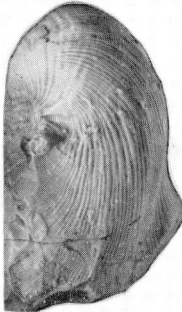

11

12

PLATE VIII

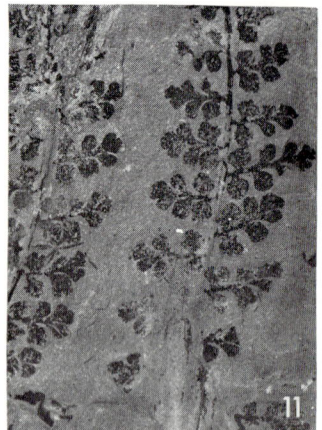

some of the limestones are of sufficient thickness and quality to be worked at present.

Although complex in detail the general structure is simple. The regional strike is north-easterly, the strata dipping gently to the south-east. Folding is mainly over axes trending north–south. The beds have been disrupted by numerous north-easterly faults with downthrow predominantly to the south-east. There has been little intrusive igneous activity apart from the emplacement of numerous small volcanic necks which now protrude above the Carboniferous strata to form prominent topographic features.

The lowest 2000 m of the sequence constitutes the Carboniferous Limestone Series (Fig. 14) which has been locally divided as follows:

								metres
Upper Liddesdale Group	.	.	.	.	.	.	.	275
Lower Liddesdale Group	.	.	.	.	.	.	.	275
Upper Border Group .	.	.	.	.	.	.	.	675
Middle Border Group .	.	.	.	.	.	.	.	425
Lower Border Group .	.	.	.	.	.	.	.	450

The base of the Lower Border Group coincides with the base of the Carboniferous at the bottom of the Birrenswark Lavas. Several flows of basaltic lava can be differentiated in the total thickness of up to 90 m. In places their outcrop forms a low range of hills with north-facing escarpments. The bulk of the group is composed of sediments which vary markedly in lithology from west to east. In the west they are arenaceous in the lower part, including the Whita Sandstone of Langholm, and pass up into thinly bedded mudstones, siltstones and sandy cementstones or limestones with very few fossils. Farther east, however, the beds are alternating mudstones and limestones crowded with *Serpula*, the bivalve *Modiolus latus* and ostracods, and including numerous prominent algal bands. Marine faunas occur near the top of the group, locally at the base of the Harden Beds, but for lack of diagnostic assemblages the age of all the strata is in doubt. They are certainly not younger than early Viséan but Tournaisian may be represented.

The Harden Beds and associated strata at the bottom of the Middle Border Group yield abundant specimens of *Syringothyris cuspidata* which invites comparison with similar faunas in the Southerness Beds and Orroland Limestone Beds of the outcrops west of Dumfries. The group locally includes

---

PLATE VIII

UPPER CARBONIFEROUS FOSSILS

1. *Anthraconaia robertsoni* (Brown). Middle Coal Measures.
2. *Anthracosia* cf. *aquilina* (J. de C. Sowerby). Middle Coal Measures.
3. *A. ovum* Trueman and Weir. Middle Coal Measures.
4. *A. disjuncta* Trueman and Weir. Middle Coal Measures.
5. *Anthraconauta phillipsii* (Williamson). Upper Coal Measures.
6. *Carbonicola pseudorobusta* Trueman. Lower Coal Measures.
7. *Naiadites quadratus* (J. de C. Sowerby). Middle Coal Measures.
8. *Posidonia sulcata* (Hind). Skipsey's Marine Band, Middle Coal Measures.
9. *Dunbarella macgregori* (Currie). Skipsey's Marine Band.
10. *Annularia radiata* Brongniart. Lower Coal Measures.
11. *Sphenopteris nummularia* Gutbier. Middle Coal Measures.
   All figures approximately natural size.

all the strata up to the base of the Glencartholm Volcanic Beds. From mudstones and limestones with marine faunas and algal bands the strata pass up through thinly bedded siltstones, sandstones and cementstones to a massive sandstone, locally called the Larriston Sandstone, which attains a thickness of 300 m in places. There is evidence of volcanic activity towards the end of the period to the east of Langholm where the 30-metre Kershopefoot Basalt caps several prominent topographical features. In the lower part of the group fossils are abundant and similar to those at the top of the Lower Border Group, but the upper part of the group is only sparsely fossiliferous. Diagnostic assemblages have not been found but the beds are considered to be lower Viséan in age.

The period during which the beds of the Upper Border Group were deposited began with a volcanic episode during which basaltic lavas, tuffs and tuffaceous sediments were laid down over at least part of the area. The rocks are known as the Glencartholm Volcanic Beds from their type-locality on the River Esk and are calculated to be about 150 m thick. They contain a poor marine fauna but are locally notable for the unusual fish and arthropod assemblages they have yielded at Glencartholm. The greater part of the group is composed of sediments. In the lower part they are predominantly marine shales, mudstones and limestones with subordinate sandstones and few thin coals and seatclays. Many of the beds are abundantly fossiliferous with rich and varied marine faunas of corals, brachiopods and molluscs. At outcrop the beds are notable for their extensive colonies of *Lithostrotion* and numerous layers of large brachiopods. In the upper part of the group the strata below the Dinwoodie Beds are predominantly arenaceous with several coals and seatclays and only a few thin marine limestones and shales. Some aspects of the fauna of the group are of interest. Several forms of *Lithostrotion* appear for the first time in the sequence and the trepostomatous bryozoa *Dyscritella nana* and *Stenodiscus* together with the bivalves *Prothyris breviformis, P. oblonga, Pteronites angustatus* and *Modiolus oblongus* seem to be confined to this group of strata. In terms of the coral-brachiopod zones the strata range in age from C_2S_1 to S_2 but the boundary between the zones is obscure.

The lower half of the Lower Liddesdale Group consists of fine- to medium-grained sandstones with subsidiary beds of marine shale and limestone and a few thin coals and seatclays. At the bottom of the sequence the Dinwoodie Beds, some 30 m of marine shales, are notable for their rich and varied bryozoa content and because the fauna contains several forms, including *Lithostrotion junceum* and *Gigantoproductus latissimus*, which have not been recorded from older strata. The upper part of the group is composed almost entirely of highly fossiliferous marine shales and limestones, collectively called the Archerbeck Beds. The fauna, which is the most abundant in the whole Carboniferous sequence, is composed mainly of bryozoa, corals, brachiopods and bivalves. It is noteworthy that *Eomarginifera, Gigantoproductus giganteus, Pernopecten sowerbii* and *Beyrichoceratoides redesdalensis* appear in these beds for the first time in the sequence. The coral-brachiopod assemblages suggest that there is some evidence for taking the base of D_1 at the base of the group.

In the Upper Liddesdale Group, which extends from the base of the Callant Limestone up to the top of the Carboniferous Limestone Series at the base of the Catsbit Limestone, the strata are all of Yoredale type facies. They have been deposited in regular rhythmic units, each unit generally consisting of sandstone, siltstone, mudstone, limestone, coal and seatearth in descending order. Some 120 m of the beds are particularly well exposed in the fine section at Penton Linns on the Liddel Water. The lime content of some of the limestones is high and several have been worked from time to time. Mining at Harelawhill near Canonbie is in the Harelawhill Limestone which is used mainly for agricultural purposes (Plate Xa). The beds have long been famous for their fossils. The limestones contain mainly corals and brachiopods while most of the forms in the shales are brachiopods and molluscs. Of the corals *Aulophyllum*, *Dibunophyllum* and *Lithostrotion* are prominent and Gigantoproductids of both latissimoid and giganteid form together with *Eomarginifera* are of common occurrence. The bivalve *Posidonia becheri*, generally indicative of the goniatite 'zone' P_1, is relatively abundant in the lower part of the group and is of common occurrence in the shales between the Tombstone and Gastropod limestones at Penton Linns. The coral-brachiopod assemblages suggest a D_2 age for most of the strata but this conflicts with a D_1 age suggested by the foraminifera from the same beds.

The Carboniferous Limestone Series passes up into the Millstone Grit Series, the boundary being taken locally at the base of the Catsbit Limestone. The strata of the Millstone Grit Series, which are thought to be about 425 m thick, are not well known because they are restricted in outcrop to small areas near Canonbie where the degree of exposure is poor. Some information from old boreholes is difficult to interpret and correlation of the beds in the upper part of the sequence can only be conjectural. The rhythmic Yoredale type facies of the Upper Liddesdale Group continues upwards in the youngest beds of the Millstone Grit Series which include the Catsbit Limestone, the thickest limestone in the Carboniferous sequence. These beds contain abundant marine faunas similar to those of the underlying strata. The Yoredale type facies passes up into a sequence of sandstones with numerous rooty seatearths and thin coals, including seams collectively called the Penton Coals which have been worked locally. Throughout these beds there are several thin bands of shale mostly with *Lingula*, and only a few thin limestones and calcareous shales with more abundant and varied marine faunas. The topmost strata of the series are dominantly arenaceous with numerous rooty beds and thin coals. Some of them display secondary reddening, which may be attributed to oxidation below a land surface which subsequently subsided as younger Coal Measures strata were deposited unconformably. That most of the Millstone Grit Series is of Namurian age there is little doubt. Likewise, although there is no goniatite evidence, it is certain, from the evidence of other fossils and correlation with other areas, that beds of E_1 and E_2 age are present in the lower part of the sequence. The age of the strata towards the top of the sequence has not as yet been established.

The Coal Measures at the top of the Carboniferous sequence are over 900 m thick (Fig. 15). They rest unconformably on the Millstone Grit Series and are succeeded unconformably by the New Red Sandstone. They crop out only in a small area around Canonbie where they are poorly exposed. Details of the sequence are well known, however, from a number of boreholes which have been put down searching for coal. The sequence is divided as follows:

									metres
Upper Coal Measures .		.	.	.	.	.	.	up to	800
Middle Coal Measures		.	.	.	.	.	.	.	180
Lower Coal Measures		.	.	.	.	.	.	.	30

The boundary between the lower two groups is taken at the base of the Queenslie Marine Band, the local name for the extensive marine band which is taken nationally as the boundary between these groups. In common with Scottish practice the boundary between the Middle and Upper Coal Measures is at the top of the local Skelton Marine Band, which is thought to be equivalent to the well-known Skipsey's Marine Band of the Midland Valley. In England and Wales the boundary between these two groups is taken somewhat higher in the succession.

Only the upper part of the Lower Coal Measures has been recognized in the area. The strata consist of sandstone with large ragged and angular fragments of siltstone which passes up into siltstones with thin bands of sandstone and seatearth and two thin coal seams. The only mussel band recorded has yielded representatives of the *Anthracosia regularis* fauna which is commonly found in the lower part of the *A. modiolaris* Zone.

In the Middle Coal Measures a typical lithological sequence in descending order is: coal, rooty seatearth, sandstone, siltstone, mudstone with shells, carbonaceous shale with plant and fish remains. The whole succession is made up of these cyclic sequences which vary in thickness from 3 to 30 m. The numerous coals range up to 3 m in thickness and are highly volatile with strong caking properties. The thicker seams have been worked out near outcrop but remain untouched where they lie at greater depths. In places some of the topmost beds have been partially reddened by secondary oxidation of their iron content. There are few mussel bands in the sequence. Nevertheless it has been established that the assemblages fall into the upper part of the *A. modiolaris* Zone and the Lower *A. similis–A. pulchra* Zone. The boundary between the two zones is taken arbitrarily at the Nine Foot Coal. The four marine bands in the succession are characteristically varied in development. The Queenslie Marine Band at the bottom yields only *Lingula* and fish remains but the associated non-marine bivalve assemblages show that it can be correlated with certainty with the Clay Cross Marine Band of the Pennines. In the Lower *A. similis–A. pulchra* Zone the Sandwich Marine Band contains foraminifera, *Lingula* and *Orbiculoidea*, the Knottyholm Marine Band yields *Lingula*, *Orbiculoidea* and the trace-fossil *Planolites ophthalmoides* and at the top the Skelton Marine Band contains all these fossils together with conodonts. These bands are correlated with the Haughton, Sutton and Mansfield marine bands of the Pennines respectively.

Practically all the beds of the Upper Coal Measures have been reddened by secondary oxidation. In places the chemical reactions involved have been so extreme that the original sedimentary structures can no longer be recognized. As a result, although there is little change in the sandstones except in colour, the different types of argillaceous sediment are, for the most part, indistinguishable. Much of the upper part of the sequence, therefore, consists of alternations of pink sandstones and red and purple massive silty mudstones. No coal has been recorded amongst these beds. In the lower part of the group normal coal seams are found amongst grey beds interbedded with reddened beds amongst which the coals have been oxidised and, in places, replaced to some extent by dolomitic limestone. All that remains in the coal position is a thin band of irony rubble or streaky limestone. Throughout the sequence there are a few thin beds of freshwater limestone with abundant *Spirorbis* and ostracods. Three marine bands are known. The lowest, the Viaduct Marine Band, contains foraminifera and *Lingula*, and above it the Rowanburnfoot Marine Band yields a similar fauna together with intercalations containing abundant specimens of *Lioestheria*. The Riddings Marine Band, the youngest band of its kind in the Carboniferous sequence, contains foraminifera, *Lingula*, *Orbiculoidea* and conodonts. These bands correlate with the *Edmondia*, Shafton and Top marine bands of the Pennines respectively. Few mussels are present and only the *A. tenuis* Zone has been proved conclusively. By implication, however, some of the strata fall into the Upper *A. similis–A. pulchra* and *A. phillipsii* zones.

Berwickshire

Carboniferous rocks crop out over an area of at least 300 square kilometres of Berwickshire. The principal outcrop extends westwards from the Border to Duns and Greenlaw and southwards beyond Kelso. A further small area occupies a narrow strip along the coast southwards from Burnmouth. Except on the coast the degree of exposure is poor and over much of the outcrop little is known in detail of sequence or structure of the strata. All the beds are considered to be of Lower Carboniferous age and are included in the Carboniferous Limestone Series (Fig. 14).

Around Kelso, where the rocks are disposed in a gentle syncline with a north-easterly axis, the oldest strata to be included in the Carboniferous are the Kelso Traps. They reach the surface in a U-shaped outcrop from Duns southwards to Greenlaw and thence across the River Tweed to the north flank of the Cheviot Hills. At least six flows of basaltic lava have been distinguished in their total thickness of 120 m which includes several beds of basaltic tuff. There is apparent thinning northwards and no igneous rocks have been found in the sequence to the north and east of Duns, where sediments of Carboniferous age rest directly on strata of Upper Old Red Sandstone facies. The sediments consist of mudstones and shales with bands of cementstone and flaggy sandstones together with bodies of cross-bedded channel sandstone up to 30 m thick. Some of the fine-grained beds are brightly coloured and sun-cracks, rain-pits and thin bands of gypsum are characteristic features. The sequence is best seen on the shore at Burnmouth where some 500 m of strata are exposed. There the lowest 45 m or so of reddish sandstone, including calcareous bands resembling cornstones, are of Upper Old Red Sandstone facies. In the Kelso and Greenlaw districts the beds succeeding the Kelso Traps include concretionary cornstones. The lowest of these beds are tuffaceous, gritty and locally pebbly. They include the Carham Stone, a cherty magnesian limestone up to 7·5 m thick, which is thought to have been accumulated by chemical precipitation from waters enriched in lime by showers of volcanic dust towards the end of the main period of volcanic action. The strata as a whole are not abundantly fossiliferous but several bands contain mainly plants, the bivalve *Modiolus*, ostracods and fish, none of which indicate the age of the beds in detail.

Strata higher in the sequence have been recognized only on the coast south of Burnmouth. Some 200 m of sandstone which crop out on the shore for

LANGHOLM

METRES FEET

0 — 0

100 —

— 500

200 —

300 — 1000

⌣   ⌣   *MUSSEL BAND*

E   E   *'ESTHERIA' BAND*

L   L   *LINGULA BAND*

M   M   *MARINE BAND (M.B.)*

MAINLY

RED

SANDSTONES

AND

MASSIVE

SILTY

MUDSTONES

SANQUHAR

UPPER COAL MEASURES

MIDDLE COAL MEASURES

LOWER COAL MEASURES

E   E

E   E

L   L   *LAGRAE M.B.*
E   E

E   E
M   M   *SKIPSEY'S M.B.*
L   L   *EASTSIDE M.B.*
L   L   *BANKHEAD M.B.*
        TARGET COAL
        CREEPIE COAL
        CALMSTONE COAL
⌣   ⌣

⌣   ⌣
⌣   ⌣   *PARROT COAL*
L   L   *QUEENSLIE*
        KIRKCONNEL
        SPLINT COAL

L   L

M   M

THORNHILL

L   L
L   L
E   E

L   L   *MARINE BAND*

SPIRORBIS
LIMESTONE

M   M   *RIDDINGS M.B.*
M   M   *ROWANBURNFOOT M.B.*
E   E
M   M   *VIADUCT M.B.*

M   M   *SKELTON M.B.*
M   M   *KNOTTYHOLM M.B.*
M   M   *SANDWICH M.B.*
⌣   ⌣   *ARCHERBECK COAL*

        6 FT COAL

⌣   ⌣   *9 FT COAL*

        5 FT COAL
        8 FT COAL
        7 FT COAL

L   L

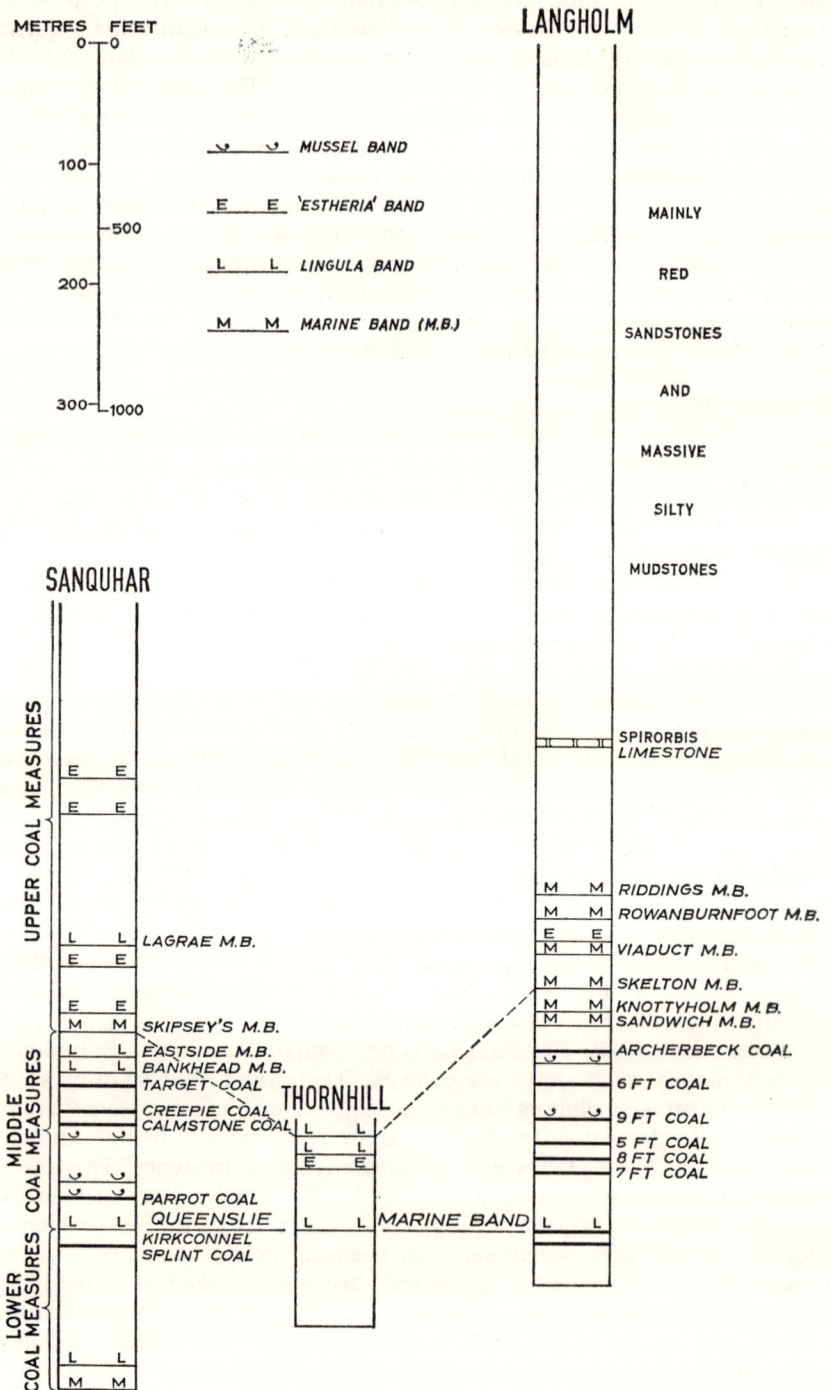

FIG. 15. *Comparative vertical sections of the Coal Measures*

nearly 2 km south from Burnmouth has been correlated with the Fell Sandstone of Northumberland. It is white, yellow and pink, and mostly false-bedded. The bedding is locally convolute and the lithology is diversified in places by bands of quartz pebbles, lenses of red sandy mudstone and ironstone nodules. On the cliffs to the south the sandstones are overlain by about 75 m of alternating mudstones, sandstones and seatearths with a few thin coals and cementstone bands. Coal from this part of the sequence was worked at Lamberton in the 19th century. Apart from fairly abundant plant remains the beds are poorly fossiliferous with only a few bands containing *Lingula*, bivalves and ostracods. Near the top of the sequence a few beds contain a marine fauna including crinoids and brachiopods. The youngest strata exposed at Hilton Bay and Lamberton include the Lamberton Limestone, which has been taken as the equivalent of the Dun Limestone at the base of the Lower Limestone Group of Northumberland. It is up to 1·5 m thick and yields a marine fauna including *Lithostrotion*, Gigantoproductids and *Punctospirifer*. It passes up into 7·5 m of marine shales closely overlain by a red sandstone with an irregular base which is up to 45 m thick just south of the Border.

South-east of Dunbar

From Pease Bay, near Cockburnspath, to within 2 km of Dunbar an upward sequence of Lower Carboniferous rocks is well exposed on the shore. The area occupied by the outcrop extends for about 3 km inland where the strata are faulted against rocks of Upper Old Red Sandstone age. The beds fall into the Calciferous Sandstone Measures and the Lower Limestone Group of the Midland Valley classification, the boundary being taken at the base of the marine beds associated with the Upper Longcraig Limestone (Fig. 14).

More than 300 m of the strata at the bottom of the Calciferous Sandstone Measures can be seen on the shore in the neighbourhood of Pease Bay and Cove. The sequence is broken only by the Cove Fault which has cut out some 150 m of beds. The arbitrary base of the Carboniferous is taken just above a prominent deep red sandstone with creamy chert lenses. The oldest beds are shales and cementstones with plant fragments. They are succeeded by the Eastern Hole Conglomerate, a distinctive 1-metre cementstone breccia, overlain by a band of cementstone yielding *Sanguinolites*. The Horse Roads Sandstone, 45 m thick, is false-bedded and near the top contains large calcareous concretions. It passes up into a series of shales with impersistent cementstones. The relationship of these beds to the Kip Carle Sandstone is obscure because the latter, a pale brown medium- to coarse-grained sandstone, is associated with the Cove Fault, the outcrop of which has not been defined with certainty. The beds beyond the fault and higher in the sequence are shales with thin coals and ironstone ribs. They are succeeded by the Heathery Heugh Sandstone, a mainly red and purple rock which forms a prominent bluff and stack at Hollow Rock. Some 12 m above it a bed of shale yields specimens of *Cardiopteris polymorpha*. The Cove Lower Marine Band is well exposed next to the southern part of the Cove Harbour sea wall and also at several localities in the Thornton Burn. It consists of up to 5·5 m of calcareous sandstone and sandy shale and yields an assemblage of brachiopods, gastropods and bivalves characterized by the abundance of *Productus redesdalensis* and the occurrence of the goniatite *Beyrichocera-*

toides redesdalensis. The Cove Upper Marine Band crops out at the north end
of the sea wall and also north-westwards along the coast at Linkhead where
it is known as the Linkhead Limestone. Up to 2·5 m of calcareous sandstone
and siltstone contain brachiopods and bivalves including *Spirifer duplicicosta*
and *Gigantoproductus*. The Cove Harbour Sandstone, a red false-bedded rock,
forms a prominent bluff north of the harbour and shortly above it in the
sequence is the Cove Oil-shale, a distinctive rock weathering bright red at the
top and containing abundant pyritized plant fragments.

The highest beds of the Calciferous Sandstone Measures crop out on the
shore northwards from Thorntonloch to Long Craig. The dominant lithology
is sandstone but two marine limestones and shales, the Lower and Middle
Longcraig limestones, occur towards the top of the sequence. The Middle
Longcraig Limestone is a particularly striking white nodular rock with a
fauna including solitary corals, abundant specimens of the brachiopod
Composita, and a Rhynchonelloid. The Limestone is characterized by large
colonies of species of *Lithostrotion*.

Inland exposures are few and of limited extent. At the south-western end of
the outcrop, however, near Oldhamstocks 60 to 90 m of basaltic lavas and
tuffs can be seen amongst sediments which are mainly sandstone. These beds
are taken to be Carboniferous in age but their precise position in the sequence
is unknown.

Over 60 m of Lower Limestone Group strata are disposed in a broad
syncline extending from Barns Ness Lighthouse to Catcraig on the coast and
inland for almost 3 km. Some of the beds are repeated in a smaller fold
cropping out along the coast towards Dunbar. In the main the sequence is a
cyclic development of sandstones and marine limestones and shales. Many of
the strata are fossiliferous and in some beds marine shells are abundant. At
the bottom of the succession the Upper Longcraig Limestone is about
5·5 m thick. It is cream-coloured and crowded with a rich marine fauna of
corals and brachiopods, particularly in the upper part. Some 6 m higher in
the sequence the Lower Skateraw Limestone, up to 0·6 m thick, is distinguished by a band of Gigantoproductids at the base. The beds above it are mainly
mudstone and seatclay with a thin coal underlying the Middle Skateraw
Limestone. It is up to 5·5 m thick and is characterized by a band 0·3 m thick
near the top containing abundant specimens of *Saccamminopsis fusulinaformis*. Above the limestone a bed of calcareous shale contains many corals,
brachiopods and bivalves, and trilobite fragments are fairly common. A
metre or so higher in the sequence a thin limestone, the Upper Skateraw
Limestone, is associated with shales yielding rich marine faunas. Later beds

---

PLATE IX
A. Anticline in rocks of the Upper Liddesdale Group, Carboniferous Limestone
Series, at Penton Linns, Liddel Water, Dumfriesshire. (Geol. Surv. Photo.
No. C4047).
B. Cliffs at Cove Harbour, Berwickshire. Steeply dipping rocks of the Calciferous
Sandstone Measures, Carboniferous Limestone Series, including the Heathery
Heugh and Cove Harbour sandstones. (Geol. Surv. Photo. No. D1151).
C. Carboniferous-Ordovician unconformity, Dumfriesshire. Rocks of the
Carboniferous Limestone Series resting unconformably on steeply dipping
Ordovician beds in the Loch Burn, Sanquhar. (Geol. Surv. Photo. No. C3570).

PLATE IX

A

B

C

A

B

are mainly sandstone but they include three poorly developed marine horizons which are in upward sequence, the Chapel Point Limestone, the Dryburn Foot Limestone and the Barness East Limestone. All these limestones are sandy and sparsely fossiliferous on the whole, but several surfaces display striking developments of 'cauda-galli' markings. The sandstones above the Barness East Limestone are taken to represent part of the Limestone Coal Group of the Midland Valley classification.

All the strata below the Barness East Limestone are of Viséan age or older. Some of the earliest beds may be of Tournaisian age but there is as yet no direct evidence that this is so. The oldest marine bands in the sequence, the Cove Lower and Cove Upper marine bands, are correlated with the Dun and Woodend limestones of Berwick and with the Redesdale Ironstone and Redesdale Limestone of Northumberland, respectively. This being so the Cove Lower Marine Band, although it does not yield a diagnostic fauna, can be taken to be of B age related to goniatites and, therefore, mid-Viséan. The youngest beds in the sequence clearly represent the Lower Limestone Group of the Midland Valley and are therefore of P_2 age or uppermost Viséan.

PLATE X

A. Limestone mines, Harelawhill, near Canonbie, Dumfriesshire. Quarry and mines in the Harelawhill Limestone (Upper Liddesdale Group, Carboniferous Limestone Series). (Geol. Surv. Photo. No. C4054).

B. Limestone Quarry, Dunbar, East Lothian. Large-scale modern quarry in the Middle Skateraw Limestone and associated beds (Lower Limestone Group, Carboniferous Limestone Series). Dunbar Works of the Associated Portland Cement Manufacturers Limited. (Geol. Surv. Photo. No. D1142).

7. VOLCANIC ROCKS OF CARBONIFEROUS AGE

Ample evidence of widespread volcanic activity in the south and east of the Southern Uplands during Carboniferous times is seen in the extensive outcrops of lavas together with the abundance of volcanic necks and intrusions of various forms (Fig. 13). The most common rock is olivine-basalt and for convenience the main characteristics of the principal types are summarized briefly below:

MACROPORPHYRITIC BASALTS
(Phenocrysts more than 2 mm in length)

Markle type: with abundant phenocrysts of labradorite and some of olivine.
Dunsapie type: with abundant phenocrysts of labradorite, olivine and augite.
Craiglockhart type: with abundant phenocrysts of olivine and augite.

MICROPORPHYRITIC BASALTS
(Phenocrysts less than 2 mm in length)

Jedburgh type: with abundant phenocrysts of labradorite and some of olivine.
Dalmeny type: with abundant phenocrysts of olivine and sporadic labradorite and augite.
Hillhouse type: with abundant phenocrysts of olivine and augite.

The ground mass constituents are labradorite, augite and iron ore.

At least three episodes of volcanic activity during which lavas were extruded have been recognized in the Carboniferous. The earliest and most extensive took place at the beginning of Carboniferous times when lavas in a series of interdigitating flows up to 120 m in total thickness were laid down over an area extending from the Solway Firth south of Dumfries to Duns in Berwickshire. In the west these rocks are known as the Birrenswark Lavas from the type-locality at Burnswark, a striking feature on their escarpment a short distance to the north of Ecclefechan (Plate XIA). Different types of basalt are present in the sequence but to the west of Langholm the Jedburgh type appears to be the most common and the Dalmeny type is well represented. Eastwards from Langholm, in Eskdale and Liddesdale, the predominant types appear to be Dalmeny and Dunsapie. Markle and Jedburgh types are less commonly found. The occurrence of glassy olivine-basalts, allied to Dalmeny type, and of a rare feldspathic Dunsapie type has also been noted. One of the most striking features of the Birrenswark Lavas is their alteration by deuteric activity in the consolidating lava and the effect of atmospheric weathering. Because of the advanced nature of the alteration of many of the constituent minerals it is commonly impossible to determine the type of basalt.

In Berwickshire the lavas at the base of the Carboniferous are known as the Kelso Traps. Although there is no evidence that they are absolutely contemporaneous with the Birrenswark Lavas to the west there seems to be little doubt that they were deposited at about the same time. The rocks are highly

86

altered olivine-basalts. A distinction has been recorded in the general disposition of the types of basalt in that the lower part of the sequence, restricted in outcrop to the area south of the Blackadder Water, consists mainly of Jedburgh and Markle types. Flows in the upper part of the sequence, which crop out in the area north of the Tweed, seem to be more basic and consist mainly of Dunsapie and Dalmeny types.

Wherever these lavas occur individual flows can be made out by the abundance of vesicles in the marginal zones associated with generally slaggy tops. In many places they are interbedded with red sandstones and shales, some of which contain a high proportion of basaltic debris. In Berwickshire some beds of basaltic tuff have been recorded but these are uncommon.

Some time later, during a second episode of volcanic activity, the Kershope-foot Basalt was deposited locally in Eskdale and Liddesdale. At outcrop the rocks cap several prominent topographic features including Windy Edge, Greena Hill, Carby Hill and Swarf Hill and they are particularly well exposed in the Kershope Burn south of Newcastleton. They are about 30 m in thickness and fairly homogeneous throughout, except near the top of the mass where the basalt is extremely vesicular and slaggy. In type the basalt varies from intermediate between Jedburgh and mugearite in the west to intermediate between Jedburgh and Markle in the east.

A short time later a further outburst of volcanic activity gave rise to the deposits known as the Glencartholm Volcanic Beds. These have been recognized at outcrop from the headwaters of the River Sark eastwards to the Liddel Water near Kershopefoot. They are about 150 m thick and consist largely of interbedded tuffs, sediments and tuffaceous sediments with varying proportions of volcanic debris. Lavas are less common and occur, up to 15 m in thickness, near the bottom of the sequence. The igneous fragments in the tuffaceous strata are mainly decomposed basaltic rocks and altered basic pumice. In places fragments of trachyte occur. The lavas are variable in type, ranging from olivine-basalts of Dunsapie and Dalmeny types to trachybasalts.

Extruded igneous rocks are also present in the Carboniferous sequence at Windburgh Hill, north-east of Newcastleton, at Catcleuch Shin on the northern shoulder of Carter Fell and at Oldhamstocks near Dunbar. Their precise age is unknown and no correlation has been made with the Kershope-foot Basalt or the Glencartholm Volcanic Beds. At Windburgh Hill and associated outcrops the strata are mainly olivine-basalts of Dunsapie and Dalmeny types overlain by beds of basaltic tuff. At Catcleuch Shin basaltic tuffs are overlain by basalts of Markle and Jedburgh type. Both tuff and basalt are present in the poorly exposed sequence at Oldhamstocks.

The vents from which these Carboniferous lavas were extruded are scattered over an area some 16 km in width extending north-eastwards from Langholm to Duns. They are mostly filled with tuff and agglomerate composed of fragments of basaltic rocks and of the country rock through which they have been blasted. Some of them are wholly or partly filled by plugs of basaltic rocks of various types. Little is known of the relative ages of individual vents. It seems unlikely that any of the Birrenswark Lavas or Kelso Traps were extruded from vents which cut strata which are clearly higher in the sequence. None of these vents cuts beds younger than the Glencartholm Volcanic Beds, however, which suggests that they were at least some of the sources of the tuffs and basalts at that horizon and probably also of the Kershopefoot Basalt.

Of the vents which are now exposed outwith the limits of the Carboniferous outcrop, those at Arkleton Hill, Pike Fell and Cooms Fell, just to the north-east of Langholm, may mark sites from which some of the Birrenswark Lavas issued. The first two are entirely filled with plugs of basalt but at Cooms Fell the vent is mostly filled with basaltic agglomerate with only a small plug of basalt intermediate between Dalmeny and Hillhouse types. In the same district the many apparently younger vents are mostly filled with basaltic agglomerate. Some of them contain angular blocks and rounded pebbles of sediments of Upper Old Red Sandstone or Carboniferous age. The largest vent of this group is at Tinnis Hill which forms a prominent topographical feature between Langholm and Newcastleton. The vent is oval in shape and is mostly filled with fine-grained agglomerate, with a small plug of basalt intermediate between Dalmeny and Jedburgh types.

Farther to the north-east in Teviotdale a varied assemblage of vents was intruded at or about the same time. Those which form the Minto Hills and others at Troneyhill and Ancrumcraig are filled with agglomerate only. More complex vents filled with agglomerate together with basalt plugs of varied proportions form the prominent features of Rubers Law, Black Law and Lanton Hill. Dunion Hill and Fatlips Crags are examples of vents filled with plugs of basalt only.

A large number of sheets and plugs were intruded in and around the valley of the River Tweed at about the same time. Some of them may have been the sources from which the Kelso Traps were laid down but others may be associated with later volcanic activity since they appear to cut at least part of the lava sequence. Olivine-dolerite is the main rock-type in the plugs at Bemersyde, Smailholm Tower and Blinkbonny. At Mellerstain the rock is a basalt of Markle type and several different basalts have been found in the composite plug at Lurgie Craigs. Basalts of Markle, Dunsapie and Dalmeny types are common in plugs at Queenscairn, Sweethope Hill, Hareheugh Craigs, Middlethird and Knock Hill. Masses of olivine-dolerite at Wooden Hill, Rutherford, Craigover, Maxton, Brotherstone Hills and West Gordon are believed to be remnants of intrusive sheets or sills. The columnar basalt of Dalmeny type at Hexpathdean Quarry has intruded sediments of the Upper Old Red Sandstone, and similar basalts which cap Duns Law and two neighbouring hills are thought to be part of a small laccolith. Insufficient evidence has been found to establish whether the basalts of Haddenrig and Lurdenlaw or the dolerite of Peniel Heugh are sills or plugs.

Some time after this widespread intrusion and extrusion of basaltic rocks a later phase of vulcanicity gave rise to the alkaline and acid igneous rocks found in the district which probably correspond in time to the trachytic lavas and intrusions of the Garleton Hills and similar intrusions in the Campsie and Renfrewshire hills. The chief types of rock represented are porphyritic and non-porphyritic quartz-trachytes, sanidine-trachyte, sanidine-porphyry, riebeckite-bearing felsite, and basalt. The areal distribution of these rocks is similar to that of the earlier basaltic phase.

Towards the known southern limit of their occurrence they are represented by a north-easterly swarm of dykes of decomposed trachyte, quartz-trachyte and phonolitic trachyte, some feldspar-phyric, together with a few dykes of decomposed felsite. In the same area is the intruded mass of phonolite at Pikethaw Hill, 13 km north of Langholm. Farther to the north-east similar rocks cap high ground at Skelfhill Pen, Skelfhill, Doecleugh and Penchrise. The associated vents in this district are mainly filled with agglomerate composed of fragments of grit, shale, greywacke and trachyte. The largest of these at Tudhope Hill, to the east of Mosspaul, is of special interest because it contains a large block of sandstone of Upper Old Red Sandstone age which has apparently fallen into the vent. The agglomerate is pierced by basalts of Jedburgh and Markle types at the southern end and by plugs of trachyte towards its northern end. Some 6 km to the north-east another large vent at Greatmoor Hill is filled mainly with agglomerate which is full of large bombs of olivine-basalt and blocks of grit and greywacke. The agglomerate is pierced by bodies of basalt of Dunsapie and Craiglockhart types and near its southern margin by a plug-like body of trachyte. A short distance to the east a smaller vent at Leap Hill is filled mostly by two plugs of non-porphyritic trachyte. The associated agglomerate is basaltic and is cut by a dyke-like intrusion of basalt of Dunsapie type.

Similar rocks thought to be of the same age are found commonly around Melrose in the form of laccoliths, sills, north-easterly dykes and in vents. The most spectacular occurrence is at the Eildon Hills which are regarded as representing the denuded remains of a composite laccolith (Front cover and Plate XIB). Rocks of slightly different type have been intruded sheet by sheet and now give the appearance of being stratified. Much of Eildon Wester and Eildon Mid hills is formed by riebeckite-felsite disposed in two layers. On the south-west face of the Wester Hill the upper layer shows magnificent columnar structures. The summit of Mid Hill is occupied by orthophyric riebeckite-trachyte overlying a sheet of augite-olivine-trachyte which crops out to the west. Eildon Hill North on the other hand consists of porphyritic and non-porphyritic varieties of sanidine-trachyte. Similar rocks are found as dykes and irregular elongate bodies with north-easterly orientation in the vicinity of White Law, Cauldshiels Hill and Bowden Moor to the south-west of Melrose. Sills or sheets form prominent features at Bemersyde Hill, Black Hill and White Hill to the east and north-east of Melrose.

The largest of the associated vents is the Chiefswood vent at Melrose. It is oval in shape with a north-easterly axis about 3 km long. It is filled with an agglomerate of angular fragments of Silurian and Old Red Sandstone sediments mingled with pieces of quartz-porphyry, trachyte and olivine-basalt. A small vent at Little Hill in the same vicinity is mostly filled with a plug of basaltic rock which almost certainly pierces the acid rocks of the Eildon Hills complex.

In Berwickshire four intrusions of felsite and associated rocks occur in conglomerates and sandstones of Upper Old Red Sandstone age. They form the hills of Dirrington Little Law, Dirrington Great Law, Blacksmill Hill and Kyles Hill. In the first three masses the principal constituent is a riebeckite-bearing rock similar to the felsite of Eildon Wester Hill, which suggests that they may be all part of a similar laccolith of the same age. On Kyles Hill, however, the rock is different. It consists of phenocrysts of feldspar embedded in an orthophyric groundmass of orthoclase, quartz and hematite and appears to be pierced by a dark bluish grey rock resembling andesite (see also p. 52).

At Southdean, 5 km south-east of Bonchester Bridge, a large plug is

G

composed of nepheline-basanite consisting of phenocrysts of olivine and pyroxene in a groundmass of pyroxene, feldspar, nepheline and iron ore. In the Midland Valley rocks of this type have been found in intrusions of late Carboniferous or, perhaps, Permian age. Further evidence of igneous intrusion in the south of Scotland in late Carboniferous times is given by a few quartz-dolerite dykes of east–west trend. One of these is well exposed as it crosses the River Esk and the Liddel Water north of Canonbie.

8. NEW RED SANDSTONE

The New Red Sandstone consists of all the rocks in the south of Scotland which have in the past been included in the Permian and Triassic systems. The twofold subdivision is retained in this account, but the boundary between the two systems is not established.

The 'Permian' system is considered to comprise all the late Palaeozoic desert-sandstones and breccias, as well as the associated lavas and intrusive rocks. This long-accepted connotation has recently been questioned on palaeobotanical grounds. Plants found near the base of the succession in central Ayrshire have been assigned alternatively to the Westphalian, to the Upper Stephanian Series at the top of the Carboniferous, or to the Autunian (basal Permian). The evidence currently available is inconclusive.

Triassic rocks occur only in an area of some 140 square kilometres between Annan and Canonbie, where they are in direct continuity with the Bunter rocks of Cumberland.

The principal **'Permian'** outcrops occupy outlying basins in the Stranraer area, in Nithsdale from Sanquhar to the Solway, and in Annandale from above Moffat to below Lochmaben. Smaller areas occur on the coast between Ballantrae and Bennane Head; in the Water of Milk, between Lockerbie and Ecclefechan; and in the Snar valley, north of Leadhills.

The Stranraer isthmus and the western shore of Loch Ryan are composed of 'Permian' sandstones and breccias which at their western boundary are seen to rest unconformably on Upper Carboniferous and Ordovician rocks, the eastern boundary, like most of the outcrop, being obscured by superficial deposits. On the Loch Ryan shore red breccias with thin beds of sandstone form cliffs up to 45 m high. The pebbles in the breccias are largely of Ordovician greywacke and chert. The outcrop, about 1·5 km wide, extends southwards to Stoneykirk, the rocks dipping gently to the east or south-east. At West Freugh, about 2·5 km north-east of Stoneykirk, a water bore proved 143 m of breccia underlain by at least 24 m of brown sandstone. The results of a recent gravity survey suggest that the rocks are mainly sandstones, which occupy an asymmetrical trough aligned north-westwards, having a maximum depth of some 900 to 1400 m in the south-eastern part of the outcrop. The eastern margin is very steep and is probably a fault.

A narrow strip of red sandstones forms the coast between Ballantrae pier and Bennane Head. At the pier they include a breccia containing pebbles of serpentinite and other rocks of the Ballantrae Igneous Complex, against which these 'Permian' rocks are everywhere faulted. In places they are cut by thin basalt dykes, probably of Tertiary age.

In Nithsdale olivine-basalt of 'Permian' age forms three small outliers, resting on Coal Measures, to the north-east and south-east of Sanquhar, and five small volcanic necks which pierce the Coal Measures nearby are taken to be of the same age. The necks are filled with angular fragments

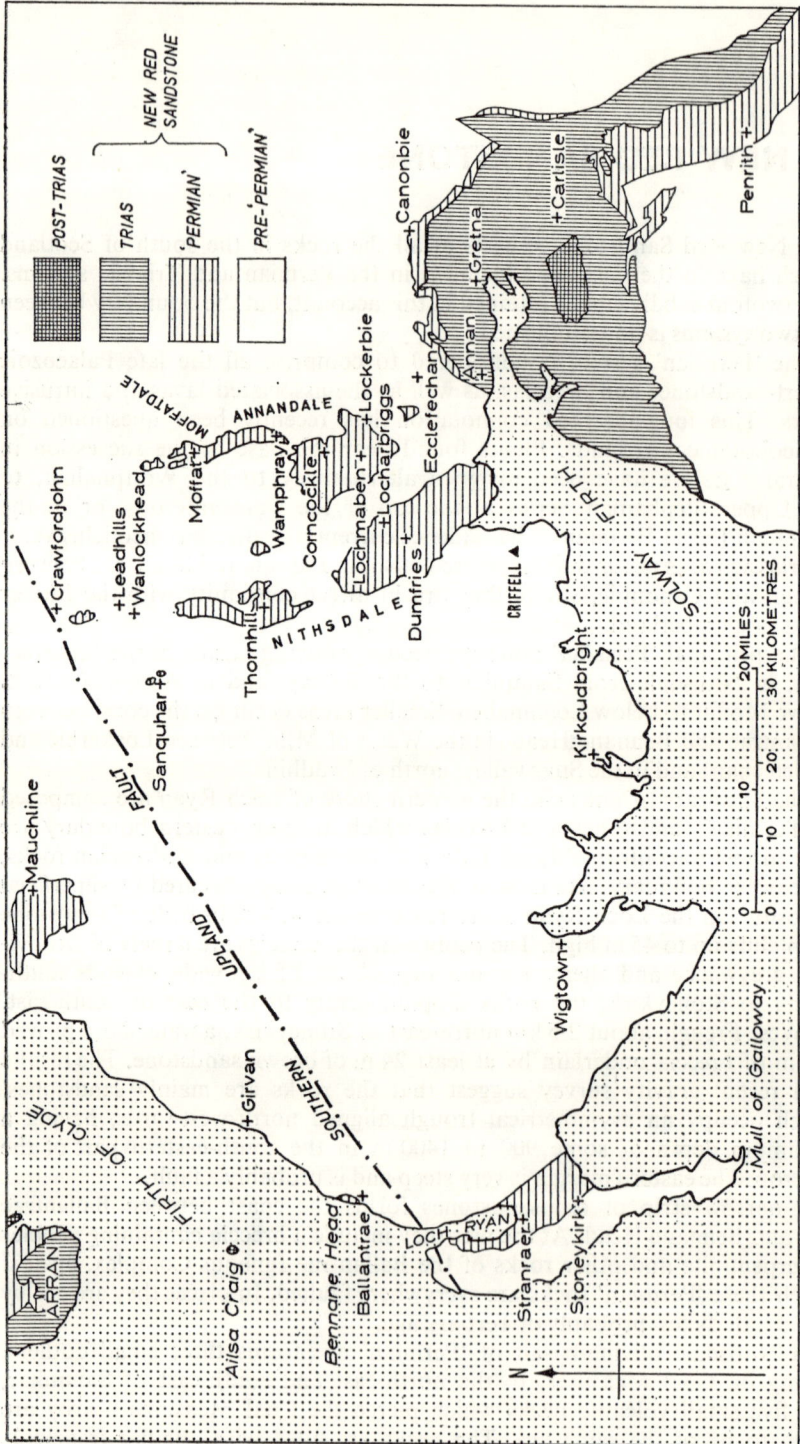

Fig. 16. *Outcrops of the New Red Sandstone in the South of Scotland and the Carlisle Basin*

of olivine-basalt and some of Carboniferous sediment. The Carboniferous rocks near Sanquhar are also cut by thin sills of teschenitic and camptonitic dolerite, and dykes of monchiquite and camptonitic dolerite with a north-westerly trend occur here and elsewhere in the Southern Uplands. A monchiquite dyke in Lauderdale has been considered to be of Carboniferous age on the basis of its pre-'Permian' north-easterly trend, but its petrographic affinities are with the 'Permian' monchiquites of Ayrshire. North-westerly dykes of theralitic essexite near Crawfordjohn and Wanlockhead are assigned to the 'Permian'.

The Snar valley outlier, some four square kilometres in area, lies about 6 km north of Leadhills, and consists of coarse breccias occupying a depression in Ordovician rocks. The rock consists of angular and sub-angular fragments of greywacke and chert, of local provenance, of which the largest are as much as 0·6 m across.

In the Thornhill basin the 'Permian' rocks rest unconformably on both the Lower and Upper Carboniferous. The basal beds are olivine-basalt lavas, probably no more than about 45 m thick, with an underlying thin conglomeratic sandstone or breccia wherever the base of the lavas is exposed. The sandstones and breccias below and within the basalts include angular fragments of greywacke, and lack the brick-red colour and the rounded grains which indicate the arid aeolian conditions of deposition of the succeeding sandstones. South of the latitude of Thornhill these sandstones overlap the underlying lavas to rest directly on the Carboniferous rocks. The lowest beds in the north of the basin often contain angular fragments of basalt, as well as of sandstone and greywacke, which may be polished and faceted after the manner of 'dreikanters'. Occasional large blocks of basalt in higher sandstones demonstrate the irregularity of the lava surface, and show that it remained exposed in places long after the process of burial began. These false-bedded sandstones were formerly extensively quarried at Gatelawbridge, near Thornhill.

The 'Permian' rocks of the Dumfries area generally dip gently to the south-west and consist entirely of red sandstones and breccias. The false-bedded sandstones have been extensively quarried for building-stone, particularly in the vicinity of Locharbriggs, and are known as the Dumfries Sandstones. They rest unconformably on Lower Palaeozoic and Carboniferous rocks and in the south-west they abut against the Criffell Granite. The breccias, which included faceted pebbles of greywacke and granite, appear to occur in the higher beds, cropping out in the south-west of the basin.

The Lochmaben basin also is occupied by red sandstones and breccias. At the extensive old quarries of Corncockle Muir the sandstones are traversed locally by thin veins of pyrolusite, and are noted for reptilian footprints on bedding planes on account of which, over 100 years ago, the rocks were assigned to the Permian. More recently the validity of correlation by footprints has been questioned.

Borings for water have proved the sandstones and breccias to be at least 200 m thick near Dumfries and 90 m, with little breccia, near Lochmaben. The maximum depth of both basins has been estimated by gravity survey to be at least 1000 m, the deepest areas being at Dumfries itself and some 6 km north-north-west of Lochmaben, and there is every indication that the

Dumfries basin, like that of Lochmaben, closes southwards and has no physical connexion with the Permian of Cumberland. The distribution of breccia and sandstone in the Dumfries basin suggests that the basin was already deformed before the breccia was deposited. The gravity information from Stranraer, Dumfries, and Lochmaben presents a consistent pattern of deposition in separate basins which were being actively deepened as sedimentation proceeded, and refutes the older ideas that the 'Permian' rocks are either the remnants of a once continuous sheet preserved by post-'Permian' warping, or the deposits of a 'Permian' valley system draining into the Solway Firth. Additional evidence of 'Permian' tectonic activity is afforded by the restriction of the volcanic necks of this age near Sanquhar to a relatively narrow zone aligned north-westward.

In the upper part of Annandale, north of Wamphray, breccias and red sandstones form a narrow outcrop and rest unconformably on Silurian rocks. The breccias in Moffatdale contain pebbles of fossiliferous Carboniferous rocks.

The Annan Series, which occupies the area between Annan, Gretna, and Canonbie, is considered to be largely of **Triassic** age. The rocks consist mainly of regularly bedded micaceous sandstones, shales, and marls, and lack the dune-bedding, and wind-rounding and polishing of grains and pebbles, which are characteristic of the 'Permian'. Ripple-marking of the marls and the occurrence of possible erosion channels are additional indications of their having been deposited in water. Pebbles of Palaeozoic rock have been found only in the basal conglomerate. Fossils are rare, but footprints of *Labyrinthodon* have been recorded from sandstones near Annan.

The rocks are poorly exposed and have been little studied. In 1916 Horne and Gregory subdivided them, and in 1942 Barrett re-interpreted the succession and correlated it with the Cumberland rocks. The table below shows the essential features of these classifications.

Horne and Gregory		Barrett
		Kirklinton Sandstone
Irregular sandstones with shales	Warmanbie Sandstone	⎫
		⎬ St. Bees Sandstone
Regular red sandstones with shales and erosion channels	Annanlea Sandstone	⎭
Gritty sandstone	Woodhouse Tower Sandstone	Transition beds
Well bedded 'typical Triassic' red marls, with traces of gypsum near the base and ripple-marked shales near the top	Robgill Marls	St. Bees Shales
Massive red sandstone, often soft, and shales	Allerbeck and Cadgill Sandstone	

Barrett discounted the Allerbeck and Cadgill Sandstone as a stratigraphical unit, and assigned the occurrences severally to the transition beds, the St. Bees Sandstone, or to the Kirklinton Sandstone. This last is characterized by the scattered occurrence of bands of wind-rounded quartz grains, and by the absence of the shale bands which split up the St. Bees Sandstone. Barrett also recognized the local development of a thin basal conglomerate with rounded and angular Carboniferous pebbles. The recent resurvey of the Langholm area by the Geological Survey raises doubt concerning some of Barrett's detailed correlations and the validity of his general classification.

The Annan Series rests unconformably on the Carboniferous and most of its outcrop is made up of St. Bees Sandstone, formerly quarried at Corsehill, near Annan, and elsewhere. The St. Bees Shales lie along the northern margin, in an outcrop which widens from the River Annan, where they are overlapped by the Sandstone, towards Canonbie. The Kirklinton Sandstone, resting locally on a small Carboniferous inlier, occupies a small area around Gretna. The thicknesses of the formations are difficult to assess, and the only estimate to which any value has been attached, even by its author, is a figure of about 120 m for the maximum of the St. Bees Shales.

The boundary between the Permian and the Triassic may properly lie within the St. Bees Shales, their basal beds having a Permian character and their stratigraphy in the north of England suggesting a correlation, in part, with the Middle or Upper Permian marls east of the Pennines. The difficulty of delineating the Permo-Triassic boundary here and elsewhere in Britain has engendered the widely held opinion that the two formations should be combined as the New Red Sandstone.

9. TERTIARY

No sedimentary rocks representative of the time between the Triassic and the Pleistocene occur in the South of Scotland. Nevertheless it is probable that Rhaetic and early Jurassic sediments were deposited in the region, at least as extensively as the Permian and Triassic rocks which now remain, and that in the Upper Cretaceous the Chalk was laid down over most of the region. Eocene basalt lavas, extensively developed in Antrim, may have spread over part of the area.

The only rocks of the Triassic–Pleistocene interval now present are basic Tertiary dykes, which cross the region in a direction which alters gradually from south-eastward to east-south-eastward as the outcrops are followed towards the south-east. They are members of the Mull Swarm and consist either of tholeiite or, rarely, of crinanite (olivine-analcime-dolerite). Several individual dykes can be followed for many kilometres, but there is an element of doubt about some cases of postulated continuity. The Eskdale-muir dyke can be followed from the southern end of the 'Permian' outlier in the Snar valley to Moffat and the vicinity of Langholm. It is of tholeiitic composition and has a width of up to 55 m. This dyke, as well as two other broad dykes within 8 km to the north-east, appears to cross the Southern Upland Fault without displacement. The most northerly of this group is the Acklington dyke, which can be followed from west of Hawick to the coast of Northumberland. The Cleveland dyke of northern Yorkshire may be linked by alignment with the Caponcraig–Coylton dyke of Ayrshire. Between Ayrshire and Cumberland there are two small outcrops of the dyke, at Troston Hill, west of Moniaive, and east of the mouth of the Nith. A branch of this dyke is believed by A. G. MacGregor to follow the Southern Upland Fault east of New Cumnock, and to swing south-eastwards along the boundary fault of the Sanquhar Coalfield. The same author has drawn attention to the similar displacement of another Tertiary dyke a few kilometres to the south-west. Other Tertiary dykes are to be seen on the shore between Girvan and Ballantrae, cutting Arenig volcanic rocks and Silurian and 'Permian' sediments.

The dykes were regarded by Geikie as the fillings of the fissures from which were extruded the plateau basalts, widely developed in the Inner Hebrides and Northern Ireland, but it is now recognized that eruption was from a number of volcanic centres, as propounded by Judd. The dykes radiate from these centres but belong to a later phase of activity than the extrusion of the lavas.

10. PLEISTOCENE AND POST-GLACIAL

The Pleistocene Period, which is defined as extending from the end of the Tertiary Era some 2 or 3 million years ago to the beginning of the Post-Glacial Period about 10 300 years ago, was a period of very marked climatic variation. On several occasions during the period large parts of the Northern Hemisphere were subjected to the most rigorous arctic conditions and, at such times, the south of Scotland was completely submerged beneath exceedingly thick ice-sheets whose outer margins lay far to the south in England. During the interglacials, the periods intervening between successive glaciations, the climate was at times considerably warmer than it is in this country at present, since fossil evidence shows that heat-loving animals such as elephant, hippopotamus and cave-lion existed at these times in parts of southern England.

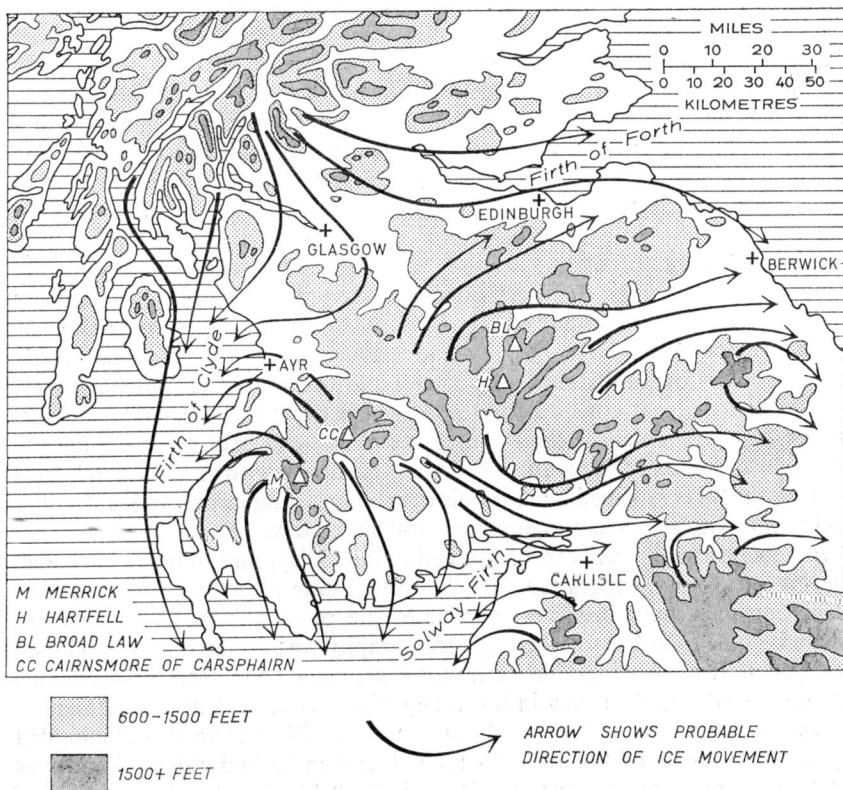

Fig. 17. *Suggested directions of ice-movement over southern Scotland*

97

Successive glaciations in Scotland probably followed a fairly standard pattern of development. Snow and ice accumulating in the Grampian Highlands and in the higher parts of the Southern Uplands formed valley glaciers which, after expanding to form local ice-sheets, flowed out from the dispersal areas and finally coalesced to form one large ice-sheet.

The dispersal areas in the South of Scotland appear to have been mainly in the high ground around the Merrick, Rhinns of Kells, and Cairnsmore of Carsphairn in Galloway, and farther north-east in the Broad Law, Hart Fell, White Coomb area where the Rivers Tweed, Annan and Clyde now rise (Fig. 17). Ice flowing northwards from these areas met ice emanating from the Grampian Highlands and the two sheets moved off as composite streams towards the lower ground of the east and west coasts. Ice moving southwards from the Southern Uplands became part of the general stream invading northern England. This pattern is confirmed by the evidence from stones carried by the ice, and by striae, the scratches made on the underlying rocks by the movement of the ice.

Later glaciations however, are liable to conceal or to remove the traces of earlier ice-sheets and there is, as yet, no undoubted evidence in the South of Scotland of the Pleistocene events which preceded the latest, or Würm-Weichsel glacial period. This glacial period, which is estimated to have lasted for some 70 000 years and is believed to have included a number of warmer spells, terminated some 10 300 years ago (Fig. 18).

The earliest Weichselian deposits in the region are tills or boulder clays, the ground-moraine of the ice-sheet, consisting of stones and boulders set with no apparent arrangement in an unstratified clayey or sandy matrix. These tills vary in colour and in composition from place to place but are often clearly related to the nature of the underlying solid rocks, indicating that a large part of their materials has not been carried very far prior to deposition. Thus, when the underlying rocks are of Ordovician or Silurian age the matrix of the till is usually brownish grey and the stones are mainly greywackes and hard shales; in areas where the solid rocks are of Old Red Sandstone or Permian age, the till matrix is red and sandy and encloses numerous blocks and boulders of red sandstone; whilst in Carboniferous areas the matrix tends to be grey and clayey, the dominant stones being brown and yellow sandstones, grey shales and Carboniferous igneous rocks. In addition to local constituents the tills also enclose a proportion of far-travelled stones which, if their source is known, can help to determine the direction of ice-movement. In some areas, particularly towards the dispersal centres, the till is replaced by morainic debris consisting largely of local stones and rubble with a sparse, rather coarse-grained matrix.

In general the till tends to be thickest in the valleys and to thin out against the higher ground, suggesting that the topography prior to the Weichselian glaciation must have been very similar to the present form of the ground. There is some doubt as to when this topography was initiated and developed but that it is of considerable antiquity is shown by the form of a channel buried beneath boulder clay in the valley of the River Nith near Sanquhar.

On the lower ground, the upper surface of the till was sometimes moulded by the movement of the ice into long, low hog-backed ridges, known as drumlins, whose longer axes are directed parallel to the direction of flow of the ice. Conspicuous examples occur on the Machars of Wigtownshire

Period	Sub-period	Thousand years B.P.	Stratigraphical zones	Climate	Relative sea-level	Deposits
FLANDRIAN or RECENT	Post-Glacial	1–3 (1 A.D., B.C.)	VIII Sub-Atlantic	Slight deterioration to present	Falling to present sea level	Recent peat, dunes of blown sand; river and lake alluvium
		3–5	VIIb Sub-Boreal			
		5–7	VIIa Atlantic	Mild to warm 'Climatic optimum'	About 25 feet higher than present sea level	Peat with remains of oak; sands and gravels of raised beach often with abundant shells. Appearance of man in the area.
		7–9	VI Boreal	Mild to cool	At or below present sea level	Peat below 'Atlantic' beach deposits in places below present high water mark; Upland peat with remains of birch, pine and hazel.
			V Pre-Boreal			
WEICHSELIAN	Late-Glacial	10	IV			
		10	III Younger Dryas	Cold	Falling gradually from about 100 feet above present sea level	Corrie morainic debris
		11	II Alleröd	Cool		Silts, brick-clays and lake-marls
		12	Ic Older Dryas	Cold		Corrie morainic debris; sands and gravels of high beaches
		13	Ib Bölling	Cool		
		14	Ia Oldest Dryas	Arctic		Fluvio-glacial sands and gravels, and boulder drift of Southern Uplands Readvance
		15–16		Sub-arctic		Fluvio-glacial sands and gravels
		16–18		Arctic		Boulder clays, shelly in some coastal districts
		68–70		Arctic		Boulder clay

FIG. 18. The chronology of Late-Glacial and Post-Glacial time in the South of Scotland

between Burrow Head and Kirkcowan, and the variation in direction of their long axes has been cited as evidence in favour of two different stages of ice-flow over this area.

There are throughout the South of Scotland numerous records of two or more superincumbent tills of very different appearance and composition but there is, so far, no clear evidence to indicate whether these are deposits of different phases of the last glaciation or whether the lower tills are relics of earlier glaciations.

The till, by its very nature, does not normally contain contemporaneou fossils. Along the coast of Ayrshire however, and on the shores of Loch Ryan and the western seaboard of the Rhins of Galloway, a boulder clay is found which contains remains of sea shells evidently picked up from the sea-floor by a stream of ice flowing southwards in the Firth of Clyde.

The erosive power of the ice that carried the till is demonstrated by rock-basins or hollows eroded into solid rock and overdeepened. Loch Doon, Loch Trool and St. Mary's Loch occupy basins of this kind as also do many of the small lochans on the higher ground. Hanging valleys—tributaries joining the main valley at discordant heights—also testify to the powers of glacial erosion. In a striking example situated 14 km north-east of Moffat, the Tail Burn issues from a hanging valley and cascades over the picturesque Grey Mare's Tail waterfall to the floor of the main valley some 100 m below.

As the climate ameliorated some 18–15 000 years ago (Fig. 18), the ice-margin, which at its maximum Weichselian extent lay across England from Yorkshire to Wales, retreated to a position in Scotland to the north of the Southern Uplands, although the uplands at this stage probably nourished a remnant of ice as a local ice-sheet. The climate again deteriorated about 15 000 years ago and the South of Scotland once more became a dispersal area for ice which streamed out to the south over the Carlisle Plain, where it is known as the Scottish Readvance, and probably contemporaneously flowed out to the north as the Southern Upland Readvance into the Midland Valley where its northern margin has been noted in the neighbourhood of Edinburgh.

The retreat of the margin of the southward extension of the ice has been studied in some detail and successive halt or slight readvance stages in the area west of Nithsdale have been named the Monreith, Kirkcowan, Newton Stewart, Minnoch and Corrie stages, the final stages being represented by morainic debris occurring high in the dispersal areas.

Much of the evidence of the retreat of the northward flowing ice lies outwith the South of Scotland region but melt-water channels have been studied in Peeblesshire.

PLATE XI

A. Burnswark, Dumfriesshire. North-westward view near Ecclefechan. In the middle distance is Burnswark, part of a prominent escarpment formed by the Birrenswark Lavas at the base of the Carboniferous.

B. The Eildon Hills near Melrose, Roxburghshire, from the east. The hills are the denuded remains of a composite laccolith of trachytic rocks intruded into the Upper Old Red Sandstone in Carboniferous times.
    (*Both photographs reproduced by courtesy of the Committee for Aerial Photography, University of Cambridge.*)

PLATE XI

A

B

Plate XII

A

B

Deposits left during decay of the eastwards extension of the ice in the Tweed Valley are conspicuous, and the later stages in the high ground near the source of the Tweed have been the subject of recent study.

During the retreat phases the increasing warmth released large quantities of melt-water and extensive spreads of water-laid, fluvioglacial materials were deposited. Outwash of this kind, consisting mainly of sand and gravel with well-marked stratification and current-bedding, occurs in the valleys of all the main rivers now draining from the former dispersal areas, the deposits in the Nith, Annan, and Tweed valleys being particularly extensive. Where the ice-margin halted, due to temporary equilibrium between wastage of ice by melting and the renewal of ice from the source, considerable accumulations were deposited (Plate XIIB), as on the isthmus connecting the peninsula of the Rhins of Galloway to the mainland. Deposits of this type were sometimes laid over and around detached masses of ice, the subsequent melting of which resulted in characteristic moundy topography of kame or 'kettle-moraine' type as at Eddleston, Peeblesshire. Deposits marking the former positions of the lateral margins of the ice and of former englacial or subglacial stream courses are also common, conspicuous examples occurring in Berwickshire between Greenlaw and Duns.

During the retreat of the ice-margin, the natural drainage was gradually re-established, but in the early stages it was in many cases obstructed or diverted so that numerous channels, probably excavated by marginal or sub-glacial streams, are found in many areas.

The latter part of the Weichselian, from about 15 000 years ago, has been named 'Late-Glacial' and is subdivided into three zones of which the first and third were arctic and the second, known as 'Alleröd', was much milder climatically (Fig. 18). The Southern Upland Readvance probably took place during Zone I times. Deposits of Zone II (Alleröd) age have been recorded from Whitrigbog, Berwickshire, and some of the higher corrie moraines were probably formed during Zone III times.

The Post-Glacial Period starts from the end of Zone III and a large part of the evidence for the events of the ensuing 10 000 years comes from the peat mosses which may attain a thickness of nearly 6 m in places but are now decaying, particularly in the upland areas. Peat mosses occupy large areas on the lower ground bordering the Solway Firth but are of no great extent in the eastern counties of the region. Elucidated first by macroscopic plant remains, later by pollen-analysis and more recently by radiocarbon dating, the climatic history of the Post-Glacial in this area may be generalized as cold to mild (Pre-Boreal to Boreal), mild to warm (Atlantic), followed by slight deterioration to the present.

PLATE XII
A. Dissected raised beach platform south of Dunbar, East Lothian. Platform of lower (Atlantic) raised beach cut in sandstone of the Lower Limestone Group, Carboniferous Limestone Series, and subsequently dissected by the sea. (Geol. Surv. Photo. No. D1144).
B. The Kaims, near Greenlaw in Berwickshire, are a well-defined kame-moraine of sands and gravels, a deposit formed by glacial streams at the ice-margin. They are also known in literature as the 'Bedshiel Kames'.
(Reproduced by courtesy of the Committee for Aerial Photography, University of Cambridge.)

Southern Scotland is believed to have been depressed by hundreds of metres by the weight of ice during the Weichselian, and after its close the land gradually recovered. At the same time world-wide sea-level rose at an irregular rate as the ice-caps melted. The combination of the upward isostatic rise of the land, which was not everywhere at the same rate, and the upward eustatic rise of the sea, caused the relative sea-level around the coasts of Scotland to vary considerably during Late- and Post-Glacial times. Peat beds formed subaerially and now occurring at levels below high water mark at Girvan and along the Solway coast provide evidence of former low sea-levels. Sea-levels higher than at present are recorded by beaches and wave-cut benches from 5 to 9 m above Ordnance Datum, with old sea-cliffs along their landward margins in places. Because of rapid fluctuations the sea-levels indicated in Fig. 18 should be considered only as very broad generalizations. Thus, a subaerial peat, now lying only 4 m above present sea-level near the mouth of the River Cree has been radiocarbon-dated as having formed 6159 years before present, that is, in the middle of the Atlantic or so-called 25-foot beach stage.

The eastern seaboard south of Cockburnspath is predominantly rocky and shows little evidence of these changes in sea-level although recent work suggests that terraces at Eyemouth may have been formed or modified by marine action in Late- or Post-Glacial times. North of Cockburnspath, how-ever, the Atlantic beach is almost continuous as far as Dunbar (Plate XIIA).

On the coasts of southern Ayrshire and Wigtownshire and along the Solway Firth the higher beaches are not clearly marked and in places may be confused with fluvioglacial features. The lower raised beach is however very conspicuous, consisting of a deposit of shingle and sand with numerous littoral marine shells and forming a broad platform the inner margin of which is sometimes marked by low cliff features into which caves have been excavated. Terraces probably related to these changes in sea-level occur along the courses of all the rivers and major streams.

Accumulations of blown sand are small except in Wigtownshire where they form an extensive area of dunes at the head of Luce Bay.

Fresh-water alluvium forms low terraces fringing most of the rivers and also occurs as flat expanses marking the sites of many former lakes.

Evidence for the presence of early man in the region, probably during Atlantic times, is provided by Mesolithic flint implements which have been found at Stoneykirk near Stranraer in Wigtownshire and at a site near the confluence of the rivers Ettrick and Tweed in Selkirkshire.

II. ECONOMIC GEOLOGY

The principal mineral products of the South of Scotland are those used in the construction industries, such as building stone, sand and gravel, and roadstone. Of more localized importance are limestone, monumental stone, coal, and clay and shale. The water resources of the region are widely, but by no means fully, exploited. Until very recently metalliferous mining was from time to time locally of great importance, but at present there is little activity in this field.

Granite

The granodiorite of Criffell and a small granite mass south of Creetown are quarried, the former near Dalbeattie, for monumental stone, building-stone, and aggregate. Synthetic stone and concrete products are also made from the crushed rock. Plans were announced in 1965 for the quarrying of road-stone in the Cockburn Law Granite in Berwickshire. The building stone is used mainly in such projects as bridges, docks, and public buildings. Other important products of the quarries are road chippings and setts.

Basalt, Dolerite, and Porphyrite

Basalt lavas of Lower Carboniferous age, and the rocks of a variety of minor intrusions, are widely quarried and crushed for use as roadstone and concrete-aggregate. The basalts are mainly in Roxburghshire and Berwick-shire, porphyrite is quarried near Kirkcudbright, and the other minor intrusions are worked at localities scattered throughout the region. In Dumfries-shire the basic rock of the Tertiary Eskdalemuir dyke was quarried recently near the Black Esk Reservoir, to be used in its construction both as building stone and as aggregate. It is at present quarried near Moffat.

Sandstone and Greywacke

The towns of the South of Scotland were generally built of local stone, of which the most commonly used were Lower Palaeozoic greywacke, Carbonif-erous sandstone, and 'Permian' sandstone. Sandstone near the base of the Carboniferous has been much quarried at Langholm and at Swinton in Berwickshire, and north-east of Kelso the dolomitic Carham Stone has been much used for building as well as being burnt for lime. The Carboniferous or Permian red sandstones of Dumfriesshire have been extensively used for building, both locally and in the Midland Valley, the principal quarries being near Dumfries, where work continues at Locharbriggs, and near Lochmaben. The stone is also used for monumental work, and the waste sand for making sand-lime bricks. In the Annan district red sandstone of Triassic age is the principal building stone.

Greywacke is much used today as a source of roadstone, and quarries, disused and operative, are scattered widely over the Lower Palaeozoic outcrop. Contact-altered greywacke is, or has been, quarried near Kirkgunzeon in Kirkcudbrightshire, at Clatteringshaws, west of New Galloway, in the porphyrite quarry (see above) near Kirkcudbright, and near Moffat.

Limestone and Dolomite

Near Girvan Ordovician limestone is quarried at Craighead and at Tormit-chell, and other limestones of this age, associated with volcanic rocks, were formerly worked in the Tweed Valley near Peebles. Limestones in the Lower Carboniferous are worked near Dunbar and in Dumfriesshire, near Ecclefechan and near Canonbie. There are old workings in the Lower Carboniferous in Liddesdale above Newcastleton, near Kelso (Carham Stone), and near Annan. The rock formerly mined at Barjarg, near Thornhill, is a dolomite of considerable purity. The principal uses to which the limestone is put are in cement manufacture in the important works near Dunbar and as fertilizer and roadstone.

Clay and Shale

The only active workings of clay in the region are near Newton Stewart. where raised beach clays are used to make agricultural drain tiles, and near Langholm, where the material is derived from a small glacial pond deposit. Old tile works are known to occur at several localities, and suitable deposits of lacustrine clay or boulder clay are probably available at some of these and elsewhere if required.

Lower Palaeozoic shales were formerly quarried at Cairnryan, near Elvanfoot, and near Stobo and Innerleithen, for use as roofing slates. Near Stoneykirk in Wigtownshire, where toughened by an igneous intrusion they are used as roadstone.

Sand and Gravel

Pits in superficial sands and gravels are scattered throughout the populated parts of the region, with a certain concentration around Stranraer, in lower Nithsdale and Annandale, and in northern Peeblesshire. The sand is used mainly in the building trade, for mortar, plaster, sand-lime bricks, and other similar purposes. Most of the gravel is used to make concrete and in road construction. Other uses of sand are in water filtration, horticulture, iron- and steel-moulding, and glass-making.

Peat

Hand-cutting of peat for local use as fuel has been widely practised in southern Scotland since ancient times. Mechanical techniques were introduced at Lochar Moss, near Dumfries, in 1910, for the manufacture of ammonium sulphate and peat briquettes, and exploitation continued until the Second World War. The Scottish Peat Committee, appointed by the Government, reported in 1962 that at that time peat was a more costly source of energy than other available fuels, and that in the immediate future the main value of the peat-mosses would appear to lie in the cultivation of farm crops and trees and in the use of processed peat in horticulture.

Coal

At present the only working collieries in the region are at Kirkconnel, in the Sanquhar basin. Considerable reserves of unworked coal have been proved to the south of the old coalfield at Canonbie. Coal was also formerly worked in Liddesdale for local use as fuel.

Iron and Manganese

Veins of hematite were worked in the last century at the edge of the Loch Doon Granite south-east of Loch Doon, and in the Criffell Granite east of Kirkcudbright. Hematite also occurs at Wanlockhead and Leadhills, in association with the lead-zinc veins. Near Lamancha in Peeblesshire a concentration of hematite, in red shales and cherts overlying Arenig lavas, was mined in the 1880's. A band 0·45 m thick, some 1·5 m above the hematite, is rich in pyrolusite. The beds are closely folded and other outcrops of the ores may occur nearby.

Copper

During the 19th century, and in the years just before and after, there were several small copper mines and trials in the South of Scotland. The usual ores are chalcopyrite and malachite, often in veins of crushed rock with calcite and quartz as the main gangue minerals. There were mines near Girvan, Whithorn, and Kirkcowan, on the coast south-east of Castle Douglas, and in the Priestlaw Granite in East Lothian. The ores were also won in the lead-zinc areas of Leadhills and between Newton Stewart and Gatehouse of Fleet. There are old trial mines near Moffat, and near Lauder and Abbey St. Bathans in Berwickshire.

Lead and Zinc

Galena has been mined at Leadhills and Wanlockhead for at least 700 years, and the associated zinc-blende at Wanlockhead from 1880. The ores occur in shoots up to 3·7 m wide in veins of brecciated Ordovician greywacke which dip at about 75 degrees towards the north-north-east, but are poorly developed, if at all, where the brecciated rock is shale or chert. Gangue minerals are mainly quartz and calcite. The mines were closed in 1929 and were reopened for about a year in 1934 and in 1957, but considerable reserves of unmined galena remain. Extraction of ore from the old tips was practised in the middle 1960's.

Both galena and zinc-blende were mined, in the last century, on the south-western flank of the Cairnsmore of Fleet Granite from Gatehouse of Fleet to north-west of Newton Stewart. Most of the veins, which occur in greywackes of Llandovery age, run in a west-north-westerly direction. Other ore-minerals present include chalcopyrite, baryte, and mispickel. There was some revival of mining at the time of the Great War but no sustained activity has taken place since then. Between 1840 and 1873 galena was worked opencast and mined at Woodhead, between the granites of Loch Doon and Cairnsmore of Carsphairn. The veins, cutting Ordovician greywackes, dip to the north-north-east at about 60 degrees. Zinc-blende and chalcopyrite are also present.

Lead and zinc have also been worked near New Luce, near Barr in Ayrshire, and near Traquair.

Silver and Gold

Prior to the 17th century silver was probably the main product of the galena mining at Leadhills. More recently it was obtained as a by-product of the treatment of galena at Leadhills, Wanlockhead, and Blackcraig, near Newton Stewart.

Alluvial gold was won in the 16th century from Glengaber Burn, near St. Mary's Loch, and at Leadhills. A small vein of gold-bearing quartz was reported from the latter area.

Antimony

Some of the galena veins of Leadhills contain jamesonite, a sulphantimonide of lead, but the main source of antimony in the region has been the Glendinning Mine, north of the road from Langholm to Eskdalemuir, where stibnite occurs in a vein 0·45m wide in a breccia of Wenlock shale which dips at upwards of 80 degrees to the south-east. Ore-minerals include galena, jamesonite, and zinc-blende. The mine was last operative in 1920. Stibnite has also been mined within a small granite mass at The Knipe, south-east of New Cumnock.

Nickel and Arsenic

Niccolite (nickel arsenide) and mispickel (iron sulpharsenide) occur close together at Talnotry, near Newton Stewart. Old trial workings exist in both ore-bodies, the former apparently a restricted lens, the latter a vein at the margin of the Cairnsmore of Fleet Granite.

Baryte

Veins of baryte occur in the Wenlock and Lower Carboniferous rocks to the south of Auchencairn in Kirkcudbrightshire, and until 1961 the mineral was worked intermittently and on a small scale at several points near the coast. Baryte has been worked, in association with copper ores, in the Priestlaw Granite in East Lothian.

Water

Most water authorities within the region, and several in the Midland Valley, draw upon the ample supplies of surface water of high quality which exist in the Southern Uplands. The Talla and Fruid reservoirs, in the upper part of the Tweed Valley, are important constituents of Edinburgh's supply-system. The 'Permian' sandstones of Dumfries, Lochmaben, Thornhill and Stranraer form the principal underground aquifers, but are heavily exploited only in the Dumfries area where 150 000 litres an hour are pumped from one of the wells. Smaller supplies are obtained from sandstones in the Old Red Sandstone and Carboniferous, and from superficial sands and gravels, and are irregularly present in open joints near the surface in greywacke and granite areas.

Sulphurous and chalybeate springs occur at a number of localities, the most famous being in the Moffat area, where Moffat Well itself has been dismantled but Hartfell Spa is still in use, and St. Ronan's Well at Innerleithen, which is also still used.

12. GEOLOGICAL SURVEY MAPS OF THE SOUTH OF SCOTLAND

(*a*) **On the scale of 4 miles to 1 inch (1/253 440)** Colour-printed.

Sheet 14   Firth of Clyde, North Ayrshire, Lanarkshire.
Sheet 15   Firth of Forth, Peeblesshire, Berwickshire.
Sheet 16   South Ayrshire, Galloway.
Sheet 17   Dumfriesshire, Selkirkshire, Roxburghshire.

(*b*) **On the scale of 1 inch to 1 mile (1/63 360)**

(i) *Hand-coloured Sheets (out of print)*
    6 (Annan); 10 (Dumfries); 18 (Morebattle); 25 (Kelso); 34 (Eyemouth).
(ii) *Colour-printed Sheets*
    These sheets show both 'solid' and 'drift' deposits. Those marked * are printed in separate 'solid' and 'drift' editions.
1 (Kirkmaiden); 2 (Whithorn); 3 (Stranraer); 4 (Wigtown); 5 (Kirkcudbright); 7 (Girvan); 8 (Carrick); 9 (Maxwelltown); 11* (Langholm); 14* (Ayr); 15* (Sanquhar); 16 (Moffat); 17 (Jedburgh); 23* (Hamilton); 24* (Peebles); 33 (Haddington).
(iii) *Colour-printed Provisional Sheet*
    26 (Berwick upon Tweed [Duns]).
Memoirs have been published describing the geology of the areas covered by sheets 1, 2, 3, 4, 5, 7, 9, 11, 14, 15, 23, 24, 33 and 34.

(c) **On the scale of 6 inches to 1 mile (1/10 560)**

The area is also covered by geological maps on the six-inch scale. In general these are not published but may be consulted at the Institute of Geological Sciences, 19 Grange Terrace, Edinburgh EH9 2LF. Uncoloured copies may be supplied on special order.

13. SELECTED BIBLIOGRAPHY

Introduction (Chapter 1)

CRAIG, G. Y. (Ed.) 1965. *The Geology of Scotland*. Edinburgh and London.

DZULYNSKI, S. and WALTON, E. K. 1965. *Sedimentary Features of Flysch and Greywackes*. Amsterdam.

GEORGE, T. N. 1956. Drainage in the Southern Uplands: Clyde, Nith, Annan. *Trans. geol. Soc. Glasg.*, **22**, 1.

—— 1960. The Stratigraphical Evolution of the Midland Valley. *Trans. geol. Soc. Glasg.*, **24**, 32.

LINTON, D. L. 1934. On the former connection between the Clyde and the Tweed. *Scott. geogr. Mag.*, **50**, 82.

—— 1951. Problems of Scottish scenery. *Scott. geogr. Mag.*, **67**, 65.

LUMSDEN, G. I. and DAVIES, A. 1965. The buried channel of the River Nith and its marked change in level across the Southern Upland Fault. *Scott. J. Geol.*, **1**, 134.

PEACH, B. N. and HORNE, J. 1899. The Silurian Rocks of Britain. **1**, Scotland. *Mem. geol. Surv.*

—— ——1930. *Chapters on the Geology of Scotland*. London.

SISSONS, J. B. 1967. *The Evolution of Scotland's Scenery*. Edinburgh and London.

Lower Palaeozoic (Chapters 2, 3 and 4)

BAILEY, E. B. and McCALLIEN, W. J. 1952. Ballantrae Igneous Problems: Historical Review. *Trans. Edinb. geol. Soc.*, **15**, 14.

—— —— 1957. The Ballantrae Serpentine, Ayrshire. *Trans. Edinb. geol. Soc.*, **17**, 33.

BALSILLIE, D. 1932. The Ballantrae Igneous Complex, South Ayrshire. *Geol. Mag.*, **69**, 107.

—— 1937. Further Observations on the Ballantrae Igneous Complex. *Geol. Mag.*, **74**, 20.

BLOXAM, T. W. 1960. Pillow-Structure in Spilitic Lavas at Downan Point, Ballantrae. *Trans. geol. Soc. Glasg.*, **24**, 19.

BULMAN, O. M. B. 1944–47. A monograph of the Caradoc (Balclatchie) trilobites from limestones in Laggan Burn, Ayrshire. *Palaeontogr. Soc. (Monogr.)*.

COCKS, L. R. M., HOLLAND, C. H., RICKARDS, R. B., and STRACHAN, I. 1971. A correlation of Silurian rocks in the British Isles. *Jl geol. Soc.*, **127**, 103.

CRAIG, G. Y. (Ed.) 1965. *The Geology of Scotland*. Edinburgh and London.

—— and WALTON, E. K. 1959. Sequence and structure in the Silurian rocks of Kirkcudbrightshire. *Geol. Mag.*, **96**, 209.

—— —— 1962. Sedimentary structures and palaeocurrent directions from the Silurian rocks of Kirkcudbrightshire. *Trans. Edinb. geol. Soc.*, **19**, 100.

DEARMAN, W. R., SHIELLS, K. A. G. and LARWOOD, G. P. 1962. Refolded Folds in the Silurian rocks of Eyemouth, Berwickshire. *Proc. Yorks. geol. Soc.*, **33**, 273.

ECKFORD, R. J. A., RITCHIE, M. and BALSILLIE, D. 1931. The Lavas of Tweeddale and their position in the Caradocian Sequence. *Mem. geol. Surv. Summ. Prog.* for 1930, Part III, 46.

EYLES, V. A., SIMPSON, J. B. and MacGREGOR, A. G. 1949. The Geology of Central Ayrshire. *Mem. geol. Surv.*

FRESHNEY, E. C. 1960. An Extension of the Silurian Succession in the Craighead Inlier, Girvan. *Trans. geol. Soc. Glasg.*, **24**, 27.

HALL, J. 1815. On the vertical position and convolutions of certain strata and their relation with granite. *Trans. R. Soc. Edinb.*, **7**, 79.

HUBERT, J. F. 1966. Sedimentary History of Upper Ordovician Geosynclinal Rocks, Girvan, Scotland. *J. sedim. Petrol.*, **36**, 677.

JOHNSON, M. R. W. and STEWART, F. H. (Eds) 1963. *The British Caledonides.* Edinburgh and London.

JONES, O. T. 1938. On the evolution of a geosyncline. *Q. Jl geol. Soc. Lond.*, **94**, lx.

—— and PUGH, W. J. 1915. The Geology of the District around Machynlleth and the Llyfnant Valley. *Q. Jl. geol. Soc. Lond.*, **71**, 343.

KELLING, G. 1961. The Stratigraphy and Structure of the Ordovician Rocks of the Rhinns of Galloway. *Q. Jl geol. Soc. Lond.*, **117**, 37.

—— and WELSH, W. 1970. The Loch Ryan Fault. *Scott. J. Geol.*, **6**, 266.

KUENEN, Ph. H. 1956. The difference between sliding and turbidity flow. *Deep Sea Res.*, **3**, 134.

—— 1957. Sole markings of graded greywacke beds. *J. Geol.*, **65**, 231.

LAMONT, A. 1935. The Drummuck Group, Girvan: A Stratigraphical Revision with Descriptions of New Fossils from the Lower Part of the Group. *Trans. geol. Soc. Glasg.*, **19**, 288.

—— and LINDSTROM, M. 1957. Arenigian and Llandeilian Cherts identified in the Southern Uplands of Scotland by means of Conodonts, etc. *Trans. Edinb. geol. Soc.*, **17**, 60.

LUMSDEN, G. I., TULLOCH, W., HOWELLS, M. F. and DAVIES, A. 1967. The Geology of the Neighbourhood of Langholm. *Mem. geol. Surv.*

REED, F. R. C. 1903–35. The Lower Palaeozoic Trilobites of the Girvan District, Ayrshire. *Palaeontogr. Soc. (Monogr.)*

—— 1917. The Ordovician and Silurian Brachiopods of the Girvan District. *Trans. R. Soc. Edinb.*, **51**, 795.

RUST, B. R. 1965. The stratigraphy and structure of the Whithorn area of Wigtownshire, Scotland. *Scott. J. Geol.*, **1**, 101.

SHIELLS, K. A. G. and DEARMAN, W. R. 1963. Tectonics of the Coldingham Bay area of Berwickshire, in the Southern Uplands of Scotland. *Proc. Yorks. geol. Soc.*, **34**, 209.

—— 1966. On the possible occurrence of Dalradian rocks in the Southern Uplands of Scotland. *Scott. J. Geol.*, **2**, 231.

SIMPSON, A. 1968. The Caledonian history of the north-eastern Irish Sea region and its relation to surrounding areas. *Scott. J. Geol.*, **4**, 135.

TEALL, J. J. H. 1894. On greenstones associated with radiolarian cherts. *Trans. R. geol. Soc. Corn.*, **11**, 3.

TOGHILL, P. 1968. The graptolite assemblages and zones of the Birkhill Shales (Lower Silurian) at Dobb's Linn. *Palaeontology*, **11**, 654.

—— 1970. Highest Ordovician (Hartfell Shales) graptolite faunas from the Moffat area, South Scotland. *Bull. Br. Mus. nat. Hist.* (Geol.), **19**, No. 1.

—— 1970. The south-east limit of the Moffat Shales in the upper Ettrick Valley region, Selkirkshire. *Scott. J. Geol.*, **6**, 233.

—— and STRACHAN, I. 1970. The graptolite fauna of Grieston Quarry, near Innerleithen, Peeblesshire. *Palaeontology*, **13**, 511.

TRIPP, R. P. 1954. Caradocian trilobites from mudstones at Craighead Quarry, near Girvan, Ayrshire. *Trans. R. Soc. Edinb.*, **62**, 655.

—— 1962. Trilobites from the *confinis* Flags (Ordovician) of the Girvan district, Ayrshire. *Trans. R. Soc. Edinb.*, **65**, 1.

—— 1965. Trilobites from the Albany division (Ordovician) of the Girvan district, Ayrshire. *Palaeontology*, **8**, 577.

H

WALTON, E. K. 1957. Two Ordovician conglomerates in south Ayrshire. *Trans. geol. Soc. Glasg.*, **22**, 133.

—— 1961. Some aspects of the succession and structure in the Lower Palaeozoic rocks of the Southern Uplands of Scotland. *Geol. Rdsch.*, **50**, 63.

—— 1968. Some rare sedimentary structures in the Silurian rocks of Kircudbright-shire. *Scott. J. Geol.*, **4**, 355.

WARREN, P. T. 1964. The stratigraphy and structure of the Silurian (Wenlock) rocks south-east of Hawick, Roxburghshire, Scotland. *Q. Jl geol. Soc. Lond.*, **120**, 193.

WEIR, J. A. 1968. Structural history of the Silurian rocks of the coast west of Gate-house, Kirkcudbrightshire. *Scott. J. Geol.*, **4**, 31.

WILLIAMS, A. 1962. The Barr and Lower Ardmillan Series (Caradoc) of the Girvan district, south-west Ayrshire. *Mem. geol. Soc. Lond.*, **3**.

Old Red Sandstone (Chapter 5)

BLYTH, F. G. H. 1949. The Sheared Porphyrite Dykes of South Galloway. *Q. Jl geol. Soc. Lond.*, **105**, 393.

—— 1955. The Kirkmabreck Granodiorite, near Creetown, South Galloway. *Geol. Mag.*, **92**, 321.

BOTT, M. H. P. and MASSON-SMITH, D. 1960. A gravity survey of the Criffell Granodiorite and the New Red Sandstone Deposits near Dumfries. *Proc. Yorks. geol. Soc.*, **32**, 317.

BURGESS, I. C. 1960. Fossil soils of the Upper Old Red Sandstone of south Ayrshire. *Trans. geol. Soc. Glasg.*, **24**, 138.

CRAIG, G. Y. (Ed.). 1965. *The Geology of Scotland*. Edinburgh and London.

DEER, W. A. 1935. The Cairnsmore of Carsphairn Igneous Complex. *Q. Jl geol. Soc. Lond.*, **91**, 47.

—— 1937. The Marginal Rocks of the Cairnsmore of Carsphairn Complex. *Geol. Mag.*, **74**, 361.

GARDINER, C. I. and REYNOLDS, S. H. 1932. The Loch Doon 'Granite' Area, Galloway. *Q. Jl geol. Soc. Lond.*, **88**, 1.

—— — 1937. The Cairnsmore of Fleet Granite and its Metamorphic Aureole. *Geol. Mag.*, **74**, 289.

GEIKIE, A. 1897. *The Ancient Volcanoes of Great Britain*, **I**. London.

GEIKIE, J. 1887. Geology and Petrology of St. Abb's Head. *Proc. R. Soc. Edinb.*, **14**, 177.

HIGAZY, R. A. 1954. The Trace Elements of the Plutonic Complex of Loch Doon (Southern Scotland) and their Petrogenetic Significance. *J. Geol.*, **62**, 172.

HOLGATE, N. 1943. The Portencorkrie Complex of Wigtownshire. *Geol. Mag.*, **80**, 171.

IRVING, J. 1930. Four "Felstone" Intrusions in Central Berwickshire. *Geol. Mag.*, **67**, 529.

LAMBERT, R. ST. J. and MILLS, A. A. 1961. Some critical points for the Palaeozoic time scale from the British Isles. *Ann. N.Y. Acad. Sci.*, **91**, 378.

LUMSDEN, G. I., TULLOCH, W., HOWELLS, M. F. and DAVIES, A. 1967. The Geology of the Neighbourhood of Langholm. *Mem. geol. Surv.*

MACGREGOR, A. G. 1939. In *Mem. geol. Surv. Summ. Prog.* for 1938, 54.

—— and ECKFORD, R. J. A. 1948. The Upper Old Red and Lower Carboniferous Sediments of Teviotdale and Tweedside, and the Stones of the Abbeys of the Scottish Borderland. *Trans. Edinb. geol. Soc.*, **14**, 230.

MACGREGOR, M. 1937. The Western Part of the Criffell-Dalbeattie Igneous Complex. *Q. Jl geol. Soc. Lond.*, **93**, 457.

MACKENZIE, R. C. 1957. The illite in some Old Red Sandstone soils and sediments. *Mineralog. Mag.*, **31**, 681.

MANSON, W. and PHEMISTER, J. 1934. On a Boring for Water at Stonefold Farm, Berwickshire. *Mem. geol. Surv. Summ. Prog.* for 1933, pt. II, 68.

MIDGLEY, H. G. 1946. The Geology and Petrology of the Cockburn Law Intrusion, Berwickshire. *Geol. Mag.*, **83**, 49.

MOULD, D. D. C. P. 1947. The Broadlaw "Granite". *Geol. Mag.*, **84**, 178.

PARSLOW, G. R. 1968. The physical and structural features of the Cairnsmore of Fleet granite and its aureole. *Scott. J. Geol.*, **4**, 91.

PHILLIPS, W. J. 1956a. The Criffell–Dalbeattie Granodiorite Complex. *Q. Jl geol. Soc. Lond.*, **112**, 221.

—— 1956b. The Minor Intrusive Suite Associated with the Criffell–Dalbeattie Granodiorite Complex. *Proc. Geol. Assoc.*, **67**, 103.

READ, H. H. 1926. The Mica–Lamprophyres of Wigtownshire. *Geol. Mag.*, **63**, 422.

WALKER, F. 1925. Four Granitic Intrusions in South-Eastern Scotland. *Trans. Edinb. geol. Soc.*, **11**, 357.

—— 1928. The Plutonic Intrusions of the Southern Uplands East of the Nith Valley. *Geol. Mag.*, **65**, 153.

WATERSTON, C. D. 1962. A New Upper Old Red Sandstone Fish Locality in Scotland. *Nature, Lond.*, **196**, 263.

WILLS, L. J. 1951. *A Palaeogeographical Atlas of the British Isles and Adjacent Parts of Europe*. London and Glasgow.

Carboniferous (Chapter 6)

CRAIG, G. Y. 1956. The Lower Carboniferous Outlier of Kirkbean, Kirkcudbrightshire. *Trans. geol. Soc. Glasg.*, **22**, 113.

—— and NAIRN, A. E. M. 1956. The Lower Carboniferous Outliers of the Colvend and Rerrick Shores, Kirkcudbrightshire. *Geol. Mag.*, **93**, 249.

CALVER, M. A. 1968. Distribution of Westphalian Marine Faunas in northern England and Adjoining Areas. *Proc. Yorks. geol. Soc.*, **37**, 1.

CUMMINGS, R. H. 1961. The Foraminiferal Zones of the Carboniferous Sequence of the Archerbeck Borehole, Canonbie, Dumfriesshire. *Bull. geol. Surv. Gt. Br.*, No. 18, 107.

DAVIES, A. 1970. The Carboniferous Rocks of the Sanquhar Outlier. *Bull. geol. Surv. Gt Br.*, No. 31, 37.

GEORGE, T. N. 1958. Lower Carboniferous Palaeogeography of the British Isles. *Proc. Yorks. geol. Soc.*, **31**, 227.

—— 1960. The Stratigraphical Evolution of the Midland Valley. *Trans. geol. Soc. Glasg.*, **24**, 32.

LUMSDEN, G. I. and WILSON, R. B. 1961. The Stratigraphy of the Archerbeck Borehole, Canonbie, Dumfriesshire. *Bull. geol. Surv. Gt Br.*, No. 18, 1.

LUMSDEN, G. I., TULLOCH, W., HOWELLS, M. F. and DAVIES, A. 1967. Geology of the Neighbourhood of Langholm. *Mem. geol. Surv.*

MACGREGOR, A. G. 1960. Divisions of the Carboniferous on Geological Survey Scottish Maps. *Bull. geol. Surv. Gt Br.*, No. 16, 127.

NAIRN, A. E. M. 1956. The Lower Carboniferous Rocks between the Rivers Esk and Annan, Dumfriesshire. *Trans. geol. Soc. Glasg.*, **22**, 80.

—— 1958. Petrology of the Whita Sandstone, Southern Scotland. *J. sedim. Petrol.*, **28**, 57.

WILSON, R. B. 1961. Palaeontology of the Archerbeck Borehole, Canonbie, Dumfriesshire. *Bull. geol. Surv. Gt Br.*, No. 18, 90.

Carboniferous Volcanic Rocks (Chapter 7)

ECKFORD, R. J. A. and RITCHIE, M. 1939. The Igneous Rocks of the Kelso District, *Trans. Edinb. geol. Soc.*, **13**, 464.

J

ELLIOTT, R. B. 1952. Trachy-ophitic texture in Carboniferous basalts. *Mineralog. Mag.*, **29**, 925.

—— 1960. The Carboniferous Volcanic Rocks of the Langholm District. *Proc. Geol. Assoc.*, **71**, 1.

GEIKIE, A. 1897. *The Ancient Volcanoes of Great Britain*, I. London.

IRVING, J. 1930. Four 'Felstone' Intrusions in Central Berwickshire. *Geol. Mag.*, **67**, 529.

LUMSDEN, G. I., TULLOCH, W., HOWELLS, M. F. and DAVIES, A. 1967. Geology of the Neighbourhood of Langholm. *Mem. geol. Surv.*

MACGREGOR, A. G. 1948. Problems of Carboniferous–Permian Volcanicity in Scotland. *Q. Jl geol. Soc. Lond.*, **104**, 133.

McROBERT, RACHEL W. 1914. Acid and Intermediate Intrusions and Associated Ash-Necks in the Neighbourhood of Melrose (Roxburghshire). *Q. Jl geol. Soc. Lond.*, **70**, 303.

—— 1920. Igneous Rocks of Teviot and Liddesdale. *Trans. Edinb. geol. Soc.*, **11**, 86.

MANSON, W. and ECKFORD, R. J. A. 1927. Note on a Xenolith in Riebeckite–Trachyte, Mid Eildon, Roxburghshire. *Trans. Edinb. geol. Soc.*, **12**, 143.

PALLISTER, J. W. 1952. The Birrenswark Lavas, Dumfriesshire. *Trans. Edinb. geol. Soc.*, **14**, 336.

TOMKEIEFF, S. I. 1945. Petrology of the Carboniferous Igneous Rocks of the Tweed Basin. *Trans. Edinb. geol. Soc.*, **14**, 53.

— 1952. Nepheline–basanite of Southdean, Roxburghshire. *Trans. Edinb. geol. Soc.*, **14**, 349.

— 1953. The Carboniferous Igneous Rocks of the Kelso District. *Proc. Univ. Durham phil. Soc.*, **11**, 95.

New Red Sandstone (Chapter 8)

BARRETT, B. H. 1942. The Triassic Rocks of the Annan Basin, Dumfriesshire. *Trans. geol. Soc. Glasg.*, **20**, 161.

BOTT, M. H. P. and MASSON-SMITH, D. 1960. A gravity survey of the Criffell Granodiorite and the New Red Sandstone deposits near Dumfries. *Proc. Yorks. geol. Soc.*, **32**, 317.

HICKLING, G. 1909. British Permian footprints. *Mem. Proc. Manch. lit. phil. Soc.*, **53**, 1.

HOLLINGWORTH, S. E. 1942. The Correlation of Gypsum–Anhydrite Deposits and the Associated Strata in the North of England. *Proc. Geol. Assoc.*, **51**, 141.

HORNE, J. and GREGORY, J. W. 1916. The Annan Red Sandstone Series of Dumfriesshire. *Trans. geol. Soc. Glasg.*, **15**, 374.

LUMSDEN, G. I., TULLOCH, W., HOWELLS, M. F. and DAVIES, A. 1967. Geology of the Neighbourhood of Langholm. *Mem. geol. Surv.*

MANSFIELD, J. and KENNETT, P. 1963. A gravity survey of the Stranraer sedimentary basin. *Proc. Yorks. geol. Soc.*, **34**, 139.

MYKURA, W. 1965. The age of the lower part of the New Red Sandstone of South-West Scotland. *Scott. J. Geol.*, **1**, 9.

SCOTT, A. 1915. The Crawfordjohn Essexite and Associated Rocks. *Geol. Mag.*, **52**, 513.

SHERLOCK, R. L. 1947. *The Permo-Triassic Formations*. London.

SIMPSON, J. B. and RICHEY, J. E. 1936. The Geology of the Sanquhar Coalfield and the adjacent basin of Thornhill. *Mem. geol. Surv.*

SMITH, J. 1900. The Permian Outlier of the Snar Valley, Lanarkshire. *Trans. geol. Soc. Glasg.*, **11**, 250.

WAGNER, R. H. 1966. On the presence of probable Upper Stephanian beds in Ayrshire, Scotland. *Scott. J. Geol.*, **2**, 122.

WALKER, F. 1925. A Monchiquite Dyke in Lauderdale. *Trans. Edinb. geol. Soc.*, **11**, 390.

Tertiary (Chapter 9)

ELLIOTT, R. B. 1956. The Eskdalemuir tholeiite and its contribution to an understanding of tholeiite genesis. *Mineralog. Mag.*, **31**, 245.

EYLES, V. A., SIMPSON, J. B. and MACGREGOR, A. G. 1949. Geology of Central Ayrshire. *Mem. geol. Surv.*

GEIKIE, A. 1880. The "Pitchstone" (Vitreous Basalt) of Eskdale: A Retrospect and Comparison of Geological Methods. *Proc. R. phys. Soc. Edinb.*, **5**, 219.

—— 1897. *Ancient Volcanoes of Great Britain*, **II**. London.

HOLMES, A. and HARWOOD, H. F. 1929. The Tholeiitic Dykes of the North of England. *Mineralog. Mag.*, **22**, 1.

JUDD, J. W. 1874. The Secondary Rocks of Scotland. Second Paper. On the Ancient Volcanoes of the Highlands and the Relations of their Products to the Mesozoic Strata. *Q. Jl geol. Soc. Lond.*, **30**, 220.

RICHEY, J. E. 1939. The Dykes of Scotland. *Trans. Edinb. geol. Soc.*, **13**, 393.

—— 1961. Scotland: The Tertiary Volcanic Districts (Third Edition). *Br. reg. Geol.*

Pleistocene and Post-Glacial (Chapter 10)

BAILEY, E. B. and ECKFORD, R. J. A. 1956. The Eddleston gravel moraine. *Trans. Edinb. geol. Soc.*, **16**, 254.

CHARLESWORTH, J. K. 1926. Glacial geology of the Southern Uplands of Scotland, west of Annandale and Upper Clydesdale. *Trans. R. Soc. Edinb.*, **55**, 1.

DONNER, J. J. 1959. The Late- and Post-glacial raised beaches in Scotland. *Annls Acad. scient. fenn.*, Ser. A, III, **53**.

—— 1963. The Late- and Post-glacial raised beaches in Scotland. *Annls Acad. scient. fenn.*, Ser. A, III, **68**.

ERDTMAN, G. 1928. Studies in the Postarctic history of the forests of north-western Europe. 1. Investigations in the British Isles. *Geol. För. Stockh. Förh.*, **50**, 123.

GEORGE, T. N. 1956. Drainage in the Southern Uplands: Clyde, Nith, Annan. *Trans. geol. Soc. Glasg.*, **22**, 1.

JARDINE, W. G. 1964. Post-glacial sea-levels in south-west Scotland. *Scott. geogr. Mag.*, **80**, 5.

LEWIS, F. J. 1906. The plant remains in the Scottish peat mosses. Pt. 1. The Scottish Southern Uplands. *Trans. R. Soc. Edinb.*, **41**, 699.

LUMSDEN, G. I. and DAVIES, A. 1965. The buried channel of the River Nith and its marked change in level across the Southern Upland Fault. *Scott. J. Geol.*, **1**, 134.

LUMSDEN, G. I., TULLOCH, W., HOWELLS, M. F. and DAVIES, A. 1967. Geology of the Neighbourhood of Langholm. *Mem. geol. Surv.*

MITCHELL, G. F. 1948. Late-glacial deposits in Berwickshire. *New Phytol.*, **47**, 262.

PRICE, R. J. 1963. The glaciation of a part of Peeblesshire. *Trans. Edinb. geol. Soc.*, **19**, 325.

—— 1963. A glacial meltwater drainage system in Peeblesshire. *Scott. geogr. Mag.*, **79**, 133.

SISSONS, J. B. 1958. Supposed ice-dammed lakes in Britain with particular reference to the Eddleston valley. *Geogr. Annlr. Stockh.*, **40**, 159.

—— 1963. Scottish raised shoreline heights with particular reference to the Forth valley. *Geogr. Annlr. Stockh.*, **45**, 180.

—— 1967. *The Evolution of Scotland's Scenery*. Edinburgh and London.

Economic Geology (Chapter 11)

GOODLET, G. A. 1970. Sands and Gravels of the Southern Counties of Scotland. *Rep. Inst. geol. Sci.* No. 70/4.

MACKAY, R. A. 1959. The Leadhills–Wanlockhead Mining District *in* The Future of Non-Ferrous Mining in Great Britain and Ireland—a Symposium. *Instn. Min. Metall., Lond.*, 49.

TEMPLE, A. K. 1956. The Leadhills–Wanlockhead Lead and Zinc Deposits. *Trans. R. Soc. Edinb.*, **63**, 85.

Special Reports on the Mineral Resources of Great Britain, *Mem. geol. Surv.*:

1915	vol. ii	Barytes and Witherite
1920	vol. xi	Iron Ores: The Ores of Scotland
1920	vol. xv	Arsenic and Antimony Ores
1921	vol. xvii	The Lead, Zinc, Copper and Nickel Ores of Scotland
1939	vol. xxxii	Granites of Scotland
1949	vol. xxxv	Limestones of Scotland

Sources of Road Aggregate in Great Britain (3rd ed.) 1960. HMSO London.

Geol. Surv. Wartime Pamphlets.

FRASER, G. K. 1943. No. 36. Peat Deposits of Scotland. Pt. I.

RICHEY, J. E. and ANDERSON, J. G. C. 1944. No. 40. Scottish Slates.

MACGREGOR, A. G. 1945. No. 45. The Mineral Resources of the Lothians.

Scottish Peat Surveys, Vol. I, South-West Scotland. 1964. HMSO Edinburgh.

Water Supply Papers, Geol. Surv. Gt Brit.

CARTER, ANNE V. F. 1966. Records of Wells in the Areas of Scottish one-inch Geological Sheets Peebles (24), Kelso (25), Berwick-upon-Tweed (26), Haddington (33), Eyemouth (34), and North Berwick (41—East Lothian portion).

CARTER, ANNE V. F. and McADAM, A. D. 1967. Records of Wells in the Areas of Scottish one-inch Geological Sheets Girvan (7), Carrick (8), Maxwelltown (9), Dumfries (10), Langholm (11), Campbeltown (12), South Arran (13), Ayr (14), Sanquhar (15), Moffat (16), Jedburgh (17) and Morebattle (18).

GAUSS, G. 1969. Records of Wells in the Areas of Scottish one-inch Geological Sheets Kirkmaiden (1), Whithorn (2), Stranraer (3), Wigtown (4), Kirkcudbright (5) and Annan (6).

INDEX

Abbey St Bathans, 105
Abbotsford, 39
—— Flags, 34, 38, 39
Abington, 23
Acklington dyke, 96
Adamellite, 52, 57
Afton Water, 24
—— —— Granite, 52, 55
Akidograptus acuminatus, Zone of, 34, 36, 45
Albitization, 15–18
Aldons Hill, 26, 30
—— anticline, 28
Allerbeck and Cadgill Sandstone, 94
Alleröd Zone, 101
Alluvium, 102
Ancrumcraig, 88
Andesite, 12, 50, 51, 89
Annan, 6, 91, 94, 103, 104
——, River, 3, 95, 98
—— Series, 1, 6, **94–5**
Annandale, 91, 94, 101, 104
Annanlea Sandstone, 94
Anthraconaia lenisulcata, Zone of, 65, 68, 71
—— *modiolaris*, Zone of, 65, 68, 69, 71, 73, 80
Anthraconauta phillipsii, Zone of, 68, 72, 81
—— *tenuis*, Zone of, 68, 81
Antimony, 106
Arbigland Group, 74
Archerbeck Beds, 78
—— Borehole, 6
Ardmillan, 30, 31
—— Series, 2, 6, **29–33**
Ardwell, —Bay, 17, 30, 31
—— Group, 28–9, **30–1**, 32
Arenig Series, 2, 11, **12 18**, 25, 26, 96, 105
Arkleton Hill, 88
Armorican orogeny, 66
Arsenic, 106
Ashgill Series, 2, 19, **22–4, 31–3**, 45
Assel Conglomerate, 30
—— Valley, 28
Atlantic raised beach, 102
—— Zone, 101, 102

Auchencairn, 106
—— Bay, 55
Auchensoul, 26
Autunian, 91
Ayrshire, 5, 6, 18, 91, 96, 100, 102

B goniatite 'zone', 67, 85
Bail Hill, 25
Bailey, E. B., 5, 6, 15, 17
Bainloch Hill, 55
'Balclatchie Bridge,' 29
Balclatchie Conglomerate, 30
—— Group, **29–30**, 31
—— Mudstones, 29, 30
Ballantrae, 4, 5, 11, 25, 91, 96
—— Igneous Complex, 5, **12–18**, 26, 91
'Balmae Grits', 41
Balsillie, D., 5, 17, 18
Bankhead Marine Band, 72
Barbae Grits, 30
Bargany Group, 35, 47–9
Barjarg, 72, 104
Barlocco Conglomerate, 74
Barness East Limestone, 85
Barns Ness, 84
Barr, 29, 30, 32, 105
—— Series, 2, 19, **26–9**, 31
Barren Mudstones, 22
Barrett, B. H., 6, 94, 95
Baryte, 105, 106
Basal Cementstones, 74
Basalt, 15, 60, 64, 65, 70, 74, 77, 78, 81, 84 **86–9**, 91, 93, 96
Basanite, 90
Bauxitic clay, 73
Beattock Summit, 39
Begg, J. L., 5
Bemersyde, 88
—— Hill, 89
Benan Burn, 26, 28
—— Conglomerate, 18, 24, 26, 28–30
—— Hill, 26, 28
—— —— syncline, 28
Bengairn, 55
—— quartz-diorite, 55, 57
Bennan Hill, 58

115

118

Dumbreddan Bay, 38
Dumfries, 6, 23, 61, 64, 69, 74, **93–4**, 103, 106
—— Sandstones, 93
Dun Limestone, 67, 83, 85
Dunbar, 2, 5, 59, 63, 64, 67, 69, **83–5**, 102, 104
Duneaton Water, 61
Dunion Hill, 88
Dunite, serpentinized, 17
Duns, 5, 52, 59, 81, 87, 101
—— Castle, 60
—— Law, 88
Dunsapie type basalt, 86–9
Dykes, 1, 6, 17, 57–8, 66, 70, 88–90, 91, 93, 96

E₁ stage, 68, 79
E₂ stage, 68, 71, 79
Eaglesfield, 76
East Lothian, 4–7
Easter Burn, 42
Eastern Hole Conglomerate, 83
Eastside Marine Band, 72
Ecclefechan, 59, 66, 76, 86, 91, 104
ECKFORD, R. J. A., 6, 25, 60
Eddleston, 101
Edmondia Marine Band, 82
Eildon Hills, 3, 59, 89
ELLIOTT, R. B., 6
Elvanfoot, 104
Enterkine Burn, 72
Entertrona Burn, 38
Eocene, 96
ERDTMAN, G., 6
Esk, River, 61, 78, 90
Eskdale, 64, 86, 87
Eskdalemuir, 6
—— dyke, 96, 103
Essexite, 93
Ettrick Valley, 38, 41
Ettrickbridge End, 22, 38
Eyemouth, 43, 50, 58, 61, 102
EYLES, Mrs V. A., 25

Fala, 59
Faltenspiegel, 9, 41
Fast Castle, 42
Fatlips Crags, 88
Fell Sandstone, 83
Felsite, 51, 88–9
Firth of Clyde glacier, 100
Fish-beds, 60
Flandrian, 99
FLETT, J. S., 5

Fluvio-glacial deposits, 100–1
Footprints, fossil, 93, 94
Fountainhall, 38
FRESHNEY, E. C., 45, 46
Fruid Reservoir, 106

Gabbro, 17
Gala Group, 2, 34–6, **38–43**, 47
—— Water, 25
Galashiels, 4, 38, 42, 69
Galdenoch Group, 24
Galena, 105, 106
Galloway, 47, 57, 58
—— granites, 5, **52–8**
—— peninsula, 11, 19, 38
GARDINER, C. I., 52, 54, 57
Garheugh Formation, 39, 41
Garleton Hills Volcanic Rocks, **64**, **88**
Garnet, 58
Gastropod Limestone, 79
Gatehouse of Fleet, 39, 57, 105
Gatelawbridge, 93
GEIKIE, A., 4–6, 96
Geological Survey, 4–7, 43, 44, 95
GEORGE, T. N., 3, 6
Geosyncline, 8, 11
Gifford, 59
Gillfoot Beds, 74, 75
Girvan, 2, 5, 11, 12, 22–4, **26–33**, 35, 38, 42, **45–9**, 50, 96, 102, 105
——, Water of, 3
—— Valley, 31, 45
Glaciation, 6, 7, **97–102**
Glen App Group, 19
Glenaylmer Burn, 24
Glencartholm Volcanic Beds, 64, 78, 87
Glencotho, 24, 25
Glendinning Mine, 106
Glenfoot Beds, 48
Glengaber Burn, 106
Glenkill Burn, 19
Glenkiln Shales, 2, 18, **19–22**, 23–6, 28, 30, 35, 36, 38; vulcanicity, 22, 24–6
Glenluce, 23, 38, 39
Glenshalloch Shales, 45–7
Glenwells Shales, 45, 46
Glyptograptus persculptus, Zone of, 34, 36
Gold, 106
GOODCHILD, J. G., 5
GOODLET, G. A., iii, 6
GORDON, A. J., 39
Granite, 2–5, 15, 18, 52, 54, 55, 57, 103
Granitization, 57
Granodiorite 52, 55, 57

Printed in Scotland for HER MAJESTY'S STATIONERY OFFICE
by Bell & Bain Ltd., Glasgow. Dd. 000315/2840   K124

heard the bad news that Dan Kyle wasn't there. Somehow, Garafolo didn't expect him to return. He was right.

The Renton Police took Garafolo's report at the Pizza Palace and found that Dan Kyle had punched his time card at three-forty-five A.M., making him the last person to leave the restaurant. In an interview with Terry Ortlip, they heard the puzzled roommate report that Kyle had bragged about never working for a living in his life, but that he wanted to try working at the pizza restaurant, and that Kyle became "obsessed" with becoming a manager there.

Ortlip, embarrassed, seemed to be holding something back. When prompted, he told the police that on the previous Sunday, December 8, at closing time, Kyle had made an odd comment. "He said he should just take the money at closing and split, or something to that effect." According to Ortlip, Kyle had scooped up the money in his hands, brought it up to his lips, and kissed it.

Asked for a description of Kyle, Ortlip said Dan was about six-foot-two, 180 or 190 pounds, frizzy dark blond hair, and had a large scar on his left wrist. Kyle had told Ortlip that he got the scar during a drug bust in Seattle.

At the end of the interview, Ortlip snapped his fingers and added something that he'd nearly forgotten. He had accompanied Kyle on a visit to the missing man's mother up in the north end of the city. "Funny thing," Ortlip said, "Dan's mom was talking to him and called him 'Charlie.' "

The windows of Renae Wicklund's immaculate white two-bedroom house, with brown trim, needed cleaning, and she'd been waiting for weather that would allow her to tackle the job. Ordinarily, gloomy December clouds would be soaking Snohomish County with rain and sleet or dusting the Douglas firs, cedars and alders with early snowfall. But today, blue sky and thin sunshine warmed damp earth and grass around the Wicklund home, perfuming the air with the fresh aroma of Christmas trees.

She'd have to hurry, though. At one-forty-five in the afternoon, only about three hours remained before the sun would drop toward the Puget Sound, leaving the hills shrouded in darkness.

Just enough chill lingered for Renae to don a black sweater over her white blouse and purple corduroy vest. Matching purple cords and winter boots would keep her warm enough to work outside. After dropping a bottle of glass cleaner into a bucket and placing it outside, she stepped back in and hummed a little song as she reached for the joy of her life, her baby, Shannah.

Sixteen months old, Shannah Wicklund had the big, liquid brown eyes, wide smile, and burnished chestnut hair of her slim, attractive young mother. Renae bundled the baby in warm clothing, carried her outside, leaned over and released her to toddle around on the lawn. As the mother straightened up, she caught sight of a tall man, in jeans and a red shirt, who had taken a couple of steps into her driveway entry, fifty-five feet away. Instantly, he stopped in his tracks, spun around, and retreated toward the two-lane paved road.

Giving it negligible conscious thought, Renae figured that he was probably looking for one of her neighbors, whose houses were difficult to see through the forest of evergreens. Maybe he'd experienced car trouble. If he had to walk to the next town, it wouldn't be too far. He'd have to descend the hill into a shallow, winding valley, climb again, and hike about a mile to tiny Clearview. A couple of auto repair shops occupied two corners of the block-long village. He would have no trouble finding assistance. If he had asked, Renae would have been happy to help if she could, but she had no telephone. Anyway, the man had apparently decided to go on his way.

The stranger disappeared, and Renae dismissed him from her mind. She stepped to the front door, intending to find some rags for her window washing task, when something, perhaps maternal intuition, caused her to look again toward the driveway.

A horrified gasp rose from the pit of Renae's stomach to her throat. The stranger, in giant ground-swallowing strides, sprinted toward her. He'd already covered half the distance, and leaped a two-rail cedar fence dividing the driveway from the lawn. Instinctively, Renae dashed to Shannah, scooped her up, and scrambled through the front entry.

For a split second, Renae thought she'd escaped. One step inside her threshold, she tried to slam the door. Too late. He threw his full weight against the door an instant before the latch caught, blasting it open and nearly knocking Renae off her feet. As he took a couple of steps inside onto the orange shag carpet, she retreated across the room, then froze in place when he ordered her to stop.

Facing him, Renae saw a man probably in his early twenties, who stood a couple of inches over six feet, thin build, with wavy, frizzy brown hair roughly parted in the middle. She thought he had brown eyes, and could see that he hadn't shaved his wide jaws and sunken cheeks for a couple of days. He wore tight, faded blue jeans, a red and black plaid flannel shirt buttoned at the collar and wrists, and dark brown cowboy boots. He also held a "thin-bladed, shiny knife."

Having placed Shannah on the couch, Renae stepped forward to form a blockade between her baby and the intruder. She already knew that no matter what it was, she would do anything to protect Shannah.

When he spoke, his voice "was not harsh" or filled with "broken language." He simply commanded, "Get your clothes off right now or I'll kill the kid . . . and I mean it." He stood next to a chair, in front of a table-mounted aquarium in which goldfish swam languidly, oblivious to the tension in the room.

Renae dropped into a black lounge chair, her heart thudding against her chest. She knew she had no choice. While he watched her every move, she leaned forward to remove her boots, then slid out of her purple cords. Looking up at him in desperate hope, she saw that there would be no reprieve. She continued removing the rest of her clothing, leaving on only her underpants. The lanky man stepped closer, reached, and yanked off the remaining garment. He halted abruptly, muttering a crude comment indicating his realization that she was in her menstrual period. Renae braced herself while he leaned forward with a sudden move, reached toward her and "pulled out" the tampon.

Squinting his cruel eyes for a moment, as if in deep thought, the intruder made a decision. He unzipped his pants, stepped forward, and thrust his hips toward Renae's face. His lust would be satisfied with oral sex.

When he was sated, he adjusted his jeans, raised his eyes toward Renae's face, muttered one word, retreated, and strode out the door. Horrified, still trembling, frightened, and disgusted, Renae couldn't believe what she heard. "Thanks," he'd said. She wanted to throw up.

Watching out the window to be sure he exited the driveway, she saw him stride west on the road, toward Clearview.

Hastily putting on some of her clothes, Renae ran to the kitchen to wash out her mouth, gargling, gagging, and purging several times. She grabbed the baby and hurried outside to her car. Terrified that the rapist might be lurking somewhere behind a tree to attack again and prevent her from calling the police, she leaped into the car and quickly locked the doors. Urgently wanting immediate help, Renae started the car, jammed it into gear, and drove fewer than one hundred yards. She reached the paved road, twisted the wheel left, immediately right again, and screeched to a halt in the driveway of Don and Barbara Hendrickson.

The Hendricksons, in their forties, had lived in the tidy bungalow-type house for fourteen years. They had befriended Renae three years ago, and rejoiced when little Shannah came along, virtually adopting the young mother and baby. At age twenty-three, Renae was twenty years younger than Barbara, but they could share conversation, jokes, and gossip just as school chums might. Barbara stood slightly taller than Renae's five-five, and weighed just a few pounds more. Her blond hair already had strands of silver, and her face, fuller than Renae's, usually glowed with a smile, emphasized by arched, penciled eyebrows and blue eyes shining behind her glasses.

When she heard Renae's car slide into the driveway, and a

sudden loud knock on the door, Barbara Hendrickson dropped her cigarette and coffee and rushed from her kitchen. It startled her when the entry door swung open and Renae charged in, breaking her usual habit of waiting to be invited inside. Barbara recalled, "Renae was very upset, borderline hysterical. She had on slacks and a little V-neck vest-type thing, sleeveless, and nothing under it. It was the type of garment that you wear something under, like a blouse or a shirt."

Shannah, Barbara observed, sobbed with fright. Putting her consoling arms around Renae and the baby, Barbara held her terrified friend and asked what was wrong. "Renae said there was a man outside and she was afraid he would come back. She looked out the window. I promptly locked the door and got out my shotgun." Barbara also called the police.

Rookie Sheriff's Deputy Kenneth O. Christensen arrived at the Hendrickson home twenty minutes after two P.M. The visit would remain etched in his memory because it happened to be his first serious felony case. He'd been dispatched to an "assault with a knife," so Christensen was surprised to observe that Renae's clothing "was disheveled as if she had put them on rapidly without concern for her appearance." He listened as Renae described what had happened, even including the perpetrator's disgusting "Thanks" before he left. She also commented that the man hadn't touched anything in the house, so there would probably be no fingerprints. Christensen asked her to write the details on a witness statement form. Renae complied, candidly writing in neat script, leaving out nothing.

Detective Lee Trunkhill, a five-year veteran of the Snohomish County Sheriff's Office, arrived at the Hendrickson home shortly after Christensen. While the younger officer left to search for the suspect, Renae led Trunkhill to her house to show him where the running man had leaped the fence, possibly leaving a footprint. Nothing usable turned up. She repeated her account of the attack, including a detailed description of the assailant, while Trunkhill took notes.

Before departing, the sheriff's officers asked if Renae needed medical treatment. She and Barbara agreed it wouldn't be necessary. They just hoped that the police would catch the swine who had terrified and violated Renae.

Back at headquarters in Everett, Lee Trunkhill sent out a teletype describing the incident and asking if any similar crimes had taken place in the region. Two days later, on Friday, he received a telephone call from police in White Center, in the southern section of Seattle, not far from Seattle-Tacoma International Airport, known as Sea-Tac.

Yes, the calling officer told Detective Trunkhill, a very similar rape had taken place in White Center just three weeks ago. The perpetrator had held a knife to a baby's throat and forced the young mother to fellate him. The suspect in that case had fled in a taxi, and been dropped off on 192nd Street, in Bothell, thirty miles north of the crime scene. *The guy must have some money,* Trunkhill thought. *That's a long cab ride.*

The following morning, Saturday, Lee Trunkhill drove down to 192nd Street and located the exact site where the fugitive passenger had exited the cab. He surveyed a row of middle-class homes, trying to decide where to start. House-to-house canvassing was often a fruitless task, but Lee Trunkhill had felt a deep sense of rage when he'd talked to Renae Wicklund, and wanted to find the creep who would threaten babies' lives as a means to force sexual favors from frightened young mothers. The sleuth started knocking on doors.

Just when fatigue began to make the task appear hopeless, his determination paid off. An attractive woman in her early twenties peered from behind a partly open door, and nodded in response to his question. Yes, she knew a man who stood about six-two and had frizzy, wavy brown hair, wide jaws and sunken cheeks. His eyes appeared greenish hazel to her, though, not brown.

"What's his name?" Trunkhill asked.

"Dan Leslie Kyle," she said.

Darlene Bolt, a student at the University of Washington, had met Dan through mutual friends two years ago, she said, and had seen him maybe a dozen times. Sometimes, he played a guitar for her.

"Did you see him this week, on the 11th?" Trunkhill asked.

Darlene felt pretty sure it was Wednesday morning when Kyle had last visited her. He'd arrived either hitchhiking or caught a ride with a buddy, she thought. But she'd had other plans that morning. "I asked him to leave and he called a cab." No, she didn't know where he lived.

Excited, Trunkhill hastened back up to Everett to initiate a records search for any more information available about Mister Kyle.

At the same time Trunkhill first heard the name Dan Leslie Kyle, investigators in Renton were taking statements about Kyle's disappearance with seventeen hundred dollars belonging to the Pizza Palace restaurant.

Detective Lee Trunkhill waited until the teletype machine stopped clacking, ripped out the yellow paper, and scanned the rap sheet. The name Dan Leslie Kyle, he read, was an alias. The suspect's real name was Charles Rodman Campbell. Charlie Campbell was well known to Snohomish County law enforcement personnel. He had a long juvenile record and adult criminal history listing infractions ranging from burglary to assault to drug possession.

On the day before Christmas, 1974, Detective Trunkhill paid a visit to Renae Wicklund. He placed a folder on the table in front of her and opened up the "six-pack" of lineup photos. She studied them for a moment, then unequivocally pointed to photo number five, a mug shot of Charles Rodman Campbell.

His records also included the address of Charlie's mother, with whom Campbell had been living. Detective Trunkhill drove to the Renton home, which was within a twenty minutes' walking distance of the Pizza Palace. Betty Lou Campbell, Charlie's mother, told the investigator that Charlie had been working for a month at the pizza restaurant. But she hadn't seen him for several days since he moved out to share a house with another guy who worked with him. No, she said, she didn't know anything about him using an alias.

At the same time Detective Trunkhill called on Mrs. Campbell, an investigator from the Renton Police Department arrived. Charlie's new roommate and coworker, Terry Ortlip, had finally remembered where "Dan Kyle's" mother lived. The fugitive's identity had now been revealed from two directions in a pincers movement of law enforcement. But the next step was to find him, and that wouldn't be as easy.

Before the investigators left, Betty Lou Campbell, depressed, humiliated, and angry, gave them a tip about her wayward son. "Charlie is an extremely dangerous man," she said. "Watch out for him."

Three

Being born in an earthly paradise, it would seem, should be the beginning of a wonderful life. Charles Rodman Campbell first saw the light of day on October 21, 1954, in a place where gentle trade winds, coconut palms, lush *pali* cliffs, and tropical beaches beckoned tourists. The *aloha* spirit still prevailed in Hawaii then, when *haoles* debarked from the cruise ship, *Lurline,* or stepped off the Pan-Am Clipper onto the island of Oahu to settle into suites at the few luxury hotels scattered along Waikiki Beach.

A strapping young marine, Oliver Campbell, who stood a muscular six-three, had brought his pregnant wife and baby daughter to Honolulu to be with his island resident parents. While Betty Lou Campbell struggled through the final days of discomfort, Oliver toured the bars along Hotel Street, listened to gentle Polynesian lyrics accompanied by ukuleles, watched the sway of hula dancers, and learned to toss back prodigious amounts of booze. She stayed with his mother, who had descended from the original Polynesian natives.

As soon as his new son could travel, Oliver Campbell took his growing family to the state of Washington. Mustered out of the Marine Corps, he found employment as a truck driver. Betty Lou had liked the tropical climate of the islands and dreaded the change back to the soggy, chilling winters of the Pacific Northwest.

She wished that other things would change, though. Oliver's drinking became habitual and so did his anger. Some people are happy drunks, but not Oliver Campbell. Liquor inflamed him, fueling an inner rage directed mostly at his wife. In desperation, she, too, took a few drinks to ease the pain, then a few more. When the bottle failed to provide solace, she found a doctor who would prescribe tranquilizers, and learned to rely heavily on Valium.

Another daughter came along one year after Charles, then a fourth daughter in 1957. The last baby was born with a congenital defect; she had no hip joints. Her disability added to the nearly unbearable stress already tearing the family apart. Even though Oliver worked regularly, financial difficulties piled up, and violent fights between the parents sent the children cowering into dark corners. The boy, Charles, had no bedroom to which he could retreat and hide. He usually slept on the living room couch or sometimes on the floor.

Too often, Charles found himself in the care of his grandparents. Oliver's mother and father, along with several other relatives, had also moved to the Seattle region to be near their loved ones. Acquaintances described the elder Campbells as "wonderful, law-abiding people." When they planned a luau, they courteously telephoned the police in advance to volunteer responsibility, and corrective action, for any problems that arose from noise or crowded parking on the neighborhood street. The couple tried to give their grandson the love apparently absent in his explosive home environment.

Children exposed to a quagmire of domestic difficulties respond in various ways. Withdrawal is common, often accompanied by health problems. Charles Campbell, who was "Charlie" to most of his family, remained healthy, with one exceptional incident. At the age of five, he developed a problem with one of his testicles, which had to be surgically removed. Psychiatrists would later speculate that the loss of a testicle "may have led Campbell to suffer some kind of inferiority complex with regard to his masculinity."

Rancor and unrest in the Campbell home, on Daly Street in Edmonds, became noticeable even to neighbors. One woman later recalled that when she was thirteen, in 1960, she lived for a few months on the same street, four houses away from the Campbells. She observed that the boy, Charles, became "a passive, withdrawn child. He was yelled at and screamed at constantly by his parents. No matter what he did, it was wrong in his mother's eyes, and I saw her hit him many times with a stick which was about the circumference of my finger." Reflectively, the woman said she couldn't understand why Charles was treated in that manner, since he didn't appear to misbehave any more than normal children, or act aggressively. The boy's younger sister, who had the hip disability, was "lavished with attention" and could do no wrong. Charles seemed to be a scapegoat.

"Almost every evening," she continued, "Charles would come to our door, a wide-eyed, withdrawn little boy, having been sent by his mother to 'borrow' some bread." His requests weren't limited to food. He also asked for cigarettes. "My aunt continued to give the family bread, fearing that the children would otherwise go hungry."

In her recollection, the woman said that Charles' father often beat Mrs. Campbell, who sometimes sought tearful refuge in her neighbor's home. "I recall quite vividly always feeling weird and sick around Mr. or Mrs. Campbell, somehow knowing something was wrong. My grandmother always prayed for 'little Chuck' and would remind us that he needed our prayers."

Police officers in the town of Edmonds thought it would take more than prayer to help Charles Campbell. His first encounter with them occurred when the boy was only ten years old. In May, 1965, a patrolman responded to a report that a two-and-one-half-ton cattle truck had been vandalized in a lot not far from the Campbell home. He found that someone had thrown rocks at the windshield and side windows of the truck, breaking all of the glass. A youthful neighborhood snitch told the officer that two boys named Charles and Tom were the vandals, and that Charles lived on Daly Street. It didn't take long to identify the rock tosser as Charles Campbell. The officer wrote that the case should be followed up by the juvenile authorities. Like too many incidents in the future of Charles Campbell, this one fell through the cracks. No follow-up was ever made.

The constant turmoil at home caused problems for young Campbell in school. He seemed unable to adjust to teachers' work requirements, and lost interest in anything they had to offer. Bored and angry, he sought thrills by joining other troubled kids in skipping school, smoking cigarettes, and sipping from cans of beer heisted at home.

The experimentation escalated to a more serious level when Campbell reached the age of twelve. He found young friends who had access to amphetamines, speed. The next year, at the age of thirteen, he injected heroin for the first time.

Betty Lou Campbell would one day write, "Charlie's father had a violent temper when he drank, so the boy's childhood wasn't too neat. His father didn't beat him or anything like that, but we used to fight a lot." Sometimes, she said, the relationship became unbearable, and she would leave the home. "Charlie's big problems didn't really start until he turned to drugs." At the age of thirteen, she said, he began to steal things.

A decade later, Charles Campbell would be asked to fill out a "social history" form. In a brief description of his childhood, he wrote, "I lived in Seattle, Mountlake Terrace, and Edmonds. Went to school, led a good life." He described his teenage years, noting, "Started getting in trouble after associating with wrong kids and using drugs."

On Friday, April 11, 1969, at eight-thirty P.M., an enraged Oliver Campbell telephoned the Edmonds Police Department. His son, Charles, hadn't returned home from school. Charlie's cousin, one month younger than his relative, suggested that Charlie had run away because he'd been expelled from school and was afraid to face his father. An officer called the vice principal of Madrona Junior High School, who said that he had "reamed the boy out" but had not expelled him. Young Campbell remained away from home until late Saturday night, then came sheepishly walking in. At that time of year, mid-April, the weather can still be frigid in Washington. Shivering, Charlie decided that his father's wrath couldn't be any worse than freezing to death. A grim Oliver Campbell telephoned the police again to report that his son had returned home.

Oliver restricted his son's activities for a few weeks, hoping that the punishment would teach him a lesson. It only made Charlie angrier. On May 22, Edmonds police picked him up at eight-thirty P.M. with a fourteen-year-old girl, in Baker cemetery. They'd been called by a woman who'd seen two kids pushing over tombstones. When she'd approached them, the young man "started acting like a madman," beating on a metal canopy used at grave sites during services, shouting at her, and making "odd gestures." As soon as the complainant left to call the police, the young couple ran into the woods behind the cemetery, disappearing into the darkness. Officers arrived, spotted the pair, gave chase on foot, and caught them. Charlie Campbell "appeared to be under the influence of drugs," but he denied either using drugs or damaging the tombstones. The police released the girl to her parents, but held Campbell in detention to be charged with malicious mischief. His parents picked him up the next day.

Charlie crossed paths with the police again, just four weeks later. After dark that evening, Patrolman John Martin pulled over a 1953 Dodge Station Wagon when he noticed that the brake lights weren't working. The four occupants looked quite young, especially the driver. Asked for a driver's license, the youth behind the wheel said that he'd left his wallet at home, but identified himself as John Sullivan, born in 1950. With a straight face, he said he couldn't remember his address. While the officer collected the passengers' names, he noticed a man standing around, observing, who seemed nervous and too attentive, so he asked for his identity as well. The new arrival gave a name and address, but Martin knew that a sixteen-acre shopping center was under construction at that location. Challenged, the young man admitted being the real John Sullivan, and that he'd been returning a truck to a friend, with "Charlie" following in the Dodge to give Sullivan a ride back home. "Charlie" turned out to be Charles Campbell, age fifteen.

The whole set of circumstances left too many unanswered questions for Officer Martin. Further investigation revealed that the Dodge station wagon had been taken without the owner's permission, so Martin had it towed while he hauled the five young men to the police station. He began calling each of the youths' parents. When he reached Campbell's home, he learned that Charlie's parents were at a Hawaiian luau being held, ironically, at the Seattle Police Pavilion.

When Martin finally reached Oliver Campbell at the luau, the father acted "highly intoxicated" and seemed to "care less." The elder Campbell became belligerent when told of his son's infractions. Martin informed him that Charlie would be released to them at the Snohomish County youth center. Oliver and Betty Lou, seething with anger, retrieved their only son at nine-thirty that night.

School, to Charlie, had become a real drag, so he gradually stopped attending. With more time on his hands, he found new ways to get in trouble.

A narrow escape occurred three days before Charles Campbell's sixteenth birthday in October, 1970. Edmonds police responded to a burglary in progress at Esperance Elementary School. Witnesses thought they saw Charlie and his buddy leaving the scene, but not enough evidence could be found to pin the crime on them. In just nine more days, though, they found him culpable for auto theft, with a more reliable witness report. It came from Oliver Campbell.

Officer Bob Greene took the call from Campbell senior. "I want my son arrested for stealing the family car," he complained. The father had been out of town because he and his wife had "split up." When he returned to the house, he discovered that Charlie had taken his father's Thunderbird for a joyride on the freeway. Unfortunately, the transmission blew up, and Charlie had to call a towing service to bring the car home. When he arrived, his father stood in the yard, hands on hips, furious. The towing charge of forty-two dollars was the last straw. Oliver called the police. Officer Greene said they wouldn't be able to come out immediately, so Oliver brought Charlie into the police station.

In questioning Charlie, Greene also asked him about the Esperance school burglary. "He just grinned at me," Greene wrote, and "denied any knowledge or involvement." Greene added, "This guy is really playing the role and thinks he is a real big con now. When Charlie was given a phone call, he told the person on the other end to shoot his father. He repeated this three times."

En route to the juvenile center with another officer, Herb Oberg, Charlie asked for a cigarette. Oberg asked, "How old are you?" Campbell responded that he was eighteen and could prove it. He produced a hunting license containing a birth date of 10-21-52. To Oberg, it had obviously been altered. When they arrived at the center, other documents on file showed Campbell's true age, barely sixteen. The officers advised him that additional charges would be filed against him for lying to an official and for a State Fish and Game violation of false information on the license.

Charlie smirked, said he had just been kidding them, and began complaining that he hadn't been advised of his rights. Greene, who had arrived at the juvenile center, asked Charlie if he knew his rights, whereupon Campbell recited the Miranda warning, verbatim.

After booking Charlie at the juvenile center, Greene transported him to the Snohomish County jail. He entered in his report, "Campbell thought it was great to get with the big boys. A life of criminal activity is the future outlook for this young adult if he does not receive treatment."

Toward the end of 1970, Charles Campbell's misdeeds escalated. When someone broke into a stereo shop, a number of people pointed at Charlie, but a paucity of hard evidence spared him. After another school burglary, the Edmonds police actually went to Campbell's home and waited for him. Charged with the crime, Campbell received only a wrist slap from the judicial system, which placed him on probation.

Oliver Campbell's frustration with his son reached the boiling point in January, 1971, when he came home to find Charlie and a group of teenage cronies smoking pot. Charlie had grown rapidly to a towering six-two with a slim, wiry build and exceptional strength. The belligerent sixteen-year-old took a swing at his thirty-eight-year-old ex-marine father, exchanged a few blows, then escaped through a back window. Two days later, with information provided by one of Charlie's sisters, officers tracked him down, subdued the struggling youth, and turned him over to his probation officer. Once again, the system released him with no jail time.

On a warm day the next spring, police spotted Campbell driving a 1962 Chevy stolen from a K-Mart parking lot. Detective Chuck Riley, in an unmarked vehicle, followed the car to the rear of an apartment building, parked behind it, and radioed for backup. He reported, "I observed the driver to be Charles Campbell, who is well known by this officer from many previous contacts." Campbell slid out of the car, wearing cut-off jeans and a T-shirt, then broke into a run, leaping fences as he went. Riley pursued, yelling at Campbell to halt, and shouting at some sunbathers around an apartment pool to help stop him. "They were just startled and went back to sunbathing," the detective later laughed.

Campbell vaulted another fence and landed in a thick bramble of thorny blackberry vines. Scrambling wildly and tearing the skin on his bare legs and arms, he made his way through the tangle, and headed for a highway. Riley could see that another officer, on the highway, had parked and started pursuing the fugitive on foot.

Officer Bob Henderson, accompanied by a college student ride-along, left his patrol car on the highway to chase Campbell in a foot race. Gasping for breath at the top of a steep hill, where they'd lost sight of the fugitive, the chasers halted. The student heard the door of a nearby house slam. Henderson asked the student to stand at the back door, while he went to the front. At his knock, a woman answered and said that a young guy wearing cut-offs, and bleeding, had asked to use the phone, but when he heard someone rapping at the door, had fled through the house toward the back. With her permission, Henderson entered in full stride toward the rear exit, and found Campbell standing outside on the top step facing the student who blocked his way.

With Campbell waving a fist and yelling, "You're not taking me in," Henderson thrust a can of Mace in his face and told him he was under arrest.

"You can make it hard, or easy, Charlie," Henderson warned.

Cursing, Campbell leaned against the house and allowed the officer to cuff him. As they walked back toward the patrol car, Campbell, seething with rage, growled, "You fucking pig. When I get out, I'm going to kill you."

At the patrol car, Detective Riley waited for them. Glaring, Campbell told Riley, "This is the second time that you've got on my list. It'll be the last time. You're a fucking pig, just like this guy, and I'm gonna kill you, too. If I had a gun, I'd do it right now."

For stealing a car, resisting arrest, and threatening to kill police officers, Campbell's punishment consisted of staying a few nights in a juvenile detention facility and extended probation. At the Edmonds police station, officers just shook their heads. They knew that Charlie was headed for bigger trouble some day and speculated that he certainly seemed capable of murder, especially under the influence of drugs. The standard joke, once spoken by Campbell himself, was that Charlie had shot up everything in his veins except peanut butter and Kool-Aid.

While most people watched fireworks, July 4, 1971, Charles Campbell devised his own method of celebrating. He invaded his grandparents' home and stole several guns and a tape recorder. Other teen associates reported that he planned to sell the weapons for enough money to run away to California. A relative notified the police. Three officers came to the Campbell home, caught Charlie lying on a couch and surrounded him to make the arrest. On the way out, he lurched over to one side and kicked out a window, sending glass shards flying everywhere. Facing family members, he shouted, "That's to thank you for what you done for me."

Some of the stolen items were found in an apartment where Charlie's drug-using social circle, teenage girls and their drop-out boyfriends, loafed away much of their time. Some of them expressed loyalty to Charlie, while others said they were afraid of him. One of his most loyal followers had been a buddy of Campbell's since junior high school. Thomas Hawkins would remain a close friend for fifteen years, until a sexual event would destroy their camaraderie forever.

The pattern of nonpunishment for Campbell's misbehavior remained consistent. His latest escapade, betraying his own family, resulted only in a notation on his criminal records that he had violated probation.

Finally, Charles Campbell stretched his good luck too far. Before July ended, he participated in the burglary of a house in Edmonds. One of Campbell's coterie informed on him, bringing the police to haul him in again. When he finally stood trial, the judge's patience had been worn out. He revoked the previously extended probation for the car theft in May and tacked on time for the burglary. Expressing hope that the youth would learn from the experience of being locked up, the judge sentenced Charles Campbell to serve one year in the Green Hill juvenile reformatory in Chehalis, Washington.

Green Hill released Campbell on parole in less than a year, early May, 1972. It took him only three weeks to get in trouble again. His father, Oliver, saw evidence that Charlie had possession of drugs in the house. That his son would risk bringing drugs into the home inflamed the senior Campbell. To avoid making Charlie suspicious, Oliver whispered to his oldest daughter to go to a nearby convenience store and call Officer Willard Anderson, whom he knew to be tough but fair. Anderson met her at the 7-Eleven, heard her story, and radioed for back-up help.

Two other officers staked out the front of the Campbell home. Accompanied by a sergeant, Anderson slipped through the kitchen door which had been opened by Oliver. In the living room, they found Charlie stretched out on a couch, sound asleep. Anderson snapped handcuffs on him before Charlie could wake up. They searched the grumpy youth and found thirty-one amphetamine tablets wrapped in the cellophane of a cigarette package and stuffed in his right boot.

After transporting Campbell to the police station, officers strip-searched him and observed his arms pockmarked with needle "tracks." A conference with juvenile detention authorities resulted in a decision not to remand Campbell for a new trial, but simply to return him to Green Hill for violation of parole.

Charles Campbell had no intention of staying cooped up in Green Hill. After four more months, on September 20, 1972, he simply walked away and returned to Edmonds. He knew that he could stay at a home just three blocks from his father's house, but he didn't know that the home owner would immediately telephone Oliver Campbell. And Oliver again notified the Edmonds police. Knowing that the suspect was the wild and violent Charlie Campbell, six officers surrounded the house at ten-thirty that night, while one knocked on the front door. Charlie looked out the window and sprinted for the rear exit. He flew out into the night amidst three uniformed officers who immediately tackled him in midair. As usual, he screamed and cursed, thrashing around on the ground until the trio subdued and handcuffed him. Charlie spent the night in the Snohomish County jail before being returned, once again, to Green Hill. The institution released him on his eighteenth birthday.

A sharp wind slanted light rain down on a cold night in February, 1973. Charlie Campbell and a buddy walked into the warmth of a Sambo's restaurant in Everett, shivering from the damp chill, having hitchhiked from Edmonds. Charlie ordered a ham omelette and coffee, while his companion had a plain omelette. They dined with gusto, lingering over several refills of hot coffee. When they finished eating, they walked right past the cash register, through the double glass doors, and ran into the dark night. But Charlie had made a critical error.

Forty minutes later, he boldly walked back into the restaurant and asked the manager if anyone had turned in some keys and a pack of cigarettes he'd left there. The manager, Greg Coleman, recognized him and accused him of walking out without paying his tab. Charlie spun around and strode out again, with Coleman following at his heels. When Charlie ran, so did the determined manager. Campbell tried to scramble over a six-foot fence at the back of the parking lot, but Coleman, twenty-two years old, six feet tall, 180 pounds, grabbed Campbell's ankles, and pulled him down. As Charlie landed, he twisted around to slam his fist into Coleman's face, bloodying the man's nose, then picked up a rock and threatened to bash Coleman's skull. At that moment, a patrol car skidded to a halt a few feet away. Campbell dropped the stone and gave up the struggle to escape.

Greg Coleman, recalling the event, said that he wasn't sure if his bloodied face came from a kick while Campbell struggled on the fence, or from a punch in the nose. He thought "Charlie was weird in the head like a scared cat. He seemed to be on drugs."

Incredibly, despite his past record of violence and encounters with the law, a judge let Campbell go with a fine of only twenty-five dollars for "defrauding an innkeeper."

That same month, Campbell met the woman who would become his wife. For many men, such an event represents a positive turning point in life. For Charlie, it only provided a new direction in which he could vent his rage.

Born in McMinnville, Oregon, six days before Christmas in 1950, Rosalie Kinner spent her undistinguished childhood and teen years in Oregon and Washington. Just after her twenty-second birthday, she attended a small gathering of friends in Edmonds. A tall youth, seemingly mature for his eighteen years, gravitated toward Rosalie and began regaling her with stories of his adventures on the shady side of the law. The couple made a stark contrast. Charlie towered over the slim, petite woman four years his senior. Despite the age difference, they found a number of interests in common, including a fondness for the effects of alcohol.

After they stood in front of Judge Rutter and recited marriage vows, they lived a shabby existence for two weeks in Brewster and Wenatchee before returning to Edmonds. Almost immediately, the police department renewed their long-standing acquaintance with Charles Campbell. Officer Esar Hasner knew not only Charlie, but he had also met Rosalie and other members of Campbell's family. "I got to know Charlie's grandparents well. They often said that I should be Hawaiian since I looked it, but I explained to them that I'm an Indian." In previous contacts with Rosalie, he developed an opinion that "she was slow and always thought that Charlie was a wonderful man."

Hasner wondered if Rosalie still felt that way when he responded to a call on October 14, 1973, a week before Charlie's nineteenth birthday. The officer entered the backyard at Campbell's grandparents' home where a camper had been removed from a truckbed and placed on the ground. Charlie and Rosalie lived in it.

Crying hysterically, Rosalie told Hasner that Charlie had roughed her up. Hasner learned that the problem had started at a drunken party. Charlie had wanted to come home, but Rosalie asked to stay longer. So he hoisted her onto his shoulders and carried her out. Tempers flared at the grandparents' home, causing Grandpa to wave a hammer at Charlie threatening to "let him have it." Charlie retaliated by screaming his intent to kill Rosalie's dog. That didn't have the frightening impact Charlie intended, so he added a threat to kill Rosalie's sister and mother.

When Officer Hasner calmed Rosalie down, she decided that she didn't want to sign a complaint. Charlie, she said, was unemployed and having a tough time. She just wanted to get some help for him, and feared that the police might shoot him. Hasner asked her about Charlie's activities during the past few months, wondering if he might be involved in some unsolved holdups. Rosalie's vague answers hinted that Charlie had told her about them, and she admitted that he probably had a gun in his possession. She denied that he'd been using drugs again.

During the conversation, Charlie emerged from the house, took one look at Hasner, and dashed into the woods behind the home. A search failed to find him. Hasner told Rosalie and the grandparents to call if Charlie caused any more trouble, and wound up the incident by informing Charlie's parole officer. He also referred the Campbells to a family counseling service. Maybe they could heal the infection that already rotted the new marriage.

Down in southern Washington that year, the family of a youngster named Westley Allan Dodd, age twelve, moved to Richland, where the Columbia River carves a big half circle in its turn westward to form the border between Washington and Oregon. Westley, the new kid in junior high school, developed a strong sexual attraction for younger boys. That urge would accelerate through his teen years, and lead him into a lot of trouble.

Rosalie Campbell's mother answered her doorbell in mid-November and confronted a red-faced, fuming Charles. "Did you give Rosalie anything to drink?" he demanded.

"No," she replied. Rosalie, now pregnant, lay asleep upstairs. Her mom worried that Charlie would come in and hurt her daughter.

"I don't want you to ever give her any alcohol," he ordered, as he marched inside, ignoring three boys who watched, wide-eyed.

Irritated at his attitude, and defensive, the mother shot back, "If I want to give her something to drink, I'll do it, especially if she asks for it. You can't tell me what to do."

Flexing his jaw, Campbell growled, "If I find out you did, I'll drag her out of here." At that moment, Rosalie appeared at the top of the stairs and said that he'd better not try, because she wouldn't go with him. The three lads, friends of the family, jumped up and offered to fight Charlie. Rosalie ran down the stairs to stop Campbell from hurting the boys. He brushed them aside, picked her up, threw her over his shoulder, and trotted out the front door.

Aghast, the mother watched him drive away in a white Dodge van, then called the Edmonds police. Patrolman Robert Hingson showed up to take the report. No actual crime had been committed, so there was little the officer could do. He filled out a form in which he noted, "It would appear Charlie is on the rampage again, and he isn't afraid of anything or anybody. He threatened to do bodily harm to everyone in the house at the time of this dispute. It probably won't be the last time we hear of him."

Campbell waited until Christmas to validate Officer Hingson's prediction. During a party that began on Christmas Eve at the grandparents' home, where a large crowd of Hawaiian guests celebrated *Mele Kalikimaka,* Charlie and Rosalie began arguing. Both of them had been drinking heavily. Just after midnight, he dragged her outside to administer a beating, and someone called the police. Officer Esar Hasner, the Native American cop who knew the grandparents, again responded.

"When I arrived," he recalled, "I could see that she was really beaten. My patience was being lost with Rosalie since she just wouldn't sign a complaint." He noted that an uncle had been slugged by Charlie with a hammer, but without any apparent injury. Charlie had fled the scene again. Rosalie's "face was red from the punches given her by Charlie, plus she was bleeding from the mouth and nose." She refused Hasner's suggestion that she should get a medical exam or treatment. He once more suggested that she file a formal charge against Charlie, but she shook her head.

Rosalie lay awake most of the night thinking about the officer's words. At last, she decided to sign a complaint against her violent husband. Immediately afterward, she left with some friends to stay with them in Okanogan, one hundred miles away, east of the Cascade Mountains.

Edmonds police found Charlie at his apartment and arrested him before Christmas day had ended. He spent the night in jail. The next morning, he faced arraignment where the judge set a trial for March 15, but allowed Campbell to go free in the interim, based on his promise that he would show up.

Charlie Campbell kept his promises with the same frequency that Mount Rainier erupted. His place at the defendant's table on Friday morning, March 15, was conspicuously empty. The judge immediately issued a warrant for Campbell's arrest.

A steady rain had been soaking Seattle all day Saturday, March 16, transforming vacant lots into lakes of mud. Edmonds P.D. Officers Ed Aksdal and Vern Elder drove through the downpour to the city, armed with the warrant to arrest Charles Campbell. They'd already checked with a member of his family who suggested a location where he might be found, but warned that Charlie might be armed with a .45 caliber automatic.

With the aid of two Seattle P.D. officers, they approached a house on Ravenna Street. Elder and one of the Seattle men covered the back door, while Aksdal and the fourth officer knocked at the front door. A scrawny, short, bearded youth, about twenty, pulled it partially open, listened to Aksdal explain the warrant, then tried to slam it shut while he yelled a warning to his houseguest. Aksdal leaned his shoulder into the door, and simultaneously heard the crash of breaking glass a few feet to his right.

Charles Campbell hurdled through the shattered front window, taking broken fragments of glass and molding with him. A razor edge caught his right hand, slashing the wrist and lacerating the palm. Blood flew everywhere. In a lightning move, Aksdal leaped toward Charlie, momentarily grasping his right ankle. But in the deep, slippery mud of the yard, Aksdal lost traction and fell to the ground, breaking his tenuous grip on Campbell, who sprinted away without ever breaking stride.

By that time, Vern Elder had circled the house. He joined a Seattle officer in chasing Campbell, while the other local cop stayed to see if Aksdal had been injured. The mud took its toll on the chasing Seattle officer. He, too, slipped and fell, dropping his drawn weapon and losing his hat. Elder, running at full speed, kept pace with Charlie, who resorted to his old tactic of scrambling over high fences. Later recalling the incident, Aksdal's eyes twinkled when he said that Vern Elder earned a new moniker that afternoon. "He is now known as 'Running Deer.' "

Following a blood trail left by Campbell, Elder continued the chase while Aksdal and the Seattle officers caught up in vehicles. Spotting Elder, they braked to a halt and leaped out near an old Victorian house, just as Campbell tore around the corner, right into a triangle formed by the pursuers. Aksdal stood rock still with his revolver at high aim, pointing directly at Charlie's head. Gasping, exhausted, and weak from the loss of blood, Campbell yelled, "Go ahead and shoot me!"

"Freeze!" Aksdal warned. "Stop right where you are."

"I'm not kidding," Campbell gasped. Pausing to catch his breath, he repeated, "Hey, fuckers, go ahead and shoot me."

In his recollection, Ed Aksdal said that he felt that Charlie really wanted to be shot. But the officers realized that the fugitive was spent and ready to drop. Blood still poured from the slashed wrist. The four officers easily subdued him, put him in one of the cars, and sped away to University Hospital. That night, the officers saw on a television news show that a photographer had somehow recorded part of the chase.

After Campbell received emergency treatment to the wound, which left a noticeable scar, he was discharged from the hospital and hauled back to Edmonds. The next day, inexplicably, he was granted probation again! Officers speculated that he had whined to a judge about wanting to be present for the impending birth of his child. They knew that Rosalie had returned from Okanogan to have her baby.

She delivered a daughter two weeks later, on March 30, 1974.

If Charles Campbell had persuaded the judge with a plea of paternal duties, his demonstration of them would have turned the stomachs of truly responsible fathers. Rosalie had complained to police several times of Charlie's mistreatment of her, which now extended to the baby as well. Seven days after her birth, police arrived at the home of Rosalie's parents in answer to a complaint that Charlie had threatened to kill the baby by throwing it through a plate glass window. In the presence of the officers, Campbell acted calm and denied the allegations. Rosalie said that he had even tried to kill the fetus before the baby was born.

Over the next few months, she suffered through a series of similar incidents with Charlie dangling his tiny child from a redwood deck, threatening to drop her twenty feet to the ground, and throwing a knife toward her play pen. The intimidation and beatings of Rosalie also continued unabated.

Campbell's reputation among Edmonds police had grown to the point where they figured each time they saw him, they might as well check him out, since he was probably wanted for something. Officer Wally Tribuzio, cruising along South County Beach on June 30, 1974, spotted Charlie driving an old Dodge pickup with a woman and a baby as passengers. When Tribuzio followed, Charlie pulled over and stopped in a graveled area. The officer rolled past and radioed for a driver's license check. Sure enough, Charlie's license had been suspended in March. Tribuzio wheeled around, pulled in next to the Dodge, and told Campbell, "Charlie, I've got to take you in for driving with a suspended license."

Campbell appeared "somewhat spooky" as he walked toward Tribuzio's car. When the officer asked Charlie to place his hands on the roof for a shakedown, Campbell jammed them in his pockets instead, hesitated for a moment, then "took off like a shot." Tribuzio knew of Charlie's reputation for running, and followed briefly. But when Campbell scaled a ten-foot fence, topped with barbed-wire, Tribuzio returned to his car and radioed for help to search the woods beyond the fence.

Back at the cars, Tribuzio found Rosalie in the pickup with the baby. She appeared "completely blitzed." Behind the seat, Tribuzio found a plastic bag containing "two dime bags, one nickel bag, and numerous loose tablets of speed." He arrested Rosalie and arranged for the baby to be taken to a foster home.

The search for Charlie in the woods that night proved fruitless. The next day, prosecutors issued a warrant for his arrest.

When Rosalie walked out of jail a few days later, she'd had all she could take. She recovered her baby daughter, left Charlie, and filed for divorce. Charlie heard about it on the run. It didn't surprise him. His mother had divorced Oliver Campbell that same year. Women, Charlie decided, were no damn good for anything.

Not long after Rosalie's departure, Charlie Campbell, a.k.a. Dan Leslie Kyle, found a job at the Pizza Palace in Renton.

Four

The narrow Okanogan River winds through central Washington and passes the tiny hamlet of Riverside thirty miles south of the Canadian border. Sheriff's Deputy James K. Weed had worn Okanogan County's badge for nearly three years of generally peaceful duty, rarely dealing with violent crimes. Even on New Year's day, 1976, he'd answered only a couple of complaints of drunken revelry. Two days later, though, things became a little rougher when he received a call requesting help for a man he knew from the nearby Colville Indian Reservation.

Tory Bearclaw, who wore his long dark hair in a ponytail, had been living temporarily in a home known locally as Old Hospital (for its use many years earlier). The owner had left town for a few weeks after hiring his pal, Bearclaw, to reside there and keep the place secure. In the early evening, Bearclaw was with four neighbor children he'd befriended, when he heard some muffled noises in another part of the house. As quietly as possible, he shooed the kids out the back door, crept toward the disturbance, and suddenly came face-to-face with a tall, lanky man wielding a sawed-off shotgun. In a cranky voice, the gunman demanded to know where the shotgun shells were stored.

Bearclaw, totally mystified about the gruff interrogation, said he didn't know of any ammunition anywhere in the house. Then, as his eyes grew accustomed to the dark room, he recognized the man as Chuck, someone he'd seen in a local tavern several times. Chuck, he recalled, had also met the owners of Old Hospital, and exchanged barroom chitchat with them at a local pub.

In a menacing voice, the intruder yelled, "I'm gonna tell you one last time, I wanna know where in hell the shells are!"

Cognizant of the gunman's obvious foul mood and disinclination to listen, Bearclaw ducked down, wheeled around a corner, and disappeared from "Chuck's" view and the weapon's range. Well hidden, he listened and heard sounds of footsteps leaving the building. Now angry, Bearclaw followed. Staying in dark shadows, he watched the thwarted burglar look over his shoulder several times, stuff the sawed-off shotgun down into his pants leg, then enter the Riverside Tavern. Bearclaw ran to a phone booth, and called the sheriff's office.

Deputy Jim Weed met Tory Bearclaw in front of the bar, and heard his account of earlier events. Just as the two men were about to enter the tavern, the gunman stepped out, carrying a paper bag containing a six-pack of beer he'd bought inside. Bearclaw pointed to him, shouting, "That's the guy!"

No small man himself, Weed had been running three miles a day, playing handball, and working himself into a solid two hundred pounds of muscle. Confronting the gunman, Weed ordered him to turn around and go back inside. Hesitating, while glaring at Weed, the suspect argued, "You step inside first."

"No, I'd just as soon you did," Weed snapped back. Chuck finally complied. In the bar, he placed the bag on the counter, and faced Weed. The deputy said, "I understand you've got a gun."

In a flash, the suspect lunged toward the exit, while Weed, equally fast, dove toward the fugitive like a blitzing linebacker. They collided in a tangle of arms and legs, tumbling onto the concrete floor and wrestling out to an exterior sidewalk. Grunting and flailing, both men rolled underneath a parked car. The bartender/owner, who knew the deputy, followed them out. During the melee, Bearclaw, who had been waiting in Weed's car, leaped out and tried to help the deputy. At last, Weed managed to pin the suspect's arms and, while trying to snap handcuffs on him, asked the bartender to pull the shotgun out of the antagonist's pants leg. Later, the bartender commented that if he'd known Chuck was packing a shotgun, he would have gone out the back door rather than follow the combatants.

Perspiring and bruised, Jim Weed finally slammed the back door of his cruiser, securing a cursing, violent suspect whom he'd be glad to see locked up. Chuck reacted in wild rage. He tried to kick the car windows out.

At the jail, officials identified "Chuck" as Charles Edward Johnston. His arrest also solved another local crime, nearly one month old. The occupant of a log cabin, down Okanogan River near the town of Omak, had complained of someone breaking and entering his domain and stealing a Remington Model 878 Wing-Master 12-gauge shotgun. The serial number matched the one found on Campbell, who had sawed the twenty-two-inch barrel down to eleven inches, violating a federal firearms act.

According to local records, Charles Johnston had a residential address in Mallot, a few miles south of Omak. He'd listed his birthplace as Oahu, Hawaii, birthdate 10-21-52, height 6'6" a slim 170 pounds, sandy blond brown hair. He'd recently worked short periods of time for a couple of local employers.

When Johnston at last sat behind bars, Jim Weed observed, "Charlie is stronger than an ox, very wiry. He's an unusual man and he doesn't fit the criminal stereotype." A couple of days later, when Weed transported Charlie to a doctor for a checkup, the furious inmate challenged the deputy to take off his badge and gun so they could settle the matter between them. Weed declined the invitation.

Another complaint came in on the following morning regarding Chuck's use of the shotgun. Georgia Hollister told Deputy Larry Hamilton that Chuck had threatened to kill her with the weapon.

"Charlie, or Chuck, or whatever they call him," she drawled, lived at a small complex motel-bar-restaurant named Elkhorn. She paused, working over her chewing gum, waiting for Hamilton's acknowledgment that he knew the place.

"Okay, what did he do?"

"Well, about two weeks ago this Monday, the twenty-second

of December . . . 'cause that was my anniversary, I was at Elkhorn with my boyfriend." They had paid a visit, she said, to a friend named Dave, who lived next door to Chuck. And Dave sulked in deep depression. When Georgia asked him why, Dave tearfully confided to his visitors that his wife was next door, in Chuck's room.

"It made me mad," Georgia complained, "because I was drinking a little bit and felt sorry for Dave. They have two little babies." She stormed next door, battered on Chuck's door, and ogled wide-eyed, with her mouth gaping open, when Chuck answered.

He stood there, with the door completely open, stark naked.

"Want do you want?" Chuck snarled.

Undaunted, Georgia shot right back, "You happen to have this other man's wife in your room. They have two little kids." Indignantly, she let him know that it just wasn't right.

Pausing for effect, Georgia continued. "So Chuck just started shaking all over, and he says, 'Get out of here, you bitch.' There was a big hassle and Dave's wife just walked out." The owner arrived, Georgia said, and told Chuck that he would have to move. Furious, Chuck packed and left that same night.

Warming up to her story, Georgia told Hamilton that a few days later, Dave's wife had met her at Elkhorn and said, "Georgia, I'm scared to death of Chuck. When he comes back, he's gonna kill me." Georgia invited her to hide out in her residence for a while.

"In the meantime," Georgia continued, "Chuck seen my daughter at Elkhorn. She's seventeen. And he drew back his hand like he was gonna hit her. He asked where I was at. Then, he came to my house, walked right through my front door without knocking." Inside, she said, he threatened another daughter, then stormed out to the front yard when the cuckolded Dave arrived. Chuck started waving around a sawed-off shotgun and held it against Dave's stomach.

With a final dramatic flourish, Georgia told Hamilton that Chuck had announced to everyone that when he found her, he planned to kill her. The deputy, having taped the entire conversation, told Georgia that Chuck was now behind bars, so she really didn't have anything to worry about. Georgia gave him a relieved sigh, rose, and sauntered out. Hamilton dutifully wrote out a report of the incident.

Deputy Jim Weed would later reveal that Charles Johnston had seriously threatened him. "A lot of guys will tell you that they're going to get you," Weed recalled, "and you would pass it off. But I couldn't do that with Charlie. I think he's vindictive and vengeful and it shows up in how cocky he is." The deputy added that he considered the possibility of Charlie escaping "extremely high." "Just the way he walks, and talks, makes me think he'd try anything. You could beat on him all you want, and he wouldn't even say ouch. I think Charlie has a screw loose, and he's about as bad a dude as I've ever seen around Okanogan."

Weed frowned and prophetically added, "I really worry about people who testify against Charlie."

While the inmate known as Charles Johnston cooled his heels in the Okanogan County jail, waiting to be arraigned, Snohomish County sheriff's officers continued the search for Charles Rodman Campbell, a.k.a. Dan Leslie Kyle, a suspect in the sexual assault of Renae Wicklund, and wanted for suspicion of theft from a pizza restaurant.

"Johnston" made the mistake of writing to a cousin in Edmonds to lament his situation in Okanogan. Word spread quickly through the family.

Betty Lou Campbell heard the news, too. She agonized over it for several days, then made a tough decision. She picked up a telephone and called Officer Bob Vaughn of the Renton Police Department. She told the astonished cop that her son, Charles Rodman Campbell, had been arrested in Okanogan County under the alias Charles Edward Johnston.

Within two days, a comparison of records confirmed the news. The King County prosecutor, in Seattle, called his counterpart in Okanogan County to advise him of the pending charges against

Charles Campbell for the Pizza Palace theft. Snohomish County officials filed a request to bring him back to face trial for the attack on Renae Wicklund.

On January 26, 1976, Campbell stood in an Okanogan courtroom and pled guilty to second-degree burglary of "Old Hospital." The judge, scanning the defendant's long record of criminal activity and the extant charges in the two other counties, wondered how this man had escaped appropriate punishment for so long. He sentenced Campbell to serve fifteen years in prison for the burglary.

Within days, Snohomish deputies arrived to whisk Campbell back across the Cascades to face another trial.

In the Snohomish County jail, Campbell pulled a very serious April Fool's stunt. A little after midnight on April 1, he rose silently from his bunk, pulled the wool blanket into his lap, and began tearing it into strips. After twisting a few of them together to form a rope, he repeated the process with his sheet. In his own words, Campbell described what he did next.

"I attempted to take my own life by hanging myself in my cell after lockup. I stood upon my bed, tied my feet together with some strips of blanket, then tied my neck to the bars with the sheet. I tied my hands together in a slip knot fashion, behind my back, and then kicked my feet out from under myself."

Deputy Ron Morrison, on guard that night, heard what he thought was the rattling of bars coming from somewhere down the dark corridor. He trotted along the front of each cell with a flashlight, trying to discover the source, but could see nothing. Waking inmates, he asked if they'd heard the sounds, but few of them showed any interest. Moving quickly into tank number 9, he heard someone shout, "Hey, the guy in the next cell needs help."

At cell 7, Morrison shined his light inside, and saw a body upright against the bars. Instantly, Morrison called for help, rushed to the control box, and opened Campbell's cell. Two other guards who had joined him by that time ran in and lifted a gasping Charles Campbell down. Charlie had done a good job tying the knots around his wrists and ankles, which held him securely while the officers attended to him. They frisked the inmate, then rushed him to another room for a strip search. No contraband turned up, so Morrison arranged for Campbell to be transported to nearby Providence Hospital where he received emergency treatment. He survived with nothing but a few scratches and bruises around his throat. If he had really tried to kill himself to escape facing trial, his effort failed miserably.

According to the laws of the state of Washington, Renae Wicklund had not been raped. Charles Rodman Campbell faced charges of sodomy, instead. In the legal language of Count I, the "defendant wilfully, unlawfully and feloniously did carnally know one Renae Wicklund, a human being over the age of fifteen (15) years, and did voluntarily submit to carnal knowledge by mouth and tongue of the victim."

Count II charged Campbell with assault with a deadly weapon.

Nervous but determined, Renae Wicklund courageously stepped up to the witness stand in the Snohomish County Court on April 19, 1976, sixteen months after the most terrifying and disgusting ordeal of her young life. Charles Campbell glared at her from the defense table, but she avoided looking at him. The thought of revealing details, in front of all these strangers, by telling how he'd violated her, made her sick. Too many women who suffer rape have difficulty finding the strength to tell the story in court, but Renae wanted Campbell punished for his outrageous conduct. And she had the courage to see it through.

Deputy Prosecuting Attorney John F. Segelbaum asked his questions softly, considerate of her discomfort. Renae described what she'd been wearing that afternoon when she stepped outside to wash some windows, and how she'd spotted Campbell in her driveway. Jurors and spectators remained hushed as she told how he'd demanded that she remove her clothing, while her terrified daughter, Shannah, only sixteen months old, watched every move and cried.

"During the act of the forced oral sodomy," Segelbaum asked, "did the defendant have an erection?"

"Yes, he did," Renae said. "He held the back of my head with his right hand and started pushing my head against him with rhythmic motions."

Segelbaum seemed reluctant to ask the next question. "Then what happened?"

With a stoic, impassive expression, Renae said, "He climaxed. It only took a few seconds."

Barely audible groans of indignation could be heard in the room when Renae told how Campbell had said "Thanks" just before he fled.

When Segelbaum asked Renae if the man who attacked her was in the courtroom, she spoke clearly and firmly. "Yes," she articulated, and pointed her finger, like a loaded weapon, toward the face of Charles Campbell. Clad in a green dress shirt and dark slacks, he gazed back at her with undiluted malevolence.

Renae told the jurors how she "halfway dressed" and took Shannah with her to Barbara Hendrickson's house.

"Why did you drive?" It was such a short distance.

"I thought possibly that, since he came from one direction (east) and left in the other direction (west) that maybe there was someone sitting at the bottom of the hill waiting for him in a car. And I was hoping to get a license number or something, or have some idea where he went."

Renae couldn't remember exactly what she had told Barbara Hendrickson. "I think I told her I'd been raped or there was someone there, or something. . . ."

Again, a quiet rumble came from the gallery when Renae quoted Campbell's threat, "Get your clothes off right now, or I'll kill the kid, and I mean it."

On cross-examination by appointed Defense Attorney Larry M. Trivett, Renae stated that she was positive what direction the intruder had taken when he left. Trivett also wanted to know what the suspect had worn. Renae described the red and black plaid shirt, buttoned at the cuffs and neck, blue jeans, and dark brown cowboy boots with pointed tips.

"Were you hysterical when you drove the car?"

With a slight frown of incredulity, Renae answered, "Yes, I'm sure I was."

Renae's protective neighbor and good friend, Barbara Hendrickson, took the stand next. "I was sitting in the kitchen having a cigarette and coffee," she said, and had heard a knock on the door. When Renae rushed in, Hendrickson recalled, "She was very upset, borderline hysterical. Shannah was crying, too."

The defense attorney had no questions, so Barbara Hendrickson stepped down. Her testimony lasted just a little less than five minutes.

Next came the rookie deputy, now far more experienced, who had responded to Hendrickson's emergency telephone call. Ken Christensen, strongly sympathetic of Renae after the crime, had taken on the roll of her *de facto* protector, accompanying her to court and sitting with her in the waiting area. He later recalled that she seemed "fearful" during the trial and afraid that Campbell would get off. She expressed concern to the officer that even if the jury convicted Campbell, he might receive a lenient sentence and come after her when released. "That's why I tried to give her moral support," Christensen said.

Two more detectives testified, detailing how Renae had identified Campbell in a photo lay down shortly after the assault, and in a live lineup just one month before the trial began.

After the prosecutor had rested his case, Defense Attorney Trivett put the manager of the Pizza Palace on the stand to describe the plaid shirt Campbell had worn to work. It might have had other colors in it besides red and black, the witness said. A secretary for the restaurant testified after the manager, and gave information about "Dan Kyle's" time card for December 11.

Betty Lou Campbell, looking depressed, took the oath next. After divorcing Oliver, who had moved to Alaska to work as a teamster, Betty Lou had worked a clerical job at Sears and Roebuck to support herself. She had mixed feelings about testifying for her son, but felt it the correct thing to do. She told jurors that she had bought most of the clothing Charlie owned, but she'd never purchased any jeans. He'd lived with her for nearly a month while he worked at the pizza restaurant.

"Did he ever have any jeans?" Trivett asked.

"When he first came back to live with me," Betty Lou answered. "But they were so shot, I threw them away."

"Did he ever wear plaid shirts?"

Betty Lou thought for a moment, then said, "He had a blue and white one, and a red, blue, and white one."

"No red and black shirt?"

"No." To the question of how he wore them, Betty Lou answered, "He always rolled up the sleeves and left the collar unbuttoned."

Charlie's boots, the mother insisted, were motorcycle boots, with rounded toes, not pointed. He had once owned a pair of cowboy boots, but not since he was about fifteen years old. To her knowledge, he had never carried a knife.

Campbell had told people that he graduated from high school, but Betty Lou said he dropped out during the ninth grade. Revealing this, Trivett strategized, would prevent the prosecution from bringing up a lie by the defendant.

"How did Charles get around when he needed transportation?"

"Hitchhiked or walked. When he stayed with me, it was about a twenty-minute walk to the pizza restaurant. Sometimes I gave him a ride. On December eleventh, he rode to work with his new roommate."

Recalling Renae's testimony that the suspect had a two- or three-days' growth of whiskers, Trivett asked Betty Lou if Campbell shaved every day.

"He didn't need to." She smiled. "He had no beard." Jurors and spectators swiveled their heads toward Campbell, but they couldn't decide if he had shaved closely or truly never needed to shave.

Prosecutor Segelbaum got right to the point on cross-examination. "Did you see Charles Campbell on December 11, 1974?" No, Betty Lou admitted, she hadn't. And she couldn't be absolutely sure that he didn't have any jeans, but thought that all of his pants, maroon, beige, and black corduroys, were kept in a drawer in his bedroom. She had not seen him after he disappeared on December 14.

The trial was not highly publicized. Most newspapers didn't bother to report it, and television reporters completely ignored it. Still, the word got around on the second morning that Charles Campbell would testify in his own behalf. Benches in the gallery held twice as many spectators as the day before.

Campbell, appearing confident and maybe a little cocky, said that he remembered December 11 only because it was a Wednesday which was smorgasbord day in the Pizza Palace. That meant all the pizza you could eat, of various types, for a set price. Yes, he said, he'd worn a multicolored flannel shirt that day, with the sleeves rolled all the way up and unbuttoned at the neck. "I have no jeans. And I had motorcycle boots on, as round at the toe as the boots I'm wearing right now." People strained to see his footwear.

Asked about his transportation modes, Campbell answered, "I didn't drive a car at that time and I didn't own one. Mostly, I hitchhiked." Usually, he said, he walked to work during November, from his mom's place to the Pizza Palace.

"How far was it?"

"About a half mile. Took me about twenty minutes." One observer thought that seemed to be a pretty leisurely pace. As if he had read the calculator's mind, Campbell quickly added that he sometimes strolled through the mall and window shopped on the way.

The defense attorney zeroed in on Campbell's time card at the restaurant, revealing that the manager had failed to adjust the machine clock to the correct date. When employees punched in on December 11, the date on the card indicated November 10. On the day of the crime, December 11, Campbell had punched in at three-fifty P.M., and out at ten-ten that night. Renae had been attacked less than thirty miles from the Pizza Palace at about two that afternoon. Could Campbell have committed the crime, then made it back to the restaurant in less than two hours? At the break, spectators figured he could have covered the distance easily, even hitchhiking.

Regarding that distance, Campbell said, "I don't even know where she lives. I've never seen her before today."

On cross, Segelbaum asked, "What do you do before you go to work?"

Campbell replied with unexpected candor, "Usually stay home and drink."

"Why did you use the assumed name Dan Kyle?"

With a smirk, Campbell shot back, "Because I chose to."

Calmly, Segelbaum asked, "Why did you choose to?"

Now a little less comfortable, Campbell answered, "Well . . . because I did not want my income tax coming."

"I don't understand," said the prosecutor.

"I did not file for income tax." Campbell sounded like a defensive kid caught misbehaving.

"What does that have to do with using the name Dan Kyle?"

His voice shrill, Campbell's reply was garbled. "Well, as far as the name goes, the job I was working under was an assumed name and there was no reason, in my particular position, to have anything where I should file anything of my own true name."

Shaking his head quizzically, Segelbaum persisted. "So you were trying to deceive the I.R.S.? Is that what you're telling me?"

"I did not state that."

"Is that why you used the name Dan Kyle?"

"No, it is not."

"Perhaps you can explain a little better, then." Trivett objected.

"Be overruled," Judge Phillip Sheridan droned.

Campbell realized he couldn't evade the issue any longer. His voice sounding resigned, he admitted, "The police were looking for me."

"Why?"

"Because I got busted for drugs in June of seventy-four."

With that admission, which the prosecutor felt gave the jury a glimpse of Campbell's true nature, Segelbaum moved on to other subjects. Charlie's access to the Pizza Parlor cash register, where he'd lived and what kinds of transportation he used came under scrutiny. Campbell admitted that he sometimes traveled in taxis, but denied ever going to Bothell.

"Do you know a young lady named Darlene Bolt?" Segelbaum asked. Campbell had blundered again, not realizing that the prosecutor had located the university student he'd visited in Bothell the morning of December 11. He admitted knowing and seeing Darlene at her Bothell home. But not on December 11, he said. He claimed that it must have been December 14.

Pressed on the point, Campbell suddenly couldn't remember anything about December 11. Wasn't sure what he did that day, except work. It was just another day, nothing special to remember about it.

"Did you wear a red and black plaid shirt on December eleventh?" Segelbaum barked.

"No, I did not."

"Are you absolutely sure?"

"Positive!"

Rubbing his chin, Segelbaum asked, "I thought you just testified that December eleventh wasn't anything particularly significant to you?"

Squirming, apparently feeling trapped again, Campbell replied, "Well . . . considering that the night I left—"

Segelbaum interrupted, "Didn't you testify to that, Mister Campbell?"

"Pardon?" Campbell stalled.

"Did you testify to that?" Louder now.

"To what?" Clearly struggling.

"That December eleventh was just another day of the year."

"Yes, I did."

Sensing that Campbell had started to cave in, Segelbaum

changed course again. "Do you remember whether you carried a knife in December, 1974?"

"Yes, I've been known to carry a knife." But, Campbell added, he didn't think it was possible that he had one that particular night.

"Did you show Darlene Bolt a knife?" Campbell started to waffle again, trying to argue about when he'd visited Bolt, then finally denied showing her a knife.

The final witness, Darlene Bolt, testified that she'd met Charlie two years earlier and had seen him about a dozen times. Yes, she had seen him the week of December 11, and she thought it was on Wednesday. He'd surprised her, showing up early that morning. After about forty-five minutes, he'd left in a cab, at her request.

"Do you recall what he wore on that day?" Segelbaum asked.

"I believe a plaid shirt . . . with red in it." She'd seen it several times before.

Asked to describe how Campbell wore it, Bolt said, "All buttoned up at the sleeves and the neck." She also recalled that he often wore cords, but sometimes he dressed in blue jeans.

"Did he ever talk about carrying a knife?"

"Yes, he said he usually carried one." He'd even taken one out of his pocket to show her. She thought it looked like a kitchen knife.

In his final argument to the jury, prosecutor John Segelbaum would like to have revealed something he considered important, but the information could not be legally admitted into the trial. Campbell had agreed to take a polygraph examination, arrogantly confident that he could beat it. The needles had jumped nearly off the graph when the polygrapher asked Campbell about specific facts related to the attack on Renae Wicklund. Afterward, when questioned about his deceptive responses, Campbell said that he had "this incident confused with another incident involving a different girl." Segelbaum knew of the other case in which a man had forced a woman to perform oral sex by threatening to kill her baby, then taken a taxi to the same neighborhood of

Bothell where Campbell had visited Darlene Bolt. Campbell's comments convinced him that the same man had committed both crimes. It frustrated Segelbaum that inadequate evidence from the other case would prevent him from prosecuting Campbell. If only he could tell the jurors, but he couldn't.

After both attorneys had completed summarizing their cases to the jury, Judge Sheridan read instructions to the panel, intended to clear up the specific laws. He explained, "Every person who shall force another person to carnally know him by the anus or with the mouth or tongue shall be guilty of the crime of sodomy. To carnally know another person includes the penetration of the mouth of a female by the sexual organ of the male. You are instructed that under the laws of the State of Washington, any sexual penetration, however slight, is sufficient to complete carnal knowledge." Regarding Count II, Sheridan commented, "A deadly weapon includes any knife with a blade longer than three and one-half inches."

The trial had started at nine o'clock Monday morning. Judge Sheridan's instructions ended by noon, Wednesday.

Before four o'clock, that same Wednesday, the jury filed back into the box and announced their verdict. Charles Rodman Campbell was guilty of the crimes of sodomy and first-degree assault.

Sixteen days later, Judge Sheridan sentenced Campbell to serve ten years in prison for Count I, sodomy, and twenty years for Count II, assault. He ordered that the sentences be served consecutively. This in addition to the fifteen years imposed by the Okanogan County judge. It sounded like Campbell would be in prison for forty-five years.

"Thank God," Renae Wicklund sighed in the arms of her friends. Her tormenter, she figured, even with time off for good behavior, would be locked up at least until he reached middle age. She would be safe from any threat of vengeance that might fester in his twisted mind.

Five

The first step for convicts entering the Washington State Reformatory system is to undergo a battery of physical and mental tests, observations, questionnaires, and diagnostic study at the Shelton Reception Center, near the capital, Olympia. Doctors and administrators try to learn as much as possible about incoming prisoners in order to place them in appropriate institutions throughout the state.

One of the fact-finding tools involves taking written statements from close relatives. On May 17, Campbell's mother, Betty Lou, wrote some very personal observations about her son. Drugs, she noted, had been at the core of his problems. She acknowledged that his home life hadn't been very "neat," and concluded the document by writing, "Charlie has some very weird ideas on women. I definitely think he has some odd sex problems and needs sexual rehabilitation." She attached an additional note, in which she suggested that he'd once had sex with a dog.

A psychologist, Doctor Felix E. Massaia, questioned Campbell about the allegation of bestiality. Charlie shrugged it off saying that it probably stemmed from having kiddingly told a relative in Okanogan that he'd had sexual intercourse with a dog. It never really happened, he claimed. Campbell did admit, though, to having once lost patience with his dog for refusing to obey his command to stop running away from him. He chased the dog down, caught it, and "choked it to death." In his explanation, Campbell blamed his cruel act on being drunk and angry.

Maybe, Campbell lamely rationalized, his mother thought killing the animal was sadistic and had confused it with a sex act.

Charles Campbell, Massaia observed, "makes use of massive denial . . . and is impaired by a high degree of emotional constriction as well as inability to resolve inner conflict pertaining to sexuality."

Massaia noted that Campbell expressed a desire to serve his time in a reformatory instead of a penitentiary because he feared hard-time convicts in the pen would brutalize him over the "skin beef," prison jargon for a sexual conviction. Rapists, or in this case, sodomizers, are the sewer rats of inmate hierarchies, on the same level as killers of children. Campbell said he would vigorously fight anyone who tried to make a "punk" of him, meaning to use him sexually.

Sometimes, inner sexual tension may be directly associated with strong religious feelings. Not so with Campbell. He stated that he thought his family was Protestant, but he wasn't exposed to any religious training or services while growing up.

He may not have feared God, but he seemed worried about how other convicts might treat him. In a fit of self-pity, Campbell told the psychologist, "I'll probably never get out of prison alive. Somebody will kill me before I ever get paroled." Massaia counseled him against the dangers of self-fulfilling prophesies he called "writing a losing life script."

Regarding the crimes for which he'd been convicted, Campbell claimed absolute innocence. He acknowledged committing a series of minor infractions during his youth, but "showed no shame or embarrassment and expressed no remorse or guilt." Massaia, noting the absence of any guilt feelings, asked Campbell why he'd tried to commit suicide.

"I had my reasons," Campbell said, refusing to explain. The bungled attempt, Massaia speculated, may have been a manipulative attempt to obtain psychiatric attention. Evidently, Campbell thought he'd been denied a fair mental diagnosis when Snohomish County authorities decided he was "in excellent contact with reality, knowledgeable of his actions, and responsible for his behavior." Charlie certainly didn't want to admit any personal responsibility.

He didn't want to admit, either, that he'd been a dropout before reaching high school. On his social history form, Campbell listed attendance in the tenth grade at Edmonds High School during 1971. The registrar there answered an inquiry, and stated that no attendance records existed for Charles Rodman Campbell, or for that matter, Dan Leslie Kyle.

Most of Campbell's statements during psychological interviews, whether lies or truth, were spoken with little emotion. The one emotion Campbell did manifest, Felix Massaia later wrote, "was a frustrated, seething anger . . . a great hostility toward his social environment." It made him "relate to other people from an aggressive stance, creating the impression he was a bellicose individual." Conversely, Massaia noted, Campbell "rationalized, projected, and intellectualized," indicating his awareness of what is expected of the individual to live in harmony with the community. In other words, Campbell could "talk the talk."

A vocational counselor also tested and interviewed Campbell. He wrote, "Charles is arrogant with an attitude bordering on insolence. He is outspoken, too loud most of the time, and frequently challenges authority. His cooperation was marginal. He claims to have experience in a wide variety of skills. Primary interests are not well established. He says (he's interested in) possibly carpentry or college." Apparently, Campbell wasn't so glib, and didn't "talk the talk" with someone who wanted to discuss putting him to work.

The Classification Board at Shelton Reception Center analyzed the data gathered on Charles Campbell and decided that he should be incarcerated at the State Reformatory in Monroe, in Snohomish County. He would be locked up close to home, not quite twenty miles from Edmonds, where he'd spent most of his youth, and less than ten miles from Clearview, the site of his attack on Renae Wicklund.

The Board of Prison Terms and Paroles set Campbell's minimum time to be served at seven and one-half years! No one bothered to tell his victims that the sentences of ten, twenty, and fifteen years, to be served "consecutively," didn't really add up to forty-five years behind bars. Many people had the impression that, even with time off for good behavior, he would have to serve at least half of his sentence.

The chance still remained, of course, that bad behavior in prison would result in Campbell staying locked up much longer than the shockingly low minimum.

Prisoner number 629817, Charles Rodman Campbell, arrived at the Monroe Reformatory in early June, 1976. He'd seen the place before, but not from the inside. It's the most noticeable structure in the town of Monroe, and occupies a promontory which overlooks the whole valley. The community is a bucolic one, straddling Federal Highway 2, surrounded by lushly forested hills. From the town center, a road climbs to a well-manicured park, then makes a big loop in front of an imposing, buff-colored edifice stretching the length of a city block. It might be a college campus, except for the high, wire fences. Behind the impressive facade of the main building, a cluster of rectangular, harsher units sit at juxtaposition and cover the remainder of the hill. They are a jarring contrast to the pastoral scene below.

Campbell's personality didn't take very long to start grating on people in Monroe, other inmates as well as "institutional staff" (their preferred description, as opposed to "guards"). By mid-July, he faced a staff committee to explain why he had refused to submit to a body search.

"I'm new here," Campbell complained. "I've only been here a month and a half, and another dude came up behind me and hit me in the mouth. I went looking for him in the big yard, and I had a stick under my coat when the officer stopped me and asked me to submit to a body search." Charlie didn't bother to explain where he'd obtained the stick. "I told him 'No,' and

I walked away out into the big yard. I caught the guy and asked him why he hit me, and he wouldn't say."

The other inmate, Campbell said, had challenged him to meet in the yard for a fight. But Campbell feared the likelihood of facing a whole gang of men in the compound. "So that's why I took the stick." As an excuse for refusing the search, Campbell said, "I was very upset."

Officer Al Gould, sitting on the committee, had a slightly different version. He revealed that he'd first met an irate Campbell two weeks earlier, when inmates had been rousted out of their bunks for a roll call after a previous count hadn't tallied properly. "Charlie was acting pissed-off." Gould reported that Campbell opened his trousers, exposed himself, and while loudly complaining about the officers' inability to count, made a vulgar demand that Gould perform oral sex on him.

Charlie had apparently decided to challenge authority, in a grossly undiplomatic manner, early in his stay at Monroe.

About the refusal to obey the order in the July incident, Gould said that he'd been warned by another officer that Campbell might be carrying a club to use in retaliation for a minor skirmish with a black inmate. When Gould found Charlie in a hallway leading to the yard, the officer saw an obvious bulge in Campbell's shirt. He ordered Charlie to submit to a strip search, but the stubborn convict blatantly refused and walked away. Fifteen minutes later, two officers escorted Campbell into a room where he complied with the request, after telling them that he'd already disposed of the stick. "Do you guys know I'm a suicide risk?" Charlie asked, during the search. "If you send me to the hole, I won't be able to handle it. I'll probably kill myself." They never found the club, and they did not send Campbell to Block 3, the isolation unit.

The committee found Campbell guilty of disobeying a lawful order. As punishment, they took away all of his evening activities (television, radio) for thirty days. They softened the sanction by applying the standard policy of suspending implementation for

ninety days, providing the individual can avoid any "major infractions" during that time.

Campbell didn't make the ninety days. On August 30, an officer observed Charlie covertly trying to carry something into
the housing area. He had it under his arm, covered by a green
institution shirt. After escorting Campbell into the lieutenant's
office, the officer uncovered the object, revealing a jug containing approximately one gallon of "pruno." Distilled from vege-
table matter, potatoes, or any fruit available, with yeast, pruno
(prison jargon for contraband homemade alcoholic beverage) is
a potent drink that has been used among convicts since prisons
first came into existence.

Again, Campbell faced the committee and received the harsh
punishment of two weeks' suspension of evening activities.

One of the differences between a penitentiary and reformatory
is the decor of the housing units (not cellblocks) for the residents
(not inmates, though guards frequently slip and use the politically
incorrect older terms). To outsiders, it's startling to hear about
curtains in the cell of a convict paying a debt to society for a
serious felony. But, two days before the end of 1976, Monroe
resident Charles Campbell once again stood before the committee, accused of removing the curtains from his "house" (prisoner
jargon for cell). He protested. "There ain't no way you're gonna
stick me with this. This is a kangaroo court." Pleading not guilty
to "destruction of state curtain in cell," he even wrote to the
reformatory superintendent to appeal his sentence of five days'
confinement in his cell. "I have been convicted for something I
didn't do," he scribbled. Maybe someone else "took the curtain
from my house." He suggested that the committee probably
found him guilty because he called them a kangaroo court. Finally, Campbell resorted to something completely out of character: tact. "I would appreciate your honesty, sir, and I know that
if you are a decent man, you will not find me guilty."

The superintendent saw no reason to rescind the finding or the sentence.

One hundred and thirty miles to the southeast, in Richland, Westley Allan Dodd, who turned sixteen that year, faced a juvenile court judge. Convicted of lewd conduct with a minor, Dodd apologized, saying, "I'm done with hurting kids that way."

Charles Campbell managed to stay out of trouble for most of 1977, with the exception of slugging another resident in November, for which he received ten days' restriction. On the final day of the year, he exploded again.

That New Year's Eve, Charlie had a cold, but had missed getting in line for medicine at the five-fifteen P.M. sick call. At six-twenty, he pounded on the closed window of the dispensations desk, then sat a few feet away, fuming and pouting. Nurse Vonnie Carney told him he would have to wait until the nine-twenty line-up. Charlie erupted. He wadded up the medical slip he'd been given, threw it on the floor, then raised his fist and leaped out of the chair in Carney's direction.

"Are you trying to scare me?" she calmly asked.

"I'll do worse if you don't give me my fucking medicine," Campbell shouted, springing toward her. A physician's assistant, Robert Lascher, stepped in and grabbed Campbell's arm, stopping him within inches of Nurse Carney. She felt sure that he intended to belt her in the face if Lascher hadn't interceded.

In a subsequent report, Carney said, "I'd been threatened before, but it wasn't like this incident. Charlie is very intimidating."

With the help of an attendant, Bob Lascher escorted Campbell to Block 3, where violent inmates could be separated from the general population. Charlie stayed there for nearly a week. Upon release, he once again came to the "medline" window to receive prescription drugs from Nurse Carney. Not quite so loudly this time, he called her a fucking bitch.

For Nurse Carney, Campbell was a nightmare. "He assaulted two other inmates," she recalled. "I heard nothing pleasant about Charlie. He extorted sex and goods from other residents."

Robert Lascher also remembered Campbell. "Charlie could become angry instantly and very aggressive. He was a 'flipper,' meaning he would lose his temper and flip out."

The thing that remained in both Lascher's and Carney's memory puzzled them: Charles Campbell's "offenses were never written up for whatever reason."

Campbell waited over three months, until mid-March, 1978, before letting his temper flare again, this time with near disastrous results. At the noon meal, in a dining hall filled with over three hundred fifty men, and forty more in line, Charlie and two buddies strolled in, walked past the line, cut in, grabbed plastic trays and demanded to be served. Campbell loudly groused about pizza being on the menu for lunch again.

A white-clad food server behind the counter, who didn't particularly like Campbell, refused to dish any food onto Charlie's tray, and growled, "You can go to the end of the line."

Because the line had stalled to a halt while Campbell argued with the server, a rumble of anger rippled among the hungry men, while those already eating stopped to see what was happening. The inmates, as usual, had segregated themselves into racial and gang groups. Campbell stood closest to a section of African American prisoners.

Recognizing the volatility of the situation, three officers rushed forward to break it up and avert a possible disaster. Campbell's two cohorts meekly complied with orders to go back to the end of the line. But not Charlie. He stood there cursing and demanding to be served. Officer Ron Gamble twice ordered Campbell to step out of line and go to the rear, and twice Charlie refused. The rumble grew louder in the entire mess hall.

As Ron Gamble moved toward him, Campbell yelled, "Keep your hands off me." Then with rounded eyes sparking fire, he raised the tray above his head and smashed it down onto an adjacent table. It shattered, sending shards flying in all directions. One African American inmate jumped up on his stool, and several more stood up. Within seconds, men sprang to their feet everywhere in the room, shouting, some standing on their stools.

Charlie's mouth twisted into an evil grin; then he capitulated and accompanied Ron Gamble out of the mess hall. The tension and furor subsided quickly as men sat back down and resumed eating their meals.

The inmate who had been the first to leap up on his stool later claimed that a sharp piece of the broken tray had struck his ankle, causing him to jump in pain. Maybe so. Otherwise, he might have been punished for contributing to a potential riot.

Officer Al Gould, who had crossed Charlie during his first two months at Monroe, witnessed the mess hall incident. He later said, "Charlie was told to go to the end of the line. His attitude was bad. One word could have set off the whole group. He always thought the rules were not for him. He knows the difference between right and wrong, but it does not apply to him."

For nearly provoking a deadly riot, Campbell got twenty days in Block 3 segregation. Five days of restricted activity were, according to policy, suspended for three months, provided no new major infractions occurred.

But Charlie couldn't stay out of trouble for a whole ninety days. On May 8, he got into a fight with another inmate, and had to serve two days of the previously levied restricted activity.

And, on May 24, he again refused to submit to a body search. An officer saw Campbell in the game room, weaving around, unsteady on his feet, and slurring his speech. "Come on to the sergeant's office with me," he ordered Campbell. Inside the office, it became obvious that Charlie had consumed something that made him woozy. But, as usual, Campbell became defiantly caustic when asked about it. He made a clumsy attempt to divert the officer's attention from one of his pockets, which had the reverse effect Charlie desired. After a violent scuffle, with Campbell kicking, biting, and head butting to resist a search, the officers restrained him with handcuffs and leg irons. Inside his jacket pocket they found a torn envelope containing three empty yellow capsules.

At the committee hearing, Campbell admitted taking three "downers" because he'd been having "stress over family problems." The punishment consisted of seven days in Block 3, and twenty days of restriction, all suspended if Charlie could stay out of trouble for ninety days. The committee seemed eternally optimistic.

Less than one-third of the ninety-day period had elapsed when Campbell walked out of the dining hall with a bulging pocket. Officer Larry Epperson stopped him for a pat down. Charlie, smiling giddily and staggering, much too cooperative, handed the suspicious Epperson a dozen cookies he'd stolen from the kitchen. The officer started to search him, but Campbell lost his temper and slapped Epperson's hand away, yelling, "Don't put your hands in my pockets." He bolted backward and ran. Four other officers chased and surrounded Campbell, struggling to subdue him. In the middle of the melee, Campbell threw a wadded envelope into a crowd of inmates who had gathered to watch.

Officer Frank Braun dove for the envelope, and after a short struggle retrieved it. Braun had previously been threatened by Charlie, who called him a "fucking pig bastard." Charlie became even more enraged when Braun just laughed at him.

The envelope recovered by Braun contained a needle and syringe. Charlie, screaming, kicking and swinging, had to be bodily lifted by four officers and carried to "three house."

This time, the committee imposed the restrictions accumulated from the previous incident, and added ten additional days of segregation. They suspended the latter sanction for ninety days, hoping again for infraction-free behavior. The more serious action by the committee included a written recommendation that Campbell be transferred to a Washington State Penitentiary. Administration officials rejected it.

* * *

The first signs of fall, 1978, colored the vine maples and dogwood around Monroe. It's a time that beckons men to tramp through the woods, inhaling the crisp air, reveling in freedom; a hard time to stay locked up. In late August a nasty rumor found its way to Monroe officials. A bulletin circulated to all watch lieutenants stating, "Reliable information has been received that inmate Campbell, #629817, may attempt to escape from this institution in the near future." All personnel were instructed to make every effort to know the whereabouts of Campbell at all times, and to watch for suspicious activities on his part. The alert included a complete description of the potential escapee, along with his tentative maximum time release date, January 23, 2000.

An officer who'd had his fill of conflicts with Campbell, Al Gould, recalled that Charlie's reputation was that of a troublemaker, a drug pusher's muscle, and a "rotten sonofabitch." He also felt that Charlie was a high escape risk, who might have been involved in two plans to bust out. One, he said, was in August, 1978, when everyone received an alert, which probably thwarted the attempt. Another, Gould thought, involved a scheme to leave via helicopter. All of the armed personnel were instructed, at the time, on how to shoot helicopters down. Fortunately for the institution, and probably for Charles Campbell, nothing ever came of any suspected escape plans. Officers thought Charlie probably worried that a failed attempt might land him in a tough penitentiary.

Perhaps afraid of being transferred to the pen, Campbell incurred no further official infractions. His most egregious criminal behavior during his remaining time at Monroe Reformatory stayed well hidden and unreported for years.

Fate sometimes has a funny way of reuniting old friends. Thomas Hawkins, who had been Charlie Campbell's best buddy in junior high school and had hung out with him in Edmonds during the mid-seventies, also found himself in hot water with the law. After the two pals left the drug-laden environment of the apartment in Edmonds, they went separate ways. Hawkins drifted over to Whidbey Island where he committed a series of petty crimes, then decided he could make more money by forging credit cards. It didn't work. When Island County police hauled him into court, he received a sentence of twenty years in the state reformatory. In mid-1978, he landed at Monroe.

The two childhood buddies met in the yard, embraced, and exchanged stories of their adventures. Within a few weeks, Charlie managed to exercise some influence and have Hawkins moved into his "house," in the C block, cell C-29.

Years later, controversy would rage over inmates wielding influence in the reformatory system. A so-called "favored inmate" system, in which prisoners "attained a special, cozy status at the old reformatory on the hill" made headlines. Accompanying articles even suggested that inmates acquired information about official corruption, and leveraged it into prison favors. State investigators probed the allegations, but turned up no proof of corruption or illegal activities. Rumors remained, however, that selected prisoners could get almost anything they wanted. It would seem impossible for Charles Campbell to attain favored inmate status, considering his outbursts against staff members. Nevertheless, his buddy, Hawkins, received permission for a transfer into Campbell's cell.

It turned out to be a real eye-opener for Tom Hawkins. "What are you here for?" he asked Charlie.

"Rape and robbery," Campbell replied, then elaborated with a story of kicking in a door where he'd raped and robbed a woman. His next comment didn't surprise Hawkins. "If I ever get out of here, I'm going to get the fuckers that put me here." Hawkins thought he meant the law enforcement people. It didn't even occur to him that Campbell might have been talking about the victims who had testified against him.

"I just laughed at him at that time," Hawkins later reported. "Because I didn't think he'd ever get out of there." Asked why he thought that, Hawkins replied, "Because of all the trouble he was always into." Hawkins explained that Campbell extorted drugs from other inmates "by scaring the hell out of them with threats of bodily harm." He also collected debts for other people, and fought all the time. Charlie's nickname, Hawkins said, was "One-punch Campbell."

Tom Hawkins' old buddy, and new cellmate, Charlie, turned out to be a rotten friend. Years later, Hawkins reported what happened.

"About two or three months before I got out of Monroe, Charlie raped me in our cell after lock-down. I was afraid to tell anybody (guards) about the rape because he would kill me if it got back to him. I got out of the cell afterward and got assigned to the fourth tier." Campbell continued to terrorize his old buddy, though. "About thirty days before I was released from Monroe, he told me that someone was going to kill me. He wouldn't tell me who (would do it), but I noticed him following me around. By that time, I was pretty afraid of Charlie Campbell, so I checked into P.C. (protective custody). I thought he was going to kill me."

Thomas Hawkins breathed a big sigh of relief when he finally walked out of Monroe, still alive, on December 6, 1978.

Hawkins was not Campbell's first rape victim in Monroe. Just two months before Hawkins settled in Campbell's "house," the previous cellmate, Jerry Peterson, experienced the same brutality.

Peterson spent about four weeks sharing a cell with Charlie, and watched Campbell use dope nearly every night, usually grass or speed. In conversations, mostly about sex, drugs, and getting out of prison, he learned that Charlie also loved to talk about violence. Physical strength, Charlie told Peterson, was the answer to everything. And women were only good for sex, kids, and cleaning the house. In an oblique reference to the crime that brought him to prison, Charlie told Peterson that "Someone is going to pay for the time I'm doing."

Charlie had been looking forward to a pending hearing that

might reclassify him to minimum custody and allow him to be transferred to the Honor Farm. On the afternoon of August 20, he came back to the cell in a foul mood. He'd been refused the reclassification. He groused, snorted, and fumed all evening, smoking dope and cursing. At about midnight, Campbell woke Peterson, abused him verbally, and ordered him to do fifty push-ups. Intimidated by Campbell's superior size and strength, Peterson rolled over onto his stomach, flattened his hands on his bed, stiffened his body, and began pushing up, then easing down. He pumped rapidly at first, slowed at twenty, and collapsed at twenty-five. He hadn't carried out the complete order, so Campbell punished him.

"I was suddenly grabbed from behind," he later recalled, "and held in a bear hug until I passed out." The next thing Peterson knew, Campbell had "yanked my pants off," and "poured oil on my butt." While pinning Peterson's arms, Campbell raped him from behind.

When he'd completed the act, Campbell growled to Peterson that if he told anyone, he'd be killed. Apparently still unsated, Campbell grabbed Peterson once more and tried to rape him again. But, according to Peterson, "He couldn't keep it up." Campbell stayed awake all night to keep an eye on Peterson and prevent him from summoning an officer.

Despite the threat of death, Peterson sought out a sergeant the next afternoon and reported that he'd been sexually assaulted by Campbell. After being cleared by the hospital, Peterson accepted reassignment to protective custody, then a transfer from Monroe.

Before long, Charlie had his eye on another new resident. Wes Hutchins arrived in Monroe in October, 1978. In later years, he described the problems of a new "duck." In prison, you can't just sit anywhere you see an empty seat. You must know someone and sit with them at "their" table. Hutchins received an invitation in the spring of '79 to join Campbell's table for a special reason.

Campbell had parted company with his "kid" (young homosexual slave, or punk) and needed a new one.

"Campbell began telling me how much he liked me, that he wanted to take care of me and make me his." The courting lasted about a week before Campbell finally cornered Hutchins and whispered that he'd better make up his mind. Nervous anyway, Hutchins noticed that Campbell had pulled his shirt aside to reveal a "shank," made from a sharpened brass bar, tucked in the front of his pants. When Campbell swaggered away, Hutchins felt gripped by real fear. "All the time before that, I thought he might be kidding." He could think of only one thing to do.

In a separate housing unit, he sought out another friend, told him of the dilemma, and asked to borrow a knife. He wanted to "end the problem once and for all." The pal didn't lend him a knife, but confided to a group who called themselves the "Lifers' Club." Members of the club accompanied Hutchins into the big yard, where the spokesman confronted Campbell and informed him that Hutchins wasn't going to be his kid, to go find himself a new duck.

Hutchins finally felt secure, having protection from the Lifers' Club. "Nobody in prison does time alone," he recalled. "It's almost a law of survival, to be associated with a group." Campbell, he said, was a real "sicko" or "ding."

The use of "punks" for sexual relief is not uncommon among prisoners. Campbell, who years earlier had beaten his wife severely for calling him a punk, might not have been one, but he seemed to have no aversion to using them.

Most members of the institutional staff agreed on critical assessments of Campbell. Officer Lonnie McGowan remembered that Charlie constantly exercised by running every day. One afternoon, McGowan watched as Campbell, during his run, repeatedly slammed himself headlong into a chain link fence. "He was strung out on drugs. I had to get help from other inmates to get him back into his cell. A nurse observed him foaming at the mouth, but said that he was just 'exhausted.' I think she didn't want to deal with him. I couldn't write it up because her medical opinion would override my lay person opinion." Campbell escaped write-ups frequently for similar reasons.

McGowan remembered hearing frequent rumors that Campbell involved himself in homosexual activities, but escaped official sanctions "because you can't convict on rumors." The officer found it frustrating that Campbell got away with refusing to obey orders, often used obscenities in face of staff, and openly collected debts related to brokering homosexual activities. "This kind of behavior," he noted, "occurs in only four or five inmates out of eight hundred and fifty."

Officer Larry Epperson described Campbell as a very violent and threatening type who would "funk up" young kids, meaning force them into homosexual activities. In psychotherapy groups, if anyone seemed to criticize Campbell, he'd deny guilt and become violent. "It had to be Charlie's way, or no way." Epperson thought he heard Campbell say one day, "that he was going to get that bitch who put him in there."

One member of the institutional staff didn't see Charles Campbell in the same negative light others saw. Ladonna Layton, an ex-nun, worked as a drug and alcohol abuse counselor at Monroe, also teaching human relations and communication skills to classrooms of volunteer inmates. Her credentials to perform the job included a Master of Arts degree in applied behavioral science, and the ability to express herself with articulation and intelligence. The program administrator pointed out that her job wouldn't be easy. "As a female developing therapeutic relationships with male clients in a maximum security institution . . . there are conditions that present a high degree of difficulty and challenge."

Not beautiful, but certainly attractive at age thirty-one, Ladonna didn't fear intermingling with nearly a thousand men who'd committed a variety of serious crimes.

Layton began her duties at Monroe in September, 1978. Before the year ended, Charles Campbell enrolled in one of her classes. His history of interaction with women included nothing but conflict, disrespect, and brutal domination. But something about Ladonna fascinated him and she began to win his interest. Officer Larry Epperson observed that Ladonna could calm Campbell down, and seemed to be the only one capable of doing it. "She talked him into being different."

He began to confide in Ladonna, who was seven years his senior. Some of the housing officers thought that Campbell showed a marked improvement in his overall behavior, while others wondered if the change was a self-serving attempt to shorten his stay in prison. If Campbell appeared "different" to Ladonna Layton and some of the Monroe officials, he didn't create that impression with an expert psychologist. During a routine psychological review in January, 1979, Dr. R. A. Maneman, Ph.D., spent an hour with Campbell and found him "cocky and challenging, almost to capricious mockery at times." He concluded that Campbell was "insensitive, blithely uncaring of others, conscienceless, malevolently intolerable of social order which imprisons him, and imminently harmful to all who directly or indirectly capture his attention or interest."

The warning bell didn't register with Ladonna Layton. After a few weeks, she reported seeing tremendous growth in Campbell. She felt that he'd taken a serious look at himself, and she complimented him for his "thoughtful, outgoing, and upbeat" participation in classes. "I feel positive about the direction he is taking himself," Layton told her boss.

At first, Campbell chose to be reticent about the crimes that had sent him to Monroe, but after several months of attending Ladonna's counseling session, he opened up to her. Easing into the subject, he told Ladonna that he'd been involved in petty offenses over the years, some of which could have sent him to jail. He'd been lucky to escape major punishment. When he finally got around to talking about the attack on Renae Wicklund, he declared his unequivocal innocence.

As the months passed, Campbell began to read more, joined a carpentry class, and continued in Ladonna's self-improvement courses. The relationship between them became more intense and emotional. Ladonna Layton found herself falling in love with Charlie Campbell, and felt that he loved her.

The growing bond with Campbell split her loyalties. She valued her job, but struggled with the idea that a relationship with one of the prisoners might violate professional ethics. Yet, she felt capable of providing objective counseling and teaching. The internal conflict caused her many sleepless nights. Should she continue working, trying to hide her love for Campbell, or simply resign?

Both Campbell's and Layton's efforts to conceal their feelings for each other had little success. Rumors ran wild among the inmates and staff. One officer commented that jealousy developed among the prison population over their perception that the relationship between Campbell and Layton involved sex. "The inmates felt that Charlie was getting some and they wanted to get some, too." The rumbles, rumors, and snide remarks grew throughout most of 1979, with increasing intensity. They finally became too much for Ladonna. In November, by mutual agreement with her employer, she left the job.

But she did not leave Charlie Campbell. If anything, the released pressure of the job conflict gave Ladonna more time to dwell on her affection for Charlie. She kept her apartment in a quiet residential section of Monroe, and visited him at least five or six times every week.

Whatever Campbell felt for Ladonna, he still wondered about his ex-wife, Rosalie. He telephoned her one evening to ask that she bring their daughter to Monroe for a visit. Rosalie said that unless he told what he was imprisoned for, she wouldn't do it. "Aw, I stole some money from a pizza place where I was working," he muttered. She waited, thinking there was probably more. Almost unintelligible, he volunteered, ". . . and sodomy."

"What's sodomy?" she asked.

In a muffled voice, he told her, "It's a head job."

Recalling his violent sexual treatment of her, Rosalie decided that Campbell didn't deserve to see his daughter, or his ex-wife. Charlie, for once, didn't argue.

Ostensibly, Charles Campbell continued to stay out of trouble. Perhaps Ladonna's influence, by staying in his life, kept him on the level. Or maybe he had learned how to manipulate authorities into turning a blind eye toward his transgressions. In either case, his behavior influenced the right people. In May, 1980, a classifications counselor wrote that Campbell's improvements deserved reward. He recommended waiving the mandatory minimum time to be served, seven and one-half years, and suggested that Campbell be scheduled for a hearing in May, 1982, with the intention of placing him in a work release program.

Campbell had hoped for a hearing in only one year, and reacted bitterly to the suggestion that he wait two years. The thought darkened his personal horizons in the same week that the Washington sky literally turned black. Mount St. Helens, ninety miles south of Monroe, erupted, blasting ash and smoke into a towerlike formation sixty thousand feet high, which soon dispersed and spread a pall over much of the state. It fittingly reflected the mood of Charles Campbell.

In reaction to the recommendation, Campbell fired a letter to the Classifications Committee, complaining about waiting two years for a hearing. He felt he had earned earlier treatment, and supported his opinion by listing his participation in various classes and programs. He admitted having many "ups and downs" during his first two years at Monroe, but pointed out that he hadn't been charged with any infractions since June, 1978.

The same classifications counselor who had suggested the two-year wait changed his mind. In November, 1980, he revised his progress report on Campbell to recommend a hearing in May, 1981. It produced results.

On May 19, 1981, the Board of Prison Terms and Paroles held the hearing, and issued an order that "the mandatory provision of the minimum term of confinement (7 1⁄2 years) to be served by Charles Rodman Campbell is hereby set aside. They also scheduled a date of May, 1983, for a full parole hearing.

Ladonna Layton sent the Parole Board a letter of appreciation. She commented that Mr. Campbell "is a good risk," and referred to their guidelines which, according to her, advise that an individual who is married or in a significant relationship has a better than normal chance for success when released from the institution. "Although we are not married," she wrote, "our relationship is a committed one and significant to us both." She would help him adjust from prison life to the community, she promised, and expressed confidence that Charlie would avoid future involvement with the criminal justice system.

Another letter arrived at the Parole Board Headquarters late that month. Oliver Campbell, responding to Charlie's request, wrote to inform the board that he planned to open a new business in Seattle, cleaning ships' bilges and tanks. He offered to employ his son upon Charlie's release from prison. He even suggested that Charlie might live with him. "It gladdens everyone's hearts to feel that there may be light at the end of a very long tunnel," the senior Campbell wrote.

Campbell's good fortune hit another high point at the end of that summer. On September 1, a screening committee accepted the recommendation of the same classification counselor who had been beating the drum for Campbell, and approved his transfer to the Honor Farm, a minimum custody adjunct to the Monroe Reformatory.

As Campbell left the main walls of the inside, several staff members shook their heads in disbelief. One of them, Lonnie McGowan, who had once stopped Campbell from repeatedly slamming into a chain link fence while running, thought that Campbell was dangerous, unpredictable, and a security risk. McGowan angrily recalled that Charlie enjoyed being disruptive, even in Block 3, and often organized group demonstrations by inciting inmates to throw food and trays, rattle bars, and burn objects in cells. Staff never wrote him up, McGowan complained, because they couldn't prove he was the instigator. "But I would overhear him speak to inmates who didn't participate and threaten to 'yard them out' which means to 'get their ass kicked.' "

McGowan also described a disconcerting situation he'd faced with Ladonna Layton when she came to visit Campbell after giving up her job. "I denied her the visit because she was inappropriately dressed. She didn't have any underwear or bra on when she came to visit Charlie." McGowan had heard that Ladonna worried about inmates thinking she "packed drugs in for Charlie." But he didn't believe Ladonna could be guilty of something that stupid. Concluding the recollection, McGowan said, "There is a strong possibility that Campbell had many more infractions than he was written up for."

Another staff member, a counselor, observed that Campbell was highly volatile, had a bad temper, and could physically carry out his threats. One inmate confided in the counselor that "Campbell was going to square accounts in the Wicklund case." Several prisoners expressed astonishment when administrators put Campbell on the Honor Farm, grumbling that others deserved it more.

At the Honor Farm, Campbell came under the scrutiny of Officer Frank Braun, who had seen Charlie more times than he cared to remember "up on the hill." But, Braun later said, Charlie seemed to make a 180 degree change. It was not unusual for an inmate to come to the farm and cooperate, but Charlie's new behavior surprised him. It didn't fit with the Campbell who had screamed and spit at officers, calling them "fucking pigs" or "bastards" and constantly threatened to get even with them.

Campbell's conduct at the Honor Farm, where he worked as a general laborer, gained him his next goal. Nine days before his twenty-seventh birthday in 1981, administrators transferred him from the minimum custody farm to outside housing at the Monroe Work Release center.

Six

The work release program is designed to provide inmates with a smooth transition back into society, and prepare them for full-time employment by allowing them to live in controlled housing, away from the prison, and work outside with certain restrictions. Participants are allowed to leave the premises only to go to work, or with furloughs or passes given by administrators. New arrivals at work release must serve a probationary period restricted to quarters before being allowed off the grounds. Charles Campbell was assigned as an in-house cook, and would have to wait until the next January before he could accept outside employment or leave the premises for any reason.

A staff member at Monroe Work Release characterized Campbell as a "game player" who manipulated people to get his way. From the start, Charlie began testing the rules and arguing with staff. His performance as a cook earned him ratings of "moderate abilities."

Bob Hall, another staff member, wrote Campbell up for several minor infractions and lectured him each time. Hall thought it strange how Campbell spoke of Ladonna Layton in degrading terms, and treated her with no respect. Another odd bit of behavior on Campbell's part, Hall said, occurred when Charlie watched television. When a movie showed someone being hit, and not hitting back, Campbell became so furious he'd have to leave the room. Hall asked him why, and Charlie said, "You should always fight for what you believe in."

Another officer, Sonia Pomeroy, who worked as a guard at

Monroe Work Release, found herself in an awkward spot. She knew that her supervisor seemed to like Charlie, and had worked closely with Ladonna Layton in counseling Campbell up on the hill. He'd gone out on a limb to accept Campbell at the work release facility, selecting him over other more-qualified cooks. But Pomeroy didn't anticipate the conflict it would cause.

Pomeroy walked into a room Charlie shared with four other men, while they were gone, and found Charlie with Ladonna, "trying to get it on." Having sex on the premises violated the rules. Pomeroy broke up the passionate encounter, and wrote a memo to her boss detailing the incident. The supervisor's next step confounded Pomeroy, who felt betrayed. He showed the memo to Charlie.

In retaliation the next day, Campbell tried to incite all of the work release residents against her by telling them how she "ratted out" on him. The men didn't harm her, but grumbled about her actions. It frightened her, and she knew that she'd better not report Campbell to her boss in the future.

Even though nervous, Pomeroy still felt it necessary to pull Campbell into the office when he'd lose his temper and yell at her. He didn't care. He'd taunt Pomeroy by snarling, "You cannot dictate to me, and your boss won't let you do it."

Any time Pomeroy complained about Campbell's behavior, the supervisor handled it by calling Pomeroy into the same room with Campbell and demanding, "You two will just have to get along." She felt that Campbell could be the most dangerous convict she'd ever seen in her fifteen years in the business and that he didn't belong in work release, much less out on the streets. She finally stopped putting anything in writing in fear for her life.

Like her colleague, Bob Hall, Sonia Pomeroy couldn't understand why Campbell treated Ladonna with such contempt. He often referred to her, the woman who'd helped him so much, and loved him, as a dog.

Pomeroy's feeling of dislike for Campbell lodged itself even more firmly in her mind just before Christmas, 1981. Three remarkably strange events convinced her that tragic disaster lay ahead for someone in Campbell's path. Pomeroy believed strongly in the supernatural, as had her mother, who'd passed away in November.

According to Pomeroy, on the night of December 10, she was wrapping Christmas gifts, using her late mother's scissors to cut the paper. A tingling sensation came over her, and the scissors began to glow with an eerie, luminescent blue light. Somewhere from the back of her mind, a message scrolled as if on a foggy screen. *Charles Campbell is going to kill someone!*

She had experienced similar supernatural events before, Pomeroy said. "It's called *materialization,* an encounter from beyond the grave."

It happened again on December 15, soon after Pomeroy had received a cash settlement from her mother's estate. She bought a short, blue coat as a last Christmas gift from her mom. When she took it out of the box at home, the impossible happened. The coat, which had been placed in the package in clean, perfect condition, had somehow been covered with kitty litter. Before Pomeroy's eyes, she said, the coat completely cleaned itself. Again, the message branded itself in her mind. *Charles Campbell is going to kill someone!*

One week later, three days before Christmas, Pomeroy had some last minute shopping to do. During her trip to town, the interior of her car inexplicably filled with the strong aroma of lilacs, her mother's favorite scent. The tingling came again, and once more the message. *Charles Campbell is going to kill someone!*

Charles Campbell did not have permission to leave the premises of Monroe Work Release, under any circumstances. Nevertheless, he decided to take the risk on Christmas day.

Rosalie Campbell hadn't seen her ex-husband since he'd gone to prison. She had written to him a few times, but had chosen not to visit him at the reformatory. Their daughter, just an infant

when Campbell went away, and now seven, could not even remember her father.

The child had stayed up late on Christmas Eve, excited about
the coming morning; then she and her nine-year-old half sister
finally drifted off to sleep. Rosalie stayed up to have a drink. At
fifteen minutes after midnight, she heard a knock on the apartment door. Surprised, she called out, "Who is it?"

"Chuck," came the hoarse reply.

"Chuck who?" she asked, without thinking.

"Chuck Campbell."

Stunned, Rosalie opened the door, whereupon Campbell
marched in, wordlessly, and began pacing in circles. His appearance did nothing to make her feel better. Greasy, long hair
reached in frizzy straggles to his neck, ripped, dirty jeans hung
loosely at his hips, and dried blood smeared both arms. He acted
very upset.

"My God," Rosalie said, "did you escape from prison?"

Reeking of booze, Campbell could only grunt, "I didn't do
it."

"Well, what are you doing out?" Rosalie felt a creepy sensation. Campbell muttered something nearly unintelligible to
Rosalie about being on a program, or a furlough, for the weekend.
"Okay," she replied, "come on in the bathroom and wash that
blood off your arms."

Still pacing, Campbell asked about his daughter, and Rosalie's
other youngster. She told him they were fine, both asleep. He
followed her into the bathroom, where she helped clean his arms,
then taped some cotton to his left wrist where a wound had bled
freely. The source of the injury would never be known to anyone
but Campbell.

"Would you like to see them?" Rosalie asked in a sudden rush
of sympathy for Charlie. He seemed eager, so she left the bathroom light on to provide dim illumination of the bedroom where
the girls slept. Tiptoeing, they entered the room, and bent over
the peaceful younger child. With a change of heart about waking
her, Rosalie bent over and gently shook the young girl. Her eyes

opened and Rosalie whispered, "This is your dad, your real dad, Chuck." Still drowsy, the girl sat up.

Campbell could think of nothing to say except, "Hi. How are you?" The child looked at him with a puzzled expression, mumbled that she was okay, then curled up to sleep again.

Back in the living room, Rosalie sat on the couch while Campbell stood and kept staring into the bedroom where he'd seen his daughter. Without a word, he turned, grabbed Rosalie's arm, pulled her into the other bedroom, and pushed her flat on her back onto the bed. Petrified, but not wanting to wake the girls, Rosalie groaned, "What are you doing? Get away from me." She tried to rise. Pinning her down with one hand, Campbell began tugging her slacks down with the other. Clawing and kicking, she tried to pull them back up, while Campbell dropped his jeans.

Astounded at his incredible strength, Rosalie tried pinching and scratching him, to no avail. Jerking her underwear down to her ankles, Campbell pressed his body down on hers and accomplished the intercourse he sought.

In a loud, hoarse whisper, Rosalie appealed to him. "My God, why are you doing this? Please stop." She tried to roll over on her side, but felt helpless against his strength. His hands groped at her bra, tearing it away.

"I've missed you," Campbell said, his first words since leaving the sleeping children. His ensuing comment confused Rosalie. "I've got a wife and two kids." She wondered if Campbell remembered they were divorced.

The whole experience was demeaning and painful to Rosalie, and she sighed relief when she thought he'd finished. She thought wrong, and his next move horrified her. Campbell rolled her over and attempted anal sex. He apparently detected her revulsion, or had already satisfied himself. He backed off, rolled over, and reached for a cigarette.

Holding back tears, and thankful that the girls had slept through the ordeal, Rosalie asked, "What did you do that for?" Campbell ignored her, glanced at a clock, and went back into the living room where he sat down and looked out the window. Still trying to arrange her torn clothing, Rosalie followed, moaning, "You'd better not ever do that again."

Campbell stepped to the door, opened it, and looked both ways outside. Over his shoulder, he said, "I'll call you soon," walked out and disappeared. Completely confused with tumbling emotions, Rosalie thought for several days about calling the police. She felt a whirlpool of conflict. On one hand, anger and revulsion. On the other, a sense of pity for Campbell. And somewhere in between, the embers of a love she'd once felt for him. She had no idea where to find him, and wondered if he would really call.

Her answer came three nights later when Campbell telephoned at ten o'clock. Apologetic, he said he'd been drunk and out of control on the Christmas visit. He wanted to know if the kids were asleep. When Rosalie said they were, he asked if he could come over. Rosalie surprised herself by saying, "Yeah." Then she quickly modified the invitation. "You can only stay for half an hour, because I have to get up early."

At precisely eleven, he knocked and walked in. Relieved that Campbell didn't appear to be drinking, Rosalie wanted to know about the crime that sent him to prison, who the girl was, and why he did it. Campbell denied guilt and claimed that people, including his own relatives, told lies about him. He answered none of her questions, just mumbled cryptically in a complaining manner. She'd hoped to learn if he'd changed. Maybe they could reestablish some rapport for the sake of his daughter.

Instead, he grabbed Rosalie's wrist, and pulled her into the bedroom again.

"You're not going to do this again," Rosalie rasped, once more trying to keep from waking the kids. "You're not going to do what you did the last time. You said you were drunk." Without a word, he threw her on the bed. "Chuck," she hissed, "this is rape. I don't want you touching me." He just looked at her, and undressed himself completely. Rosalie leaped for the door, but he grabbed her and began stripping her clothes off. "For God's sake, Chuck, let me go," Rosalie appealed, knowing very well that it was hopeless. Ignoring her pleas, he tore away the rest of her clothing and raped her again. In a final, desperate attempt to avoid the inevitable, she even grabbed his pubic hair and pulled sharply. Hopeless. It didn't even slow him down.

Campbell's first words during the act came while she struggled. "Don't you ever . . . haven't you ever had a climax? Don't you enjoy sex?" Rosalie didn't answer, she just bit his arm, clawed at him, and tried to think about something else until he finished.

When Campbell left, Rosalie felt more confused than ever. On January 6, she packed a few things, took her two daughters, and drove to a ranch in Eastern Washington to think things over. It would be ten weeks before she decided what to do.

No official at the Monroe Work Release center had noticed Charles Campbell's absence during the week of Christmas. It would later be speculated that he'd paid another inmate, who had a legitimate furlough but no place to go, to sleep in Charlie's bed. That way, the officer making the night count would never notice that Campbell had slipped out to visit his ex-wife, all the way over in Lynnwood, twenty miles to the west.

Two weeks into 1982, administrators of the Monroe program demonstrated implicit faith in Charles Campbell by upgrading his classification to full work release status. They also promised efforts to schedule a full parole hearing if he could successfully complete three months of the program with no problems. That meant a target date of April 14 to knock down the final barrier to freedom. Campbell branded that date into his brain. April 14, 1982.

Of course, Campbell would be required to work. His supporters searched for an employer willing to risk hiring a convicted felon, and found one before January ended, in Campbell's old stomping grounds, Edmonds. A sea foods processing company expressed interest in hiring Campbell as soon as an opening developed. They put his name on a waiting list. Everything seemed to be working in Charlie's favor. Ladonna Layton, now his official sponsor, would be permitted to escort him on social activities away from the facility premises. With an administrator's permission, he even acquired an old car. The 1973 Ford Torino, a rusty orange color, would provide transportation when the job materialized.

Proud of her ward and lover, Ladonna took Campbell to meet her mother. His conduct during the visit, according to the mother, "was nice, but he talked a lot about himself." He gave the appearance of trying to impress her with his own importance. He would fidget for a while, then get in a hurry to leave.

The relationship between Ladonna and Charlie became more serious. They talked about getting married and having a baby when Campbell finally won his parole. By the end of January, they'd already made a good start on the second half of the goal. Ladonna was pregnant.

In a show of domesticity, Campbell even adopted a pet. A woebegone dog, a mixed-breed female, apparently lost or abandoned, wandered onto the Monroe Work Release grounds, where Campbell spotted it. He fed the skinny, brown dog a few times, then decided to adopt it. Perhaps comparing his own life to the dog's, he named his new pet "Loser." When Campbell accompanied Ladonna off campus, he took Loser along. He appeared to have more affection for the dog than for most humans.

With more freedom, and newly acquired access to stores in town, Campbell fell back into his old habit of drinking too much. Work release rules prohibited alcohol consumption, but that didn't seem to matter to Campbell. Ladonna tried to discourage the backsliding, but with very little success. He drank steadily while at her apartment, and with increasing frequency found ways to smuggle booze into his sleeping quarters at the facility.

A document came to light much later showing that Campbell broke another rule. An "adjustment report" filed in January, 1982, contained a disturbing entry: "Campbell had a dog in his bed, under the covers. He was, by all appearances, sexually molesting the dog. Evidence shows this to be true. He wasn't supposed to have dogs or cats in bed. This is against the rules." The paper also contained a notation that "Campbell wasn't given a violation."

His resumption of the drinking habits had the same old effect on Campbell. He began snapping at Ladonna during telephone conversations and while spending time with her. During his drinking episodes at her apartment, before he'd pass out, she heard him express animosity toward Renae Wicklund, but thought little of it. He just needed to work off steam over his frustrations, she rationalized.

Campbell may have been feeling too much stress on the night of January 28, when he checked back into the work release facility. Appearing bedraggled, he told the officer he'd been in an auto accident in which the driver had slammed into a telephone pole. Fortunately, Campbell said, no one had been injured. A state trooper who responded to the scene of the wreck found an abandoned black Volkswagen Rabbit smashed against a utility pole, damaged enough to make it undriveable. A check of the registration revealed that it belonged to Ladonna Layton, but subsequent investigative efforts failed to prove who had been driving.

One of the frustrations for Campbell came from the elusiveness of employment. He needed a job in order to complete his three-month program. April 14 edged closer. The fish processing company, where his name had been placed on a waiting list, had experienced financial problems and couldn't add any new help. His father's job offer was based on the contingency of being paroled. Applications at other companies failed to generate any positive responses.

The most serious problem nagging at Campbell came via rumors. The Monroe Work Release center, people said, was scheduled to be closed. It turned out to be true. Inmates on the program, insecure and nervous about their futures, inquired about relocation to the centers in Seattle or Everett. Campbell strongly preferred Seattle. But Everett expressed a willingness to accept him.

On February 24, Campbell arrived at an old two-story house in Everett, diagonally across the street from the courthouse where he'd been convicted, to join twenty-three other men in the work release program. An officer assigned him to share an upstairs bedroom, room number 7, with another inmate.

Not very happy anyway, Campbell sank into a deeper melancholia a week after his arrival at Everett when his dog, Loser, wandered off. Within a few days, he learned that the dog had been picked up and euthanized at an animal control shelter. According to a psychologist, Campbell put a symbolic twist on the dog's death, convincing himself that it had been executed for being free. It gave him a reason to seek solace in the bottle. The old volcanic anger simmered inside him.

A bright spot did emerge in early March. An Edmonds landscaping company agreed to hire Campbell as a laborer. He began working on March 8, renewing the potential for him to meet his commitment of performing a job, trouble free, before the three months' probationary period ended on April 14.

The phone rang on the morning of March 16 in the office of Snohomish County Sheriff's Detective Rick Bart. A solidly built six-foot-three, fair complected with friendly eyes, Bart partly compensated for a receding hairline by growing a neatly trimmed mustache. He kept his square chin closely shaved revealing a Cary Grant type dimple. Bart had been with the department since 1973, successfully investigating assault and homicide cases during the last four years. A quick sense of humor and pragmatic outlook helped him cope with the stress known to every cop in the world. He picked up his phone, and heard the slightly slurred drawl of Rosalie Campbell. She wanted to report that she'd been raped by her ex-husband.

For Rosalie's convenience, Detective Bart agreed to meet her at the Lynnwood Police building, close to her apartment, and arrived there at ten-forty-five A.M. While Bart listened patiently, she described the whole history of her relationship with Charles Campbell, including the marriage and divorce. He'd been in prison, she said, since 1976. Somehow, he'd left Monroe early

Christmas morning, came to her apartment drunk, and raped her. Three days later, she said, he called and asked to come over. This time, he sounded sober, so she had agreed to allow him the visit, but for a short time. He raped her again, she complained to Bart. And, Rosalie added, a few weeks ago, he did it again!

Rick Bart asked Rosalie for more details about the third, and most recent, attack. She couldn't remember it very clearly, she admitted, because she'd been drinking a lot herself. Ever since he'd sexually assaulted her on Christmas, she'd been extremely upset. Afterward, she'd gone over to Eastern Washington to try to cope with her alcoholic problems. But lately, she'd been drinking again, and her memory had become hazy.

"Do you recall the date it happened?" Bart asked.

"No, I'm not even sure about that," Rosalie murmured.

The long interval of time Rosalie had waited to report the assaults, added to the possibility that she had consented to sex with him, would present a real problem for the chance of successful prosecution, Bart realized. He asked her why she'd waited so long. Rosalie said she feared that Campbell would retaliate by harming her or her children. She had thought it over, though, after some counseling help, and decided that he should be punished for his brutality. "I want him prosecuted," she said, "and I am willing to bear any hardship to see it through."

Not wishing to discourage Rosalie, Bart told her that he would do his best to help her. He also recommended that she seek help from Rape Relief, an organization for victims of sexual assault. Rosalie agreed.

After spending two weeks looking into the criminal history of Charles Campbell, which covered several pages, Bart contacted Rape Relief to see if Rosalie had, indeed, sought help. It pleasantly surprised him to learn that she had. He asked the RR agent to tell Rosalie he'd appreciate her contacting him again to talk about prosecuting Campbell.

Another week passed by, and Rosalie hadn't called or shown up. By sheer coincidence, while off duty, Bart ran into her, chatted about the case, and secured her promise to come in soon to discuss the case.

Charlie Campbell, meanwhile, faced troubles at the Everett facility. On a Wednesday evening, he approached the duty correctional officer, a woman, and told her he needed a "business outing" pass, but wouldn't be specific about the reasons. Instead of answering her questions, he became evasive, sarcastic and argumentive. She shrugged and denied the pass.

Another female officer, on a night following an argument with Campbell, conducted a room check after midnight. She found a partially empty can of beer on Campbell's bunk, in which he lay sound asleep. The whole room smelled of alcohol. She confiscated the can and wrote a report citing violation of the no drinking rule.

Angry at what he perceived as mistreatment, Campbell left one night and drove to the home of the Monroe supervisor who had given him a series of breaks. Charlie complained that he wasn't sure he wanted to stay in the Everett program. The supervisor calmed him down and promised to look into the matter. The next day, he called an official at Everett, heard the other side of the story, and came to the conclusion that Campbell had overreacted. Charlie, he decided, would be very lucky if the Everett people allowed him to stay.

On Friday, March 19, Thomas Cornish, the Everett supervisor, held a "termination hearing" with Campbell and his case counselor, to determine if Campbell's deteriorating behavior should result in returning him to Monroe Reformatory. Cornish, noting that Campbell "seems to have had some problems adjusting to the structure of Everett Work Release," asked Campbell if he had difficulty accepting the authority of female officers. He also wanted to know if Campbell would be able to change his behavior and follow the rules.

Evidently realizing he had seriously jeopardized his status, Campbell admitted that he'd had "a discussion" with a female officer, but asserted that he had no hard feelings against any of the officers, including the women. He admitted not only drinking several beers on the night the can was found in his room, but confessed to doing it at other times, too. "I promise I won't take another drink as long as I'm in work release," he told the two men. In addition, Campbell committed to abiding by all rules, and telling the truth. "I want another chance to show I can complete the program," Campbell pleaded. "I have a fiancée with my child on the way. I want to earn my parole and take on the responsibilities of raising a family."

After the hearing, Cornish decided to keep Campbell on the work release program, and not to recommend any disciplinary action by the parole board. Instead, he assigned Campbell extra duty, to clean out the attic of the house, ordered that he be disallowed any immediate furloughs, and placed him on house restriction for one week.

The magic date of April 14 could still be a turning point in Campbell's life.

Seven

Jamestown, North Dakota, nestled in an ancient lake bed, sits in the southeast quadrant of a state known for wide-open spaces, bone-chilling winters, and a wonderfully low crime rate. At the confluence of the James River and Pipestem Creek, the peaceful town of fifteen thousand residents is known as "Buffalo City" in recognition of millions of bison that once thundered across the prairie, and as a tribute to today's small remaining herds. The world's largest buffalo statue, measuring twenty-six feet high and forty-six feet long, was constructed of concrete there in 1959. In blue-sky summers, the surrounding plains ripple green and gold with crops of wheat, corn, and sunflowers, then turn blinding white during winter blizzards. It's less than a two-hour drive east, on I-94, from the state capital, Bismark, and only 135 miles south of the Canadian border. A community of harmony and solid values, Jamestown is a place where a man could settle down, and raise a family.

Five years after the end of World War II, Ahlen Ahlers, naturally called "Al" by everyone who knew him, settled in Jamestown for the second time with his new bride, Hilda, a lifelong resident of the community. She had two sons from a previous marriage, and Al had a daughter, but that presented no obstacle for a couple in love, just a ready-made extended family.

The first child from their union came along on February 20, 1951. They named the gorgeous brown-eyed girl Renae Louise. Nineteen months later, a baby sister, Lorene, rounded out the family. Al had worked for the railroad for years, but decided to try his hand at tilling the soil and raising crops in the rich North Dakota farmland. He bought a small place, cheap because it had no running water, and moved his wife and kids to the country. In today's world of cyber-paced technology, instant gratification, and jet set transportation, youngsters laugh at parents who tell childhood tales of walking through deep snowdrifts to a one-room school. For Renae and Lorene, it was no laughing matter. They really did it, until Renae reached the fifth grade, when Al, Hilda, and the children moved to a more modern home, with up-to-date plumbing and expanded space, where a school bus provided transportation.

Several relatives of the family called Jamestown home, too. Hilda's brother had a daughter, Jan Wegenke, the same age as Renae, who admired her cousin. "Renae could always make do, despite not having a lot of money when she was little. She sometimes had to wear old clothes that had been 'rehabilitated,' but somehow, she looked terrific. I think it really made her a strong person, and able to be competitive in whatever she tried."

Those were precious years for Renae and Lorene. They had their own horse, named Star, and a pet raccoon, called Chico. Both girls loved the farm, the country life, and worked like hired hands with little complaint. They had a great deal in common, including slim, delicate beauty, brown eyes, perfect skin that tanned easily under summer Dakota skies, and unlimited energy. They varied, though, in personalities. As they reached their teen years, Renae remained introspective and stayed with a close circle of carefully selected companions. She joined the 4-H organization, where she won several special achievement medals, some of them with *Renae Ahlers* engraved into the silver. In her spare time, she practiced sewing (making most of her own clothes), cooking, and working on intellectual pursuits that kept her grades at high levels all through school. With no musical background, she took up the flute while still in the seventh grade, and became an accomplished musician. Her talents qualified Renae to attend the International Peace Garden Music Camp three consecutive years, from 1966 through 1969. She had little time for flirtatious boys, but finally did accept her first date during her junior year in high school.

Lorene, on the other hand, no less bright, became gregarious and fun loving. She spoke in a lilting, rapid-fire, yet melodious voice, and liked nothing better than to join a large group of laughing chums for a hayride or to go ice skating. The more people, the better. The difference in their social outlooks didn't impair the relationship between the two sisters, though. They loved each other intensely, and would do so for the rest of their lives.

Renae's one compromise to glitter and excitement came with being selected as a Jamestown High School drum majorette. In her tall, white furry hat, held tightly with a white chin strap, and matching spangled costumes made by Hilda, she marched at football games or town parades, expertly twirling the baton. In 1968, she traveled to Rapid City with the band to perform for the "Dakota Days" festival. The next year, she attended the Mecca for majorettes, the Casavant drum school, where she studied field conducting and honed her skills with the baton. Her dual activities made for an interesting dichotomy. Renae could often be seen sitting quietly alone with her flute, reflectively lost in thought, while on other occasions, she strutted athletically in front of the blaring musicians, eyes shining and teeth sparkling in a wide, joyous smile.

Her music teacher loved Renae, and selected her to direct the massed bands covering the entire football field at the 1968 Jamestown College homecoming half-time performance. That success led to Renae conducting all Jamestown High School marching band half-time shows for football games in the 1969-1970 season.

The overflowing energy did not end there. On long summer evenings, or on weekends, Renae could be seen placing a two-by-four on two battered old sawhorses, and using it as a balance beam to practice gymnastics. She didn't belong to the school gymnast team; she just wanted to prove to herself that she could do it. Acquaintances called her a "goal-oriented" girl. Renae packed her flute along wherever she went so she could practice in spare moments. While hauling the grain crop one autumn, she'd accompanied the syncopation of the truck engine with sweet warbling from her flute. Her expertise with it won her a scholarship.

Following high school graduation in 1970, Renae attended Valley City State College, which had recruited her as a majorette and a flutist. There, too, she took on the duties of drum majorette for the marching band. As she left her teen years behind, Renae's pretty facial features matured into delicate beauty, with eyes the color of polished walnut and the slim, sculptured face of a porcelain figurine.

Renae had completed one year at the school and was wondering just what to do with her future when her half brother brought his wife from California for a visit. Renae returned to the Golden State with them, where she took a job and worked all summer to earn enough money to buy a car. Her half sister lived in Washington, so Renae drove up to see her. Enchanted by the beautiful environment surrounding Puget Sound, Renae found another job and extended her stay. She met Jack Wicklund in Seattle, and for the first time, felt seriously romantic about a man. Like Renae's own parents, Jack had children from a previous marriage, but they were in the custody of their mother. Maybe Renae felt attracted to his maturity, being fourteen years younger than Jack. It certainly wasn't his money that interested Renae. Jack sold cars for a living and paid healthy child support payments. Whatever the attraction was, it soon became serious.

Lorene Ahlers, back in Jamestown, accepted her sister's invitation to travel to Seattle and attend the wedding at St. Peter's By The Sea, on February 18, 1973, two days before Renae's twenty-second birthday.

After living temporarily in apartments, Renae and Jack managed a down payment on a cozy little rectangular, one-story house, nestled among evergreens in the rolling hills of Snohomish County, near Clearview. Renae decorated it in warm colors complementing the orange shag carpet and polished hardwood hallway floors. She used parts of brass farm implements, brought from Jamestown, to adorn the walls. With three bedrooms and a fireplace, plus an expansive yard, it seemed the perfect place to raise the child Renae expected.

Little Shannah arrived on August 20, 1973, beautiful, brown-eyed, and perfect. Renae had every reason to expect an idyllic, wonderful and safe life. They even acquired two big Doberman pinschers to provide a measure of companionship and security.

But the luster in the marriage had already started to fade. The used car sales business is subject to wild fluctuations with commensurate drops in income. It's often feast or famine. Jack Wicklund found more of the latter. His various jobs took him away from home with increasing frequency. The periods of separation grew longer each time Jack left. A neighbor who knew them quite well heard that Jack sometimes returned from an absence, slipped into the house, and stole money from his wife.

Needing a respite from the growing tension, Renae took Shannah to Jamestown in the summer of 1974. Her spirits soared again in the hometown atmosphere, and she even helped her old music teacher by training a new drum majorette for the high school band.

Back in Washington, Renae hoped that Jack could spend more time with her and Shannah, but it didn't work out. A young mother and daughter being left alone in the country so often could create a forlorn existence, but it was just the contrary for Renae and Shannah. With a widespread circle of friends and close relationships with neighbors, they felt a rich sense of belonging. Next door, Andrea Warner included them in family gatherings and activities, and Shannah regarded Patty Warner, three years older, as a big sister.

Perhaps the warmest relationship developed soon after the Wicklunds moved into the neighborhood. Across the main road, 180th Street, S.E., Don and Barbara Hendrickson had occupied a tidy home since the mid-sixties. Visitors always felt welcome and comfortable in the Henderson living room. The amiable, good-hearted Barbara, twenty years older than Renae, became a surrogate mother and confidante to Renae, and happily accepted the role of a third grandmother to Shannah. Don Hendrickson extended his affection equally, once writing a letter to Lorene expressing his love for them. In one sense, he was Shannah's godfather, since he'd taxied Renae to the hospital when she gave birth to her daughter.

With strong feelings of mutual respect and affection, Renae and Barbara frequently visited each other to chat over coffee and cigarettes; Renae's Virginia Slims and Barbara's Benson and Hedges. The older couple listened to problems Renae needed to share, offering comforting advice or help. Renae knew she could turn to the Hendersons in any emergency.

The emergency came on the clear, sunny afternoon of December 11, 1974, when a tall, bushy-haired stranger forced his way into the Wicklund home.

In Jamestown, Lorene learned about the brutal attack when Renae wrote her a letter. In it, she gave no details, saying only that she'd been raped, but that she was "taking the matter under control," meaning that she would cope with it in her own private way. Renae asked her sister not to tell their parents. She didn't want them to worry, and realized there was little they could do.

Lorene, of course, telephoned her sister immediately to offer sympathy and encouragement, but Renae said, "You know, sis, we don't get to talk very much. We want to talk about the happy things going on in our lives, not the bad things." Years would pass before Lorene, or any of the family, would learn about the details of the attack, the trial, and the imprisonment of Charles Campbell.

During the year following the traumatic event, Renae appeared outwardly to adjust well, but those who knew her saw signs of inner turmoil. She developed a near phobia about Shannah, worrying that the child would be the victim of another attack, perhaps by the same man, who at that time hadn't yet been apprehended. Renae even hated to leave Shannah in the care of a baby sitter. Frequent visits from Renae's mother, Hilda, helped considerably.

Hilda sometimes even accompanied Renae on her business rounds, taking Shannah along with them.

When investigators finally arrested Charles Campbell and brought him back from a jail cell in Okanogan, Renae felt some measure of relief, but not completely secure. And she dreaded the trial. When she finally had to go to court, in April, 1976, Hilda had traveled west to stay with Renae, still unaware of the rape. Renae chose to shield Hilda from the pain, and casually mentioned, without giving any reason, that she had to go to court.

It helped Renae a great deal when Ken Christensen, the first deputy to arrive at Barbara's house after the assault, voluntarily stayed close to her during the trial. When she stepped into a hallway en route to the courtroom, she froze in fear as she saw Campbell being escorted in. She bolted to run, but Christensen soothed her shattered nerves, and sat next to her while she waited to take the witness stand. Trembling and fighting back tears, she told the deputy of her fear that Campbell would walk out of there, free to come after her again. Christensen admired her courage and determination.

Even after Campbell was convicted, though, Renae still didn't feel entirely safe.

The marital discord between the Wicklunds escalated. Financial problems contributed to simmering stress, so Renae applied for a job with a public relations firm, then later accepted a position as a financial consultant with the owner of twelve beauty schools. Her income sometimes exceeded Jack's, which may have been one factor in the ongoing dissention between them. It finally became apparent that the marriage to Jack couldn't be saved. Renae continued a harmonious relationship with his parents, but she and Jack filed for divorce.

Renae focused all of her energies on raising Shannah, and on her work. She became executive assistant to the beauty school owner, traveling among the schools to counsel students on financial matters, provide advice on securing student loans, and to conduct audits. Gradually, Renae organized her work into a system that allowed her to perform many job duties at home, giving her more time with her growing daughter.

Another wedding in the family gave Renae a good reason to take Shannah to Jamestown in August, 1977. A handsome young man named Jerry Iverson had proposed to Lorene, and she'd accepted.

Still concerned about her daughter's safety, Renae let Shannah stay with her aunt and grandparents the remainder of that summer. Hilda and Lorene, years later, would laugh with tears in their eyes, recalling the wonderfully childish antics of Shannah during that period. The child loved the farm, just as her mother and aunt had. One afternoon, she watched in awe as her grandfather prepared to change the oil in his tractor. He removed the drain plug, letting the used oil pour into a pan. Little Shannah bent over, looked in wonderment at the stream of black oil, and asked, "Grandpa, is the tractor going potty?" At other times, when given gentle instructions, Shannah calmly replied, "My momma doesn't want me to do that," or, "My mom wants me to eat candy in the morning."

Hearing Shannah announce that she was hungry, a relative replied, "Well, what would you like, for instance?"

With a clearly perturbed expression, Shannah corrected the woman. "I'm not For Instance, my name is Shannah."

The family enjoyed her stay so much, they insisted that Shannah return in the summer of 1978 and the following two summers.

Lorene and her husband, Jerry, spent the 1977 Christmas holiday with Renae and Shannah in Clearview. One evening that week, while they all sat around the crackling fireplace, talking and laughing, Renae's telephone rang. A nurse from a Seattle hospital told Renae that Jack Wicklund had been injured, and was asking for her.

Jack had been in his Seattle apartment when a burly man barged in carrying a package that might have been construed as a Christmas present. Without warning, he overpowered Jack and tied him to a chair. No one would ever know the reason for the barbaric act, but while Jack struggled in terror, the assailant doused him with gasoline and ignited the volatile liquid. Searing flames charred the skin on most of Jack's body. Fire department emergency medical technicians rushed him to a hospital, where doctors miraculously saved his life. He spent an agonizing time in burn wards undergoing surgery and physical therapy. He would be scarred for the short remainder of his life.

Police were never able to solve the mysterious ambush. Jack denied any knowledge of the intruder's identity or reason for torching him.

During the months following the bizarre attack, Jack Wicklund underwent a remarkable change, becoming a completely different person. For years prior to his ordeal, he'd damaged relationships with his family and friends. Now, he did everything possible to repair them, frequently visiting his parents and looking up alienated acquaintances to renew lost harmony. It was too late to restore the marriage, but Renae admired his efforts to make amends with his family.

Sometimes, people have intentions to make changes like Jack did, but wait too long. Jack accomplished his fence mending just in time. In April, not quite five months after the mysterious torching episode, Jack had dinner with his parents near Kingston, across the Puget Sound from Edmonds. He said good night to them and headed out along the dark Hansville Road. On a dangerous curve, his car spun out of control and slammed headlong into a tree. He died instantly.

Renae maintained contact with Jack's family, even after the period of grieving, continuing to join them for holidays and social functions. Family ties meant everything to Renae. She relished visits from her beloved Jamestown kin, spent time with her half sister in Washington, stayed in touch with a half brother in California, and drove down to Oregon to call on her other half brother. In her spare time, she researched her genealogical roots, and often expressed an abiding determination to prevent her family from drifting apart.

Shannah had inherited physical characteristics from her pretty mother, along with many of her personality traits. She adored animals, just as her mom had back in North Dakota. Renae had to find another home for the Dobermans, but still took her daughter to visit and pose for photos with them. Later, she bought a beautiful Afghan hound. Shannah named it Alex and showered it with affection. They also acquired a little cat, called Sammy, who quickly became a huge cat. Lorene, during visits, couldn't stop taking photos of Sammy because she thought he resembled a pudgy bear.

Besides the love for pets, Renae passed on her interest in the flute to Shannah and was delighted how well the youngster mastered it.

In a horrifying 1977 event, Renae thought she'd lost Shannah forever. While driving along the busy, six-lane I-5 freeway, Renae caught peripheral sight of her four-year-old daughter just as she tumbled out the passenger door. Shannah rolled under the fast-moving vehicle, barely avoiding being crushed by the wheels. From the traffic behind Renae's car, drivers swerved wildly right and left to avoid hitting the fallen child. Renae screeched to a halt and ran back to Shannah, who lay still on the pavement. An ambulance raced them to a hospital where doctors worked feverishly to stem the damage from her injuries. They encased her entire body in a full cast which would stay on for months. Renae hoped the doctors' warnings were wrong in cautioning her not to be too optimistic when the cast came off. Shannah, they said, might be partially disabled or walk with a limp. But within minutes of its removal, she astonished her mother and the doctors by walking and moving normally. After a few weeks, she demonstrated near miraculous progress by excelling in gymnastics classes.

Shannah's thankful grandparents visited often during her recovery, and as frequently as they could over the years. Ahlen traveled to Washington six times, and Hilda made at least a dozen trips. Renae once proposed that her parents stay in North Dakota during the mild summer months, and live with her in Clearview during the frigid Dakota winters.

Another family member journeyed from Jamestown to Clearview in 1979. Cousin Jan, formerly Wegenke, now Barnes, spent two weeks with Renae. While Shannah and Jan's son played, the mothers hugged, giggled, reminisced about times spent together in childhood, and gossiped about old acquaintances. They'd both gone through divorces, but didn't spend much time commiserating. Jan recalled, "Renae and I were experiencing some emotionally hard times, but didn't talk in depth about it. . . . In a silent way we both knew what the other was going through." Their whirl of activity included having a drink in Seattle's landmark Space Needle, a hop over the border to Vancouver, Canada, and picnicking by Lake Washington, where laughter echoed and sunlight sparkled from the rippling water's surface. "It was really fun for us."

Jan couldn't get over the dramatic changes she saw in her cousin. "Renae had changed immensely from a 'country girl' to a sophisticated woman in the business world." Some of Renae's clothing, Jan noticed, included suits and dresses "rehabilitated" by Hilda. It made no difference. "Renae looked like she had just stepped out of *Vogue*. She was very slim at that time and very attractive . . . with those large brown eyes."

During the second week, Jan's mother and Hilda joined the reunion. "It was kind of like old times again, having us all together again." The visit ended too soon. With lumps in their throats, Jan and her mom left with the usual promises of more-frequent repetitions of the joyous time.

Religious training played an important roll in Renae's life. She took her daughter regularly to the Shepherd of the Hills Lutheran Church in Snohomish. Even as a preschool child, Shannah earned the nickname "Little Missionary" by influencing her playmates to come to church with her. Don Hendrickson affectionately described Shannah: "She was special. A fearless little punkin'. She had one of those sparkling personalities (and) great, huge brown eyes. She was so bright and perky. The neighborhood dogs would gather by her front porch and wait for her to come out and play with them."

Cathcart Elementary School was just a few miles from the Wicklund home, and when Shannah enrolled there, she impressed teachers and staff alike with her good manners and study habits, just as her mother had at a one-room country school outside of Jamestown. Shannah didn't have to walk to school, though. Renae chauffeured her in the car for most of the first year, then finally allowed her to board a yellow school bus for the round trip. The bus always delivered Shannah home safely at three-thirty in the afternoon.

As the new decade began, Renae remained busy with her job and Shannah, and appeared happy to her circle of loved ones. Her job and parental duties filled most of her time. In the summer of 1980, at a party, she met a computer software engineer, Glenn Douglas, who captivated her attention. He really seemed nice, and could keep up with her intellectually. They agreed to get together again, and began dating regularly, twice a week on the average. Douglas considered proposing marriage to Renae, but waited for the right timing.

Sometimes, Douglas observed, she had a faraway look in her eyes. She discussed it once with him, confessing her worry that someone might want to harm her and Shannah. But she never told Douglas about the rape. She did mention being nervous about a financial consultant from New Jersey, a Mr. Pissaro, who blamed her for losing out on some business. Also, she confided, she got strange telephone calls now and then that frightened her. Douglas asked for details, but Renae changed the subject and never told him any more.

The relationship grew closer, and Douglas hit it off perfectly with Shannah, too. Because Renae wanted her daughter to feel included, the couple spent many nights at the house, eating, watching television, or just laughing and talking. One Saturday night, Renae brought out a box of jewelry she wanted to show Douglas, wondering if it had any value. She sorted it on the living room table, and they spent nearly an hour examining and chatting about each piece, even her engraved 4-H medals. One item particularly caught Glenn's eye, a small, unusual sea shell in a matrix of gold. He also recognized a gold leaf on a chain he'd seen her wear, and some square design earrings. It was a warm, sharing evening that he would always remember.

The look in Renae's eyes caught the attention of Hilda, too, during a Christmas visit in 1981. One night, Alex, the big Afghan, normally quiet and well behaved, began barking and howling furiously at something, or someone, outside. It was too cold, dark, and spooky to go out there to investigate. But Hilda could see that certain expression in her daughter's eyes.

The next time she saw it, Renae looked even more frightened. "I saw Renae looking out the window at the road, with the strangest look on her face," Hilda recalled. Alarmed, she asked, "What do you see out there?"

"Oh, that . . ." Renae tried to shrug it off. "That was just some kook that used to drive past here a lot."

More troubling signs appeared in January, after a snowfall that left the hills and trees mantled in pure white. Don Hendrickson, doing some chores outside his house, saw some large footprints in the snow, near a window. Later that day, Barbara mentioned the discovery to Renae, whose face darkened. She, too, had found footprints under one of her windows.

Good old Alex, the big playful Afghan, seemed to feel the tension. He nipped at some neighborhood children. Afraid that he might bite someone, Renae felt obligated to find him another home, as she had the two Dobermans.

Glenn Douglas spent Saturday, April 10, 1982, with Renae and Shannah, stayed overnight, and lingered until late Sunday afternoon. He didn't detect anything wrong. At about four-thirty he kissed them goodbye, and left. Renae took Shannah over to

Don and Barbara's to have dinner with them. She told them she
felt a little sick, like maybe she was getting the flu.

Generally quite healthy, Renae had once nearly died because
she dismissed symptoms as the flu. It happened during a visit to
her half brother in California. He insisted on taking her to a
doctor, where they wheeled her promptly into the emergency
room for surgery. She had a ruptured appendix.

Don and Barbara expressed concern, but Renae was reluctant
to go to a doctor. When she admitted to Don that she'd had a sore
throat for two days, he wouldn't allow any more resistance to
medical treatment. He coaxed Renae into his car on Tuesday
morning and drove her to Snohomish, where she received a prescription for a codeine-based throat medication.

On the cool Wednesday morning of April 14, Barbara told
Don she was still worried about Renae, and walked over to the
Wicklund house. She convinced her friend to sip some chicken
broth, but Renae couldn't keep it down. Barbara saw Shannah
off to school, bundled Renae into bed, and promised to return
later that day to make some throat-soothing Jell-O for her.

At four-twenty that afternoon, Barbara tucked a thermometer
into her sweater pocket, borrowed Don's watch, and walked
across the road on her mission of mercy.

Eight

A few minutes after Barbara left to check on Renae, Don Hendrickson switched the television to channel 5, slumped into his comfortable recliner chair, and settled down to watch the news. He shook his head at the litany of negative reports. The Seattle Mariners had lost a baseball doubleheader, a poor start for the new season. The Seattle Supersonics basketball team had dropped a close game to the San Francisco Warriors. Another reporter reminded viewers that income tax forms must be filed before midnight on April 15th. The Hendricksons had completed the dreaded process weeks ago.

One news item would have upset Don if he'd been concentrating on the report. A two-year-old girl had been beaten to death over in Spokane four months earlier, and her stepfather was recently acquitted of murder charges. The baby's mother had testified against him in exchange for immunity. Now, no one would be held accountable. In a press conference, the Spokane County coroner called it, "one of the most brutal child deaths I've seen in a decade," and demanded passage of new, tougher laws to curb child abuse before it results in death. Few crimes were more despicable than violence against children.

Andrea Warner, next door to Renae, had mentioned to Don earlier in the day that Patty saw a stranger lurking around, and there'd been those footprints in the snow in January. They all needed to stay alert.

Don's thoughts drifted from the reports of political corruption, crime, taxes, and death, to Renae. She seemed to be really suf-

fering from the strep throat diagnosed yesterday by the doctor.
He didn't even question the idea of Barbara walking over to
Renae's house to care for Renae. Of course Barbara would do
that. Shannah should also be home by now to help attend to her
mother. Don glanced at a clock. His wife had been gone for more
than an hour.

Absentmindedly, Don watched the national news report end,
and the second edition of local news begin at six-thirty. Feeling
a vague sense of worry, a little knot of tension in his stomach,
he lifted himself from the soft comfort of his chair, and began
puttering around the house, cleaning things that weren't dirty,
straightening magazines and ashtrays that didn't need rearrange-
ment. He checked the clock again.

Maybe he would just wander over to Renae's house and see if
everything was okay.

After carefully locking the front door, Don traversed his front
yard, crossed the road, and walked the length of Renae's driveway.
Past her dark red and white Ford LTD she'd parked in front of
the house, Don turned right, took several steps, and knocked on
the front door. No answer. He knocked again, and with the knot
in his stomach tightening, he leaned over to the window and
peered through a narrow gap in the drapes. Recalling that Renae
usually kept most of the house lights on at night, Don's alarm
grew. Complete darkness obscured the whole interior of the
house. By pressing his face to the glass, Don could make out
another oddity. The rear sliding glass door stood wide open.

Quickly circling to the backyard, Don leaned into the open
slider, and heard the loud splatter of water running in the stainless
steel kitchen sink. Almost instinctively, he stepped into the
kitchen to shut off the valve. Complete silence.

A flurry of thoughts raced through Don's mind. Questions
formed, answers materialized, then faded in the face of logic;
new explanations emerged, images ebbed and flowed. In the short
space of microseconds, a myriad of possibilities tumbled in his
thoughts like the interior of a spinning clothes dryer——none of
it easing his rising tension. Had Barbara, Renae, and Shannah

gone somewhere else? Not likely. The Wicklund car sat cold in the front driveway. Maybe Renae had needed more medical treatment, and someone had taken the trio to the doctor. No, that didn't make sense. Barbara would have returned and asked Don to take them. Wait . . . possibly another friend had already been visiting, and all of them had hurried to take Renae for emergency care. Still, Don figured, Barbara would have telephoned him to let him know. Unless they were in a frenzied rush. Or worse. . . .

Better look around inside, Don thought.

First things first. Don stepped toward the entry and flipped a wall switch, flushing away the dark shadows. He blinked at the bright illumination, and noticed that one of the kitchen chairs lay on its side. A few dishes had been placed in the right half of the divided sink, and an amber drinking glass sat on the counter. Otherwise, the kitchen appeared clean and orderly.

Ever optimistic, Don mentally sought and sorted through possible explanations, trying to reason away the silence and apparent absence of the women. His eyes scanned the adjacent living room. Nothing out of place. He stepped through it and looked into the hallway.

Don Hendrickson's world exploded! His mind reeled and the room seemed to whirl about him. A shriek of horror lodged silently in his throat. This couldn't be . . . !

Barbara Hendrickson reposed on the floor as still as a statue. On her back, she faced the ceiling, her head toward Don, her eyes closed, her lips slightly parted. Both arms, unbent, extended at slight angles outward from her sides, with each motionless hand lying about six inches from her hips. The white sweater gapped open revealing her light brown pullover blouse and the thin leather shoulder strap of her purse still looped over her upper right arm.

Bright crimson blood pooled around Barbara's gray-blond hair on the honey-colored wooden floor and seeped in a stream reaching eighteen inches away. A gaping red wound in her throat had drained her life away.

Now beginning to tremble in horror, Don found himself kneeling at Barbara's side, touching her right cheek and her neck. "She felt cold," he later cried. Trying to overcome the confusion and tumbling emotions, Don spotted the living room telephone. Without really thinking about it, he picked it up and automatically called 911. While responding to the dispatcher's questions, he asked that in addition to the emergency medical team, sheriff's deputies be sent to investigate a murder.

After hanging up the phone, Don Hendrickson stepped outside. He desperately needed to gulp some of the clean night air, and to try to clear his head. The scene didn't seem real. It had to be a horrible nightmare.

In a few moments, he forced himself back inside the house, knelt again by his beloved wife, leaned forward, and kissed her forehead. In that kiss, he tried to express the profound love he felt for Barbara, her importance in his life, and to apologize for all the times he hadn't clearly articulated his deep affection for her.

Once more, Don moved outside, into the night, and wandered to the front of the house. While he stood in the driveway, a noise pierced the darkness, startling him. Car tires rumbled on the eastern neighbor's gravel driveway. "I was scared," he recalled. "I didn't know what to expect." Without knowing why, he moved toward the noise.

"When I got to the top of the driveway, I noticed it was Andrea and her daughter in their pickup truck. I don't recall exactly what I told Andrea, but I think I said that a terrible thing has happened and Barbara was killed at Renae's." Without knowing if the neighbor had heard or seen him, Don Hendrickson returned to the Wicklund driveway, where he saw red and blue emergency lights flashing the arrival of fire department vehicles. He waved them into the driveway. When uniformed figures hastily emerged from the cabs, Don led them to the back of the house, and pointed at the still open sliding door. "I was a little abrupt with them," he remembered. "I told them to get their ass to the back door. When we got there, one man went in and another man stayed with me, outside."

While the emergency team leaped into action, and other vehicles and men arrived, Don Hendrickson stood outside, in a daze of incomprehensible shock. Somewhere in his subconscious, he wondered where Renae and Shannah were, but he couldn't focus on that. His tidy, safe world had erupted like a blood-spewing volcano, and his life was irretrievably shattered. Nothing would ever be the same.

REPORT OF LT. WILLIAM RAY SPALDING, CLEARVIEW FIRE DEPARTMENT

"At 1851 hours on 14 April, 1982, District 7 was alerted for a possible unattended (injury victim) at . . . 180th St., S.E. Upon arrival I found a Don Hendrickson in driveway. He showed us where the patient was. Myself, my partner, Randy Weiss, and Fire Chief Richard Eastman entered the rear of the house through sliding glass doors. The doors were wide open. Upon entering the hallway I found a white female lying on the floor with what appeared to be a slashed throat. I went out to the kitchen to ensure that nothing would be disturbed. . . ."

Behind the wheel of Rescue Unit R-711, Randy Weiss flipped on the siren switch and accelerated. A few minutes before seven P.M., the country roads were enveloped by darkness. In a tunnel of light created by the vehicle's headlamps, he steered between the rows of evergreens lining 180th Street, S.E. He probably would have passed the address for which he and Lieutenant Spalding searched, but Randy spotted a middle-aged man at the mouth of a driveway, gesturing frantically. Weiss slowed, turned into the long, gravel drive, and braked to a halt near Don Hendrickson. Leaping from the driver's seat, Weiss grabbed his medical kit, and in lock step with Spalding, followed Hendrickson to the open sliding door.

Fire Chief Richard Eastman arrived at the Wicklund home

almost simultaneously with his two subordinates, and caught up with them as they entered the kitchen. Hendrickson then led the trio to the grisly sight of his wife lying on the hallway floor. The officers had no difficulty deciding that she was beyond the need for any emergency medical help.

Pale and shaken, Don Hendrickson fought to hold back tears while telling Spalding that the woman on the floor was his wife. He and Barbara lived across the street, he whispered, his voice breaking. Finally, he also remembered to tell the chief that Renae Wicklund and her young daughter lived in the house where Mrs. Hendrickson lay dead. He didn't know where Renae and Shannah were.

As Hendrickson dejectedly shuffled back outside, Bill Spalding whispered to Randy Weiss to go with the older man, and to watch him carefully. The officers had no way of knowing how Hendrickson might react, or even if he might be a possible suspect. Weiss carried his emergency case to the back patio, put it down on the cement, and waited while keeping his eye on Hendrickson.

In the bloody hallway, Dick Eastman and Bill Spalding edged carefully around the still body of Mrs. Hendrickson, exercising extreme caution to avoid disturbing any possible evidence. They both observed that someone had piled an array of multicolored clothing over Barbara's feet. That oddity held their attention until both men had moved past the body and the clothing. Then they looked through the entry into a bedroom. Eastman gasped and gritted his teeth. Spalding groaned a nearly silent, "Oh, my God!"

A completely nude woman lay on her back, her head on the floor within two feet of Spalding's shoes. Her alabaster body and thick dark hair contrasted sharply with the orange shag carpet. Both arms were akimbo, bent at the elbows, with the hands resting on her breasts. The legs were splayed apart, the left one jutting away from the body, bent at the knee. A pillow and a sheet partially pulled from the disarrayed bed covered her right leg from the knee to the foot. Smears, spatters, and rivulets of blood marked the arms and legs. Her face, painted in ghastly puddles of scarlet, had been battered to a pulp.

Both men grimaced when they caught sight of the woman's throat. Thick, dark, gelling blood had stopped oozing from the yawning wound which had nearly decapitated her.

Taking a tentative step into the dimly lighted room, they looked into the dark shadows beyond the woman's feet. Eastman spotted it first, and his gasp brought Spalding's eyes to the same point. Between a tall mahogany chest and a blue mattress, nearly obscured by more scattered clothing, another thicket of long brown hair, above a red garment, rested in stillness on the carpet.

The child lay facedown, her head completely hidden by the matted, tousled dark hair. A long-sleeved red sweatshirt covered her upper torso and arms, which reached in both directions, angled away from the body. She wore a gray skirt, red knee socks, and tennis shoes. Massive amounts of blood had soaked into the carpet around her neck. Even though neither man could see the wound, they both guessed what it would look like.

Spalding and Eastman gently made a cursory examination of both bodies. Like the one in the hall, the motionless flesh felt cold. None of the three victims would ever need any human help again.

Now investigation of the tragic deaths would be handed off to homicide investigators. Fire Chief Eastman made his way from the abattoir carefully into the kitchen, picked up a dish towel from the countertop, and used it to hold the telephone while he called the sheriff's department.

While waiting for the arrival of the police, Eastman and Spalding talked to Don Hendrickson, and listened as the distraught survivor explained again that the victim in the hallway was his wife. He recited the sequence of events leading up to his discovery of her body. She'd left their home before dark, he said, and when he later became worried, he'd walked over and discovered her body.

Paying close attention to Hendrickson's statement, both officers became especially attentive when Hendrickson paused to control his emotions, then told them of an occurrence almost eight years earlier. Renae Wicklund, he said, had been raped at knife point. Both she and Barbara had testified at the accused man's trial. The rapist, Hendrickson said, had vowed he would come back and kill the two women.

No matter how hard he tried, though, Don Hendrickson could not remember the guy's name. "But," he added, "the woman who lives next door saw a man hanging around in the area earlier today."

Snohomish County Sheriff's Deputy Doug Pendergrass received the call at 6:58 P.M. to proceed to 180th Street, S.E. En route, a voice crackled over the radio for him to upgrade the call to a Code 3 He arrived at the Wicklund residence at 7:07, just eight minutes after the fire department rescue team.

Chief Eastman met Deputy Pendergrass near Renae's parked car, and briefed him on the discovery of three female bodies, all expired from throat lacerations. Within a couple of minutes, two other deputies also squealed to a halt in the already crowded driveway where official vehicles parked in various juxtapositions. The new arrivals also listened to the briefing.

While Doug Pendergrass entered the house through the open slider to verify the observations of the fire department trio, the other two officers set up a crime scene perimeter with yellow plastic tape. One of them, Deputy John Hinds, pondered Hendrickson's comments about the neighbor having seen a suspicious person in the area. He left his partner on guard while he walked next door to the neighbor's house, on the east side, to determine if they had, indeed, heard or seen anything.

When the front door of the residence opened, Andrea Warner, Renae's friend, gave the officer a quizzical look. Hinds explained that he was investigating an incident in the neighborhood, without giving any details. Curious, Mrs. Warner invited him in.

"I was told," Hinds said, "that someone at this address may have seen a suspicious-looking individual in the area today."

Mrs. Warner replied that her daughter, Patty, had noticed a man, whom she didn't recognize, walking around. Not too many strangers took walks around here, she added, then introduced Hinds to Patty. "She's eleven years old," Andrea said, "but she's mature for her age."

Deputy Hinds asked Patty if she could tell him about her observations, and perhaps describe the man.

"Sure," Patty replied, overcoming the natural shyness of a child giving a report to a police officer. "I'm not sure just what time it was, but I looked out my window this afternoon, after school, and saw a tall, dark man walking down the gravel road on the side of the house. Then he went to the very end of our property and started walking alongside the fence until he got to the gate that borders Renae's yard, and started walking alongside her house."

The story came in such a rush that Hinds had some trouble taking down notes. Her pause to take a breath helped him catch up. "Do you recall what he looked like?" Hinds asked.

"He had curly, short black hair and a mustache," Patty replied, without hesitation, impressing the deputy with her excellent recall. "He had a sports jacket. And jeans. I think he weighed about a hundred and fifty or maybe a hundred and seventy pounds. He was tall . . . about six-two or six-four. I think that the sports jacket was blue with a yellow stripe."

Few adults ever provided such detailed descriptions. Hinds had made notes, but because the youngster seemed so capable, he asked her to fill out a witness statement form. Patty readily complied, neatly printing the same details she'd reported.

Tipping his hat with a smile, Hinds thanked Andrea and Patty Warner, told them that a detective would probably pay a visit soon to ask a few more questions, and returned to the crime scene. The crowd of officers, officials, and the curious had grown.

Nine

Detective Joseph W. Ward had been home from work a little over an hour, just starting to unwind, when the jangling phone startled him. Unexpected calls to the home of a homicide detective rarely bring good news. Ward answered, listened for a few moments with a grim expression gradually darkening his Nordic, bespectacled face, hung up, and told his wife not to expect him back very soon.

Twenty minutes later, at seven-fifteen P.M., he angled his car into the crowded Wicklund driveway and found some difficulty locating a place to park. The scene around the house appeared almost surreal in the bright glare of emergency floodlights provided by the fire department. Blazing, uneven light contrasted sharply with the murky night, casting long, distorted shadows and exaggerating the criss-crossing movements of deputies and other officials. A couple of news media reporters milled around outside the yellow-taped perimeter hoping for interviews.

Under the supervision of Sergeant Joe Belinc, Ward was the first arrival among ten detectives from the Snohomish County Sheriff's Office who would eventually work on the gruesome homicide case. Most of the work would be shared by Ward, Robert "Rick" Bart, and Tom Psonka, three of the four-man homicide team. The others would be borrowed from separate units.

A native of Everett and graduate of the local high school, Joe Ward, thirty-three, had spent four years in the U.S. Air Force before entering law enforcement. Following his military stint, while attending Everett Community College, he saw a classified help-wanted ad placed by the Snohomish County Sheriff's Office. They needed a dispatcher. Ward applied, took the test, and got the job. Shortly afterward, he also became a reserve deputy. Excellent scores on another written test allowed him to become a full-time deputy in 1972, increasing his salary from five hundred dollars a month to a handsome seven-fifty. He spent five years on patrol, then accepted an invitation to become a detective in 1979.

Making his way through somber-faced officers who secured the crime scene perimeter, around to the north side of the house, Ward found Deputy Pendergrass near the sliding glass door.

"Can you fill me in, Doug?" Ward asked. The deputy summarized what he knew and added descriptions of his personal observations of the bodies. "There was so much blood," he added.

"Who found the victims?" Ward wanted to know.

"The husband of the one in the hall. He's over at his home across the street." Pendergrass described the brief conversations he'd had with Don Hendrickson.

Ward borrowed Pendergrass's flashlight, having left his own in the car, leaned inside for a moment to be sure that no one was in the house to disturb evidence, exited, and slid the door closed. The sliding glass moved stubbornly because it had been derailed from its track.

"Don't let anyone else in there, Doug," the detective ordered, and walked into the darkness toward the Hendrickson home.

Don Hendrickson seemed relieved to finally sit in his own living room and tell the details of the nightmarish evening to an investigator. Ward listened, jotting entries into a notebook that would be bulging before the night ended. Just as Hendrickson wound down his story, still holding his emotions in check, his daughter, Peggie Ann Stein, walked in. Somehow, her presence threw the grieving man off balance, and he began sobbing uncontrollably. Joe Ward knew that the father and daughter needed some time alone. He asked if he could take the slippers that Don wore for comparison of footprints, then told Peggie that he would return in a couple of hours to ask her some questions.

At the north side of the Wicklund house again, Ward met detective Rick Bart. Also a native of Washington, Robert "Rick" Bart had started work with the massive Weyerhaeuser "lumber king" Company following his high school graduation in 1966. Within a year, the specter of being drafted into the military and being shipped to the jungle hell of combat in Vietnam loomed on Bart's horizon. Instead, he paid a visit to an air force recruiter who suggested that he could become an "aircraft patroller." Sounded great to Bart, so he signed up. A few weeks later he found himself in an assembly hall with 180 other recruits. An officer walked in, divided the group in half and announced, "This half are cooks and this half are cops."

"I was a cop," Bart later recalled, describing his experience in the military police. "I didn't like it, but there was nothing I could do. They sent me to Alaska, where I spent a year in the Aleutian Islands at a radar installation, freezing and waving at Russian pilots flying overhead." A reassignment came along, to North Dakota. "I thought Alaska was cold. Nothing's as cold as a North Dakota winter. I didn't even know I was in the United States. A sergeant had to show me on a map."

He didn't know it at the time, but he wasn't very far away from the hometown and the family of a young woman named Renae Ahlers.

Washington climates seemed warm by comparison when Rick Bart mustered out in 1971. While working at Weyerhaeuser again, and wondering what he was going to do with his life, he decided to use the G.I. Bill to attend Shoreline Community College in Seattle. In retrospect, he decided that his military police experience wasn't so bad after all, so he chose classes in that specialty. "Got a degree in law enforcement there. Went to work as a jailer while I was still attending school."

Bart found that work in law enforcement, over a period of time, agreed with him. Following graduation he took the test to become a deputy sheriff in Snohomish County and scored higher than anyone else in the group. Accepted as a patrol officer in early 1973, he went back to school part time to earn a B.A. The degree helped advance him to detective status where he worked burglaries. "At that time, there were two homicide detectives, and I was invited to join them; but didn't especially want to." His reluctance didn't discourage the captain in charge. "In '78 one of the detectives got promoted, and the other guy was working a murder scene alone where there was a burglary involved. They called me to help him out. When I got there, the captain told me I was now a homicide detective." Bart laughed as he recalled, "We didn't solve that case for several years."

The two-man homicide team had handled an average of ten or fifteen murders annually for several years. The year Bart joined the team, "We worked our butts off," he remembered. The county experienced a sudden jump in killings in 1979, so the captain added two more detectives to the unit. One of them was Joe Ward. Bart and Ward became partners in 1981.

Now, on April 14, 1982, Rick Bart also grimaced when his phone rang. "I was exhausted from another murder case I'd been working on." He also had other cases in the mill, including the charge of sexual assault reported by Rosalie Campbell, who hadn't yet returned to discuss the case with Bart.

"My wife and I were lying on the bed, watching television," Bart recalled. "She picked it up, listened, then threw it at me!" As he hurried back into his work clothes, he couldn't believe what he'd heard. A triple homicide, in Snohomish County? That just didn't seem possible.

It took Bart only ten minutes to arrive at the Wicklund house. A patrol sergeant briefed him, and had just finished when Joe Ward returned from his visit with the sobbing Don Hendrickson.

"I haven't been inside yet, Joe," Bart told his partner. "Thought I'd wait for you. Chief Eastman and his two guys are getting ready to leave. Do we need anything else from them before they take off?"

"Yeah, I think so." Ward nodded. "There are some bloody

smears on that hardwood floor in the house. We'd better get some photos of the shoe soles of everyone who's been in there."

So, one at a time, Fire Chief Eastman, Lieutenant Spalding, and Randy Weiss knelt on the ground facing away from Joe Ward. Each man held a piece of yellow paper, inscribed with his name and shoe·size, next to his shoe bottoms, while Joe Ward snapped pictures. The same procedure would be used for every one of the officers who entered the house.

As the fire department team left, Joe Ward and Rick Bart made ready for more photography. Ward wrote in his summary of investigation report, "At 1949 hours (7:49 P.M.) Detective Bart and I began to photograph our way into the residence, from the sliding glass door area. We first observed that the sliding screen portion of the door was bent, as though it had been forced open at one time." That damage, he noted, was in addition to the glass door being off track.

Step by step, into the kitchen, they progressed while Bart's strobe light flashed. He took nearly a hundred shots while Ward made notations. Just inside the door, "We observed an orange throw rug, bloodstained footprints, a Frisbee, and an overturned chair," Ward wrote. The two detectives also noticed that the faucet handle to the kitchen sink appeared to be bloodstained. Ward scribbled an observation that Don Hendrickson had admitted turning the water off when he first entered the house.

They moved forward to make a complete photographic record of each room before beginning the evidence collection process. With meticulous care, they inched toward the three bodies, assembling the first pieces of a ghastly puzzle. A scenario of brutal, bloody violence began to emerge in the minds of the two sleuths. As they worked their way into the hallway, they noticed blood spatters' and smears in several places on the walls. More "possible" footprints showed up on the shiny, varnished hardwood floor. Clothing had been scattered everywhere.

As the bodies came into view, deep shock registered with both men. "It was vicious," Bart would later tell a journalist. "It was a horrible mess. The worst I've ever seen. I'd been in the military four years, but nothing compared with this. On patrol, I've seen mothers and kids killed in car wrecks, but it wasn't the same. There were different factors here. This little girl . . . I had a daughter five years old and Joe had two daughters. My God, her head was almost cut off. . . ." He felt the anger rise up inside him, he said. "I was so mad at what I was seeing. We would go in a room where they were; then we'd have to come out and just sit for a while . . . talk about it, then go back in. I hated whoever did this. I felt I would personally kill him if I could."

Containing his fury in order to get on with the job, Bart concentrated hard on the process of lifting blood samples from the floor by moistening sterile cotton swabs with distilled water and rubbing them on the stains. He even lifted one off the fallen chair in the kitchen.

Joe Ward's reaction to the savage execution of Barbara, Renae, and Shannah sounded very much like Bart's. "That was the most shocking crime scene I've ever seen," he would recall. "The number of bodies, the amount of blood . . . the damage to the bodies. And the child's age. . . . All women." Ward told how he, too, tried to shake off the emotional reaction and concentrate on the job at hand. "You just immerse yourself in what you have to do. After a while, it becomes a routine. I try not to think about the victim's suffering, try not to focus on that."

Despite himself, though, Ward couldn't help but relive his reaction to the agonizing, brutal way the three died. "The killer made Renae suffer horribly. Having your throat cut is not a quick death. One other victim I can recall, a woman, lived for five or six minutes, running around a bus stop trying to get someone to help her. It's not quick."

When they'd completed making a comprehensive photographic record, the two detectives were free to move whatever was necessary to begin collecting evidence. Perishable items would necessarily take first priority. Because Renae's body was nude, had been battered, and lay with the legs apart, Bart and Ward agreed that "a potential sexual assault had taken place." This meant that they would be required to take swabs of fluids, place them on glass slides, and preserve them for future testing to determine the presence or absence of sperm. Police organizations in large cities generally use criminalists for such specialized work, but in smaller towns and rural areas, homicide detectives must develop expertise in a variety of functions. Ward and Bart could do the job as well as anyone.

As soon as that delicate task was finished, the two men launched into the procedure that predated Sherlock Holmes: picking up clues. Any item that potentially could point to a suspect must be identified, tagged, bagged, protected, and transported. Minuscule material such as a thread of fiber or a hair, or the other extreme, such as the chair, pieces of carpet, doorknobs, even a bloodstained section of wall, are often collected.

Among the myriad of artifacts detectives Bart and Ward bagged were a piece of broken fingernail found on the dining area floor, two cigarette butts, one of them from the floor between Renae's legs, a variety of loose hairs, and other mundane minutiae that might, or might not, help in the investigation.

To preserve any potential evidence the three victims may have touched or grabbed, they placed paper bags over each of the stilled hands, and tied them at the wrists. Before covering Barbara Hendrickson's left hand, they observed that she had very long fingernails, with the exception of the ring finger. That short nail appeared to be, "rather squared off at the end and ragged. . . ." It had probably been torn off in a struggle. This missing nail tip, they realized, had been picked up a few feet away and placed in a paper envelope.

In the pocket of Barbara's white sweater, they found her husband's watch, an open package of Benson and Hedges cigarettes, a gray cigarette lighter, and a pitiful symbol that mutely testified to the good-hearted intent of her visit . . . a thermometer in a black plastic case.

Both men dreaded the next task. The child, Shannah, had been discovered lying facedown. With their jaws clenched, making a mask of impassiveness, they gently turned her over onto her back.

The hearts of two fathers thudded and their breaths came in short gasps.

Shannah's neck had been sliced through, draining her life-blood onto her red, soaked zippered sweatshirt and smearing the lower part of her face. That was bad enough, but the most gut-wrenching blow came when they looked at her beautiful, large brown eyes. They were wide open! Shannah's last view in the world had been of a monster slashing at her throat with a razor-sharp knife.

"I try not to think about the victim's suffering, try not to focus on that," Joe Ward would say, his voice even, trying to mask emotions. But at this moment, neither he nor any other human being could avoid it. Joe Ward and Rick Bart felt the intense pain. And neither of them would ever forget it.

One of the officers gave the duo a welcome interruption when he asked them to step outside. He'd found something interesting.

Following the deputy diagonally across the backyard, toward an opening in the white wooden fence that delineated the neighbor's property, they stopped about seven yards from the house. On the ground, they saw a small gold-colored chain and a metal stickpin. Both items had probably been taken from a jewelry case found on the orange carpet in a bedroom, the small drawers emptied and scattered on the floor. The killer, in his haste to leave, had apparently dropped them, leaving a directional arrow pointing to his escape route. The chain and stickpin, too, were photographed and placed in an envelope, and Sergeant Belinc laid a paper bag on the ground to preserve any other possible evidence until a daylight search could be made.

Back inside, Bart and Ward made a closer examination of some strange marks on Renae's right leg. After studying the wavy lines of blood imprinted on the skin, they realized that the impressions had been left there by a sports shoe. Someone had stepped on her after she'd fallen to the floor. Both men looked at each other, and silently moved over to Shannah's body.

No conversation was necessary. Joe Ward gently lifted the

girl's left foot and examined the sole. With horror, they shared a mental scenario of what happened.

Shannah had left the school bus, walked innocently up the long driveway, routinely entered her quiet home, and been confronted with a knife-wielding monster. Screaming, the horrified girl scrambled for her life. She ran through the hall, into the bedroom where her nude, executed mother lay. In abject terror she tried to escape her pursuer, and had stepped in a spreading puddle of blood on the floor, then tried to leap over Renae's body, but came down on her leg with one tennis shoe. The savage killer caught the child after only one more desperate stride.

Some time elapsed with the killer still in the house before Barbara Hendrickson appeared. Inside, she'd confronted a maniacal slasher, who took her life, too.

No one, except the killer, would ever know precisely what had happened, but the two detectives knew they weren't far off the mark.

Instead of returning across the street to interview Don Hendrickson's daughter, Joe Ward decided to stay with Rick Bart and continue processing the crime scene. He asked Tom Psonka to question Hendrickson and Peggie Ann Stein.

Standing over six-three, burly and muscular, with reddish blond hair, Tom Psonka had recently transferred to Snohomish County from Chicago. Even though he was experienced, his peers still regarded him as a rookie on the team of detectives. He'd been working sexual assault cases prior to the triple murder, and had gradually gained the respect of the group.

Despite his imposing appearance, Psonka could still be gentle in handling a grieving relative. He made Hendrickson feel comfortable repeating the whole story again. Sometimes, it pays to hear a witness statement more than once. It confirms repeated points, and frequently adds important details. Psonka listened with compassion as Hendrickson concluded his recollection of the day's events.

Three hours had passed since Hendrickson had discovered the

ghastly horrors across the street, and it already seemed like three days.

At a little after ten P.M., Psonka turned to Peggie Ann Stein. Frowning, she told the detective that her mother had recently described a disturbing "situation" between Renae and a distressed man. "My mom said that Renae told her she was being pressured to give some work to another person, but she refused. Later, Renae told Mom that she felt sure she was being followed . . . tailed by someone."

Renae, Stein said, thought that the man following her had some relationship to "an older gentleman who lived in Portland, who had interest in several schools Renae did work for."

After some thought, Stein continued. "The tail only lasted a short time. Renae didn't seem to be too worried by the whole situation because there was no further trouble over her work with the schools. But my parents and I were concerned for Renae and Shannah because they were lax in locking their doors."

"When did this take place?" Psonka asked.

"I think it was about six months ago," said Stein.

At Psonka's request, Peggie Stein filled out a witness statement form detailing her story, and gave it to the detective at eleven-thirty P.M. He thanked Hendrickson and his daughter, then hurried across the street to tell Ward and Bart of the possible lead to a suspect.

Several more detectives had arrived by the time Psonka returned. One of them, Herb Oberg, worked busily applying black dust to nearly every surface in the house that might contain a latent fingerprint.

Well after midnight, the coroner's van rolled out of the yard, carrying the three bodies away. The weary team of detectives continued the evidence search for three more hours. Finally exhausted, they closed the crime scene for the night at three-thirty A.M.

One last responsibility remained to be completed that night. One of the toughest duties of homicide detectives is notifying the families of murder victims.

* * *

The phone rang well before dawn in the home of Lorene Ahlers Iverson, Renae's sister, and her husband, Jerry Iverson, in their country home just outside Jamestown, North Dakota. Lorene picked it up, groggy and half-asleep. A male voice asked, "Is this Lorene?" She said it was. "Is Jerry there?" Now confused, Lorene woke her husband and handed him the phone. The voice asked to speak to him privately, suggesting that Jerry pick up the phone in another room. A fearful rush of adrenaline melted away any sleepiness, and Jerry went into the kitchen to an extension. Lorene heard him ask her to hang up the bedroom phone. Wondering what all the mystery was, she complied, but felt rising alarm. The caller identified himself as a police officer from Everett, Washington, who had once met the Iversons when they'd traveled to visit Renae.

Now realizing something must be terribly wrong, Lorene walked into the kitchen. Jerry sat on a chair listening to the caller, his head bowed, one hand grasping his forehead. When he carefully replaced the handset in the cradle, he looked into his wife's eyes, and said, "Oh, honey, I'm so sorry." He paused to control his trembling voice. "It's Renae and Shannah. They've been murdered."

In a nightmarish spin of horror, Lorene and Jerry wondered what on earth could have happened. They'd been given no details. Where and how were Renae and Shannah murdered? Why? Nothing made any sense.

Lorene gathered her thoughts. She realized that her mother, Hilda Ahlers, must be told. Lorene called her pastor, gave him the sketchy news, and asked him to meet them at Hilda's Jamestown apartment. She and Jerry gathered up their three young children, Amber, Treven, and Kama, all under five, put them into the car, and drove through the predawn darkness.

With Pastor Hutton, they knocked lightly on Hilda's door. She asked who was there, and Lorene answered, "It's me."

By the time Hilda opened the door, the sun hadn't yet crawled over the horizon. To wake her at this hour, something must be terribly wrong. The first question to pop in her mind involved her grandchildren. Had she lost one of them? She felt momentary relief when Jerry stood there holding two sleepy babies, and Lorene held the third.

Thank God! Hilda thought. *They're all here.* It was then that she focused on Pastor Hutton standing behind the group. Hilda's mind raced to Renae. It must be her. She voiced her question. "Airplane accident?" Lorene's eyes filled with tears as she shook her head no.

"Car accident?" Another choking shake of the head.

It took all of Lorene's courage and strength to form the word, ". . . Murdered."

But what about Shannah? Who's taking care of Shannah? The questions filled Hilda's thoughts before she uttered the name, "Shannah . . . ?"

Nothing Lorene had ever spoken before, or would ever speak again, came harder.

"Shannah, too."

Ten

Reporters had rushed away from the Wicklund house Wednesday night in time to beat deadlines and file short articles. On Thursday, early risers opened newspapers and suddenly stopped yawning when they read the headlines: "Three Found Slain Near Clearview." The accompanying text, though, contained scant information, simply listing the names and ages of the three victims, telling who discovered them, and promising more details after the pending autopsies. A Seattle radio station scooped the other media, announcing the victims' throats had been slit.

The news described early morning reactions from neighbors who "huddled together, consoling each other, watching officials come and go." One woman asked a sheriff's deputy posted at the crime scene if it was safe for her children to wait at the school bus stop. Another said the "frightening" crime made her nervous because she'd heard nothing, not even any screams. She and her family had recently moved to Clearview from California to "escape this kind of thing."

Later newspaper editions added more particulars about Renae Wicklund, Shannah, and Barbara Hendrickson.

Other than stories about the triple murder, April 15 was a slow news day. Reminders appeared below the fold, prompting readers to file their income taxes before midnight. A bridge had collapsed in Chicago, and Argentine ships headed toward the Falklands war zone. Another homicide article appeared in national papers that day. In New York, a judge sentenced Jack Henry Abbot to serve fifteen years in prison for killing a waiter. It was the second time around for Abbot. He'd gained national fame for authoring a book, *In the Belly of the Beast,* while imprisoned for a previous murder. The book caught the attention of author Norman Mailer, who spearheaded a sympathy movement for Abbot, eventually leading to his release on parole. Now, he'd killed again, generating a tidal wave of controversy across the nation over the issue of freeing convicts too early. Many argued that such a policy led to the deaths of even more innocent victims.

Sheriff's investigators at Renae Wicklund's house hadn't told reporters everything on the previous evening. That would have led to premature speculation. Besides, detectives usually hold back certain details that only the killer would know, setting up the chance that when he is apprehended, he might blunder into mentioning the details, thereby incriminating himself. Several leads had developed, buoying investigators' hopes that a suspect in the grisly triple murder might be identified soon.

First of all, they had a pretty good idea which way the killer left after the bloody spree. Items of jewelry found on Wednesday night near an opening in the backyard fence pointed the way, so Detective Bart asked for help from a K-9 unit, on the chance that a dog could pick up the trail. A handler, Deputy Terrance Green, arrived before ten P.M., accompanied by a handsome, pure black Shepherd-mix named "Ace." The scent had been preserved when Sergeant Joe Belinc placed a paper bag over the spot where the gold stickpin lay on the pine needles. Green commanded Ace, "Seek him out, get the crook." Bright-eyed and enthusiastic, Ace trotted to the bag, put his sensitive nose to the ground, and "alerted" (tensed his body to let his handler know he'd picked up a scent).

Police dogs love their work. To them, it's like an exciting game, so they play it with wonderful enthusiasm. With his snout to earth, ears high, and running with abrupt zigzag turns, Ace moved through the fence opening, detected the track, and headed through the adjacent backyard, where the Warners lived. The handler and detectives followed, probing the darkness with powerful flashlight beams. Across the yard, Ace came to a narrow gravel road, crossed it, and worked his way through a thicket of heavy brush. Scrambling to keep up, the men aimed their lights in the direction Ace took them, and could see freshly trampled grass and twigs, evidence that someone had recently plowed through the shrubbery, on foot. The trail led them back onto the main road, 180th St., S.E. There, unfortunately, Ace lost the scent. But his efforts had not been wasted. The trail Ace followed would tie in closely with witness reports being taken at that very moment by other detectives.

In the Warner home, where Ace had just led his team across the backyard, Detective Wyatt Weeks followed up on the earlier visit by Deputy John Hinds. Weeks wanted to see if the little girl, Patty, could add anything to the statement she'd given earlier in the evening. Patty repeated most of her previous recollections, adding that the tall stranger she'd seen in her backyard that afternoon had paused to look at rabbits the Warners kept in a cage. He'd then turned through the fence opening, and walked into the Wicklunds' yard.

Detective Weeks asked Patty if she could be a little more specific in describing the man. "Sure," she replied, perky and unafraid. "I looked out my window and saw him." She closed her eyes in deep thought, and recited again her mental picture of the intruder. The detective smiled at her confident precision, and asked how old she thought the man was. Patty pondered for a moment, and guessed he was between eighteen and twenty-two. "My sister saw him, too," Patty volunteered.

Patty's sixteen-year-old sister, Deanna, had also glanced out the window while the stranger stood near the rabbit hutch, and thought it might be someone she knew. She didn't have her glasses on, though, so couldn't make him out clearly. When she'd stepped outside for a moment, he turned his back to her and walked away. Deanna couldn't recall any details about his appearance.

A new arrival at the Warner home appeared distraught to the

detective, so Weeks turned his attention to the man, Glenn Douglas, Renae's boyfriend. Mrs. Warner had telephoned Douglas as soon as she knew enough about the tragedy next door to let him know what had happened. He'd hurried over, sick at heart.

Douglas told Weeks about the last time he'd seen Renae, Sunday when he'd visited her at home. He said he'd tried to call her this afternoon, at about five-thirty, but no one had answered the phone. As Weeks took notes, Douglas seemed concerned about something else. Weeks asked about it.

"Well," Douglas said, "Renae was afraid of a man named Pissaro. He's a financial consultant from New Jersey, and she was responsible for keeping him out of some work in this area." Other than Pissaro, Douglas couldn't think of anyone else Renae had feared. "She did get some threatening phone calls some time ago, but she couldn't recognize the guy's voice."

The topic of the sexual assault, over seven years ago, came up, and Douglas's face registered confusion. As he heard about Renae's ordeal of December, 1974, his expression darkened in dismay. She had never told him about it. His grief over her death took on an added burden of sympathy and sorrow.

Other local residents to be questioned that night remained on Detective Weeks' list. Detective Psonka took over while Weeks left to locate other possible witnesses.

At one of the listed homes, on nearby Cedar Road, Weeks' pulse rate speeded up as the home owner told of seeing a stranger that afternoon, driving a small orange or red two-door coupe. At about four-fifteen, the car had rolled slowly along Cedar, with a dark-haired young man in a blue coat behind the wheel, acting "suspicious."

The next person Weeks interviewed, also on Cedar Road, described deep mud tracks on his property where someone, probably unfamiliar with the area, had gouged holes in the ground by turning a car around too quickly.

A third resident in the same row of homes punctured holes in the possible leads from the first two statements. His own visiting son drove an orange two-door coupe, and had turned it around that afternoon in some mud, nearly getting stuck. "This accounted for the only out-of-place vehicle seen on Cedar Road that day," Weeks wrote, a little disappointed. In movies and mystery novels, every clue is a piece of the mosaic that finally bags the culprit. In real life, only a small percentage of the leads, if any, turn out to be useful.

By the time Rick Bart and Joe Ward closed the crime scene in the predawn hours of Thursday, April 15, a pair of leads to possible suspects had been developed. Don Hendrickson, who had discovered his wife's body, had mentioned to Deputy Pendergrass the sexual assault on Renae back in December, 1974, but he couldn't remember the name of the guy who did it. And Detective Weeks, in conversation with Glenn Douglas about that same attack, had heard of a man named Pissaro who possibly had a motive for revenge on Renae.

Detective Bart knew it would take only a few minutes to pull the name of the sexual assault perpetrator, and check out his current status. He also planned to learn more about Mr. Pissaro.

The final indignity for murder victims is the autopsy. It is a scientific process in which there is little room for tender compassion. Still, for the detectives who witness the postmortem in order to collect evidence in a murder case, it is impossible to set aside the sympathy and emotional pain associated with senseless loss of innocent lives.

Before Dr. Clayton R. Haberman began the surgery on Barbara Hendrickson Thursday morning, Rick Bart snapped a series of photographs while Joe Ward kept a list of the evidence gathered. Carefully packaging Barbara's clothing, pocket contents, hair samples, and pink slipper (the mate had been picked up at the crime scene), the detectives also collected her jewelry, with one exception; they left her wedding rings on her finger. Observing that she wore only one earring, they noted that the other had been torn from her pierced right ear.

In addition to the gaping throat wound, the detectives observed the swollen right side of Barbara's upper lip, where a hard blow had landed prior to her death. While Dr. Haberman conducted the surgical exam, he dictated his scientific observations. Later transcribed, his medical terminology of the neck wound alone covered two full pages of single-spaced type. The autopsy report cover sheet summarized Barbara's injuries: 1) Massive incision of anterior neck with severance of carotid arteries and oro-pharyngeal area, 2) exsanguination (bleeding to death), 3) an-temortem (before death) manual strangulation, and 4) blunt trauma to scalp and face.

On Renae Wicklund's body, there were no clothes to be re-moved and packaged. A delicate gold chain around her neck had been hidden in the gore of her wounds. Examination of the mas-sive trauma covering her entire body revealed savagery almost unimaginable to the sane human mind. No one could have seen the horrifying results without flinching and feeling visceral anger boiling from within.

Renae, too, wore only one earring, on the left side. The other one had been ripped out. A gold ring decorated the bruised and bloody third finger of her right hand. Her facial, throat and bodily injuries were so extensive, the typed report took eleven single-spaced pages to describe. Ward and Bart grimaced when they saw that the killer, before slashing her throat, had stabbed her in the neck repeatedly. One final discovery stunned the two detec-tives even more. Dr. Haberman found that as Renae died, her killer had sexually assaulted her with an unknown object ap-proximately one and one-half inches in diameter, and ten inches long! Renae Wicklund had suffered: 1) Massive blunt trauma to the face, fracturing the nose, jaw, and crushing the soft tissues, 2) manual strangulation, fracturing her thyroid cartilage, 3) blunt trauma to the abdomen and right chest causing internal hemor-rhage and a fractured rib, 4) blunt trauma to the right side of the head, 5) multiple bruises and abrasions of her arms, sustained while she tried to shield herself from the blows, 6) multiple stab wounds to the lower neck, 7) massive incision of the neck, with severance of trachea, esophagus and carotid arteries on each side, and 8) laceration of the vagina, probably "agonal."

In layman's terms, the summary told of her painful suffering from savage multiple injuries inflicted with the most barbaric violence conceivable.

One more extremely difficult phase remained for the detectives. Most homicide officers claim they are able to develop an aloofness to watching autopsies, but invariably agree that the greatest difficulty is experienced when the victim is a child. Bart and Ward, two fathers of young daughters, agreed. Bart, however, received a phone call that spared him from the ordeal. Sergeant Joe Belinc wanted to see him as soon as possible.

Shannah Wicklund's red hooded sweatshirt and blouse were "massively" soaked with blood, which had also stained the gray woolen skirt. She, too, wore only one heart-shaped gold earring on the right side. Joe Ward noted it, wondering if the killer had some maniacal urge to collect trophies.

The mortal wound to Shannah's throat equaled the trauma suffered by the two women. Dr. Haberman took vials of blood samples from each of them, but Shannah had bled so profusely that he had difficulty filling even one vial of blood from her desiccated body. He summarized her injuries: 1) Massive incision of neck structures, including airways, esophagus and both carotid arteries, 2) multiple lacerations of the scalp secondary to blunt trauma, 3) strangulation and multiple bruises of the face, 4) exsanguination, and 5) bilateral vocal cord hemorrhage from the strangling.

Joe Ward left the coroner's lab with renewed determination to find the beast who had killed so brutally, and see him hanged if at all possible.

Eleven

Even though detectives had worked the crime scene until the wee hours of Thursday morning, most of them returned by dawn to continue evidence collection. Detective Herb Oberg had already lifted thirty-five latent fingerprints late Wednesday, but knew he could find more. Twelve of them came from the rear sliding glass door, three from a coffee cup in the kitchen, and the balance from a variety of furniture, doorknobs, mirrors, and surfaces in the bathroom. When he resumed the task, he dusted and taped jewelry, a fuse box, windows, bathtubs, and walls. In the kitchen, next to the sink, he saw an amber-colored drinking glass, purple-stained with what appeared to be grape juice. Oberg took it to test for prints, but decided to package it for mailing to the F.B.I., on the remote chance that the stains could be blood.

The detective knew, full well, that most of the prints he found would be from innocent people, the victims, friends, neighbors, or relatives. But the possibility that just one of them had been left by the killer made the entire effort worthwhile.

Most of the fingerprinted objects, after Oberg's processing, were packaged, booked, and sent to the property room at headquarters. This included sections of carpet, pieces of walls, and even doorknobs unscrewed from their sockets.

While Oberg worked his technical skills inside, big Tom Psonka and Wyatt Weeks searched the yard. Psonka then led the way for another investigator, Ken Crowder, to the Warner home. Detective Crowder had learned how to assemble composite pictures of suspects, using descriptions from witnesses. By asking

questions, he selected celluloid prints depicting the right size
and shape of noses, ears, eyes, mouths, facial shapes, eyebrows,
hair, and any moles, scars or other marks. Stacking them on a
white background, Crowder could add or change features until
the image resembled the suspect. Crowder and Tom Psonka went
to the Warner residence hoping that young Patty could pick out
the characteristics of the man she'd seen.

Patty seemed to enjoy the picture-puzzle challenge. When
they'd completed the composite, a sparkling smile lit her face.
She said the picture looked exactly like the man, then decided
that maybe the nose should be a little more "triangle-shaped"
and flatter at the base. Finally, she wanted the hair to appear
fuller, then gave her approval. Crowder took the finished product
to be reproduced and distributed.

A member of the investigative team responded to a telephone
call from a family on Waverly Drive, less than one-half mile from
the Wicklund house. Mr. Victor Gray, his wife Jane, and his two
sons, Gary, thirteen, and Dale, fifteen, all contributed some
promising information.

The father, Victor, while driving home on Wednesday afternoon, at three-forty P.M., had seen a strange automobile backed
into the woods, a hundred yards up Waverly Drive. It looked like
an older model Ford Torino, a "very dull orange-reddish color."
Then, on Thursday, he and his wife Jane, while walking their
dogs along Waverly, saw "what appeared to be the contents of a
woman's purse spilled" alongside the road. Among match books
and facial tissues, they'd noticed two 4-H medals. A burglar had
stolen jewelry and medals from the Gray home in 1981, after
which Jane had developed a habit of always looking for her lost
treasures. She heard about the neighborhood tragedy, and wondered if the discarded items might somehow be associated with
the murders, so she picked up the medals. At home, Jane cleaned
them, and found one inscribed with the name Renae Ahlers. Vic-

tor and Jane knew of "a neighbor girl" named Renae, but didn't recognize the last name.

The older brother, Dale, while riding the school bus home at two-fifty that afternoon, had looked out the window just after passing a lumber mill, and noticed a faded red car backed into "an inlet." A tall man, with his back toward the bus, stood looking into the car, which Dale thought might be a Duster or Impala, but warned, "I'm not sure of the make." The stranger had "sandy-brown, naturally wavy hair, and stood about six-two."

Gary, the younger son, had a story even more interesting to the officer. The youth said that on Wednesday afternoon, at three-thirty, he and a pal were riding bicycles to a third friend's house, when they observed something unusual. They spotted the same car seen by Gary's father, parked in an "awkward" spot, backed into a dirt road that led to an old dump ground. "I've never seen a car parked there before," Gary said. It was faded red, similar to a Chevrolet Duster, he said, but admitted, "I don't know much about cars."

At the home of their buddy, they played badminton in the spacious backyard. At about four-forty-five, they caught sight of a man about eighty yards away walking rapidly toward the parked car. He had "black, wavy hair, a thick mustache, and was about five-foot-eight." Slung over his shoulder, he carried a "red blanket with small white and yellow stripes, that appeared to be stuffed with something." The man wore blue jeans and possibly a jacket, and carried the bundle "like Santa Claus."

When Gary returned home alone, at five-fifteen, he noticed that the car was gone.

At headquarters, Sergeant Joe Belinc studied file records containing the name and criminal history of Charles Rodman Campbell, who had been convicted of sexually assaulting Renae Wicklund in 1974. He saw a certain irony in the dates. Renae had testified against Campbell on April 19, 1976. She was murdered on April 14, 1982, just five days short of the sixth anniversary of her testimony which sent Campbell to prison.

Belinc also held a motor vehicle report indicating that Campbell owned a 1973 orange Ford Torino. The last part of the rap sheet sent Belinc's pulse racing. Campbell had received a long prison sentence, but had been placed on a work release program a few months ago, and transferred recently to the same program in Everett. It appeared to Belinc that Campbell might very well have had the opportunity to commit the murders. He picked up the phone and called the supervisor at the Everett facility, only to learn that Campbell had violated rules against drinking alcohol, and had been returned to the reformatory over in Monroe.

The lead seemed to be evaporating until Belinc asked when they took Campbell to Monroe. "Just last night," the supervisor replied.

Belinc heard the details of exactly how Charles Campbell had destroyed his work release privilege and chance of parole:

A few minutes before six o'clock, on Wednesday evening, April 14, the day Charlie Campbell had been anticipating for so long, he and Karl Popovich, a fellow inmate, logged out of the Everett house to drive over to Marysville. They told the duty officer they wanted to arrange transportation for Popovich to go to work on Thursday. Campbell had already been out for several hours, but the officer approved the request. An hour later, Campbell returned, alone, saying he had dropped his companion off in downtown Everett. His words sounded slurred, drunken.

Another officer, conducting a resident check in Campbell's room a few minutes later, saw him sound asleep on his upper bunk, fully clothed and still wearing shoes. Oddly, his jeans were soaking wet from the knees down. She tried to wake him, calling his name and shaking his bed, but got no response. He smelled strongly of alcohol.

She telephoned the facility supervisor, Tom Cornish, who advised her to let Campbell sleep until his parole officer, Gary Whitinger, came to work. Whitinger, the supervisor said, should collect a urine sample from Campbell. When Whitinger arrived at about nine-thirty, he managed to awaken Campbell and asked for the urine sample. Campbell sprang up, yelling obscenities about his sleep being interrupted, and after some resistance, went into the bathroom. There, he insisted that he couldn't urinate, and sullenly headed back toward his bunk, muttering angry threats to Whitinger and complaining about being singled out for harassment. Whitinger warned Campbell of the possible consequences of such behavior, and walked downstairs toward the operations office, with Campbell following right behind, complaining bitterly.

Once more, Whitinger asked for the sample, but Campbell said he had just relieved himself a short time ago, and couldn't do it again. At last, the angry resident agreed to a balloon test. With a smirk, he said he'd seen on television that balloon tests didn't work anyway. No trace of alcohol could be found. Whitinger called supervisor Cornish, who agreed that the refusal to cooperate with the request for a urine sample violated the rules. He gave Whitinger instructions to obtain police help and transport Charles Campbell to the Monroe Reformatory.

The recalcitrant Campbell had finally gone too far and exhausted the patience of work release officials. Ironically, it came on April 14, the magic day he should have become eligible for a full parole.

While being escorted into the police car after the officers had searched him, Campbell yelled at Whitinger, "I'll remember this." Whitinger delivered Campbell to the Monroe Reformatory at eleven-sixteen P.M. that Wednesday night. Early the next morning, Tom Cornish went to Campbell's Torino, parked across the street from the Everett house, and looked inside. He saw piles of trash, partially eaten food, bottles, and beer cans littering the car's interior. Cornish confiscated the beer containers.

A single earring lay in plain view on the front seat. Fortunately, Cornish didn't touch it.

* * *

As soon as Joe Belinc heard that Campbell's time was not clearly accounted for during the time of the murders, he and another detective quickly walked the two blocks to the work release house, where he found supervisor Tom Cornish.

Describing the events of the previous evening, Cornish advised Belinc that Campbell had been returned to Monroe for either being drunk or under the influence of drugs, a violation of the work release rules. Cornish said he'd removed some beer containers from Campbell's car, parked across the street. Belinc asked, "Did you see any jewelry inside it, or anything else of a suspicious nature?" Cornish answered that he had seen some jewelry on the front seat.

All three men crossed the street to the parked Torino, and looked inside through the windows. Belinc saw what he described as "one earring, post type, with what appeared to be a pearl on the end of it." He wondered if it would match the one found on Renae Wicklund's ear. Circling the car, Belinc observed a red stain, possibly blood, on the driver's side door handle. He also saw mud and debris clinging to the underside of the trunk, the tires, and inside the rear wheel wells, "indicating that the vehicle had been in a muddy, gravelly area and had taken off at . . . a high rate of speed."

Joe Belinc returned to his office and hurriedly wrote out an affidavit requesting approval for three search warrants to examine the contents of the Torino, the interior of Campbell's room at Everett Work Release, and to search the cell and person of Charles Rodman Campbell at the Monroe Reformatory. He wanted to find out if Campbell had possessed or hidden any jewelry, knives, or anything else that could be identified as coming from the murder scene. Within an hour, he obtained underwriting from a deputy prosecuting attorney and approval from a judge.

Belinc telephoned the coroner's office, and asked that Rick Bart return to headquarters as soon as possible. Then he had the Torino impounded, towed to the sheriff's garage, and sealed in preparation for a subsequent search.

Meanwhile, Tom Psonka and Detective Weeks, armed with the warrant to search Campbell's room, hurried to room 7 at the Everett house. They seized a blue nylon jacket, bedding, a pair of tennis shoes, and a clump of soil stuck to the end of the bunk, where Campbell's shoes would have made contact.

Rick Bart and Detective Roger Johnson had the pleasure of traveling over to Monroe to execute the warrant on Charles Campbell. They drove through the quiet town, up the hill to the imposing edifice, and through the sally port. No free person enters a prison without feeling a little chill. Inside, Bart spoke first to a sergeant who gave him the clothing that Campbell had worn on his return to the reformatory. It included a purple jacket, blue jeans, a pair of Nike sports shoes, and a pullover shirt.

The detective faced Charles Campbell for the first time a few minutes later. Cocky as usual, Campbell glared at Bart, who promptly read him the Miranda warning. Campbell responded with a sullen grunt. The warrant provided for the taking of blood samples, saliva, hair, and allowed an inspection of Campbell's body for injuries he might have sustained during the violence in Wicklund's home. Rick Bart methodically collected two vials of blood, hair trimmings, and the saliva, then ordered Campbell to strip nude. He took a series of color photographs from every angle. During the whole process, Campbell sneered and hissed insulting comments. When Bart had completed the task, he faced the contemptuous inmate. With undisguised loathing in his eyes, Bart spoke, forming each word with controlled enunciation, as if they were chiseled from cold steel. "I'll be back. I'll be back with a warrant in hand to arrest you for three counts of aggravated murder."

Campbell stood still, speechless. His shoulders slumped as he turned away to return to his cell.

Ladonna Layton heard from Campbell that same afternoon. He telephoned to ask her to move his Torino from the street over at the work release house in Everett. Still loyal to him, she drove from Monroe to Everett, and asked the duty officer about the car. Sergeant Joe Belinc, who had returned and happened to be standing nearby, overheard her, and introduced himself "That vehicle has been impounded," he told Layton.

Appearing distressed, Layton explained that she was Charlie Campbell's girlfriend and asked what was going on. "Is he in trouble again?"

Giving no answer, Belinc asked when she'd last contacted him. She told the sergeant about Campbell's telephone request, then inquired again if Charlie was in trouble. Belinc informed Layton that he was conducting an investigation of "a situation" in which Campbell could be involved. "Did you have any contact with him at any time yesterday?" he asked.

Layton said that she had. Campbell had arrived at her Monroe apartment in the morning, about nine-thirty, and stayed until a little after noon, when she had to leave for work. She didn't want to be late for her new job in Seattle at a halfway house for convicts. Charlie, she said, drank a full six-pack of Budweiser that morning. As she prepared to leave, Charlie said that he planned to buy some new tires for his car and have them mounted that afternoon.

"Did he do that?" Belinc asked. Layton didn't know. She hadn't heard from Charlie again until nine o'clock last night, she said, when he called her place of employment. She couldn't get to the phone right then, so he left a message for her to call him back at the Everett house. But when she tried, an officer informed her that Charlie had "passed out" in his bunk. And then he called this morning to ask her to move his car. Ladonna Layton's face twisted with worry.

The sergeant tried to word his next question tactfully. "Did Charles Campbell ever mention to you, or make any reference to the victim, or witness, of the crime he committed in 1974, the one he went to prison for?"

Layton's answer reflected equal caution. "Yes, he did. He talked about it a few times, and he always said that he was innocent of any of the charges."

Belinc thanked her, and left to continue the investigation. Ladonna Layton learned from someone else at Everett that Campbell had been taken to the Monroe Reformatory for violating the rule against drinking. She still didn't know that detectives suspected him of murder.

Twelve

Karl Popovich had met Charles Campbell at the Monroe Reformatory in 1981, and the two spent time together commiserating about being locked up. When Campbell transferred to the Honor Farm, Popovich was sent to the Everett Work Release house. Reunited in February, 1982, they teamed up again.

On Wednesday, April 14, Popovich spent most of his day lounging at the facility, then left in the late afternoon to apply for a job. A company that installed fences hired him, so officers at the house didn't chastise Popovich when he returned a few minutes late that afternoon.

Feeling pretty good about the new job, Popovich sauntered into the television room where he found his buddy, Chuck. They chatted for a while, while Campbell rubbed the fingers on his right hand, saying he thought he'd broken the hand. He seemed slightly "loose" to Popovich, as if he'd been drinking, but not enough to be drunk. The pair decided to leave the house for a little celebration. Campbell said he also had something else he wanted to take care of. They requested a pass to leave, saying they needed to arrange transportation for Popovich to get to work the next day.

After changing his clothes, Popovich went up to room 7, and gasped in surprise. Campbell had actually taken a shower, something he habitually avoided. It didn't make sense to Popovich, then, when Campbell dressed in dirty blue jeans, a soiled shirt, and old tennis shoes. Campbell also picked up five or six articles of dirty clothing from the floor, bundled them together, and told his buddy that he was ready to leave. The duty officer filled out a pass for one and one-half hours which should give the men enough time to make the transportation arrangements.

Campbell threw the bundle in the trunk of his Torino, and they climbed into the cluttered interior. Popovich laughed at the mess: an open potato chip bag, a shoe horn and some beef jerky on the dash, plus moldy remains of a lunch on the floor. He also noticed fresh mud on the driver's side floor, and the broken rearview mirror. To his question about the mirror, Campbell said he'd broken it off with his hand when he "went off" a couple of days ago.

A few blocks from the house, Popovich expected Campbell to stop at a convenience store for some beer, but Campbell turned instead toward the Snohomish River. "I've got to go to the river," he told Popovich several times. En route, they finally stopped at another store where Popovich hurried inside for a quart bottle of Budweiser. Rolling again, Campbell told Popovich to reach under the car seat where he had a half bottle of tequila hidden. Popovich asked, "Where'd you get it?"

"I took it from a woman today," Campbell replied, without elaborating. They drank from both bottles as Campbell continued to drive. Feeling nervous, Popovich twice asked Campbell to slow down a little. They'd been driving ten or fifteen minutes when Campbell turned onto a dirt road leading to the river. Popovich recognized it as the Lowell boat launch area. They rolled to a stop near a youth straddling a parked motorcycle, who tried to make conversation with them. Campbell whispered to Popovich, "I can't do what I have to do while this guy is here." Amused, Popovich told him to relax. The motorcycle rider produced a "bong" and some marijuana, which he shared with the men in the car. When they'd finished inhaling the potent weed, the youth fired up his bike and sped away.

Campbell asked his companion if he'd mind "taking a little walk down the road," by himself for a while. Popovich shrugged, grabbed the Budweiser, stepped out of the car, and headed back toward the road. He stayed away about ten minutes, smoked a cigarette and finished the beer. From the direction of the river, he heard tires spinning in the dirt, saw the Torino skid from around a bend, and hopped in when Campbell reached him.

On the way back to Everett, Campbell had nothing to say about the mysterious stop. They finished the tequila, and Popovich tossed the bottle out of the speeding car. He asked to be dropped off at another friend's house in Everett, so Campbell returned to the facility alone.

When Popovich arrived back at the house, he found Campbell in the television room, slumped in a chair, nearly passed out. He helped his staggering buddy back to room 7, trying to prevent the officers from noticing Campbell's advanced state of inebriation.

Karl Popovich lay awake most of Thursday night, wrestling with his conscience and his urge for self-preservation. He'd heard enough of the news to figure out what his fellow inmate had done. Popovich had to report to a job the next morning, but he decided to make a phone call first.

While driving to work on Friday morning, April 16, Rick Bart answered a radio call from Joe Belinc. The sergeant said that a work release inmate, who was working near Lake Stevens, had asked to talk to a detective. Bart agreed to detour over to the lake and meet the guy, Karl Popovich.

The convict had no trouble convincing Bart of the value of his trip. "I want to talk to you about what happened in Clearview," Popovich said. After a short conversation with Popovich, the two men climbed into Bart's car and headed to the Lowell boat launch area. At the river's edge, Bart wondered about Popovich. The detective later told of his thoughts: "When I walked up to the bank with him, I was trying to figure out this guy's involvement in the murders. Is he the murderer? Did he help Campbell? What's his motive? All he could say is he's a three-time loser. He didn't want to make any mistakes."

When Popovich told Bart that he'd been at the river on Wednesday night with a fellow work release resident, Charles Campbell, the detective wasn't surprised, being quite familiar with the name. Popovich volunteered his reason for deciding to inform. He cited the age-old rule of convicts, "You don't kill kids."

Popovich hadn't seen exactly what Campbell did at the river, or where he did it. He simply suggested to Bart that he thought the purpose of the trip was to dispose of some evidence. Perhaps fate stepped in at that moment to lend a hand. Rick Bart glanced down at the mud just above the water's edge, and zeroed in on a silver bracelet. He felt like leaping into the air, turning cartwheels, or shouting. "I was really happy, but trying to contain myself," Bart recalled. He'd made a rash promise to Campbell over in Monroe. Now, "I knew I had the son of a bitch."

As soon as he could get back to his car, Bart radioed for help. He wanted a scuba team to make a thorough search of the area. By early afternoon, a team of seven divers and a boat operator went into action. They found four more pieces of jewelry before darkness halted the search.

The depth of the Snohomish River, where it empties into the Puget Sound, is affected by the ebb and flow of tides. During the search on Friday, high tides pushed the water up the banks, perhaps ten or fifteen feet. The team, led by Deputy Dallas Swank, a former U.S. Navy SEAL, scheduled additional dives for low tide periods. During one of the expeditions, Bart recalled, he developed extreme admiration for a big, shaggy dog that he thought was a Saint Bernard. "They brought this dog up. I brought a blouse from the murder scene, let the dog smell it, and he went straight to the river. He jumped in, barking, growling, and carrying on, swimming upstream and downstream. The handler knew his dog was onto something, and yelled, "Your stuff's in the river." When the tide went out, we found pieces of pottery, more jewelry, a brass wall ornament, and clothing. The dog knew it was there. I don't know how he did it. I was so impressed with him smelling stuff right through the water."

Bart may have been enthused with the dog's performance, but his opinion of "a certain sergeant" was considerably less exuberant. Back at headquarters that afternoon, the sergeant began pressuring Bart to arrest Charles Campbell for the triple murder, so it could be announced immediately to the press. Bart felt they needed more solid evidence to seal the case. All they had so far was circumstantial evidence, he argued. The sergeant insisted and ordered Bart to take the newest detective, Tom Psonka, the recent transfer from Chicago, with him and make the arrest. That would enable the sheriff to make the announcement at a press conference, scheduled within the hour, and let the public hear it on the evening news. Bart all but refused the direct order, snapping back at the sergeant, "You go arrest him."

Furious, the sergeant turned to big Tom Psonka and ordered him to go to Monroe, and arrest Campbell. Bart thought, *Oh, great, the rookie will probably go do it.* Psonka looked at Bart, turned thoughtfully to the sergeant, and said, "No." Suppressing a grin, Bart turned to Psonka and said, "You're okay. C'mon, we've got some more investigating to do." To the red-faced sergeant, he chided, "You guys have your press conference, and do what you want. I'm going to go search that car."

On the way out of the building, Bart and Psonka ran into the sheriff, Bob Dodge, who asked, "How's it going?"

"Not good," Bart replied.

Frowning, the sheriff asked, "What do you mean?"

Bart felt sorry for the top cop. "Look, in that press conference, are you going to tell the public that Campbell is our suspect?"

"Yes."

"Are you going to tell them that we're going to arrest him?"

"I'd planned to."

"Don't do it," Bart urged. "We're not ready yet. You're the sheriff, so you can do what you want, but I sure wouldn't recommend it."

Sheriff Dodge walked away, looking worried. Bart and Psonka left, searched the Torino, and returned after three hours. Bart learned from a livid sergeant that Dodge had danced all around the issues during the press conference, saying nothing of substance. The sergeant accused Bart of going over his head, and Bart resented the way he said it. "They had to separate us," he later recalled. With a twinkle in his eye, he remarked that maybe he should run for sheriff someday, and avoid silly problems like that.

In searching the Torino, Bart and Psonka recovered an assortment of items including soiled clothing, beer bottles, papers, the rearview mirror, and the front seat adjustment knob smeared with a suspicious red stain. They also found the pearl earring on the front seat. After bagging and logging the material, they toted it to the sheriff's evidence room, where an accumulation of other jewelry and possessions waited for identification by the victims' relatives, friends, and witnesses. Some of the viewing process would have to wait for a week, until April 24, when the heartbroken members of Renae Wicklund's extended family in North Dakota planned their sad journey to Washington.

One of the first witnesses to arrive at the evidence room that same evening was Glenn Douglas, Renae's distraught boyfriend. Tom Psonka and Joe Belinc showed him assorted bracelets, earrings, and medals gathered from the Snohomish River, recovered from Campbell's possession, and found at the crime scene.

Douglas recognized a pair of earrings Renae had once shown him. They had been found among Campbell's clothing at the Everett house. Visually examining each piece of jewelry, Douglas positively identified a locket and two 4-H pins Renae had earned in her hometown. One of the pins, inscribed with the name Renae Ahlers, had been found by the Gray family while walking their dog.

On Saturday morning, while corporate employees took a weekend off, the team of detectives started work early, and would continue without a day off for weeks. Andrea Warner, Renae's close friend and neighbor, along with another female acquaintance, came to the evidence room. Psonka and Bart displayed the jewelry, and Andrea's eyes filled with tears when she saw the red-beaded Indian necklace and matching earrings divers had pulled from the river's depths. Shannah had proudly shown the trinkets to Andrea, announcing that her grandmother had given them to her. Both women recognized a broken portion of a coffee cup, also found in the river, as one Renae often used.

Renae, the two friends told Bart, wore only 14 karat gold or silver jewelry because she had an allergy to most other metals.

While the identification process took place, other investigators spread out over the county to collect more proof in the growing case against Campbell, still looking for badly needed physical evidence. Detective Wyatt Weeks visited Campbell's employer at the landscaping firm in Edmonds, where the suspect had worked part-time as a laborer since March 9. On Campbell's last day there, the company owner said, he showed up reeking of beer, and had a few cans of Budweiser with him. "I told him about our policy about drinking on the job, and warned him not to do it again. He got upset, but told me he understood the policy."

Weeks asked if Campbell had worked on Wednesday, the 14th. "No, he didn't," the owner replied. "He called me at about nine o'clock that morning, and told me he would be late for work. He and his girlfriend had to have the snow tires on his car changed. He assured me that he would be at work before noon that day. But he never showed up."

"Did Campbell use, or have access to, any sharp tools?" the detective asked.

"No, not really. He mostly used shovels, rakes, hoes, wheelbarrows, stuff like that, to perform earth moving, sod laying, brush cutting, or just loading debris into a truck."

On his way back to Everett, Weeks felt good. The interview had eliminated Campbell's workplace as an alibi for the time period during which the murders occurred.

Elimination of other potential suspects also took place that weekend. Barbara Hendrickson's daughter had told Detective Psonka of a man who'd had some conflict with Renae related to her work, and might even have been following her. And Renae's boyfriend, Glenn Douglas, had suggested that a man named Pissaro, a financial consultant from New Jersey, had been angry at her for preventing him from contracting some work. Both possible leads turned out to be the same person, who was unmistakably cleared of any involvement in the crimes. One man remained on the list as a possible accomplice or independent killer. Suspicions still clouded the actions of Karl Popovich, who had led Detective Bart to the Snohomish River cache of evidence.

Because they felt that Ladonna Layton might shed more light on the activities of Campbell, a pair of detectives drove to her Monroe apartment on Saturday afternoon. She wasn't home. Later in the day, they telephoned, found her there, and asked if she could come over to the sheriff's office in Everett to discuss Campbell. She stated that it would be impossible for her to come right then. Would she mind talking to a detective at her residence? Ladonna let a long moment of silence elapse before saying that she was too emotionally upset over the situation, and couldn't give a good statement right now. Could the detectives have her permission to search the apartment? She didn't hesitate this time. No. It wouldn't do any good, she said, because Charlie didn't have anything at her home. After hanging up, the detectives began filling out an affidavit for a search warrant. It would never produce anything important to the case.

Two more inmates of the Everett house agreed to talk to investigators. One of them reported overhearing a conversation in which Campbell had told Karl Popovich that "he raped the woman before killing her." While interesting, and convincing to the detective, he realized that it wouldn't be useful in court because it would be categorized as hearsay.

The second informant had less dramatic information, but possibly helpful. He said that Campbell rarely bathed, maybe once every two weeks. But when he came back to Everett house on Wednesday, at about five P.M., he hurried to the showers. Afterward, acting very "boisterous and unusually nervous," Campbell carried "a bundle" to his car.

The bundle, also seen by Karl Popovich, probably contained the items later dredged from the river.

Rick Bart and his partner heard from a loquacious, plump, middle-aged woman who thought she had seen someone possibly involved in the murders she'd heard about on television. Vera Norton worked at a small grocery store in South Everett, and chuckled a lot while rambling nonstop in her booming voice. On either the 11th or the 14th, she couldn't remember exactly, a tall, thin man in his mid-twenties came into the store and asked for directions to Clearview. The detectives listened as Vera told her story:

"I remember I laughed and said, 'Clearview, what's in Clearview?' and he kind of laughed and said, 'Not much.' After I waited on a couple of customers, I asked him, 'What's the address?' and he didn't have one. So I asked him if it was a private residence or a business, because whenever anyone comes in and asks for a place, I always try to find that out. I'm fairly familiar with the area. Well, he never answered me.

"He said that he'd been there before, but it had been a long time and he couldn't find the right road from Murphy's Corner, and that things had changed. He'd gotten off the freeway at 128th, but everything was different. I agreed with him that things sure had changed.

"I asked him then, 'Well, you must know where the Bothell highway is?' And he said yes, he knew there was a road to turn off to Bothell, but he couldn't find it, 'cause it was different. I said it was, and there was lots of new homes and a new shopping center. So we have a big map on the door behind the counter, and I said, 'Well, come over here and I'll show you how to get there from the Bothell highway, since you're confused about Murphy's Corner.'

"So, on the map I found 180th and showed him and he looked very confused, and I asked him again, 'Well, don't you have an address?' He kept looking at the map, then he said something about Highway 9, which he was pointing at. I told him that was the main way to Clearview, and about all there is in Clearview is a burnt-down tavern on one corner and a store close to it.

"I was really starting to wonder, at that point, where he was going. My daughter used to live in a trailer park close to there, and she moved because there was lots of drugs there. So I thought to myself maybe that's what this guy is looking for, and that's why he doesn't want to give me an address. Anyway, I finally came out and asked him if, by any chance, he was looking for the trailer park. He said no and kept looking at the map. He said he would know when he got there and saw it. He started to leave, but then he got a couple cans of beer. I said 'I hope you find what you're looking for,' and he said, 'Thanks a lot, lady.'

"I'm pretty sure he got into a small type car. It was parked directly in front of the big windows, and I could plainly see him through the windshield. He was alone. There was another customer in the store at the time, and we remarked that we hoped he knew where he was going. He was so vague about it. I remember the conversation plainly, 'cause I did most of the talking. He wasn't saying much, and I thought at the time, 'How'd he get from Murphy's Corner to our store, when we're a little out of the way?' "

If Vera Norton's story hadn't been connected to such a serious investigation, the detectives might have found it amusing, because of her candid and homespun way of telling it. They wondered, if the man asking directions had been Campbell, was it on the day of the murders, or three days earlier? Perhaps he drove out to the Wicklund house in advance to plan the crime. The small car Vera Norton had seen could have been Ladonna Layton's black Volkswagen Rabbit, which had been repaired after the wreck in January.

They asked Vera if she could return on Monday, April 26, when several witnesses would view a lineup to see if they could identify Charles Campbell. She agreed to be there.

* * *

Rick Bart realized that the search for physical evidence to link Campbell to the murders must be intensified. So far, all they had were witnesses reporting a man who resembled Campbell lurking around the area, and even those descriptions varied somewhat. A car had been spotted that roughly matched his Torino. The recovery of jewelry and other items taken from the Wicklund home didn't prove that Campbell had wielded the murder weapon, nor did the pair of earrings taken from his pocket. Campbell could conceivably have acquired the jewelry from someone else, maybe Karl Popovich. Popovich took Rick Bart to the river, and had been in the Torino a number of times. Could he be the real killer? Not one eyewitness had seen the murders, or the killer in the Wicklund home. Everything unearthed so far was only circumstantial, and it wouldn't take a particularly skilled defense lawyer to punch holes in the case.

No, they still needed at least one piece of physical evidence before Charles Campbell could be brought to justice in a murder trial.

Thirteen

By Monday morning, April 19, Detective Rick Bart still thought he needed more evidence before officially arresting Charles Campbell. The suspect certainly wasn't going anywhere, being locked up in the Monroe Reformatory. Nevertheless, public pressure and political expedience won out. With arrest warrant in hand, Bart drove over to Monroe, up to the edifice again, and through the sally port. Waiting in between locked gates, Bart watched as two correctional officers escorted Campbell, wearing chains, into the yard. Other inmates stood in the background, silently observing.

"I told you I'd be back," Bart said, in a crystal clear tone. He handed the warrant to Campbell, who wore his usual sneer. The inmate scanned the pages, and handed it back without a word or a sound. His escorts guided him into Bart's car. No conversation took place on the way back to the Snohomish County jail in Everett.

The news media desperately wanted something else to feed public hunger for updated information on the case. They agreed, however, to avoid publishing photos of Campbell until investigators completed identification lineups. Witnesses scheduled to pick out the man who'd been seen near the crime scene might be influenced by published photos of the suspect. While waiting for new developments, articles speculated whether Campbell, if convicted, would be eligible for the death penalty. But the news hounds needed something more dramatic.

Rosalie Campbell gave it to them.

In an interview with reporters, Rosalie said that she'd been having recurring dreams in which Campbell slashed her with an ax. She pointed out the irony of Renae and Shannah Wicklund's ages compared to her own and her daughter's. Renae was thirty-one and Shannah was eight. Rosalie was thirty-one, and her daughter (by Campbell) was eight!

Rosalie chilled the reporters with her next comment. "I think that woman was supposed to be me, and her little daughter was supposed to be my daughter. We were meant to be those people." Had Charles Campbell vicariously killed his own ex-wife and daughter?

The thought presented a repugnant possibility. If Campbell's mind was that twisted, could a sharp defense attorney plead guilty by reason of insanity, get him committed to an institution for a few years, and then seek freedom when Campbell returned to sanity? Rosalie added fuel to that fire with her description of Charles Campbell as, "Possessed."

Then she gave the reporters another explosive comment to stir up readers, and embarrass officials of the work release program. "Charlie raped me last Christmas Eve," she said, and added that he'd done it again a few days later.

Penal system administrators scrambled to examine records of Campbell's stay at Monroe and Everett. He wasn't supposed to leave the premises for any reason. How could he have raped his ex-wife in her Lynnwood apartment? Blushing officials said that Campbell had not been granted any authorized furloughs from the time he went to the Monroe Honor Farm to the time he was transferred to Everett. Although Campbell "could have been away from Monroe house without authorization" they said, it would have been "difficult" for anyone to leave without the absence being noted.

An officer at Monroe house stated in writing, "If Campbell did leave the Monroe Work Release unit on the morning of De-

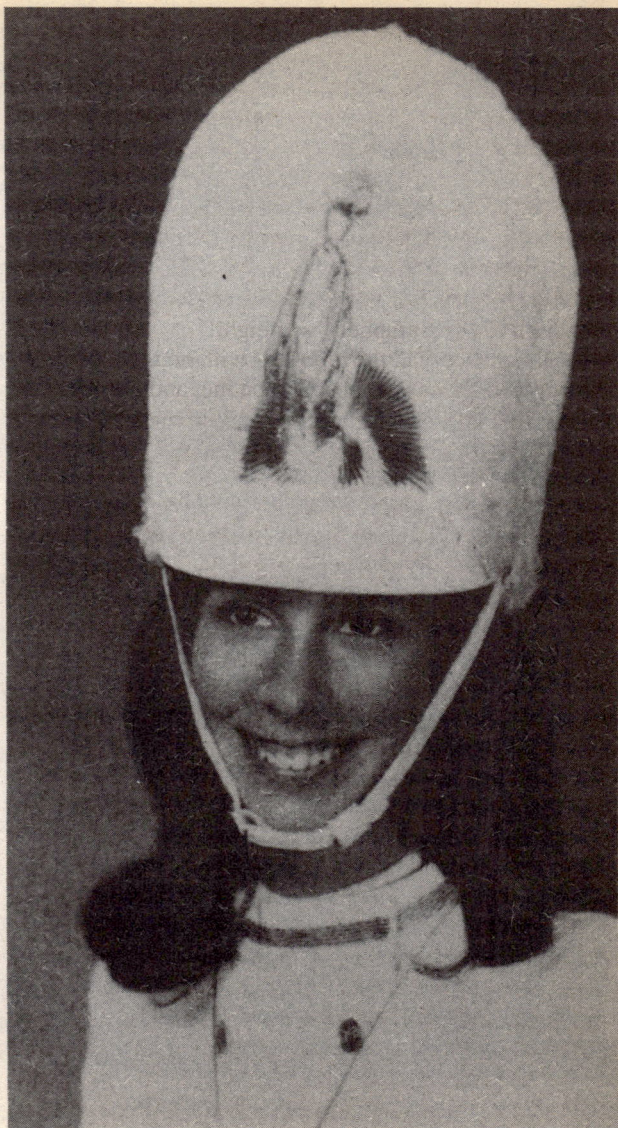

High school yearbook photo of Renae Wicklund.

Renae and daughter Shannah at Christmas.

Renae at Christmas.

Shannah and Renae outside their Clearview, Wash. home, shortly before they were killed.

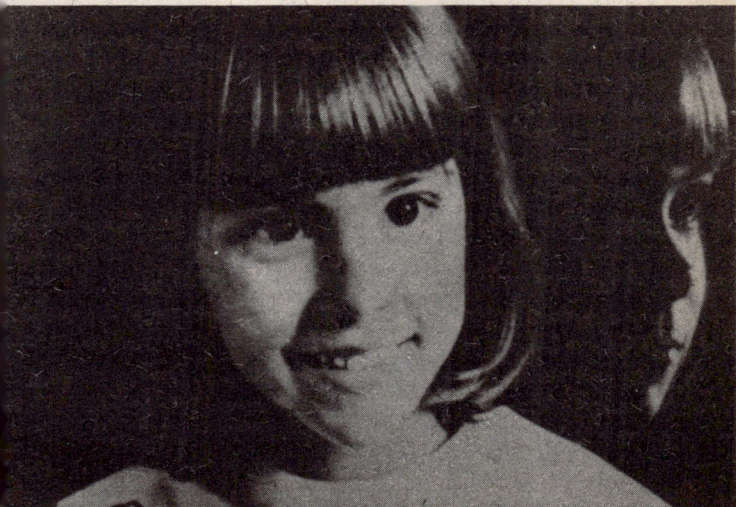

Shannah Wicklund.

Shannah's bedroom.

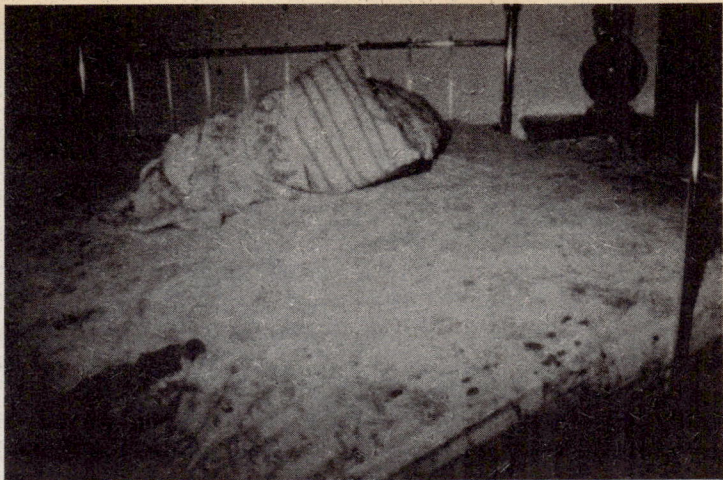
Renae's bloodstained bed.

Blood on the wall of Renae's bedroom.

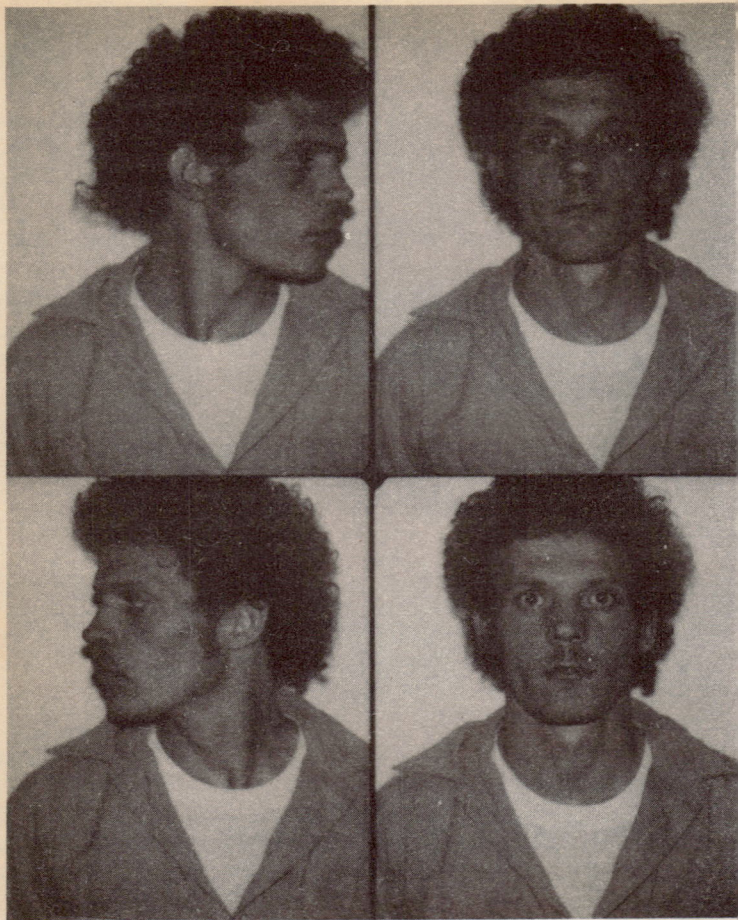

Mug shot of Charles Rodman Campbell.

Campbell entered the Wicklund's house through the kitchen. The glass (right) on the countertop helped police place Campbell at the crime scene.

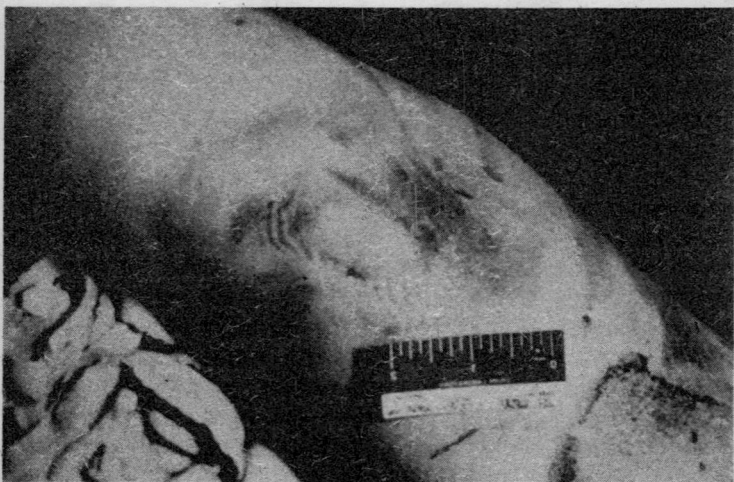

Shannah's shoeprint pattern in blood on Renae's leg.

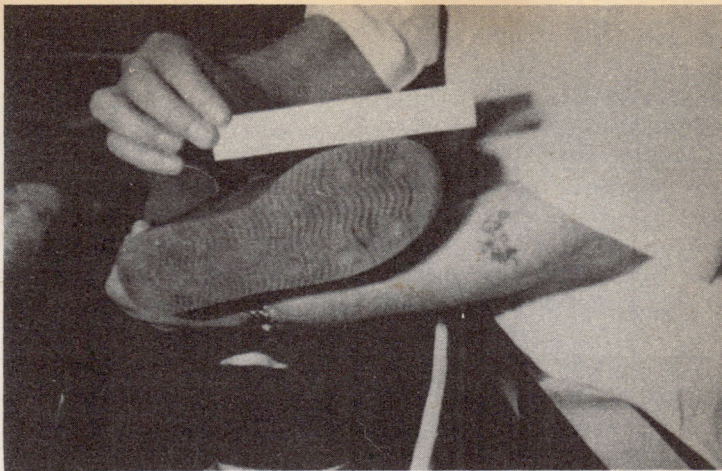

The sole of Shannah's shoe, showing pattern found in blood on her mother's leg. This indicated that Campbell chased the girl around the room before killing her, after he'd already killed her mother.

Campbell being led into courtroom during his trial.

Lieutenant Rick Bart. *(Courtesy Gary C. King)*

Detective Joe Ward.
(Courtesy Gary C. King)

Sergeant Joe Belinc
(*Courtesy Dreams in Still Photography*)

Washington State Penitentiary in Walla Walla, Washington.

Campbell being led from his cell on Death Row to a
court hearing.

cember 25, 1981, he would have to have had an accomplice. I made my hourly bed check by shinning (*sic*) my flashlight above his bed. There was a living, breathing body in his bunk as well as all the other bunks that were supposed to have inmates."

To add even more controversy, Rosalie told reporters that Campbell had been delivered and picked up, both times he raped her, by a woman wearing a uniform that looked like a security guard. That allegation couldn't be proved, or disproved, and went nowhere.

A fallout of the news reports made work release inmates furious at Charles Campbell, when new controls were imposed upon them.

Exactly one week after the murders, Detective Rick Bart convinced Campbell's girlfriend, Ladonna Layton, to give him a statement. She told Bart that Campbell came to her apartment in Monroe at about nine-thirty on the morning of April 14. She hadn't expected him, and assumed he was on his way to work with the landscaping company. He had some Budweiser beer with him, "the only kind he drank," she said, and had apparently been drinking already. They spent the morning together.

During the morning, Ladonna told Bart, Campbell made telephone calls trying to find some tires he could afford to buy for the old Torino. She left him in her apartment about fifteen minutes before noon, to be at work by twelve-thirty.

"Was he alone?" Bart asked. Yes, Ladonna said, and he was "slightly inebriated." Bart shook his head. He realized that Ladonna, as an ex-employee, knew very well that a work release inmate shouldn't be drinking, or lounging around in his lover's residence without authorization. Love is blind.

Ladonna said she talked to Campbell the next morning on the telephone. He called her from the Monroe Reformatory to let her know when she could visit him, and to ask her to move his car out of the limited parking zone in Everett. "He did not relate to me anything about what had happened," Ladonna asserted, "except that he was in W.S.R. for drinking, and that he would be out in a couple of weeks and everything would be okay."

She had tried to visit Campbell that afternoon, but officers wouldn't allow her to see him. He'd left telephone messages Wednesday evening at her workplace, but she'd been unable to make contact with him.

Bart sensed that Ladonna had reached a point in her story where she was reluctant to continue. With a little coaxing, she spoke again. Ladonna told Bart that after her return from Everett, where she'd gone to move the Torino, only to learn that it had been impounded, she noticed that something appeared to be missing from her apartment. A wooden block in the kitchen holding her butcher knives had a conspicuous absence, like a missing tooth. One of the knives had been taken, but Ladonna wasn't quite sure when it had happened. At Bart's request, she even sketched a picture of the knife.

There was no doubt in Rick Bart's mind that Campbell had taken the knife, and it was the murder weapon. But it would be impossible to prove unless they could find it. He didn't know it right then, but the knife would never turn up.

"Did Campbell ever discuss any of the murder victims with you?" Bart asked, deliberately omitting the names.

Again somewhat hesitant, Ladonna replied, "Chuck felt tremendous resentment toward Renae Wicklund." Hastily, Ladonna explained that she knew Renae's last name from reading the newspapers. "He felt that way because he said he'd served six years in prison for a crime he did not commit. Chuck had talked to me about this, and told me he wanted her to feel everything he felt. He'd talk this way when he was drinking, usually."

Ladonna said that Campbell had looked up Renae's place on a map "to sort out in his own mind how he could have done the crime . . . when he was at work in Renton at the time." She had apparently never seen the documentation on his case proving that his time during the assault was unaccounted for. She seemed to believe every word that "Chuck" ever spoke.

Campbell had seen Renae recently, Ladonna admitted. Concealed behind some trees, he watched her "taking groceries inside her home."

Good Lord, Bart thought. *Campbell really was stalking her.* He asked Ladonna if Campbell had used his own car when he saw Renae.

She didn't think so. "He has borrowed my car, a black Volkswagen Rabbit, many times. He has free use of it."

How generous of her to help him break the rules by running around in a borrowed car.

"I would like to add," Ladonna said, "that he has indicated to me that revenge was not the answer in dealing with his anger about being in prison for six years. He came to this conclusion while drinking, as well as when he hadn't been drinking."

Rick Bart thanked Ladonna Layton for her help, and drove back to Everett, mulling over in his mind the relationships some women choose. Hard to understand.

Maybe Ladonna Layton wouldn't have had such unconditional faith in Campbell if she knew of his other activities during his tenure in the work release program. His ex-wife revealed that he'd raped her two or three times. Correctional officers alleged Campbell having sexual activity with a dog. And on April 14, when Ladonna had left him in her apartment, he had promptly driven over to Snohomish and tried to have sex with a friend of Ladonna's, Ellen Tremaine.

Big Tom Psonka had located Tremaine, who wasn't particularly happy to see him. He'd obtained her name as the result of a sequence of interviews starting with convicts at Monroe. Ellen Tremaine had sometimes visited certain men in the reformatory, and had met Campbell in the visiting room about two months before his transfer to the Honor Farm. Psonka didn't beat around the bush. He asked Ellen if she'd seen Charles Campbell on April 14. She admitted she had. Psonka said, "We received an anonymous letter stating that there was an attempted rape of you on the day of the slayings."

Ellen wanted to know who sent the letter, but Psonka deflected her question. "We can't divulge that information. Was Campbell here?"

"Yes," she answered. "Chuck was here."

"Could you tell us what happened?"

Looking around as if she needed some help, Ellen replied with a question: "Shouldn't I talk to some counsel first?" Psonka assured Tremaine that she had nothing to be afraid of, that she was not a suspect.

"Well," Ellen said, more at ease, "I know I was a victim, and I'm not afraid." It was all so "mind boggling" and distressful, she said. "How would you like it if a friend of yours was accused of a triple homicide?" Ignoring her rhetoric, Psonka asked Tremaine to give him a detailed statement. She began talking, and didn't stop for nearly half an hour.

Ellen Tremaine told of meeting Chuck Campbell in the Monroe visiting room, then hearing from him, and Ladonna Layton, after he moved to Everett Work Release. "Him and his girlfriend would come out and walk in the woods." Later, Campbell came by himself. On April 14, he knocked on her door at about one-fifteen in the afternoon. She'd said, "Hi, Chuck. Come on in." But she wanted him to be quiet because her daughter was asleep in the loft.

Campbell seemed to be turned on by visiting women while their children slept. His behavior at Tremaine's apartment held true to form. "He proceeded to make advances toward me. I told him to just stop, because I didn't want him. He was *extremely* intoxicated. Before I knew it, we were on the floor. He was rough and tried to take my clothes off. I started to cry and said, 'Chuck, please don't.' " Ellen didn't want her daughter to see what was happening.

"Then it was like something snapped in his head, and he instantly backed off. I got up and sat in my rocker. I was still crying and upset. He said he didn't mean to hurt me. I started washing dishes, and he saw a knife I had just rinsed."

According to Ellen, Campbell said, "Why don't you just take

that knife and slit my throat. I'm no good. I'm no good. I'm a sinner."

She had calmly responded, "That won't solve anything."

"Then give me some booze," Campbell retorted.

"No, Chuck, just please go now."

Tremaine told Psonka that Campbell became more agitated, banging the chair with his hand and mumbling, "I can't have anything else. I want the booze." He was referring to a bottle of tequila she had in a cabinet.

Disgusted and wanting Campbell to leave, Ellen told him, "Look, Chuck, if you have to take my booze, just take it and please go." She also warned him that he'd better not come out alone anymore.

Campbell finally left, Ellen said, at two P.M., grabbing the tequila and stumbling out the door mumbling to himself.

Detective Psonka couldn't resist asking her one more question. "Did it occur to you that you might have been one of those murder victims?"

"Only for a moment," Ellen said. Then added, "If Chuck did commit those crimes."

Tom Psonka had inserted one more important segment of the puzzle detailing Campbell's activities on the fateful day of April 14, but like Rick Bart, he knew that the missing link was still out there somewhere. They needed physical evidence.

In Jamestown, North Dakota, Lorene Iverson and her family attended a church service for Renae and Shannah on April 22, and left that same evening to drive to Washington. It seemed like an endless trip, during which Lorene's mind kept drifting back to something a cousin had said shortly after the nightmarish telephone call. With a stunned, astonished look on his face, the relative had lamented, "This doesn't happen to us. This happens to other people, not people like us." Now, on the sad trip west, Lorene pondered the tragedy. She felt as if her family had been slapped in the face with harsh reality. It had awakened them, all too quickly, to what goes on in the real world.

Two days later, on Saturday, the family gathered in Snohomish, Washington, at Shepherd of the Hills Lutheran Church. One hundred and twenty mourners gathered where the "Little Missionary," Shannah, would no longer bring her playmates to Sunday School. They came to pay respects and say goodbye to Renae and her daughter. Pastor Larry L. Reinhardt conducted the service in which he posed the question, "How could a loving God will such a thing?"

"Let me set the record straight," Reinhardt said. "What happened here in Clearview WAS NOT GOD'S WILL." Peace, harmony, love, and the commandment "Thou shalt not kill" are God's true will, he explained. "Unfortunately, man uses his free will to oppose the will of God, and then tragedies take place, like murder."

Grappling with the question of why didn't God prevent the murders, Reinhardt offered several thoughts, including, "He permits such tragedies in order to bring out that which is human in all of us . . . sympathy, sensitivity, and caring. Such tragedies show us how fragile our lives are . . . and teaches us to show more love and concern for one another." Reinhardt concluded the moving half-hour ceremony by pointing out that "Some questions surely remain for us," then offered the promise of faith to bring comfort and hope after tragedy.

Detective Rick Bart welcomed Hilda and Lorene into his office on Monday morning. It was the first time they'd met face-to-face, and the start of a permanent mutual admiration and respect. Hilda gave Bart some photographs she brought, at his request, showing Renae and Shannah wearing certain items of jewelry. With gentle and sincere compassion, Bart conversed with the two women before escorting them to the basement property room to identify recovered jewelry. He knew the heartbreak they suffered, and that the sight of Renae and Shannah's personal treasures would be emotional.

With courage, and moist eyes, they identified the pearl earring, recovered from the Torino, several other pieces of jewelry, and an item pulled from the river, a brass wall ornament Renae had brought from the Jamestown farm. The grieving women left to attend to estate business, and Bart joined Psonka to drive once more to Clearview, and escort the prosecutor and a newly appointed defense attorney through the crime scene. Later that day, the detectives joined divers for a new search of the Snohomish River. They found some pottery and water-soaked clothing, but nothing that promised to be the sorely needed physical evidence of Campbell's presence in the Wicklund home.

That week, Renae's family returned to Jamestown, then made the long trip again in a rental truck to haul her possessions back to the farm. At last, Renae and Shannah came home, too. The caskets were closed, but Lorene wanted one last look at her sister. She needed the closure, the final assurance that Renae was, indeed, gone. Lorene had flown back from Seattle, and had seen a woman on the plane, from behind, whose features strongly resembled Renae's. *Maybe this is just a horrible nightmare,* Lorene had thought. *Maybe she'll suddenly show up and be with us again.*

The open casket revealed a restored face that didn't look very much like the sister Lorene remembered and would always cherish. But it closed the book, ending the hope that the tragedy would evaporate, like the morning mists on the peaceful Jamestown prairies.

Shannah and her mother were buried side by side, next to Renae's father, Ahlen Ahlers, who had passed away three years earlier. At least he had been spared the heartbreaking burden borne by the rest of his family.

* * *

Rick Bart sent several cartons full of collected evidence to the Federal Bureau of Investigation laboratories in Washington D.C. Packed in the boxes were items of clothing, swabs, glass smears, blood samples, and assorted other materials. Also included were fifty-eight fingerprints, along with exemplar prints from Campbell and his buddy, Karl Popovich. Maybe, somewhere in that assembly representing the intensive work of many investigators, F.B.I. technicians, with state-of-the-art methods, would turn up that coveted piece of physical evidence so desperately needed.

Fourteen

Detectives Herb Oberg and Bob Quay stood on the bank of the Snohomish River late one afternoon, near the Lowell boat launch area, ready to provide assistance to a group of divers searching for sunken evidence. Two noisy dirt bikes roared to a halt near the detectives, and the pair of riders, both scruffy-looking men in their mid-twenties, stood astraddle their motor-cycles to see what was going on.

Recalling that informant Karl Popovich reported meeting a young man on a bike at the river that night with Campbell, Quay sauntered over and asked, "Do you come down here very often?"

"Yeah," the shorter of the two said. "I ride down here pretty often." Focusing his attention on the divers in the river, he asked, "Are you guys collecting more stuff for that homicide investigation?"

"You've heard about it?"

"I heard over the news that some jewelry's been found here by the boat launch. You guys need any help? I'd do anything to help you guys out if I can."

"Were you here at about five in the evening on the 14th?"

The bikers both shook their heads in the negative. Quay, not entirely convinced of their honesty, asked if they knew of anyone else who had been on a bike at the launch that evening.

"No," said the shorter one, "but I'll sure snoop around, and see if I can find out who it was."

"You do that." Quay nodded. He didn't expect to ever hear from either man on the subject again. He was right.

During the first full week of the investigation, a number of witnesses came into the sheriff's office to identify evidence. Detectives descended from the fourth floor of the courthouse building and escorted them to the basement property room. There, the officers laid out items of jewelry along with other possessions of Renae and Shannah found on the roadside, at the river, or in the Torino.

Another important step followed. Detectives hoped witnesses, at a lineup, would be able to identify Charles Campbell as the man they'd seen lurking around the Wicklund neighborhood. Tom Psonka greeted the first group, all youngsters. Patty Warner had seen the tall stranger in her backyard. Gary Gray, thirteen, had spotted someone walking along Waverly Drive carrying a bundle "like Santa Claus." And his older brother, Dale, had observed a gangly man standing by the oddly parked Torino, also seen by the two boys with whom Gary had played badminton that day. All five sat nervously waiting for the crucial moment.

After separating the witnesses so they couldn't influence each other, Psonka marched six men, all with similar physical characteristics, onto a stage. They could be clearly seen, but couldn't see the witnesses. Charles Rodman Campbell, on the way in, spewed vitriolic insults at Rick Bart, and said, "I'm not going to stand up in there."

"That's okay," Bart replied. "We can just have these two guys hold you up." He nodded in the direction of big Tom Psonka and a deputy of equal size. Campbell changed his mind, and stood in position number one.

Patty Warner had probably seen the stranger more closely and longer than the boys had. She studied the sullen line of men, and made her pick. Then came Gary, Mike, and the other two boys.

The final two lads were unable to find anyone with familiar features in the lineup. Gary Gray thought he did, and picked man number 4, while his brother, Dale, picked number 5.

Except for one selection, detectives thought, the process was a disaster.

* * *

Patty Warner, age eleven, filled out a witness statement to support her pick. With perfect penmanship and spelling, in large letters, she wrote, "I went into a lineup room and saw 6 guys. I picked number 1. The reason I picked him was because I was sure that's the guy I saw wandering in my yard. Because of his hair, moustache, height, build, and color. On 4-14-82, 3:30 P.M., I saw this man walk up our fence line and through the gate to Renae's yard. I am 90% sure that he is the guy."

Why couldn't all witnesses be like Patty Warner? Psonka admired her and felt sure she'd do a terrific job on the witness stand.

A second lineup, conducted by Detective Joe Ward, brought Vera Norton, the loquacious store clerk who had chatted with a tall man asking for directions to Clearview. Again, Charles Campbell stood in the number 1 position. Vera studied the six men carefully and talked her way through a process of elimination. She asked to hear their voices. Each man, reading from a placard held by an officer, twice spoke the words, "Yes, would you give me some directions?" Gradually, Vera eliminated numbers 2, 3, 4, and then number 6.

Finally, Vera Norton said, "No . . . I think number five's nose and hair aren't right." She settled on number 1, Charles Campbell.

Detective Joe Ward would eventually find another woman who had crossed paths with Charles Campbell, in an incredible coincidence:

Gloria French, thirty, couldn't remember the exact date, but recalled being on a Seattle city bus with her six-year-old daughter. They'd boarded in the late afternoon to go home, in the Magnolia area, where they had lived for over three years. Gloria and her daughter took a seat which faced across the aisle, near the front of the bus. Opposite them, sat a tall man with "a light-colored Afro and some facial hair." He wore dark blue overalls that reminded Gloria of a uniform, and carried a lunch pail.

"I was talking to my daughter," Gloria recalled, "about where her grandmother lived, in North Dakota, when the man asked me if I was from North Dakota." Gloria didn't make a habit of speaking to strange men on the bus, but saw no reason to be rude. She said yes.

"My wife's from North Dakota," he volunteered. Gloria hadn't paid much attention to him before, but now noticed that he "would snicker spontaneously to himself, and appeared drowsy." She asked him which town his wife was from.

"Jamestown," he said.

"Really?" Gloria said, surprised at the coincidence. "I'm from Jamestown. What's her name?"

"Renae Wicklund."

The name didn't sound familiar to Gloria, so she asked, "What was her last name before she married you?"

"Ahlers was her maiden name," he replied without a moment of hesitation.

"That sounds familiar," said Gloria, pressing her fingers to her temples trying to recall. "But I can't quite place it."

The friendly stranger changed the subject to ask about Gloria's interests. He inquired about where she lived. A little apprehensive at his peculiar habit of snickering, she gave him a false surname, and said that she lived in an apartment complex on 34th Street. In her statement to Joe Ward, she said, "I remember feeling vaguely threatened." She hated to lie, she said, but felt safer not giving the man her real address.

A sense of relief engulfed Gloria when the bus pulled over to the curb at her stop, but it melted away quickly when the inquisitive stranger stepped off behind her. Maybe he detected her fear, because when she turned north on the sidewalk, he walked south.

A couple of days later, Gloria began receiving phone calls with no one making a sound on the other end, one in mid-afternoon, the rest of them in evenings. A couple of days had passed, and she had begun to relax, when she saw the strange man again. She and her daughter were walking near her home when they passed a group of men, including the bushy-haired man, landscaping a corner lot. He snickered as they passed by. During the next few days, she saw him striding along the sidewalk in front of her house, sometimes going in one direction, and sometimes in the other.

Her doorbell rang one afternoon, and Gloria realized immediately that she'd made a mistake when she opened the door without looking outside first. The man with the "Afro" stood there at her threshold. And she nearly froze in her tracks when she glanced downward. "I saw that he had a hunting knife in a leather sheath in his right hand down by his right leg. It was about ten to twelve inches long from the end of the handle to the tip of the sheath."

Trying to avoid showing her fright, Gloria forced herself to answer his questions, but not very truthfully. In her mind, she pictured herself slamming the door in his face, but couldn't summon up enough nerve to try, for fear that he could force it open before it latched.

He stood there, looking over his shoulder frequently, and spoke. "I've been working down the street on a work release program, and I'm looking for odd jobs. Do you have anything I could do?"

"Not really," she said, trying to keep her teeth from chattering. "My husband works part-time, so he has plenty of time to take care of our odd jobs. He'll be home any minute." Gloria regretted her answer immediately. She'd just told this guy that her husband wasn't home, and she knew it sounded phony that he'd arrive any minute.

"Maybe you could use some painting," he suggested. "There's always some painting to be done." No, Gloria said, nothing needed painting. He then wanted to know if she'd ever lived on 34th Street, and if so, how long. No, she said. She'd lived in this house for over three years.

His questions became more nerve-wracking. She wanted to run, to call for assistance, but felt numb and helpless.

"Are any of your neighbors home during the day?" Responding as if she believed he was really seeking a job somewhere in the block, Gloria said that many of her neighbors were retired, enabling them to always be at home and take care of their own maintenance chores. There are always husbands and boyfriends around to take care of odd jobs, she told him. Again, she thought her answer sounded too obvious.

"Do you have a gun in the house?"

"No, but the woman across the street has a shotgun." The implied threat didn't sound very scary. A loud barking echoed from the backyard, and Gloria silently thanked her big Irish wolfhound for the distraction.

"Is that dog friendly?" he wanted to know.

"Only to our family. He's very aggressive to strangers."

"What kind of a dog is it." She told him the breed, trying to make it sound like a grizzly bear.

"Can he get out, over that fence back there?" He'd apparently scouted around the house.

"Yes, he can jump over it quite easily."

His next question completely confused Gloria. "Is there an elementary school around here?" Maybe he was a pedophile, looking to kidnap a child.

"It's a few blocks away," she said, trying to discourage that idea.

"Does your daughter go there?"

"No, she's too young." A large truck passed by at that moment, which seemed to make the interrogator nervous. Holding the sheathed knife in his right hand, he raised it up to chest level, "slightly out from his body, horizontal," and he started to fondle the sheath with his left hand. "He did this very slowly and carefully," she recalled. He looked uncertain, and kept fingering the sheath. Gloria described it as tooled leather.

At that instant, an act of fate may have saved her. A police car rolled by.

"Do the police come by here very often?" he demanded.

"Yes, they do," Gloria lied.

With a burst of courage stimulated by the presence of the patrol car, Gloria blurted out, "I don't know of anyone in the neighborhood who needs odd jobs done." She slammed the door, and bolted it as quickly as her shaking hands would allow.

Gloria told Joe Ward that she didn't usually watch the news, or read papers. But she'd recently seen some publicity about the killings up in Clearview, and figured out that the weird stranger might be Charles Campbell.

That last burst of courage, allowing her to slam the door, may have saved the lives of Gloria and her daughter. She didn't know it, but she perfectly fit the image of the victims Campbell obsessively stalked.

Another woman inside the dangerous circle of Campbell's life hadn't been so fortunate. His grandmother, the woman who descended from ancient Polynesians, had collapsed when she heard of her grandson's arrest for murder. She spent six weeks in intensive care recovering from a heart attack. "He almost killed me," she later declared. "Charles is nasty tempered. Yes, I'm a little bitter, I guess." Suggesting that Campbell may have serious psychological problems, she said, "I don't think he's all there."

In a small grocery market in tiny Clearview, Rick Arriza, the store owner, bristled at newspaper stories speculating about a possible death penalty for Charles Campbell. Possible death penalty? If anyone ever deserved to die for murder, the killer of the Wicklunds and Mrs. Hendrickson certainly did, Arriza figured. He'd often seen the victims at his checkout counter, smiling and chatting with other customers. Beautiful, friendly people. Their deaths had struck him like a blow in the stomach. Something should be done about it. The bearded owner, in his red apron, had an idea.

The next morning, motorists stared at a large sign posted outside Arriza's store. They saw, in six-inch letters, "WE WANT DEATH PENALTY. PETITION INSIDE STORE."

The response pleased Arriza, as several hundred people came in to sign the petition in just four days. Many of them expressed the community outrage in their comments to the grocer. "I think he ought to be thrown in a pit and raped," said one furious young woman. Another woman signed because her daughter had been a classmate of Shannah's.

"I'm afraid now," one customer said. "I just went out and bought a gun."

A resident of the community for thirty-three years softly noted, "I've had a hard time coming to grips that something like this could happen in our rural area."

Some of the comments centered on disillusionment about the failure of "the system" that released a man convicted of sexual assault back into the neighborhood of the victim. Rick Arriza summed it up, saying, "Renae was a beautiful woman and Shannah was a cute little girl, and Barbara was a nice lady. They don't have to be afraid anymore. But at least, they should have the satisfaction of justice." He worried that his efforts might be futile, though. "A lot of people said it (the petition) isn't going to do any good, but they signed it anyway."

Maybe he was right. In the entire history of Snohomish County, only four men had ever been executed. In 1905, Angus J. McPhail, a woodsman, went to the gallows for shooting a saloon owner. Five years later, Richard Quinn gunned down his wife in a drunken rage, and dangled at the end of a rope for several minutes, begging to be dropped again, before he died. In 1940, Ed Bouchard axed and strangled two victims, then faced Washington's hangman. And in 1949, Wayne Leroy Williams beat his wife with a rock before pushing her, along with his four-year-old daughter, over a cliff. The child survived, the wife died. Williams resisted while being led from his cell, so officers strapped him to a board and carried him to the gallows.

The state of Washington hadn't executed anyone in nearly

twenty years. Five murderers had their death sentences reduced to life in prison when the U.S. Supreme Court overturned the state's capital punishment law in 1981. Since passage of the new law, only two men had been sent to Walla Walla's death row.

Elsewhere in the U.S., it had been seventeen years since any killer had been hanged. In 1965, Richard Eugene Hickock and Perry Edward Smith, whose story Truman Capote magnificently told in his genre creating book, *In Cold Blood,* met their joint fate on a gallows in Kansas. On a cold, rainy morning, just after midnight, Hickock walked up the thirteen steps, spoke briefly, then dropped through the trapdoor. Thirty-eight minutes later, Smith followed his partner in crime to their final destiny. The month and day they died meant nothing to a very young Charles Campbell, but it would take on greater significance later.

It was April 14!

Citizens doubted that Campbell would ever face a hangman. Undeterred, Rick Arriza delivered his petition to the county prosecutor.

The F.B.I. reported to Snohomish County Sheriff Robert Dodge that fingerprints in the Torino belonged to Charles Campbell and Karl Popovich. All others were still being examined. The agency offered to send an expert to testify, if necessary, in the trial.

Still needing at least one piece of physical evidence, Rick Bart and Joe Ward kept digging. Bart had faith. "Joe and I, and most detectives, will tell you that when you've got the right guy, things will go your way. We had the right guy, and we knew it." They might have a slim chance to win a conviction in court with the circumstantial evidence, he said, but really needed more. County prosecutor, Russ Juckett, and Jim Roche, the deputy named to present the case in court, agreed. Some of the lineup identifications had been pretty shaky, and the lawyer feared that Karl Popovich, who had led detectives to the river evidence, would be cut to shreds in court. A clever defense attorney might even make a jury believe that Popovich, a three-time loser, had really committed the murders. Or maybe the jurors could be persuaded that a random burglar had entered the house and killed all possible witnesses. The case could sink faster than a dinghy on stormy Puget Sound. No, they had to have something more solid.

At the end of June, Bart received a telephone call from an F.B.I. agent who'd previously worked with the detective and wanted to give him an advance tip. They were sending a teletype, and the caller thought Bart might want to be on hand to read it as soon as it arrived.

Bart stood by the teletype machine in suspense. As soon as the clacking stopped, he ripped the yellow paper out, read it, and hurried down four floors, taking the steps three at a time. He ran into the prosecutor's office, and asked, "How good do you feel about this case?"

Jim Roche stared at the grinning detective, and said, "You know we've got to get around some problems." He expressed special concern about Popovich. Russ Juckett nodded.

"Well," Bart declared, "I've think we've got around them."

"What?" the prosecutors asked.

Handing them the teletype message, Bart waited. He later recalled, "You've never seen a happier bunch of sharp lawyers in your whole life."

"This is great," Roche shouted.

The teletype contained a summary of information spelled out in a letter that arrived the next day. Under a bold letterhead reading FEDERAL BUREAU OF INVESTIGATION, Washington D.C., the text told Sheriff Robert M. Dodge that a number of fingerprints had been analyzed. The technicians had examined "62 lifts" from several items, including two doorknobs, a steering wheel, a drinking glass, a lunch bucket, and a rearview mirror. They had compared the prints to exemplars from the three victims and from Charles R. Campbell. They had matched Campbell's prints with latents lifted from the Ford Torino. That came as no surprise to the detectives.

But the next paragraph caused them to celebrate.

The F.B.I. had examined the amber-colored drinking glass recovered from Renae's kitchen counter, the one apparently stained with grape juice. They'd confirmed the grape juice stains, but also found bloodstains on the glass!

And, on the surface of the glass, in the grape juice and blood, they'd found palm prints consistent with the ridges and whorls from the hand of Charles Rodman Campbell!

Even with the single item of physical evidence now built into the case against Campbell, investigators wouldn't rest. The more evidence they could find, the better.

Hurrying to collect as much additional information as possible before the trial started, Rick Bart took additional statements from Campbell's ex-wife, Rosalie, Everett Work Release Supervisor Frank Cornish, and from a man who had worked with Renae, and admired her jewelry.

In the latter part of September, as a trial date edged close, a married couple came forward to tell the detectives what they'd seen. Rick Bart listened in admiration.

Victoria Ibison and her husband, Harold, lived in a comfortable mobile home on Waverly Drive, one-quarter of a mile from the Wicklund home. Bart later described them: "They were great," he said. Hal was a "tough old war hero," and Vickie "was a naturalized citizen from Holland."

The couple told Bart that they'd seen someone on April 14, near their home, who resembled the man they'd recently seen on television, Charles Campbell. Early the following morning, the Ibison's daughter had told them of the murders and advised them to call the police to report seeing the stranger. They made the call, and a deputy came out on Thursday. He took notes and walked with them along the route the stranger had taken.

Bart hadn't learned of the couple's sighting of a suspect until September. Somehow, the notes taken by the responding deputy had been misplaced. Fortunately, their story came to Bart's attention before the case went to trial.

Vickie Ibison told her half of the account first. She'd been standing with some children, by a sandbox in the front of her daughter's home, at about five P.M., when she noticed a man with "reddish brown hair" carrying a big "bedroll" on his back, walking toward the lumber mill. Her dog, a Sheltie named Cody, barked furiously, and Vickie had to hold him back. The bundle carried by the stranger looked like a red patched quilt, with something heavy rolled up inside. She ran into her home, behind her daughter's house, and breathlessly told Hal what she'd seen. Hal grabbed his military style binoculars and watched the man until he disappeared into the woods.

Hal Ibison picked up the story from there. He said that Vickie had rushed into the house and told him about a guy out front with a funny-looking pack on his back. He'd looked out the window, and could see the fellow carrying a bedroll across his shoulder, with a "large lump, about the size of a basketball" in it. Through the binoculars, he watched the guy stop at a thicket of blackberry bushes, look around, then continue. "The guy acted like he was doped or intoxicated because he was wobbly, staggering." After crossing the road, he struggled up an embankment, and turned so that Hal could see his profile. Describing the man's face to Bart, Ibison said, "He had a dark, short chin beard, was six feet tall or better, and had brownish hair, not too long."

After he printed their stories, and had them sign the witness statement form, Bart asked the Ibisons if they'd be willing to testify in court. They said they certainly would.

Long before any trial could get under way, a tangle of legal issues required sorting out. Royce Ferguson, a young attorney contracted by the county to represent indigent defendants, inherited Charles Campbell as a client. He would be assisted by an Everett attorney, Ken Lee. Defending Campbell wouldn't win either man any popularity contests in Snohomish County. The general mood of the citizenry seemed to be that a trial was a foolish waste of time and money. Just take the killer out and hang him.

The first conflict Ferguson encountered came from Campbell himself. During Campbell's years in the reformatory, he'd learned some basics about the law, and now imagined himself qualified to form the strategies for his defense. Ferguson tried hard to compromise with the intractable con, but found it difficult.

Despite Campbell's meddling, Ferguson found an early basis to request dismissal of the charges. Through informants, the lawyer heard that a guard at Monroe had concealed himself in a dark room and eavesdropped on Campbell's meetings with Ferguson and Lee. Eventually, a judge dismissed the motion due to inadequate supporting evidence, but at least it was a starting point.

It turned out to be the ending point as well. The intransigent Campbell quarreled so frequently with the attorneys, they finally requested, and were granted, permission to withdraw from the case.

New lawyers shouldered the burden, and prepared for trial before the end of the year.

Fifteen

Trials had been held in the Old Mission building in Everett
for four decades. Just two stories high, the structure sat on top
of a hill south of the town center. An attractive light tan example
of Spanish architecture, decorated on the west face with a domed
clock tower, gracefully arched capstones, and overhanging tile
roofs, it housed the sheriff's and prosecutor's offices for years.
In 1967, a four-story modern annex on the north side added badly
needed space for the sheriff's growing force, plus plenty of new
courtrooms.

Judge Dennis J. Britt, Department 6, presided in the large
courtroom on the second floor of the old building. It had a row
of arched windows overlooking a lush green quadrangle shaded
by lofty, ancient deciduous trees, through which afternoon sunlight filtered into the court. Britt sat behind a high desk, the
windows to his left, the blue padded jury chairs to his right. He
faced toward counsel tables and three long pews of curved, high-
backed light oak benches for the gallery. Walls of the same light
oak color kept the room luminous, unlike the somber atmosphere
of many courts. Orange pads on the chairs for counsel added to
the bright appearance.

Near the end of October, 1982, Judge Britt had a tough decision to make. Tall, bald, and gaunt, he resembled the character
actor John McIntire who appeared in forty-two movies and
countless television plays, often as a judge. In Britt's seventeen
years on the bench, he could be compassionate with frightened
witnesses, or scathing when attorneys strayed from the path of

correct court procedure. His craggy features wrinkled when he pondered deep problems, like the one that confronted him during jury selection in the Campbell trial. It soon became obvious that jury candidates from Snohomish County had been inundated with news about the case, making it nearly impossible to seat an unbiased panel. The judge finally agreed to travel all the way across the state to find objective jurors, and bring them back to Everett. He arranged to join the lawyers and the defendant for a journey to Spokane.

Just prior to their departure, Charles Campbell announced that he didn't want to go. He would just stay in his cell in Everett, while the judge and attorneys traveled. "You guys go ahead without me," he insisted.

Jim Roche, chief deputy prosecuting attorney, and his new assistant, Eric Lind, strenuously objected. "You're playing into his hands, Your Honor." They wanted to avoid giving him any ammunition for future appeals. Campbell's attorneys had no problem with him staying behind.

Surprised by Campbell's request, Judge Britt weighed the decision. "I was amazed," he later said. "I didn't expect it to happen. Defendants are always (in court) unless they are unruly." In the final analysis, Britt could see nothing wrong with conducting jury selection without the defendant, as long as he was properly represented by his attorneys, and had knowingly made the decision himself to skip participation. It was a decision Judge Britt would live to regret.

With twelve Spokane citizens, good and true, plus three alternates, the trial of Charles Rodman Campbell got under way on November 8, 1982. The six men, six women jury, plus the three women alternates, would be sequestered in an Everett hotel for the whole trial. They hoped it would conclude by Thanksgiving, but if it didn't, maybe the judge would allow them to go home for traditional family dinners.

Judge Dennis Britt turned to the jury, who were well dressed and coiffed as all juries are on the first day of a trial, and said, "At this time, ladies and gentlemen, Mr. Roche will make the opening statement on behalf of the State in these proceedings." Attorneys' statements are *not* evidence, and should not be considered by the jury during deliberations. They are supposed to be nothing more than a figurative road map of where the trial is going. Nevertheless, both sides try hard to make a good first impression.

Prosecutors Jim Roche and Eric Lind still felt somewhat apprehensive about the circumstantial nature of the evidence available to them, and the weaknesses of some of the witnesses. Lind, just one year out of law school, had a look of intense exuberance on his youthful face, topped by thick, dark hair matching a full mustache that drooped over the corners of his mouth. The young lawyer had just recently visited the crime scene, which would haunt his memories. "It's the only experience I've ever had where the walls of the house seemed to speak to you. . . . It was like the house was screaming that there had been a sudden burst of evil, maniacal violence that had swept through the place."

Roche, soft-spoken, with dark hair crowning his round face, not quite six feet tall, immaculately dressed in a dark suit, stood before the assembled court, took a look at Campbell, and greeted the expectant jurors.

"Morning, ladies and gentlemen," Roche began in a voice hard to hear from the gallery third row. "I'm glad that you could all make it from Spokane, and I hope you had a nice trip over. He advised them of the limited purpose of his statement, then launched into a fundamental description of the murders, pausing over each of the three victims' names and emphasizing the age of the little girl, Shannah.

"Renae Wicklund and Barbara Hendrickson," he said, ". . . testified against Charles Campbell, the defendant, in 1976, because of crimes he committed against Renae Wicklund . . ." Roche couldn't tell the jurors what the crimes were, yet. He could state that Campbell went to prison, and "was still serving the sentence, although nearing completion, on April 14, 1982."

After describing Campbell's participation in the work release program, Roche began laying out the step by step events. ". . . Mr. Campbell checked out . . . at seven-nineteen in the morning, saying he was going to work. However, he never arrived at work. He called his employer at approximately nine A.M. . . . saying he was going to be late. Instead, . . . he went to his girlfriend's house in Monroe. She will testify in this case."

Campbell had told Ladonna Layton of his "resentment" toward Renae, Roche said, and wanted Renae to feel everything that he had felt in prison. The prosecutor revealed how Campbell had resumed drinking, and had stalked the victim. The defendant then had tried to rape another woman, Ellen Tremaine, and failing, had invited her to cut his throat.

At about three o'clock, Roche continued, a young girl, Patty Warner, "saw Mr. Campbell cutting across her backyard, and enter . . . the yard of Renae Wicklund." Shannah Wicklund, he said, arrived home on the school bus at about three-forty-five. "The evidence will show that Mr. Campbell most probably entered the Wicklund residence through a sliding glass door in the rear of the house and that he attacked Renae Wicklund in the bedroom of the house. Renae was home sick in bed. She'd been to the doctor the day before and she was still ill.

"It appears from the evidence that Renae attempted to defend herself. There were bruises on her hands . . . but it was very clear that she was overpowered by her attacker. She was very brutally beaten and stabbed. Her jaw was broken during the beating."

The only sound in the courtroom was the soft voice of Jim Roche, spellbinding everyone with the tale of grotesque cruelty. "Her nose was broken during the beating. She sustained a broken rib and stomach injuries with the beating as well. She was stabbed several times. Finally, her throat was cut with a knife and she bled to death."

Observers in the gallery who knew about the case dreaded the next segment: "Shannah Wicklund suffered much the same fate as her mother, with one exception. Renae Wicklund was raped right around the time of her death. Her attacker raped her with some blunt instrument. There was evidence of a torn vaginal vault (found by) the doctor who did the autopsy. . . . The evidence will show that Shannah was most likely attacked as she entered the home in the living room-dining area. Some of her blood was found in that area near the hallway leading to the bedroom. Her body was found in the bedroom. She also tried to resist her attacker."

Soft moans of horror escaped pursed lips and drifted through the courtroom. "She had some bruises on her hand where she tried to defend herself as well, but being eight years old, of very small stature, there wasn't much she could do. The evidence will show she was beaten on the head." Roche told of the child being bludgeoned with a sharp-edged instrument and being forced into her mother's bedroom, where she was killed. "Her throat was slashed." She bled to death, Roche almost whispered. "It occurs very quickly when both arteries are cut. Her throat was slashed with such a vengeance that she was almost beheaded." The prosecutor deliberately used the shocking words to create the grisly mind picture. "There was only a very small amount of flesh in the back of her neck that was holding her head on."

He paused for a moment. People who had been holding their breath sighed. "Barbara Hendrickson left her home across the street from the Wicklund residence at about four-twenty in the afternoon." Her husband, Roche said, had just arrived home from work and heard Barbara say she was going to check on Renae and Shannah. She entered the Wicklund home, and "She was beaten less severely than Renae, less severely than Shannah. However, she attempted to resist as well. It appears that she was attacked in the same area as Shannah. She also was forced down the hallway toward the bedroom and her throat was cut, and she was left lying in the hallway. Her throat was cut so severely . . . her attacker cut into the bone surrounding the spinal cord."

Now Roche slowed down, emphasizing each word in describing the evidence. The defendant, he said, "left a very crucial piece of evidence. A palm print was found by the sheriff's office on a drinking glass in the kitchen where water was left running . . ." Roche promised that testimony from an F.B.I. agent would prove Charles Campbell had left that palm print. If the jury heard nothing else, Roche hoped they clearly heard about that palm print. It was the nucleus of his case.

Roche told jurors that the defendant also robbed the Wicklunds, and briefly listed the things taken. Painting a word picture, the prosecutor described the defendant's route back to the Torino, and how he dropped some of the loot on his way. Much of the jewelry, Roche said, had belonged to Renae since high school.

The search of the Torino, and recovery of the pearl earring, came next, followed by the items recovered from the river. A number of people, Roche said, witnessed the defendant fleeing from the crime scene, and will so testify.

The defendant checked back into the work release facility at five-seventeen that evening, took a shower, packed the clothes he'd been wearing, and went out again that night, Roche told the jurors. At the Snohomish River, the defendant dumped some of the jewelry and his clothes into the water, but the investigators recovered much of it. Roche mentioned jewelry, a piece of china, and a "candle holder wall ornament" that would be identified by relatives. A witness from the work release house was with the defendant, Roche revealed, and will give all the details in his testimony. They both drank tequila and beer, in violation of the work release rules, he said, resulting in the defendant being sent back to the reformatory.

"I have tried to capsulize and put in a nutshell basically what our case will show. I've only summarized the evidence and I just kind of highlighted things, and there's going to be a lot of other things that are going to be presented. I would just ask that you please carefully consider every bit of evidence that comes in during this trial and that you give us a just verdict in this case."

Campbell sat beside his two attorneys. Anyone who had seen news photos of the scrawny man with bushy hair, a straggly beard, unwashed and ragged, wouldn't recognize him. Bathed, trimmed, and shaved, wearing a neat suit and tie, he looked different, but his face still exuded malevolent arrogance.

Beside him sat Anthony Savage and Mark Mestel, two highly successful and well-known defense attorneys. Campbell had already fired a set of appointed defenders over differences of opinion on trial strategies. The taxpayers would foot the bill for this exceptionally well qualified pair, Savage with a clean-shaven affluent look, and Mestel sporting a light brown beard matching neatly styled hair, and large, shining eyes with a look of readiness for intellectual battle.

Britt asked if the defense wished to present an opening statement or reserve the right to do so. Anthony Savage stood and tersely announced, "We'll make an opening."

Making immediate and intimate eye contact with jurors, Savage began in a strong, articulate voice. "Ladies and gentlemen, this is the first chance Mr. Mestel and I have to address you on behalf of our client, Charles Campbell, and I welcome the opportunity to respond to Mr. Roche's opening remarks. . . . We do not agree for one minute that Mr. Campbell is responsible for these terrible and brutal murders that did indeed occur. It's our hope that at the end of all the evidence, we will have proved to you, not that it's our burden, that Mr. Campbell did not commit these offenses and, at the worst, the gap between reasonable doubt and the proof of . . . guilt is so wide that there can't be any question as to what verdict should be returned. That is our hope."

Conceding that the victims died at the hands of "somebody," Savage warned jurors they would see some distressing photographs. He acknowledged that Renae and Barbara had testified against Campbell "several years ago," then abruptly left that topic. Campbell, he said, was in a program, "working his way back into society," and was "at liberty on the afternoon in question."

Tilting his head in the direction of Detective Rick Bart, Savage told jurors that law enforcement authorities had "almost immediately leapt to the conclusion that Mr. Campbell was responsible" for the murders.

Savage described it as, "People with probably good intentions have tried to pound square pegs into round holes on the theory that Mr. Campbell must have done this, so let's kind of push it a little."

Attacking the massive publicity surrounding the case, Savage suggested that witnesses for the prosecution had been influenced by it. He singled out Karl Popovich, the informant, as "one of the most important witnesses," who was a "professional burglar," and whose testimony would be "at best, extremely inaccurate," and in some instances, "outright falsehood." Popovich, Savage said, had tried to ingratiate himself with the law enforcement officials to help himself out of his own difficulties.

The most important thing, Savage asserted, would be that 99.9 percent of the evidence, such as blood, hair, and tracks, would "point away from Mr. Campbell and point to the commission of these crimes by somebody else."

"Now, indeed," Savage concluded, "you can't take my word for these things any more than you can take Mr. Roche's, but each piece of physical evidence is going to be tested by us to the limits of our intelligence and training, in the hopes that we'll be able to demonstrate to you, beyond any doubt, and again, it's not our burden, that Mr. Campbell is not the one responsible for the deaths of these three women. Thank you very much."

The prosecution team noted that Savage avoided mentioning the amber drinking glass, and wondered how he planned to neutralize the impact of Campbell's palm prints at the crime scene.

Sixteen

Following opening statements, on that same Monday morning, prosecutor Roche called his first witness, Lorene Ahlers Iverson, Renae's sister, who had traveled with her mother, Hilda, from North Dakota. Both of them would testify.

Lorene made her way up to the witness stand, and forced herself to look at Campbell. She wondered why the system allowed him to appear so different, almost as if he wore a disguise. Was it really fair to deceive the jurors by creating the image of a clean, decent person? Why couldn't they see him as he always looked, or as witnesses saw him on April 14, with dirty clothes, unkempt hair and a scruffy beard? She'd watched him walk into the courtroom, the first time she'd ever seen him in the flesh, wearing a nice suit and tie. He gave the impression of being "very confident with a smirk on his face," as if he knew it was just a matter of time until the trial ended and he could walk out, a free man. When he'd glanced over at Wicklund and Hendrickson family members seated in the "pews" he had a "cocky" grin. Lorene's stomach tightened, wondering what kind of a grotesque person could have committed such vile acts and show no sign of remorse.

After she'd been sworn in and identified herself, the prosecutor handed her some photos of Renae and Shannah to use in telling jurors, officially, who the victims were. Lorene felt grateful that gruesome crime scene photos, depicting the grisly damage inflicted on them, would be viewed only by the jurors, sparing her that heartbreak. Next, she verified that a silver bracelet, recovered from the river, was one Renae treasured from her college days back in Jamestown. Lorene identified a 4-H pin, a delicate locket containing Shannah's picture, and a pendant. The latter item framed a gold "J" embedded on it. Lorene, trying courageously to keep her voice from quaking, said that it stood for several things: Jamestown, Jays . . . bluejays . . . the school symbol, or Jamestown High School. Yes, it certainly belonged to Renae.

Jim Roche asked gentle questions, in his naturally soft voice. Lorene said she'd visited her sister at Christmas and other occasions, but their mother had visited more frequently. She recalled that Renae had decorated the house with "old items from the farm, old brass ornaments" like the one fished out of the riverbed. She fondly held a broken pottery bowl, and told the jury that it belonged to her sister.

Lorene would always remember that when she first sat down in the witness chair, she'd looked over at the jurors and felt sympathy for them, wishing that they didn't have to go through this terrible ordeal.

The defense team wisely chose not to cross-examine Lorene.

Hilda Ahlers, her graying hair styled in a neat cut, short at the neck, bravely walked through the gallery gate, adjusted her glasses, and took the stand. She gave a brief background of her life in Jamestown, and the names of her two sons and two daughters. Renae, Hilda said, had lived in Clearview for eight years. "I visited her every six months. I came there last December, on the ninth, and stayed until the middle of January."

Hilda, too, examined several pieces of jewelry handed her by Jim Roche. She gazed nostalgically at the pearl earring and said it belonged to Renae. Sadness crept through Hilda's attempted mask of equanimity when she examined a bracelet. "I bought that for Renae in North Dakota." She also recognized another 4-H pin. Her time as a witness was blessedly brief.

Defender Savage spared her, too, any cross-examination.

The next two witnesses had participated in the sexual assault trial in April, 1976. A court clerk described logistical matters, and prosecutor John Segelbaum filled in specifics about the charges and the conviction. Following him, a Department of Corrections manager reported the dates of Campbell's incarceration, emphasizing that he was still a prisoner, although on work release, on the day of the murders.

The widower, Don Hendrickson, came forward and swore to tell the whole truth. Emotional pain etched his face. It could be seen in his demeanor, and his slow walk. Hendrickson's health had obviously deteriorated, making him look older than his fifty-four years. He would later recall that he hadn't laughed one time since the death of his beloved Barbara.

His voice shaking in grief and anger, Don Hendrickson first sketched a verbal picture of his life with Barbara who was fifty-one when she was murdered. On April 14, he said, "I worked all day, then got home about four-fifteen. Barbara left in about five or six minutes to go check on Renae and Shannah." He'd gone over to the Wicklund house, worried because Barbara had been gone a long time, and found her body in the hallway. About the other two victims, he said, "I have no mental image of Shannah or Renae in the bedroom."

With undisguised distress, Don identified the pink slippers Barbara had worn the last time he saw her alive, and her eyeglasses. "Yes," he said in response to Roche's question about whether Barbara smoked. "She liked Benson and Hedges Green, the green pack, mentholated."

Roche's examination lasted only a few minutes, and Savage limited his cross-exam to a couple of innocuous questions before they excused the emotionally torn man.

A parade of officers followed to describe their arrival at the crime scene, discovery of the bodies, and first steps of investigation. Fire department members, Chief Richard Eastman, Lieutenant William Spalding, and Randy Weiss preceded sheriff's officers, Doug Pendergrass, James Keightley, and John Hinds. Deputy Hinds recalled he'd been the first one to interview little Patty Warner next door, and heard her describe a tall stranger lurking behind her house, wearing a blue jacket.

Near the end of the court day, Detective Joe Ward took the stand. The defense attorneys finally bared their fangs. When prosecutor Roche attempted to qualify Ward as an expert in taking blood samples, the defenders attacked. Even though Ward had successfully collected blood in more than one hundred cases, with no problems, they wanted to plant doubt in the jurors' minds that he possessed, or used, real expertise. The day ended on an acrimonious note.

As they would every day when the courtroom emptied, Lorene Ahlers Iverson, her mother Hilda, Don Hendrickson, and his daughters all walked down one flight of stairs to the ground floor and assembled in the office of Steve Eckstrom. He and his organization had been, and would continue to be, their savior. Eckstrom occupied an office supplied by the Snohomish County Prosecutor, right across the hall, as a representative of the Victim-Witness program, and an ambassador of a group called Families and Friends of Violent Crime Victims. The nonprofit, all volunteer organization had been formed in 1975 following the disappearances and murders of several young women in the Seattle area, to provide counseling, emotional support, and guidance to grief-stricken survivors of the wreckage left by barbaric criminals.

One of Don Hendrickson's daughters had been approached at Barbara's memorial service by a member of Families and Friends, who gave her a business card. She called and heard about the compassionate, empathetic help available for distraught relatives of murder victims, and thought her dad might benefit from it. It turned out to be a life changing experience for Don Hendrickson. He, with the help of Steve Eckstrom, extended the group's support to Hilda and Lorene.

Hilda would one day write the best possible expression of the help they received. "As we stood feeling helpless, frightened and numb with grief, Families and Friends put their collective arms around us. The value of their guidance, protection and understanding, through the entire . . . judicial process, can never be measured."

Before Joe Ward resumed his testimony on Tuesday morning, a heated battle took place out of the jury's presence. A few unidentified hairs had been found in Barbara Hendrickson's hand, hairs that did not match samples from Campbell. Maybe they'd been on the carpet, or possibly from her own clothing. No proof existed that they were even human hairs. The defense, though, expressed the intent to introduce the hairs through the testimony of Joe Ward, to suggest that Barbara had plucked them from someone other than Campbell, thus suggesting someone else was the killer. Both sides had tried to obtain sample hairs from Karl Popovich, but with the help of a lawyer, he'd refused. The defense wanted to imply that Popovich might have committed the crimes.

Prosecutor Eric Lind objected vehemently to the defense tactics, citing legal precedence. "You've got to have evidence, other than hearsay, that points in the direction of someone else," Lind complained. "You can't just say, 'well, geez, we don't know who did it, but it must be somebody else because these hairs don't fit.' "

"Your Honor," Mestel countered, "we are pointing to someone else. There is only one person who ever professed knowledge of where the proceeds of the alleged burglary were." That person, he said, was Popovich.

The defense knew, Lind insisted, that all the fingerprints at the crime scene were analyzed, and none of them matched Popovich. It was only speculation that he was even tangentially involved. Now, Popovich had said, "Wait a second, the defense is trying to pin this on me! I need a lawyer." He got one, and refused to give hair samples.

The judge postponed any ruling on the matter pending the laying of some foundation to admit the hairs into evidence.

Joe Ward pulled the jury back into the murder investigation by describing his and Rick Bart's search for a murder weapon, which they'd never found. They'd collected a large assortment of things from the house interior, including a Benson and Hedges cigarette that had never been lit, a Holly Hobby lunch box in the hallway where Shannah had probably dropped it as she fled in terror, some eyeglasses, a Virginia Slims cigarette found between Renae's legs, and a pink slipper. The slipper, found in another room, matched the one they saw on Barbara's foot in the hallway. They'd picked up some earrings in the house, which Ward characterized as the start of a "trail of jewelry."

Ward had thought it peculiar, at the autopsy, that each victim had only one earring, the mates having been torn out of the ears. It was another mystery that would never be explained.

Jim Roche asked Ward one last question. "Detective Ward, why is it that two vials of blood were taken from the bodies of Barbara Henderson and Renae Wicklund, and only one vial from Shannah Wicklund?"

The answer chilled everyone in the courtroom, with the possible exception of the defendant. "There just wasn't any more blood left in her body."

Defender Mestel, on cross, managed to squeeze in a question about collecting hair from the hands of Barbara, and the other two victims, but halted there without planting the implication that the hairs belonged to someone other than the defendant.

Some bloody smears on the hallway hardwood floor might have been footprints, Mestel's questions implied. But Ward said they were too indistinct to be characterized as shoe prints.

Stepping down at three-thirty, Joe Ward gave way to Dr. Clayton Haberman, the pathologist who had conducted the autopsies. After establishing credentialed expertise, the witness's *curriculum vitae,* Jim Roche elicited from the doctor a detailed description of the injuries he'd discovered, and his opinions on how the wounds were inflicted. It was a spine-chilling recitation of horror that left the gallery sickened as they filed out at the end of the day.

* * *

On Day 3, Wednesday morning, a defense objection caused
Dr. Haberman to cease referring to the death weapon as a knife.
He had to find other words, such as a "sharp instrument." Court
watchers grunted their displeasure at the infinite technicalities
of the law. He spent the rest of the morning discussing the extensive injuries to Renae Wicklund. He could not pin down the
exact time, in relationship to her death, that she'd been subjected
to trauma by sexual penetration with a blunt object. The defense
attorneys paid close attention to the imprecise time frames and
took copious notes.

When Dr. Haberman concluded his testimony, another meeting took place out of the jury's presence. Anthony Savage wanted
to contest the allegations of rape. "Mr. Roche said that he was
going to prove that this woman was raped before she was killed.
They had the doctor on the stand. He testified (the rape) could
have occurred as long as two hours after the cessation of circu-
lation. There is no rape! You cannot rape a dead person."

Eventually, Judge Britt ruled in favor of the defense. Techni-
cally, the victim had not been raped.

The jury became acquainted with "Ace" the police dog
through the next witness, his handler, Deputy Terrance Green.
Green had trained Ace himself, and clearly held his K-9 partner
in very high esteem. The enthused dog had led detectives to the
first segment of the killer's trail.

Sergeant Joe Belinc, Homicide Squad supervisor, when asked
about his duties, said, "I observe the detectives; I don't direct
them." He detailed his visit to the Everett Work Release facility
where he interviewed a supervisor and impounded the Ford
Torino.

The Wednesday session closed after the landscaping company owner revealed Campbell had failed to show up for work
on April 14.

Charles Campbell surprised everyone on Day 4, Thursday, by
announcing that he wanted to personally cross-examine Ladonna

Layton, his girlfriend, and Ellen Tremaine, the woman he'd tried to rape and then invited to cut his throat. In the chambers, Judge Britt asked, "Is it your desire to examine these two individuals and to be responsible for both the direct and the cross, and dealing with objections and any physical evidence?"

"Yes, it is," Campbell replied.

"Have you discussed this with your attorneys?"

"Yes, I have."

"Do they agree with your decision in the matter?"

"Well, they're accepting it." Campbell acknowledged they had counseled him against it. Judge Britt asked a few more questions regarding Campbell's understanding of the correct procedures. Campbell said he understood, but raised one issue. He didn't want to sit at his chair, where his ankle was ordinarily connected to a chair leg with an inconspicuous chain. He wanted to stand at the lectern because he felt that he worked better on his feet. The judge realized the allowance of that much freedom could create a security problem. Campbell promised not to make any sudden movements, so Britt relented based on one condition. Campbell must move to the lectern while the jury was still out, and remain there until they left. A guard would be posted nearby to be ready in case of any sudden moves by the defendant.

Ladonna Layton, the new mother of a month-old baby boy, answered the questions posed by Jim Roche, relating how she'd met Campbell four years earlier in Monroe Reformatory where she was a drug and alcohol counselor. "What's your relationship now?" Roche asked.

"Fiancée, I guess," Ladonna said, not sounding very positive. She recited the events of April 14, in which "Chuck" came over at nine A.M., lugging some Budweiser beer, and stayed at her apartment after she went to work. He drank beer the whole morning. She worked a late shift, stayed overnight on the job, and missed his evening telephone message. The next day, he called

her from the Monroe lockup, and asked her to go to Everett where
his car needed to be moved.

"Did you make a statement to Detective Bart saying that you
had some property missing?" Yes, she said, a knife was missing
from her apartment. It was about a foot long, half blade and half
handle. She answered a series of questions about the car, then
heard Roche ask the question she'd been dreading. "Had you
ever heard the name Renae Wicklund?"

"Chuck had mentioned that name to me."

"When?"

"Quite a while ago. Probably before he left the reformatory."
Several times. She'd also seen transcripts of the rape trial in his
possession.

"Did Mr. Campbell ever express a feeling of resentment toward Renae Wicklund?"

"Yes, but I can't give you specific times he mentioned it."

"Did he ever tell you he wanted her to feel everything that he
felt?"

"Yes." And he had admitted being at Renae's house after being
transferred to the Honor Farm in January. He said he drove past
her house and watched her removing groceries from her car.

At ten-twenty A.M., Roche announced, "No more questions."
It was Charles Campbell's turn.

"Good morning, Miss Layton," Campbell said, playing the
role of attorney to the hilt. "You gave a description of a knife. I
don't recall that you said how wide it was."

"It was about an inch, inch and a half wide." Ladonna seemed
uncomfortable. It seemed so strange to be cross-examined by the
father of the infant she'd delivered just four weeks ago. Campbell
asked her to repeat the answer, then requested more details about
the knife. She did her best to answer his questions objectively.

"Okay," Campbell continued, "you said that you were employed in West Seattle, and that you're no longer working there."

"Yes."

"Did you quit or resign?" Roche objected, citing irrelevancy.
Instantly, Campbell shot back, "I'd like to make an offer of proof

outside the hearing of the jury." He'd obviously been paying attention to the court protocol. Judge Britt excused the jurors for a few minutes. Campbell's offer of proof consisted of complaining that police had harassed Layton, and threatened to take her to court, causing her distress which led to the loss of her job. Judge Britt sustained the objection.

Resuming his formal cross-examination of his new son's mother, Campbell questioned her about moving his Torino. "Did I ask you to clean it out?" She said that he hadn't. Maybe the jury would think that he couldn't be guilty if he hadn't even directed his lover to remove evidence from the car.

Campbell turned the subject to his drinking, drawing from Ladonna the comment that he appeared "inebriated" when she left him in her apartment.

"Could you tell me what inebriated means?" She said he was lucid, not "falling down drunk, but difficult to communicate with."

A quibbling match ensued about whether in discussions prior to the murders, he had used Renae's full name. Layton couldn't recall. He followed up by drawing definitions from her of the work release program, and his activities during the six months he participated in it. Rambling, he returned to her views of his escalated consumption of beer and booze. Ladonna admitted, "I didn't like how you got when you were drinking."

Once more, Campbell returned to the subject of Renae. "You said that I expressed resentment toward Renae Wicklund. Do you find that unhealthy?" Judge Britt sharply sustained the objection, pointing out that her feelings about the matter were irrelevant.

"Did I ever express that I wanted to hurt her or her child, or Barbara Hendrickson?" Ladonna said that he had not. "No more questions, Your Honor," Campbell declared, resonating with self-admiration.

On redirect, Roche wanted to know if Ladonna, knowing the rules of work release, had ever reported Campbell for drinking. She could only utter a simple, embarrassed, "No."

Ellen Tremaine seemed even more nervous than Ladonna Layton had. Perhaps she worried about Campbell seeking revenge if she said the wrong thing, or maybe she felt she was betraying a friend. She certainly dreaded being cross-examined by the man who had wanted to have sex with her last spring.

Deputy prosecutor, Eric Lind, asked Ellen to point out that man. She raised her arm, gestured in Campbell's direction and described him as, "the one with the nice beige suit on." Ellen had met him while visiting other inmates at Monroe, she said, and befriended him and Ladonna. He'd shown up "pretty drunk" at her apartment on April 14 at about one-fifteen that afternoon. Lind inquired about the degree of drunkenness, and Ellen said that he could walk and talk, but "not like a sober person." He'd made a couple of passes at her, then became "more amorous."

Irritated that Tremaine seemed to be toning down the allegations of rape she'd made to a detective, Lind reminded her of her statement. Ignoring the contradictions, she now recalled that when she and Campbell dropped to the floor, she might have offered to give him a back rub.

"Once you were on the floor, what did he try to do?" Lind inquired, remembering her previous angry comments about Campbell trying to disrobe her while she cried in fear.

"Well, he started tugging at my clothes, but then I got a little upset and asked him not to . . . and then he backed off." She sweetly added that it hurt her feelings, but she hadn't been physically hurt. She'd started washing dishes after he sat down, Ellen said. And Chuck had confided that he was no good, and depressed.

Disgusted, Lind asked, "Did he say anything in relation to the knives you were washing?"

Ellen couldn't soften this answer. "Yes, he said he was no good, and why didn't I just take that knife and slit his throat." Then, before he'd left, he asked for her bottle of tequila.

Lind questioned Ellen about whether she knew that Ladonna Layton and Campbell were romantically involved at that time. Ellen said she "had no idea."

"Did you consider yourself a friend of Mr. Campbell's on April 14th?"

Sarcasm creeping into her voice, Ellen said, "Well, if I didn't, I wouldn't have said, 'Hi, Chuck, come on in.' "

"I have nothing further," Lind said, plopping into his chair.

If anyone had been anticipating the novelty of Campbell doing the cross-examination again, they were disappointed. He decided to let the experts take over once more. But neither Mestel nor Savage chose to ask Tremaine any questions. Instead, Mark Mestel promptly moved for a mistrial.

"On what grounds?" the judge asked.

Mestel said the prosecution had made a representation that Ellen Tremaine would testify that Campbell had attempted to rape her. That certainly was not her testimony, the defender protested. Judge Britt denied the motion.

Two prosecutors breathed a sigh of relief.

With precious little to do while sitting in jail at night, Campbell decided to write his infant son a letter:

"My son. . . . I am writing to you from a jail cell and although you are too young to understand exactly what a jail cell is, one day you'll know.

I want to tell you that there are a lot of rough roads in life's highways, as well as some pretty smooth ones, too. What we make of ourselves is what's important, and it is up to each one of us to decide what he or she is going to be and to take the responsibility for that.

Sometimes in growing up we each hit a rough spot in the road and we trip, stumble, or fall. No matter how hard it is or how bad it seems, we have to get back up and keep going because that is what life is about, surviving."

Campbell lavished his love on the child with the written word. He concluded with, "I am not always going to be in your life, but (I) will be as long as I possibly can. . . . I have to take the

responsibility for what I do and some times that is a pretty heavy
burden. . . ."

No one but Campbell knew if he referred to the horrific crimes
for which he faced trial, or if the letter was just his usual exercise
in self-serving rhetoric.

Seventeen

The witness chair looked too small when big Tim Psonka settled into it on Thursday afternoon. Detective Psonka took prosecutors through his serving the search warrant at the Everett Work Release center, on the second floor, far southeast room. There, he said, he seized a blue jacket from the top rail of the bunk Charles Campbell occupied. Jim Roche hoped that jurors would imprint that color in their minds, as other witnesses would recount a stranger in the vicinity of the murder scene wearing a blue jacket.

Psonka described other search warrants he'd help serve, and his participation in searching records regarding the 1974 sexual assault after Don Hendrickson had mentioned the incident but couldn't recall the name of the perpetrator.

Jurors next heard from Deputy Dallas Swank, the leader of the scuba divers who'd scoured every inch of the muddy Snohomish River bottom. Swank's qualifications impressed them. He'd been a diver for fifteen years, first certified in beautiful Maui, Hawaii, and later a member of the famed SEALS of the U.S. Navy. He was a charter member of the county's underwater research unit. The officer fascinated observers with his knowledge of watery search procedures, and the success of his team's efforts in recovering jewelry, blue jeans alleged to be Campbell's, and other evidence.

Herb Oberg, the detective who'd taken a myriad of fingerprints, followed Swank. Defining "major case prints" as "the rendering of the entire skin surface on fingers and palms of the subject's hands," Oberg said he'd covered fifty pieces of paper with exemplars from Charles Campbell, "because I wanted to do a good job."

At the bloody and tragic home of Renae Wicklund, Oberg had worked seven hours the first night, and twice that much on subsequent visits, taking latent prints.

"Will you define what a latent fingerprint is?" the prosecutor requested.

"It's a mark left by moisture on your fingers, perspiration on your palms or fingers." Sometimes it's visible, and sometimes it's not, Oberg said.

The prosecutor handed Oberg a small cardboard box and asked him to examine it and the amber drinking glass inside. The detective complied, and said it was the glass he'd removed from the Wicklund kitchen. In order to protect the glass, he'd made the box from cardboard and tape. Before inserting the glass into it, he'd started to dust it for prints, but noticed traces of prints in the "reddish-purplish" substance on the outer surface. Not wanting to contaminate the existing prints, he'd discontinued dusting, and secured the glass inside the box to protect it for subsequent examination by the F.B.I. Oberg had taken the package to the evidence room, and "booked" it, meaning stored it on his table in the property room, but not "logged" it with property room personnel.

The defense bored in on that oversight, suggesting that not logging it made the glass vulnerable to contamination by other people who might have access to it.

Anthony Savage felt that the procedures for access to evidence stored in the property room lacked strong controls. He spent the final half hour of Day 4 attacking security measures.

That issue continued on Friday, Day 5, when Evidence Control Officer Margaret Smiley testified about the booking and logging procedures. Savage not only brought up the potential for evidence tampering in the property room, but asked Smiley how she knew that tampering didn't take place while evidence was in the custody of the F.B.I. in Washington D.C. She couldn't speak for other agencies. Perhaps the next witness could.

Steven Kasarsky, an F.B.I. fingerprint expert, was sworn in. He disclosed that items needing fingerprint analysis are sent to them from all over the United States by registered mail. The major case prints he'd received from Detective Oberg were of "excellent quality."

Among the items he examined in this case was a child's lunch pail. It contained only the fingerprints of Shannah Wicklund.

During Kasarsky's testimony, Jim Roche watched the defense table in dismay, then jumped to his feet and objected to Savage and Mestel "fondling and rolling" the amber glass on which the critical prints had been found. The judge settled the problem by having the glass placed on the clerk's desk.

Regarding the conclusion that the prints on the glass belonged to Charles Campbell, Kasarsky said, "I found fifteen distinct points of individuality in this particular print . . . which could have been made by no other person." The standard for conclusive identification, he said, was nine points.

To acquaint the jury with the forensic use of fingerprints, Roche asked Kasarsky a series of questions on the subject. The expert, using terms such as "papillary ridges" and "friction ridges" said that latent prints originate not only from perspiration, but a thin film of oil on human skin as well. He delivered a detailed explanation of how prints are compared for identification purposes and on the permanence and individuality of fingerprints. "Permanence," he said, "means that fingerprints . . . well, and palm prints, and footprints, and toe prints, are actually formed before a person is born, usually about the third or fourth month of fetal life. They remain unchanged for life. 'Individuality' refers to the fact that no two person's prints have ever been found to be exactly alike."

On cross-examination, Mark Mestel bored in on the possibility that another agent had unpackaged the glass and handled it before Kasarsky. In a sidebar, he asserted that such an event would destroy the chain of custody and cause possible contamination of the prints.

Eric Lind argued that F.B.I. procedures provide for such things. Every person authorized to handle evidence knows how to avoid contaminating it, and how to reseal it to maintain chain of custody. An agent named Richard Reem, a blood expert, had indeed opened the box, checked the glass for blood, and replaced it with proper sealing. No chain of custody abrogation had occurred, he said. The glass hadn't been rolled around all over a table, like Mr. Mestel had been doing. Lind gave the defenders a wry little smile.

In front of the jury, agent Kasarsky used poster-sized enlargements of the prints, along with detailed technical explanations, to demonstrate how he concluded they matched Campbell's exemplars.

To a query on the possibility of forging a fingerprint, Kasarsky replied, "Generally speaking, it's not impossible to forge a print," explaining that it might be done by taking a print from someone with tape, and transferring it to an object. "But that person would have to know more about fingerprints than I do," he remarked.

On the proposition that a print on a drinking glass might be distorted, Kasarsky agreed that this particular one was distorted. "I think that when this particular latent palm print was left on the glass, that there was an unreasonable or undue pressure applied that would tend to distort some of the ridges." But the distortion did not prevent the identification.

Because the print on the amber glass was a key to the prosecution case, the defense hammered away at agent Kasarsky until mid-afternoon. No one but jury members knew how effective either side had been.

Another detective testified next. Wyatt Weeks had taken a statement from little Patty Warner, and had later been one of the divers in the Snohomish River. During a heated sidebar, before Weeks was excused, defender Savage complained about police procedures again, to which prosecutor Roche objected, "It sounds like the Sheriff's Office is on trial."

Judge Britt simply said, "That objection is not well taken."

Eleventh grader Dale Gray marched confidently to the witness stand, was sworn in, and promptly began to wilt. Jim Roche showed him an aerial photo of the Waverly Drive region, asked the boy if he recognized it, and suggested he speak right into the microphone.

Dale asked, "What am I supposed to say?"

Caught off guard, the prosecutor replied, "I'm not here to tell you what you're supposed to say."

Regaining his poise, Dale spoke rapidly, "Okay, this is my house, right over here. You can't . . . my house is right here, you can't see it. It's in the shadows, okay?" He pointed out the school bus route and where the bus turns off 180th to Waverly Drive. "Right around the corner, at the bottom of the hill, that's where I get off."

To the next question, the lad recalled that on April 14, near the sawmill on Waverly, he looked out the bus window and saw a tall man near a rusty red car. He'd thought the car was a "Duster, Nova, or possibly an Impala."

Dale Gray's father, Victor, replaced him on the stand, and repeated the account he'd given to detectives about walking his dogs and finding some jewelry on Waverly Drive.

The final witness of Day 5 spoke only long enough to identify herself, give her age, and mention school. Patty Warner had just turned twelve the previous month, and was in the seventh grade. Her favorite subject, she said, was math.

Judge Britt alerted the assembly that court would be in session tomorrow, Saturday, November 13.

On Day 6, before Patty resumed her testimony, Anthony Savage asked the judge to consider taking the jury to the crime scene. He agreed to take the matter under consideration.

Patty listened carefully to each of Roche's questions before answering. She'd been sick on April 14, and hadn't gone to school. At about three-thirty that afternoon, she'd looked out the window, and seen a man "wiggling around in the bushes," she said. "He went down the trail, then stopped at our rabbit cages."

Asked if anyone else had seen him, Patty said that her sixteen-year-old sister, Deanna, had, and thought the man might be a friend of hers, but couldn't see him clearly because she wasn't wearing her glasses. Deanna went outside to say hi; but the man "turned around so she couldn't see him," and Deanna, who thought "he was pretty weird," had returned.

Jim Roche asked Patty if anyone in the courtroom might be the stranger she'd seen. Without hesitation, she pointed out Charles Campbell, but said, "He got his hair cut."

Yes, she said, she'd been Shannah's friend, and rode the same school bus with her. It always got them home at about three-thirty each afternoon.

When defender Savage cross-examined, he got an acknowledgment from Patty that when she was first interviewed, she mentioned that the man might be black. That sent Savage into a scathing criticism of the prosecution for a discovery violation, never revealing that bit of information to the defense.

When Roche had his chance again, he asked Patty if Mr. Campbell's complexion might look a little different now than it did in April. Roche gambled on his knowledge that Campbell's deeply tanned skin had faded to the pasty fish-belly white of most convicts.

Patty said, "Yes, he looks much lighter."

After Patty left the courtroom, the third member of the Gray family came forward. Gary, now fourteen, and in the ninth grade, proudly mentioned that he was the center on the Valley View Junior High School football team.

He said he rode his bike to his friend's house at about three-ten P.M. on April 14, and saw a car parked on an old dirt road. Trying to guess the make of car, Gary had told a detective he didn't "know much about cars." At a later meeting with investigators, he looked at a series of car photographs, and picked out two that might resemble the one he'd seen, but neither of them was a Ford Torino.

On cross-examination, Savage let the jury know that Gary had also picked out the wrong man in a lineup.

Roche drew from him that when Gary had returned home, after five o'clock, he'd seen a man carrying a bundle, "like a reddish-colored quilt and it was wadded up like it had something in the middle."

Gary's friends, with whom he'd played badminton that afternoon, testified next. They had been unable to pick anyone in the lineup; but they, too, had seen a quiltlike bundle the man carried, and one boy observed that the stranger wore a blue jacket. The defense, to test the lad's recall ability, tried an experiment, but it backfired. Mestel asked him to describe the detective who'd interviewed them. He did it quite accurately.

At a break, the defense renewed a standing objection they'd already lodged in an attempt to preclude the next two witnesses from being allowed to testify. Harold and Vickie Ibison had reported seeing the stranger on Waverly Drive; but police had lost their notes, and detectives hadn't interviewed the couple until late September. Mark Mestel had already convinced the judge to force the deputy who'd lost the notes to testify. He would prefer, however, to suppress the couple's testimony entirely. Overruled, said Judge Britt.

Victoria Ibison clearly recalled standing near a sandbox, calling her grandchildren in for dinner, when she spied the stranger. "He was kind of bent over, and he had a bedroll on his back, carrying it. It seemed like it was quite heavy and he was kind of shuffling along, you know, going down the road." She could still picture the bright red patches on the quilt he'd folded into a bundle. She'd had to hold back her dog twice, then rushed inside to alert her husband, Harold. Vickie gave Roche all the details he asked for, with vivid recollection.

Mark Mestel questioned Victoria at length, but couldn't find any inconsistencies in her narrative. Observers stifled chuckles at her description of Campbell's unusual hair. "I remember he had reddish brown, high wavy hair, kind of wooly-curly."

Countering with his own talents for description, Mestel asked if she remembered giving a statement to Detective Bart. "You remember (Bart); tall, thin guy, large forehead?"

"I don't think he's that big," she dissented. "But he's tall, yeah."

Judge Britt reminded counsel that he planned to recess at one P.M., so Vicky Ibison stepped down, and the jury filed out for the remainder of the weekend.

Before the lawyers left, they discussed the possible admission of two additional witnesses, Deanna Warner, who'd seen the stranger, but without her glasses, and Thomas Hawkins, Campbell's boyhood pal whom he'd raped in prison. Campbell entered the legal fray about Hawkins, insisting that he be present in a planned preliminary interview with Hawkins. The judge denied his demand. It didn't matter. Neither Deanna Warner nor Thomas Hawkins would testify in the murder trial.

Eighteen

Victoria Ibison's stay on the witness stand, on Monday morning, Day 7, turned out to be very short. Her husband, Harold, replaced her within fifteen minutes.

Both of them had seen the fleeing suspect on Waverly Drive. Eric Lind asked Harold if the previous witness was his wife, and what was her name. With obvious pride, Hal said they were married, her name was Victoria but he called her "Vic," and "She's a Dutch war bride."

"Were you a Dutch war husband?" Lind smiled.

"Well, something like that, I guess. I'm part Dutch."

What happened on the late afternoon of April 14?

Hal had been sitting on the divan, reading a newspaper, when Vickie came in, asked, "Did you hear Cody making all that racket?" and said there was a man going down the road. He got up, and looked out the window. The man, over six feet tall, was about forty yards away. Ibison ran for his binoculars.

"They were your binoculars while you were in the service?"

"Yes. They were for ack-ack spotting, airplanes and one thing or another. Very valuable." He'd focused them on the stranger.

"Do you remember what color hair he had, and what style?"

"Kind of sandy brown probably. He had sort of an afghan. His hair stood up, only he wasn't black." Observers again stifled laughter at his characterization of the hair as "afghan."

Hal had watched the man walk for over 125 yards, "until he went into the bushes. He stopped three different times behind clumps of blackberries along the road."

Lind wanted to know if Ibison had ever seen pictures of Campbell on television or the newspapers. Hal said he had. Could Hal identify Campbell as the man he'd seen, independent of the photos he'd seen in news media. Hesitating, Ibison first explained that when he'd seen the man through the binoculars, he'd noticed a beard. But news photos showed Campbell without one. Lind decided to push for an unqualified answer. "Do you see anybody in the courtroom today that looks like the fellow you saw on April 14, 1982?"

"Guy over there looks a little like him." Ibison gestured toward the end of the defense table.

"Could you describe what he's wearing?"

"Well, he's got a light tan jacket on." Judge Britt agreed that Ibison had identified the defendant, Charles Campbell.

Ibison had called the police, he said, and given details of the incident to a uniformed officer who came out to the house. He'd even accompanied the deputy in a walk along the roadside, and up an embankment, retracing the route taken by the stranger, until they came to the place the man had disappeared. The next day, he'd shown another officer, who had a dog with him, where the guy had walked. Hal hadn't heard from the sheriff's office again until late in September, when detectives Ward and Bart came out.

The cross-examination consisted mostly of questions related to the suspect's beard, or absence of one. Ibison had described a short, dark chin beard. Photos of Campbell, unshaven, showed straggly, curly dark brown hairs, hardly thick enough to be called a beard. Mestel and Savage hoped the jurors would regard the difference as significant. The Ibisons had given a more detailed description to the deputy on April 15, and defenders would have their chance to confront that officer, who would be the next witness.

In the deputy's testimony, he acknowledged interviewing the Ibisons on Thursday, April 15. He mentioned some of the physical characteristics of the suspect he'd entered into his notebook, as described by the couple. That same day, he thought, he'd given his notes to one of the detectives, but later, no one could track them down. He'd be willing, he said, to testify from memory and tell the jury what else he'd written.

A vitriolic debate followed, out of the jury's presence, in which the defenders argued that the deputy should not be allowed to testify from memory. He might modify the descriptions he'd heard. This was a deliberate effort by the prosecution to play games, defenders argued. They moved for a mistrial.

Judge Britt rejected the mistrial motion, but agreed that the deputy would not be allowed to tell the jury what he'd allegedly written in his notes. With the jury back in the box, Britt instructed them to disregard any description the deputy had already given in his testimony.

The last witness on Day 7, a male friend and professional colleague of Renae Wicklund, had visited Renae at her home a few times. He had admired some of her jewelry and specifically remembered some of the pieces she'd often worn. Roche showed him a bracelet and necklace recovered from the Snohomish River, and the witness unequivocally said they were Renae's. On cross, Anthony Savage asked how he could be so positive. The witness explained that the necklace, with pieces of coral in it, was "very distinctive," and he could still conjure up a clear mental picture of that necklace around Renae's neck.

After the jury had been excused for the day, Judge Britt held a brief meeting with the lawyers, Campbell included. The worried judge expressed concern over a timing problem. He could see that the trial would probably not conclude before Thanksgiving, only a week away. During jury selection, in Spokane, he'd hinted to the panelists that if the trial overlapped the holiday, he would consider allowing them to go home to their families during the four-day period.

Judge Britt was concerned about the fifteen jurors who were 170 miles from home, and worried about the effect of their missing out on such an important family holiday. After briefing the attorneys, and Campbell, Britt suggested some possibilities, including giving the jurors four or five days off to be with their families. He wondered if they should propose some of the options to the jurors for discussion.

Charles Campbell jumped in first. "I'd like to state my preferences . . . I don't even agree with them going anywhere in (this) town. I watch TV and I see news flashes of the case. I have a hard time believing that anybody seeing that stuff won't be affected by it." Campbell opposed the suggested trip to the crime scene, too, worried about signs such as the one Rick Arriza had posted at his store, petitioning for the death penalty. "It's human nature," Campbell said, "to be curious about these things." He didn't want the jury going anywhere until the trial was over.

"Well," Britt said, "I'm concerned about these things, too. I'll have to make the final decision, then I'm the one they can be angry with."

While he had the floor, Campbell wanted to complain about something else. He thought that working the jury six days a week might be too much for them. It only gave them Sunday to digest what they'd heard all week, to "go over things in your mind." Maybe that was too stressful for them.

Patiently, Britt explained to Campbell that "the jury is not supposed to be going over the evidence in their minds or between themselves at this point." And it might be "a greater burden on them" to believe that their sequestered time is not being used to the maximum.

Campbell argued that it would be impossible for jurors not to be going over the evidence in their minds. Mark Mestel interrupted to paraphrase Campbell's intent. "I think Mr. Campbell's concern is he'd rather have the trial five days a week."

Sounding discouraged, the judge said he appreciated any observations. He'd have to make the decisions himself. The meeting hadn't accomplished very much.

* * *

Years later, Rick Bart would express his tremendous admiration of Victoria and Harold Ibison. "They were killer witnesses," he chortled. "Absolutely great. They got on that witness stand, and if you've ever seen right over wrong, good over evil, it was that couple. They were so proud. Especially her. She's a naturalized citizen from Holland, and here she is on the witness stand in a murder trial. She got up there and just crucified him. They were terrific."

The detective also had comments about Patty Warner's testimony. "The kid did very well, but the parents were terrified. The mother (Andrea Warner) was so scared. Campbell knew who they were. What if he gets out of prison again? What if he's found not guilty and walks? They said, 'You couldn't keep him in prison the first time.' " Bart wondered what he could tell them. "We couldn't give them an answer, but they all made brave decisions and testified. They did a wonderful job. You've got to hand it to the parents to make that decision."

It remained to be seen if Andrea Warner's fears were justified.

Day 8, Tuesday, opened with brief appearances by a deputy sheriff and Sergeant Joe Belinc. Then came a surprise witness, at least to reporters and observers.

Trudy Young, a clerk typist at the Everett Work Release center, lived in Monroe and commuted every workday. To Jim Roche's questions regarding her method and route of travel, Young said she usually left work a few minutes before five P.M., and drove her car along Highway 2 toward home. That's what she had done on April 14.

"And did you see Mr. Campbell along the way home?"

"Yes, I did." She'd spotted Campbell driving a red car, alone, near a dairy farm just outside Monroe. That would put him within a five-minute drive of the Wicklund home.

Another employee at the Everett house, who had the duty of knowing the whereabouts of residents on April 14, told the jury that Campbell had logged in at five-thirty P.M., requested a busi-

ness pass at five-fifty, and left with fellow resident Karl Popovich. Campbell had returned, alone, at 7:08 that evening. No
records accounted for his activities during the hour before or
after the murders.

An inmate-resident at Everett, who'd been convicted of burglary and forgery, evidently wanted to demonstrate his verbal
skills and vocabulary when he took the stand. He testified that
he knew Charles Campbell and had seen him leave with Popovich. Roche asked about Campbell's demeanor that Wednesday
evening, to which the witness replied, "Mister Campbell showed
a marked behavioral aberration as if intoxicated."

Roche countered. "So he looked drunk to you?"

"That's right," replied the deflated inmate.

Gary Whitinger, the Everett parole officer, recalled for the
jury that he'd requested a urine sample from Campbell, and then
transported the furious inmate back to Monroe Reformatory. He
had observed three police officers, who'd been summoned to
help arrest Campbell, search the inmate that night and confiscate
a guitar pick, a one-dollar bill, and two earrings from his pockets.
Whitinger had sealed the items into an envelope and left them
on supervisor Tom Cornish's desk.

The testimony of a corrections officer from Everett agreed
with Whitinger's account, and brought the blue jacket into play
again. She'd seen it in Campbell's possession.

Judge Dennis Britt took a time out from the witness parade
to address the jurors. "Ladies and gentlemen of the jury, as you
will recall, I indicated it was my hope . . . that I could allow you
to go home to your families for Thanksgiving." He complimented
them for "exceeding his expectations" in insulating themselves
from all outside influences during the trial so far. The media
attention, he was sorry to say, had not abated as he hoped it
would. "For that, and other reasons, I find myself in a position
where I am not going to . . . allow you to go home for Thanksgiving." He'd had a lingering hope, he said, that he could give
them better news, but he didn't think it fair to keep them waiting.
"There is not much more I can say. I am truly sorry. This is not

my wish. The risk of allowing you to go home is just too great. We will try to make your Thanksgiving as pleasant for you as we possibly can under these trying circumstances." He also announced his intention to continue holding court sessions on Saturdays, and on Friday after the holiday. He did not tell them what he had up his sleeve to enliven Thanksgiving day.

On Day 9, Wednesday, Everett supervisor Tom Cornish told the jury that on the morning of April 15, he'd found the envelope left by Whitinger on his desk. He'd turned it over to Detective Tom Psonka, along with the blue jacket.

Mark Mestel objected to admitting the earrings as evidence, arguing the chain of custody requirements had clearly been violated. Psonka offered testimony countering the objection, and informed the jury that he'd taken the blue jacket to the river, on the third dive expedition, to provide a scent for the "bloodhound."

Detective Robert R. (Rick) Bart dreaded his time in front of the court. "The whole process was gut wrenching," he later told a journalist. "At that point in time in my career, I did not enjoy taking the witness stand and testifying. I didn't like it. It was the part of being a homicide detective I didn't enjoy." Years later, he said, he learned to be comfortable in front of a jury. But at that time, being in the spotlight's glare made him uncomfortable. "Here are all these cameras, and people, media coming up from Seattle and second guessing our investigation."

Clenching his jaw muscles, Bart eased into the chair and glared at Campbell. The detective probably would have been even more distressed if he'd known his appearance was only the first of four he would have to endure.

Jim Roche took Bart through the discovery of the bodies, his initial investigation with Joe Ward, and the arrest of Campbell at Monroe. Anthony Savage asked a long series of detailed questions about the search of the Torino, and each item taken from it. He launched into a microscopic examination of Bart's arrest of Campbell, wanting to know if the detective had noticed any bruises or injuries to the defendant while photographing him in the nude. The inference was that a killer couldn't stab or slash victims to death without being wounded in a struggle that surely would have occurred.

Had Bart tried to find trace evidence under the defendant's fingernails? Yes. Did Bart take all of Campbell's clothing at the reformatory? Yes. Just to be sure, the defender asked a separate question for each item. His shoes? A pair of Nike tennis shoes? A pair of socks? A pullover shirt? A purple jacket? Key rings for his car? Was it all sent to the F.B.I.?

Finally, the first session, lasting over two hours, came to an end.

Washington D.C. had sent another F.B.I. agent, Richard E. Reem, to testify about blood. Maybe the trial would have run longer if deoxyribonucleic acid, D.N.A., had been used in forensic science in 1982. But Reem's testimony focused on simple blood types. The jurors still were treated to esoteric terms like "phosphoglucomutase enzyme, phenotype 1-1, esterase D, hepatoglobin, and secretors." Blood evidence wasn't exciting then, and never would be. But conscientious jurors listened, and tried to sort out the importance of the evidence.

They looked more attentive, though, when Eric Lind brought out the amber drinking glass. "What were you looking for when you examined it."

"I was looking for human blood," Reem replied.

"And did you locate any human blood on that glass?"

"Yes sir, I did." But he hadn't been able to type the blood adequately to identify the donor.

Another piece of evidence Reem had examined would have been more useful if DNA technology had been available. He'd found traces of sperm on a glass slide containing fluid samples lifted at the crime scene. He had no way of telling who had left it there.

Mark Mestel, for the defense, bored in on how the glass was packaged when Reem received it, trying to return to the chain of evidence problem. Holding up a small cardboard box near the glass, Mestel asked, "How was this glass packaged when you received it?"

"As you see it, sir," Reem said, nodding toward the box.

"You're sure of that?"

"As far as I can recall, yes sir."

"What would you say if I told you that this box is from my office?"

"Then I would say that maybe you're right. But I received it contained in a package."

"But how was it packaged?"

"I don't recall."

"Why do you think it was this box?"

"Because we get a lot of items in boxes." Mestel, with a trace of a smile, placed the box, which had once contained a steam iron, back on the defense table.

Turning to the jeans and shirt pulled from the river, which had contained no bloodstains, he read from a book titled *Crime Investigation.* "As many as four successive washings, hand washings in cold or hot water, with and without detergent, have left residual blood detectible by chemical test." Agent Reem, an expert in blood analysis, disagreed with the hypothesis.

"How many times have you personally conducted experiments removing bloodstains from garments?"

"Several times." Mestel spent the next ten minutes trying to get an exact number from Reem, but the agent never varied from his estimate of "several." But Mestel had made his point. The jury would have to decide if the river current could have washed clothes clean that might have been worn during a bloody massacre. Or wait to see if the defense would bring in their own expert.

Jurors, the press, and gallery observers had been wondering if Karl Popovich would testify. That question was answered in the afternoon of Day 9, when the wiry, thin ex-con made his way to the front of the courtroom. In answer to Jim Roche's questions, he informed listeners that he'd been paroled last August, and now worked as a janitor in Everett. Yes, he knew Charles Rodman Campbell during the time they both served at Everett Work Release.

"Mr. Popovich, did you have a beard on April 14, 1982?" No, he didn't. The implication was clear; nearly everyone who'd seen the stranger lurking about the crime scene had described whiskers or a beard. Nor did Popovich have frizzy hair.

The witness had been away from the Everett house between two-twenty-five and four P.M. on the day of the murders, searching for a job, on foot, because no car had been available to him. The last of the three victims to die, Barbara Hendrickson, hadn't left her home until after four o'clock, so Popovich appeared to be an unlikely suspect.

Roche made it clear that Popovich had checked out again, right after his return to the facility, but had gone to a job counselor who could attest to his presence.

When Campbell had returned that evening, according to Popovich, they discussed going out for some booze. Under the guise of seeking work transportation for Popovich, they had left about six P.M., in the Torino. They'd bought a quart of "Bud," and gone to the Lowell boat launch area of the Snohomish River. "Chuck was carrying a bundle of clothes."

Now, Roche brought up the subject of injuries to the defendant. "Did Mr. Campbell discuss his right hand at all?"

"Yeah, he thought he broke it that day."

Outside the courthouse, an emergency vehicle sped by, sirens screaming, momentarily interrupting the growing tension inside.

At the river, Popovich said, a guy on a bike talked to them for about fifteen minutes, sharing a couple of "doobies" with them. They'd also consumed the beer and a fifth of tequila, half-full. Chuck said he'd taken it from some woman that day. At Chuck's request, Popovich had taken a little walk, leaving Campbell alone. "Apparently, he didn't want me to see what he was doing."

"Objection."

"Sustained. The jury will disregard that part of the answer."

After ten or fifteen minutes, Popovich said, during which he heard tires spinning in dirt or gravel, Campbell picked him up. Back in Everett, Chuck had dropped him off at a friend's house. Popovich arrived back at the house about seven-fifteen.

When Popovich heard news about the murders on Friday, he'd told supervisor Cornish, "I believe I might have some knowledge of some important things." Detective Rick Bart arrived shortly afterward, and Popovich directed him to the boat launch area.

Popovich testified that no promises or rewards had been made for the voluntary information he gave. That ended the court's day.

Nineteen

Returning to the witness stand on Day 10, Thursday, November 18, Karl Popovich faced the fiery, brutal stare of Charles Campbell and the caustic interrogation of his defense attorney, Anthony Savage.

With his first salvo, Savage established that Popovich had not been with a job counselor for the full time he'd implied under direct examination. After "about a half hour or forty-five minutes" with the counselor, Popovich admitted, he'd walked one block over to a friend's house, who had subsequently taken him back to the work release center. He'd asked the pal to give him a ride to work the next day.

"What day did you go to the river with Detective Bart?"

"It was the morning of April 15th."

"Are you sure?"

"Yes."

"Now the 15th, Mr. Popovich, that is the very day after . . . you and Mr. Campbell were down there. You were back there within eighteen hours?"

Popovich instantly realized his blunder, misstating the date. "It was the morning of the 16th." He knew he looked like a liar in the eyes of the jury.

Savage elicited from the witness every detail of what happened on the trip with Bart, including the detective's discovery of an earring and bracelet at the water's edge. Savage's questions seemed to suggest that Popovich knew, in advance, exactly where to look for the discarded baubles.

Redirecting the nervous witness back to Everett house, Savage wanted to know, minute by minute, Popovich's activities on the crucial Wednesday evening. If Popovich's answers seemed colored at all by guesswork, Savage pulled him up short and asked for explicit recollection, not guesses. He asked about the arrangement to go out for a drink with Campbell, and the bundle of clothes Campbell took with him. And he wanted to know exact times and distances. Popovich disclaimed any ability to estimate distances, and never carried a watch. Savage made abrupt switches in the subjects of his inquiries, waiting for Popovich to contradict himself.

Had Campbell smoked marijuana that night at the river? "He took a hit or two," Popovich said, "but he told me he didn't like marijuana."

What was the weather like at the river? Was it light or dark? What were you wearing? The witness answered several times that he didn't remember. Defenders usually don't mind that answer. It can sound like deliberate evasion.

On the river visit with Bart, neither man recalled seeing any motorcycle tracks. Was the fellow on the bike a figment of Popovich's imagination? The witness admitted alcohol and drug problems, including the use of LSD. Maybe his memory and imagination were irreparably scrambled.

He did recall being interviewed by a defense investigator, Sylvia Matthews.

Popovich proved his poor ability to estimate time. He guessed that the trip to the river had taken fifteen minutes, they were with the biker about ten minutes, he waited for Campbell fifteen minutes, then they'd returned to his friend's house, arriving at about six-thirty. How could that be if they'd left the Everett house at six? Appearing consternated, Popovich shook his head. "Well, like I said, I didn't have a watch. I didn't time this, but I knew where I went. I know what I did."

Savage wondered what else Popovich was guessing.

When Popovich was finally excused, Rick Bart took center stage again. He recalled that two pieces of broken pottery had been found, one on Waverly Drive, the other at the river, and sent to the F.B.I. for comparison to another bowl the detective had taken from the crime scene.

Relieved, Bart stepped down after only ten minutes on the hot seat.

The third F.B.I. agent took the oath. Ronald C. Rawalt, qualified as an expert in the "mineralogy unit, which deals in evidence composed of geologically derived material." He knew about pottery.

Examining the two pieces Rick Bart had just handed back, Rawalt said they were comprised of fired clay with a ceramic glaze. He explained the technical process of analysis, concluding that "these two pieces were at one time the same bowl." In addition, the sample bowl Bart had taken from the Wicklund home contained the same physical characteristics of the broken bowl, in size, material, coloration, style, and other similarities. Rawalt offered his opinion that the shards and the bowl were originally from the same set.

If Rick Bart thought he had a long reprieve from testifying, he was mistaken. He eased himself back into the chair immediately following the F.B.I. agent. This time, Eric Lind started at the beginning. He asked Bart to recite, step by step, how he'd heard about the crimes, and precisely what he did upon arrival at the Wicklund residence. Trying to conceal his emotions while recalling the grisly scene, Bart created a horrifying word picture, and a clear report of police procedures. Mark Mestel objected to the "cumulative" nature of the testimony. The judge called counsel up for a sidebar, and apparently satisfied the matter there, because he issued no ruling on the objection.

It soon became evident what Lind was leading up to. "Did you recover, in the bedroom, the cap of a pill bottle?" Bart said he did, a little later that night. The jury would learn that Renae Wicklund had some codeine-based prescription medicine for her sore throat. Detectives hadn't found it. Campbell's blood had contained traces of codeine.

Eric Lind also tackled the issue of hairs found in, or on, the hands of Barbara and Renae. "Now, what kind of carpeting is in the northeast bedroom?"

"Oh, I'd call it shag." Anyone experienced with shag carpet knows stray hairs abound in it.

"Now, were there any hairs grasped in (victims') hands?"

"No, not in my opinion." Barbara Hendrickson, Bart recalled, had a few hairs lying on her hands, adhered with a red stain. The same with Renae Wicklund. He didn't think any hairs were found on Shannah's hands.

Lind took Bart through the events of the next day, April 15, focusing first on booking procedures in the property room, about which the defense had left some issues hanging. Bart said he'd ordered personnel in the room to delay some of the booking so it could be completed in chronological order. He vouched for the security of all evidence stored there.

The questioning progressed through the autopsy and to Monroe, where Bart had served the search warrant on Campbell. It abruptly halted for a sidebar when the defense wanted to prevent admission into evidence of a cardboard earring holder from a jewelry box. The holder had been found in a pocket of Campbell's clothing at Monroe. Protesting that Campbell had already been searched at the Everett house when he was arrested for being drunk, the defense suggested that anything subsequently found in his clothing could have been planted there. Lind argued that the jacket had been in a secure place at the reformatory, thus preventing tampering.

Judge Britt ruled the cardboard inadmissible.

Questioning Bart again, the prosecutor tried to establish that the jeans seized at Monroe belonged to Campbell, but ran into another sustained objection.

A meticulous coverage of events at the Snohomish River followed, including the diving expeditions and each piece recovered. Moving on to the Torino search, Bart itemized everything seized from the car.

After another sidebar, Lind produced two photos Bart had

taken of Campbell trying on the shirt and jeans pulled from the river.

"Did that shirt fit?" Lind asked.

"Yes, it did."

"Did those jeans fit?"

"Yes, they did."

"How would you describe the fit?"

"Like a glove," Bart asserted. "They fit perfectly."

More examination of the boat launch area ensued, as Lind showed Bart an enlarged photo. He pointed to some tire tracks in the picture, and asked Bart if he'd found more than one set of tracks. The detective had. One of them led all the way down to the water. Another, Bart described as a "burn-out," meaning rough gouges in the ground where tires had spun. The irregular nature of the burn-outs had made those particular tire impressions unsuitable for plaster casting.

Starting with a question about Bart's responsibilities as leader of the investigation, Mark Mestel conducted the cross-exam. "Why don't you explain to me what your function is as the chief investigating officer?"

"I suppose I would be the man, since I work homicide, who would take evidence at the scene along with evidence elsewhere, and help other officers in the case."

"Is it your job to put the case together?"

"Yes, it was."

Directing the subject back to hairs found on the victims' hands, Mestel said, "I believe you testified that none of the victims were grasping any hairs in their hands." Bart agreed. He scrutinized a photo Mestel had handed him, and said it depicted a single strand of hair in the left hand of Renae Wicklund. Another picture showed a hair in her right hand. A third one had captured a hair on the hardwood hallway floor.

"Is that one in a bloodstain?"

"It's in a red-colored stain." He'd bagged them, and sent them to the F.B.I. to compare with samples from the victims and from Campbell. Observers waited for Mestel to ask for the results of the analysis, but the defender left the subject and never came back to it. Instead, he chose to chip away at property room security again. Bart agreed that certain detectives could check into the room where evidence is stored, but anyone touching items from his case would be accountable to him. No, he didn't have a key to the room, he had to go through security officers just like anyone else.

From there, Mestel bounced from subject to subject. He lingered for a while on the glass, but elicited nothing new. He may have scored a few points with the jury when Bart said that he hadn't noticed much of a beard when he'd first seen Campbell, only a little stubble on his chin, as if he hadn't shaved for a day or two. More than one witness had referred to a beard. Bart finished his third session on the stand at three-forty-five P.M.

At 4:04, Glenn Douglas, Renae's boyfriend, faced questioning by Eric Lind. He told jurors that he'd met her in the summer of 1980 at a social gathering, and they soon developed a "very close, warm, and comfortable relationship." After the tragedy, when he'd been summoned to identify her jewelry, he'd recognized a locket lying facedown on a table. He knew it contained a photo, so asked them to turn it over and said, "That's Shannah."

Douglas had also seen a familiar gold box and told the detectives, "Look inside, you'll find 4-H medallions that belong to Renae." When they did, they found her name engraved on some of them.

He'd also identified some earrings, a gold leaf, and a small shell.

A bittersweet image replayed in Douglas's mind, of a cozy night sitting with Renae at her living room table, while Shannah played quietly. He could hear the faint echos of their voices; Renae held up the gold leaf. "Do you like it?"

"It's very nice."

"I'm very proud of it. It was a gift. . . ." The voice and image faded away like a dream.

Sharp, arguing voices snapped Douglas back to reality, as lawyers quibbled over an objection. On cross-examination, Mark

Mestel asked Douglas how often he'd seen the jewelry. Most of it he'd seen just once, Douglas said, when Renae put it on the table one Saturday night.

Mestel wound up on the subject of Douglas's visit to the property room, and how he had identified each item for the detectives. At four-thirty-six P.M., Judge Britt declared court adjourned until nine-thirty tomorrow morning.

Back to the hotel, en masse, the jury trooped, under the watchful eyes of uniformed officers. They had no complaints about their treatment. On the contrary, they felt very well treated by the officers and staff. But there was something about their censored world, chopped up newspapers, off-limit television and radio programs, and monitored phone calls that anyone would find difficult. Judge Britt had offset the tedium with orders to provide the jury with sightseeing jaunts, games, and shopping trips. They just hoped it wouldn't last a long time.

Day 11, Friday, November 19, opened with another dispute out of the presence of the jury. Mark Mestel contended that witnesses had been mistaken about which dates they'd been in the property room to identify evidence, and that some of the jewelry had never been properly identified. Eric Lind shook his head. "Your Honor, we keep going over and over this, the name calling, this, that, and the other thing. The simple fact is Mr. Mestel is trying to cloud the issue."

Thirty minutes of contentious volleys solved very little.

Although Jane Gray's husband and two sons had already testified about finding jewelry on Waverly Drive, and seeing the bundle-carrying stranger walk to a red car, Jim Roche wanted more substantiation of the sightings. She replicated the story told by her husband, Victor, about walking their dogs and finding the 4-H pin by the side of the road. For the first time, though, jurors learned that the medallion had a photo on it. After she'd taken it home and placed it on a table, the witness testified, "I noticed there was a picture of a little girl that I figured was probably taken in the late fifties." It seemed to be a 4-H award, and had the name "Renae Ahlers" on it. She handed it over to the detectives, along with the other items Gray and her husband had picked up.

Gray couldn't recall the date she'd gone to the property room, when Mestel asked on cross. After a few more questions, he excused her.

The last in the long line of police officers for the prosecution settled into the chair. Deputy David Zander had been dispatched to Waverly Drive to pick up some evidence from the Gray family. His main purpose was to show the jury an unbroken chain of custody. But Anthony Savage unveiled a weak link in the chain in Zander's report of enclosing several pieces of unmarked jewelry in the same bag, and dropping that bag in a property room bin without observing completion of the booking process.

Only three witnesses remained for the prosecution's case in chief.

A professional associate of Renae's, who'd known her three years, clearly remembered purchasing a pair of "good quality" pearl earrings for Shannah. Examining the one detectives had seized from the front seat of Campbell's car, he said, "This earring is the same size and has the same coloring on the pearl as the one I gave to Shannah." The post, he felt sure, was from the set, too. He had also bought jewelry for Renae. "Yes," he said, "that appears to be a gold leaf that Renae and I purchased at the gold show in Seattle."

Answering Mark Mestel, the witness said he'd bought the earring for Shannah's last birthday. Mestel, a puzzled expression on his face, asked, "Can you tell me how it is you can recall the post of an earring?"

"The earrings that I purchased were fine quality gold, fourteen karat. Very good looking, and as I mentioned, I do enjoy good jewelry and I recognize good jewelry, and that is good jewelry."

Mestel wasn't going to let him off that easy. "I understand that, sir, but what I want to know is how can you remember what the post of an earring looks like?"

"Well, I do a lot of ear piercing at the beauty school and we see a lot of earrings, so I am just able to recognize the post of an earring."

Boring in, Mestel wanted a more concise answer, but the witness held that he'd carefully examined the gold before he bought it. At the prosecution table, Jim Roche suspected foul play and asked for a sidebar. The judge sent the jury and the witness out.

Indignant, Roche said, "Your Honor, I anticipate what Mr. Mestel is doing, I believe." He knew the defender had checked the earring out of the property room and kept it for over a week. "I believe he bought a pair, as identical as possible, and is going to see if this witness can distinguish the difference. That is improper cross-examination."

"I don't see what's improper about it," Mestel argued. The witness, he said, had positively identified the earrings. The purpose was to cast doubt on his credibility. He admitted that his investigator, Sylvia Matthews, had purchased four similar pairs.

Judge Britt decided to allow cross-examination by open comparison, but warned the defense not to try to confuse the jury by secretly substituting the purchased earring for the true exhibit.

Contentious verbal exchanges between counsel accompanied the witness's examination of several earrings, but he still believed the prosecution exhibit was the earring he'd bought for Shannah. The ones introduced by the defense, he said, didn't have the same sheen, and the pearl was not as translucent. Jim Roche appeared relieved that his witness held solidly to his convictions.

Fear had been a constant companion of Andrea Warner, little Patty's mother, since the murders, and it could be seen on her face as she took the oath. She positively verified that exhibit 185 was a necklace belonging to Shannah. It had been in her house two weeks when Patty borrowed it. She had also seen Renae wearing the earrings marked as exhibit 9, and eaten from plates, in Renae's house, now shown as broken pieces of pottery.

Another neighbor woman had seen the necklace, exhibit 185, and recognized it as Shannah's. She also had seen Renae wearing exhibit 9, the earrings, and a matching necklace. When she stepped down, Jim Roche announced, "Your Honor, we have no further witnesses and we're prepared to rest."

Twenty

The defense case-in-chief opened on Saturday morning, Day 12. Their investigator, Sylvia Matthews, had interviewed Patty Warner. Frequently referring to her notes, Matthews testified that little Patty had said she'd picked Charles Campbell at the lineup because he was the only guy who looked at all like the stranger she'd seen. Patty had also stated, Matthews said, that she'd seen Shannah get off the school bus at three-forty-five on the afternoon of April 14, contradicting her testimony that the bus always delivered them home at three-thirty.

Regarding Karl Popovich, whom she'd also interviewed, Matthews said that he'd admitted it was his idea to go somewhere that night with Campbell. Observers wondered why she brought that up, because Popovich had openly acknowledged in court that he'd made the suggestion to go for a drink.

Matthews told the jury that she'd bought the similar pearl earrings shown earlier to Glenn Douglas.

The prosecution, on cross, got an admission from Matthews that her notes of the interview with Patty Warner, to which she referred during testimony, were not a verbatim record of the conversation.

Everett Parole Officer Gary Whitinger testified that he'd observed the search of Charles Campbell by police officers when they arrested him at Everett. But Whitinger did not see exactly where the guitar pick, the dollar bill, and the earrings had been in Campbell's clothing.

"You did see the search, didn't you?" Eric Lind asked on cross-exam. And, "The three items were handed directly to you?" Whitinger answered yes to both questions.

The next defense witness surprised court watchers. Patty Warner walked primly back through the gated barrier between court officers and the gallery.

"I hate to bring you back here, on a Saturday when you're out of school," Mestel apologized, "but I just have a few questions for you." Lawyers always have only a "few" questions for witnesses.

Many attorneys are notoriously bad estimators of quantities and time. Mestel asked Patty exactly 101 questions.

First, he wanted more details regarding the blue jacket she'd seen on the man in her yard. Then he asked her to recall her relationship with Shannah. Patty had known her for five years. Were they close friends? Yes. Had they played together? Yes. "Did you both have pierced ears?" "Yes, but Patty's had closed up. Did you trade earrings and necklaces back and forth?" Yes. But she couldn't identify or remember the pearl earring.

Two jackets had been shown to Patty in the sheriff's property room, but she couldn't say that either of them was the one worn by the prowler. Regarding the "faded" blue jeans he'd worn, Patty said they were the same color as the ones she had on at that moment. Mestel asked her to stand and demonstrate to the jury. They seemed darker than one would normally call "faded."

Trying to describe the process of assembling prints of celluloid facial parts into a composite, Patty said, "He showed me a bunch of noses and told me to pick out one that I thought was his (the prowler), and ears and stuff like that, and then he put it together." Mestel produced the composite, and Patty recognized it. It bore very little resemblance to Charles Campbell. Patty realized it, and commented that the man's hair was really longer and his face was shorter. Mestel asked why that hadn't been incorporated into the original by the officer, and Patty explained, "He couldn't make hair."

"Do you recall telling the officer that the man you saw had short, curly black hair?"

"Yes," Patty answered with a little blush.

Now Mestel came to a point he wanted the jury to hear clearly. He asked Patty, "Are you certain that the person you saw was wearing a blue jacket?"

"No." A buzz rippled through the gallery, drawing a stern look from Judge Britt.

"Can you just tell me why you chose blue as the color?"

"Because that's what I thought he was wearing, and I put, 'I think.' " Mestel decided to leave well enough alone, and turned her over to the prosecution.

Jumping right in for damage control, Jim Roche asked, "Do I understand that to the best of your recollection, the individual you saw in your yard wore a blue coat?" He held a blue jacket in his hands.

"Yes."

A furious skirmish took place after the jury and witness were temporarily excused. Mestel growled, "I find it to be the most clearly objectionable form of examination to knowingly suggest to the jury that this is the jacket (the prowler wore). She could not pick it out in the property room." The defender suggested that Roche was placing false evidence in front of the jury and made another motion for a mistrial, saying "I've asked you to abort this trial eight times based on this type of error."

Agreeing that it was a thorny problem, Judge Britt at last said he would instruct the jury to disregard the cross-examination with reference to the jacket, and read them a statement of stipulation that the jacket was not the one worn by the man Patty Warner saw on April 14.

With the little girl back on the stand, Roche wanted to rehabilitate her comments about the composite drawing. Patty recalled that she had told the detective the hair was bushier and nose was "flatter at the base." Happy to step down, Patty finally walked out of the courtroom for the last time.

The detective who had interviewed Patty and taken a description of the man lurking in the rear yard, Wyatt Weeks, recalled for Mark Mestel some of the conversation he'd had with Patty while she selected facial features to make up the composite. His testimony lasted only a few minutes.

Continuing to select police officers as defense witnesses, Mark Mestel called Detective Ken Crowder. He had been dispatched by Sgt. Joe Belinc to take his Identa-Kit to the crime scene on April 15, and assemble a composite likeness of the man Patty Warner had seen. Mestel commented that on television, they usually have people talking to a police artist and making sketches. "Is this a newer and better way of doing it, or do you just not have police artists there?"

Crowder said no police artists were employed by the sheriff. He explained to the jury, through answers to Mestel's questions, how the process worked. He'd assembled more than one hundred of them during his tenure as a detective. The celluloid sheets containing various facial features, called foils, would be stacked on a white metal background, to make up a complete face. Sometimes, he had to use a grease pencil to enhance the likeness, according to the witness's description.

Was Patty happy with the final result? Yes, except for the nose, which she wanted a little wider and flatter at the base. And she had difficulty with the hair. "I tried using the grease pencil." She described it as being longer, fuller, and bushier. His efforts with the pencil hadn't worked to her satisfaction.

Patty had given him a general description of the man, then modified it by adding his age and height, making him about twenty-five and six-two. Although it couldn't be depicted in the black and white composite, she'd said that the stranger's eyes were either hazel or green, which was remarkably accurate considering she'd been no closer than thirty feet away. But Crowder hadn't recorded that in his notes, and Patty hadn't recalled eye color in her testimony.

Judge Britt excused the jury at twelve-fifty-five P.M. until Monday morning. That weekend, the sequestered group was treated to some entertainment that may have pleased the six men more than the nine women, including the three alternates. They boarded vans, traveled south on the I-5 to Seattle, and marched into the circular Kingdome where they watched a Seattle Supersonics basketball game. They felt a sense of relief to be part of the normal world again, away from the depressing world of murder.

Monday morning, Day 13, got off to an unlucky start for the defense. They'd brought in a forensic scientist to testify about fingerprint evidence. Eric Lind, during *curriculum vitae* questioning, cast doubt on the witness's expertise in the field, and the judge also expressed doubt. Mestel capitulated. He had another expert waiting in the wings.

Within the first hour of Raymond Davis's testimony, Mark Mestel brought out the amber glass. The expert said he thought it was odd that he could find very few traces of black dusting powder on it, and wondered why the investigators hadn't photographed prints they'd found on it.

Mestel turned to the jeans fished from the river and asked Davis if he thought blood traces, had there ever been any, would have remained on jeans despite being immersed in the water. Davis referred to a book, *Crime Investigation,* and read aloud. "When bloodstains are washed, the blood is rarely totally removed. . . . As many as four successive washings of bloody clothing by automatic washers, commercial laundries, hand washing, in cold or hot water, with or without detergent, have left residual blood. . . ." To Mestel, the jury would have to believe that a mere river current, then, could not remove the stains. Thus the jeans couldn't possibly have been used in a bloody murder.

Regarding the absence of fingerprint powder, Eric Lind, upon cross-examination, noted that both he and the witness held the glass very carefully, in a manner that would not contaminate or remove evidence. He asked, ". . . if people running their hands all over it, rolling it on the counter during examination of other witnesses, and things like that, isn't it highly possible that the fingerprint powder would be removed . . . ?"

"Probably remove a great deal of it," the witness hedged.

"Do you still have that book you used?" Lind wanted to talk about the jeans. Davis opened it to the page he'd read. Lind asked if it said that blood was *rarely* removed. Yes.

"So there are cases where it could be totally removed?"

"It would be possible," Davis conceded.

The final witness in the case-in-chief trudged to the stand again. Rick Bart still didn't like testifying. Mestel inquired if Bart had been present when Campbell tried on the jeans and shirt. Bart had. Did you have him try on a thermal shirt? Yes.

Bart concurred that he'd taken photos of Campbell. About the Torino search, Mestel and Bart agreed that the interior was a complete mess and that the detective hadn't removed everything, just what he regarded as items of evidentiary value. Testimony covered once more the trip with Karl Popovich to the river, hair evidence, and examination of jewelry in the property room. Rick Bart made a welcome exit at two P.M.

In every murder trial, there is a great deal of speculation about the possibility of the defendant testifying in his own behalf. Most defense attorneys advise against it, and most prosecutors rub their hands in greedy delight when defendants ignore that advice. The general public is usually skeptical about a defendant who is not willing to step up and declare his innocence. "If someone put me on trial for murder, and I wasn't guilty, you couldn't keep me off of that witness stand." The debate will continue as long as trials are conducted.

Charles Campbell had certainly not been reluctant to speak during the trial, even conducting the cross-examination of Ladonna Layton. Now the public, press, and prosecutors waited for his decision.

After sending the jury out on Monday afternoon, November 22, Judge Britt questioned the defendant. "Mr. Campbell, I assume you have discussed with your attorneys your right to testify in this case. Have you?"

"Huh?"

"Have you discussed with your attorneys your right to testify?"

"Yes."

"You have the right to decline to testify. You do not have to. Do you understand that?"

"Yes."

Trying to give the defendant every chance, Britt repeated, "You can if you want to, but you don't have to." Campbell nodded silently. Britt asked, "You are fully aware of the choice that's available to you?"

"Yes, I am."

"Have you made a choice in that regard?"

"Yeah," Campbell grunted. "I don't wish to."

Mark Mestel announced that the defense would rest. Jim Roche said he would decide tomorrow if he would present a rebuttal case.

Judge Britt spent the next hour discussing with the lawyers and Campbell the options related to taking jurors on a trip to the crime scene. They agreed to allow it the next morning, on a circuitous route, avoiding roads or byways that had been named in testimony.

Day 14, Tuesday. In welcoming the jurors back from their field trip to Clearview, the judge explained why they had not taken direct routes, and cautioned them against using any mental notes they may have taken of distances or travel times.

Jim Roche stood to inform everyone that he would not present a rebuttal case. The only thing left now would be instructions from the judge, final arguments by the attorneys, and deliberation by the jurors.

A quandary faced the judge, though. If he completed delivering legal instructions to the jury, and the attorneys finished arguing by Wednesday afternoon, the jury would begin deliberations that day, and be forced to continue on Thanksgiving day. That would destroy some very special plans he'd made. So, apologizing for wasting the remainder of Tuesday, and all day Wednesday, he announced to the jurors they would be in recess until Friday.

Because the jurors hadn't seen their families since the beginning of the trial, and would miss being with them on Turkey day, Judge Britt unveiled his special surprise that Thursday, November 25. He had arranged for every member of the jury to see and talk to their loved ones via closed circuit television. The judge personally monitored each hookup, and the conversations, to assure that no one communicated anything about the case. It was a remarkable and generous gesture by Britt, who gave up time with his own family to implement the project.

Twenty-one

Day 15. The first order of business for Friday morning was the reading of the lengthy instructions to the jury by the judge. Juries must hear the litany of legal instructions they are required to follow in weighing the evidence and reaching a verdict. The lawyers and judge pluck selected standard instructions from extensive volumes, then massage and supplement them according to applicable conditions. Some judges can accomplish an oral presentation of this material in a palatable, interesting manner. Others drone on in a stultifying monotone for eternity, virtually guaranteeing that the benumbed, drowsy jury understands very little of it. It's not an easy job to deliver the ponderous language in an interesting manner. Judge Britt accomplished it as well as it can be done.

When he'd completed the reading, Britt announced, "You will now hear the closing arguments of counsel." Like judges, some attorneys are masters of this stage, delivering a summary of the evidence that evokes outrage, righteous indignation, chills, tears, anger, and the entire gamut of emotions. It is the ultimate test of speaking ability, since a person's life can literally rest in the balance.

Eric Lind would go first for the prosecution. Young, handsome, vigorous, and enthusiastic, he stepped in front of the jury box with all the confidence of a seasoned veteran.

Nearly always, closing arguments begin with an explanation that the lawyer's words are not evidence, only an interpretation of the evidence that has already been presented. A second element usually presented is acknowledgment to the jurors of the fine job they've done, and respect for the tough job they face. Lind tagged both of these bases smoothly.

"You have to make the law live and breathe again in Snohomish County," he intoned, "because on April 14th of 1982, the law died in Snohomish County." The protective structure of the law, for Renae Wicklund, Shannah Wicklund, and Barbara Hendrickson, failed. . . . Their right to be free, safe, and secure in their homes, and the law died, Lind said. "You have to bring it back to life."

He wouldn't cover every piece of evidence, or each witness, Lind promised, but would highlight the most important ones. Lind kept eye contact with jurors, saying that Campbell's 1976 conviction for sexual assault, a crime against Renae's person, and his "burning hatred" of her, provided a second fingerprint at the crime scene. The defendant's girlfriend had revealed a lot about him: the resentment toward Renae, his knowledge of where she lived, his keeping a transcript of the trial, and his stalking her. "Ladies and gentlemen, he had been there, he'd watched her, and he knew she'd be home. He did that with the intent of coming back and killing her."

Reminding jurors that Ladonna Layton had also spoken of Campbell's drinking on April 14, when she testified about her missing knife after he'd left, Lind said that knife matched the death implement described by the pathologist. Evoking mental pictures of "terror, pleas for mercy, screams of horror," the attorney asked jurors to look at the photos and "you can hear the screams."

"Campbell couldn't just kill Renae, he had to savagely beat her first. He enjoyed it. He took pleasure in it. . . . Killing her wasn't enough, he had to . . . sexually mutilate her as well."

Shannah, "the beautiful eight-year-old child who won't grow up, won't know what it's like to be an adult because her life was stolen from her," was beaten and murdered by Charles Campbell and it was premeditated, Lind said. "Shannah Wicklund came home after Campbell was seen at three-thirty, and was subdued in the hallway by Campbell, and dragged back into the bedroom where he killed her. Why did he drag her back there? So she could see what he'd done to her mother, ladies and gentlemen."

Barbara Hendrickson, Lind said, came into the house after four-twenty, and was killed in the hallway. And the really sick thing about these horrible, hideous crimes was that he had to take trophies, the earrings missing from each body. Lind emphasized the time span, from Campbell entering the property at three-thirty to Barbara leaving home at four-twenty. What was he doing between four and four-twenty? "The answer screams out. He was waiting for Barbara Hendrickson!" Lind theorized that in her terror, Renae had told Campbell that her daughter and friend would be there soon, hoping the threat of witnesses would scare him away. Instead, that excited the "demon fire" in him for "sheer animal vengeance." The vengeance factor pointed directly at Campbell as the killer, and no one else.

Granted, nearly all the evidence was circumstantial, Lind said, but the judge's instructions said it "is every bit as good as any other type of evidence."

Campbell left a "trail of jewelry" the lawyer continued, still spellbinding jurors. The private citizens who identified it have no reason to lie. Patty Warner, a "brave little girl," had positively identified him. Others saw him on Waverly Drive, where the Torino registered to Campbell was parked. The most damaging jewelry evidence, Lind said, was the earring found on Campbell when he was searched. Glenn Douglas recognized that earring. "Mr. Campbell did it. There is no doubt."

"They tried to trip" the witness who identified Shannah's earring found in Campbell's car, by getting one that looked like it. But it didn't fool the witness; he saw the difference. He had no reason to lie.

Lind cited the contribution of Karl Popovich leading detectives to the river where more of the trail of jewelry led to Campbell. "Everywhere Campbell goes, there is evidence that links him with this hideous act." Reminding the jury of promises made in the opening statement by the defense, to reveal evidence that

Popovich lied in return for favors from the state, Lind indignantly asked, "What evidence? What favors? He testified truthfully. He was unshaken." Campbell had to go to the river that night to dump evidence of his guilt. "Every piece of evidence leads directly to Mr. Campbell."

The State, Lind said, had also alleged aggravating factors in this case. He listed them: committing murders while serving a term of imprisonment, murdering former witnesses who testified at a trial, murder in the course of flight from a burglary, and murder of more than one victim. It was all part of a plan that had developed while he was in prison, burning with hatred for Renae Wicklund, hatred that consumed him and led to death for three innocent people. Campbell festered in hatred. "The hatred you must punish him for."

"Now, one point I want to make. The defense told you what they were going to do in the opening statement . . . and you must hold them to that. They said that ninety-nine percent of the evidence in this case would point away from Mr. Campbell. I have yet to see one single piece of evidence that points away from Mr. Campbell."

The jewelry, the jeans, the witnesses, motives, premeditation, all these things "I've talked about," Lind said. "But there's one piece of evidence that I haven't talked about yet. It's the single piece of evidence you could base a conviction on if you had nothing else."

The glass.

Lind spoke slowly, clearly. "It had Mr. Campbell's palm print on it." The chain of evidence was unbroken.

"Does the glass point away from Mr. Campbell? Does the jewelry point away from Mr. Campbell? Does anything else point away from Mr. Campbell? No! The very nature of the crime itself with a maniacal, sadistic attack on Renae Wicklund points directly to one person and one person only, and it points to this man right here." Lind's voice rose to an indignant crescendo. "This man killed those three women. This man did it with premeditation. This man did it because she had testified against him.

This man inflicted the carnage upon that house, the screams of agony." Pointing at Campbell, Lind let his voice tremble. "That man did it. Every piece of evidence points at that man and to no other."

Clarence Darrow would have been proud.

Lind paid tribute to the witnesses who bravely testified against a violent, vengeance seeking bully. He acknowledged that some mistakes may have been made, but downplayed them. Were they the type of thing that should lead to an acquittal, in light of the evidence? "The answer is clearly NO."

"I will get to address you one more time," Lind said. The prosecution has the burden of proving the case, so always gets to rebut the closing statement of the defense. But, Lind pointed out, his job was not to incite anger, hatred, or revenge. "There's been enough vengeance."

His job, the articulate young lawyer said, was to bring the law back to life in Snohomish County. To make it live and breathe for Renae, and Shannah, and Barbara. "Nobody has the right to steal the lives of that beautiful woman and her beautiful child, and her caring neighbor." Lind paused for a long breath, and concluded. "I'm asking you, ladies and gentlemen, after carefully considering the evidence, as I know you will, make the law live once more. Make it live for Renae. Make it live for Shannah, and make it live for Barbara. Thank you."

Eric Lind had spoken for nearly two hours. The jury recessed for lunch.

At one-thirty, before the jury filed back in, Mark Mestel had a request to make. "Your Honor, Mr. Campbell would like permission to address the jury as part of closing argument."

Jumping to his feet, Eric Lind had to control his voice to keep from shouting. "I'm going to strenuously object, Your Honor."

Judge Britt, with his usual calm patience, said, "Give me an indication into what regard." Mestel assured the court that Campbell only wanted to speak as part of closing argument, not to argue anything not already admitted into evidence or to testify in his own behalf. But to questions by the judge, Mestel could

only say, "It hasn't been thought through, Your Honor." A perturbed expression crossed Britt's face, then passed. He suggested
that the defense lawyer present the statement, then they would
take a recess for the judge to hear what supplemental information
Mr. Campbell might want to offer the jury. Mestel quickly
agreed.

With the jury reseated, Mestel rose, and opened by thanking
the judge, jury, and opposing counsel. "This is the last time I'll
get to address you, ladies and gentlemen." As Lind had, he reminded them this segment was a summary, not evidence. "I don't
plan on being theatrical, or using flowery phrases, or to confuse
you with legal terms." He would discuss it, he hoped, "as if we
were sitting in your living room," appealing to their common
sense.

"We concede nothing," he asserted. "We concede only that the
State has not proved their case." Reminding jurors of the essential
presumption of innocence for his client, Mestel said, "Now the
easiest thing would be for you to go back into the jury room, say
that you feel sorry for the beautiful child, the loving mother and
the kind neighbor, and that there's enough evidence to demonstrate that Mr. Campbell may have done it, or could have done
it, and in tribute to their memory you'll find him guilty." But, he
said, jurors must uphold the law and remember presumption of
innocence. The prosecution was required to prove guilt, and it
was not incumbent on the defense to bring any evidence into
court. "The whole purpose . . . is to make these two gentlemen
show you beyond a reasonable doubt that Mr. Campbell is in fact
the person who committed the hideous crimes."

Mestel apologized for his frequent objections during the trial,
many of which required the jury to leave the room, but explained
the necessity as part of his responsibility to see that justice was
done.

"I'm not here to solve the crime for you," he emphasized.
"I'm here merely to demonstrate why Mr. Campbell is not
guilty." He called the prosecution's efforts "just a cheap attempt

to get to your emotions," and expressed hope that he would not argue in that regard.

Tackling the always elusive definition of reasonable doubt, Mestel said, "There is no good example as to what is a reasonable doubt. When you see it, you will know it. And in this case you should know it well."

Mestel lauded Eric Lind. "He argued eloquently." But the defender felt the prosecution's case "has been one heated, headlong race down a slippery slope to get Mr. Campbell to the gallows without respect for the evidence, the investigation, or any of the facts. It is based on the worst tradition of appealing to emotionalism to cloud the issues and to convince you that Mr. Campbell deserves whatever it is the state has in store for him because he's a bad person."

Attacking the prosecutor's opening argument, Mestel said Mr. Roche promised to demonstrate that Campbell had attempted to rape Ellen Tremaine. Actually, "there was nothing except a man becoming overly amorous with a lady friend.

"Then he (Roche) said he would show you how Mr. Campbell brutally raped Renae Wicklund as she lay dying. Well, you don't have to take my word for the fact he didn't do it because Judge Britt threw it out."

The testimony of Campbell's fiancée, Ladonna Layton, Mestel noted, reported Campbell's admission of feeling resentment, but that he never wanted to hurt anyone. Yes, he'd been out there, and yes, he was convicted of the 1974 crime. "I will talk to you until I can't talk anymore to convince you *that* is the reason Mr. Campbell is on trial today."

"By the evening of April 15th, . . . the police had already decided that he had done this act because he was convicted in 1976. . . . There never has been an investigation. Campbell was selected and now Campbell is on trial . . ."

Critical of the sheriff's office for losing notes taken by the deputy who wrote down descriptions provided by Harold and Vickie Ibison, Mestel wondered aloud if the loss was deliberate. Investigators knew that Campbell didn't have a black beard, but

Ibison had described a full, dark chin beard. The defender suggested that a detective had just put the notes in his pocket or threw them in the garbage. "Don't you imagine," Mestel asked the jury, "that if (the notes) would have said six-foot-three, faint mustache, brown curly hair, thin medium build, whatever fits Mr. Campbell, that those notes would have been here?" The witness, "looking through his binoculars saw somebody who was not Mr. Campbell."

On the matter of the composite drawing, Mestel excoriated the officer who took the description from Patty Warner for "some of the most incredible testimony I have ever heard," and suggested that the little girl had been unfairly influenced to modify some of the features she described. "When you start changing evidence to fit the suspect," Mestel said, "you're not upholding the law. . . . This is what I call reasonable doubt."

Leading up to the crucial prints on the glass, Mestel noted that Detective Oberg "took fifty-six lifts from every imaginable place in that house," and "not one immovable object had a fingerprint on it." Scanning the implacable faces of the attentive jurors, Mestel continued. "So now we have the *moveable* glass. On the 14th, when everybody was searching the house, nobody seemed to notice this glass with the reddish-purplish stains all over it and the fingerprints visible in the stains."

Mestel drew an objection from Eric Lind when he said, "Oberg said he saw a latent fingerprint."

"That's not what Detective Oberg testified to at all."

Judge Britt imperturbably deflected it. "The jury will recall what the testimony was. Proceed."

Ignoring the interruption, Mestel continued, questioning the amount of fingerprint powder on the glass and suggesting its vulnerability to tampering in the property room. "It seemed like the property room was the public library where you just go down to whatever you want, take whatever you want and nobody really cares about it. Supposedly, Oberg just left this glass lying around for seven days. He didn't log it in until after he had taken Campbell's fingerprints and, then he took all this material at the same time and brought it into the property room."

They put the glass in a box and sent it to the F.B.I., Mestel said. Observers knew what was coming next, and they were right. Mestel recalled Agent Reem's testimony, in which he had mistakenly agreed that he'd received the glass in a box the defender had held up, which was actually a steam iron box. The implication seemed to be that if Reem was wrong on that answer, he might have been wrong on other answers.

By the time the glass arrived at the F.B.I. labs, Mestel said, it had no stains or dusting powder on it. "If this glass was in the property room, why had it changed so dramatically by the time it got to the F.B.I.?" Perhaps it had been manipulated or substituted.

"I ask you, when you pick up a glass to drink, whether you even touch your palm to the glass . . . ?" Some observers wondered if the attorney was inviting the jurors to experiment, which is not proper. They are required to weigh only evidence they hear or see in the courtroom.

Attacking the fingerprint expert's testimony, Mestel continued to chip away at the single piece of physical evidence. He challenged the "points of similarity" of the print to Campbell's exemplar. He blasted salvos at the procedures for lifting the print on the glass. Asking the jury to reject the testimony, Mestel added, "You need not get that far because this glass is *not the glass that was in the Wicklund home.*"

Switching to earrings, Mestel asked, "Where did the earrings come from that were supposedly taken from Mr. Campbell?" The police officers who arrested Campbell at Everett, and reportedly took earrings from his pocket, had not been called to testify. "The reason those police officers aren't here is because there were never any earrings found in Mr. Campbell's pocket . . ." Mestel said that Gary Whitinger, the parole officer, had listed nothing but a guitar pick and a dollar bill in notes he'd dictated one-half hour after the search.

"Let's discuss what the State has to prove the case against

Campbell." First, Mestel said, they had Patty Warner, a child, whose description of the stranger did not match Campbell. Then, the young boys couldn't pick Campbell out in a lineup. And they had a lot of confusion about a blue jacket, which Mr. Campbell did not wear that day, according to testimony from more than one person. And from the photo montage of cars, no one had been able to conclusively pick the Torino.

Mestel asked, "What about the pearl earring in the car? Is it Shannah Wicklund's? I don't know. The truth is I had Sylvia Matthews go out and buy a similar earring, not an identical one, so I could use it for cross-examination." He asked the jury to compare the two during deliberations and see if they could tell them apart.

The final link in the State's case, Mestel said, was Karl Popovich. There was a dispute about whose idea it was, Campbell's or Popovich's, to go out that night, and Mestel thought Popovich had lied on the stand. Many questions remained, too, he said, about what they did when they went out. "We do know that Campbell came back without him. We know that he lied to work release people. We know that he carries marijuana . . . and that he drinks. No big deal, but we know that he's certainly not above breaking the rules." Mestel implied that Popovich had planted the jewelry at the river for Detective Bart to find.

Who committed the murders? Mestel said, "Now, we have (Mr. Popovich) and we have his picture and we have the composite. I'm not here to tell you that he did it, that one of his friends did it, because I don't know. I'm here to tell you that Mr. Campbell did not do it." Mestel was positive that the police should have investigated Popovich as a potential suspect. "Popovich carried Campbell up the steps on the evening of the 14th, and supposedly earrings are found in Campbell's pocket. Popovich goes into Campbell's car on the evening of the 14th, and there's a pearl earring found . . . in the passenger seat where Popovich was sitting. Popovich clearly has as much involvement with this as Campbell possibly could have, yet nothing is done about it." All these questions, Mestel said, hadn't been answered. "I call them reasonable doubt."

The hairs found on the hands of two victims also bothered Mestel. "Whose hair is this? I'll bet you my entire fee that if it was Mr. Campbell's you would have had another special agent up here telling you that this was Mr. Campbell's hair." Or Mestel asked, was it Popovich's hair. "You'll never know, because the State decided not to present that evidence."

Invoking "the search for truth" four more times, Mestel accused the State of simply ignoring evidence that did not point to Campbell. The jeans pulled from the river, he said, would fit a number of people, and if they'd been used in a gory murder, there would have been blood on them.

"Let me tell you what happened as best I can make out from the facts that you heard. . . . Mr. Campbell wanted to get his tires changed. He had to get his studded tires off and he went out and started drinking early in the morning, as was his habit. He went to Ladonna Layton's house, in Monroe, drank some more, got kind of 'rasty' with her and obnoxious, went to get his tires, ended up at Ellen Tremaine's house drunker than he started off, had his little to-do with her, took a bottle of tequila, went back to Ladonna's house and drank the half bottle of tequila."

Taking a deep breath, Mestel continued his narrative. "Why can I say that to you? You'll have to look at the map. It will show you that she lived in Monroe, and Ellen lived in Monroe, and he was seen between five and five-fifteen coming back from Monroe. . . . He got into his car drunk and came back to the work release facility, never going to Clearview, checked into work release dressed just the way he left, right past guards who noticed nothing unusual. The man who has just left what Joe Ward calls the scene of a massacre, blood everywhere—he just walks in . . . and sits down in the TV room and watches television. Popovich says, 'Let's go out and get loaded.' Campbell says, 'Fine,' goes up and showers, puts some stuff in a bag or under his arm, and leaves.

"To begin with, don't you think Campbell would have known

that he would have been the most likely suspect? Don't you think anybody would know that if they had a crime six years ago with somebody and that person turned up dead while they were out in the street, that they would be the most likely suspect? Why go back to the work release facility so as not to break the rules, so as not to be late? I mean, obviously, he would have headed for the hills. If you were in your bloody clothes, somebody is going to see you. If he changed before he went into the work release facility, why is there all this talk about taking stuff and putting it in a bag and taking it out to the car? Why would you bring back the proceeds of the crime, these earrings, the (brass) candle holder, all this other jewelry? What purpose would it possibly serve to bring it back to the work release facility? Why not just take it and dump it on the way back? NONE OF IT MAKES SENSE!"

Mestel threw more questions at the jury, and reemphasized that you just don't kill three people and not get blood all over you. The crime, he said, suggested a burglary gone bad.

"Mrs. Wicklund was beaten," Mestel said, "and all the blows fell on the right side of her body. The other two victims had bruises on the right side of their bodies. . . . If you walk up and hit somebody on their right side, you use your left hand. Everybody says that Campbell was rubbing his right hand."

The dimensions of the knife taken from Ladonna Layton's house, Mestel asserted, were not consistent with the wounds on the victims.

Reminding the jurors that this was his last opportunity to speak to them, Mestel ridiculed the logic of the case against his client. He suggested they should make Mr. Lind, for the prosecution, answer some questions. Make him explain where those lost notes were. Make him explain why the police who supposedly searched Campbell weren't there. Make him explain why there's no hair evidence for them to consider. Make him explain the absence of tire prints and footprints evidence.

"If the prosecutor wants to do justice, make him explain why he did not present all of the evidence to you. If he can't explain those to you, ladies and gentlemen, if he can't come up with something just a little better about this glass, I submit it's just because the case is no good. I would ask you, on behalf of Mr. Savage and Mr. Campbell, to do justice for Mr. Campbell, to stop the slide to the gallows based on the law as you've been instructed to hold onto the presumption of innocence, recognize reasonable doubt when you see it, and return verdicts of not guilty. Thank you."

Twenty-two

After a twenty-minute break, and while the jury was still out, Judge Britt and the lawyers worked out a few housekeeping details regarding evidence. That completed, the judge said he'd like to resolve the matter of Mr. Campbell wishing to address the jury.

Mark Mestel eased the judge's concern. "Your Honor, I've discussed Mr. Campbell's earlier request with him and Mr. Savage, and he has decided to withdraw his request."

Judge Britt, wise in the way of appeals problems, wanted to be sure. "You'd made the request on his behalf. He did not personally make it. You think he ought to personally withdraw it? Mr. Campbell, your attorney has indicated you do not wish me to consider further a request that you address the jury. Is that correct?"

Sullen, and not bothering to explain, Campbell said, "Yes, it is."

When the jury had taken their seats, Judge Britt invited Eric Lind to make his concluding arguments.

Observers in the gallery thought Mark Mestel had raised some interesting points, and were anxious to see how the prosecution would counter them.

Lind counter attacked with gusto. "Ladies and gentlemen, I hope I don't disappoint you in my concluding argument when I don't personally attack the defense, when I don't call anybody stupid, talk about sloppiness, or come out and call people liars."

He said he wouldn't resort to low blows, to accuse "Mr. Mestel of trying to lie to you. He's trying to do as good a job as he can."

Starting with the fingerprint on the glass, Lind seemed to laugh at the defense implying that it must have been planted. There was certainly no other way they could explain it, he said. And the earrings found on Campbell during the search? It wouldn't make sense that they were planted before he was even a suspect. Yes, Mr. Whitinger, had left them off his report. He'd left *all* the items off the report the defense referred to.

The questions posed by Mr. Mestel, Lind said, were easy to answer. Tire track evidence? Campbell had skidded and spun the tires in soft, muddy earth. No casts could be made. The hairs? Detective Bart testified that there were loose hairs in the shag carpet, and the hair on the victims' hands hadn't been "grasped." Besides, Lind pointed out, the defense expert had the same opportunity to examine the hairs. If they were exculpatory, he would have brought it out.

"The police aren't on trial. The State isn't on trial. The prosecutors aren't on trial. That's the way it sure sounded like, but we're not on trial. So let's look at the evidence as it existed." The glass, for example. Lind summarized the testimony regarding the palm prints, and concluded, "There's nothing wrong with it. There are no inconsistencies." And Lind ridiculed the proposition that if F.B.I. agent Reem was mistaken about the box the glass was packaged in, he must be mistaken about everything.

The blood. Evidence showed that blood *could* be washed out with cold water, Lind said, leaving no trace.

No investigation was perfect, Lind acknowledged, and mistakes were made. But the loss of some notes shouldn't be reason to acquit Mr. Campbell.

"These aren't reasonable doubts, ladies and gentlemen. They are problems that Mr. Mestel would *like* to be reasonable doubts".

Karl Popovich, Lind said, was never a suspect in this case, because he was never involved in the crime. His time was clearly documented on the work release log. "No way. Not one

shred of evidence has been presented to you that points anywhere near him."

Bringing the focus back on Campbell, Lind reminded jurors
that the defendant's jeans were wet from the knee down when he
returned to the Everett house that night. It was obvious he'd been
to the river. And Popovich had been with him, as shown by his
fingerprints on the passenger side of the Torino, and no place
else. He'd never driven that car, nor been near the crime scene.

"Mr. Mestel did point out a correct distinction between (our)
opening and closing arguments. Yes, the State did tell you that
we were going to prove that Renae Wicklund was raped. And we
didn't do that. We did prove to you that after she died, she was
sexually mutilated." Lind didn't trouble the jurors with the technical details of the law.

Disputing Mestel's comments about the probable murder
weapon, Lind said that the butcher knife missing from Ladonna
Layton's apartment could have made the gruesome wounds.

"I'm not asking you to convict Mr. Campbell in the memory
of Shannah Wicklund or Renae Wicklund, or Barbara Hendrickson. I do think it's important that you understand what type of
people they are, and get to know them a little bit. We sometimes
forget who was killed, people who have lives, goals, people who
have aspirations—"

"Objection, Your Honor," Mestel interrupted. "It's not proper
argument to argue about the character of the victims as a basis
for finding guilt."

"The objection is sustained."

"But they are people," Lind continued. "The fact that they are
people isn't why you should find Mr. Campbell guilty. It must
be based on the evidence, which points to the fact that Mr. Campbell is guilty of three counts of first-degree, aggravated, premeditated murder."

Listing more of Mestel's rationale for reasonable doubt, one
by one, Lind contradicted each one. "When you can't explain
evidence in one way, try to explain it in another. And their explanation for all the evidence in this case is that it was planted.

Well, ladies and gentlemen, if we were going to plant evidence on him, we'd have done a lot better job of it.

"If we were going to plant fingerprints, it would make sense to plant them all over the house," Lind argued. "We'd have a murder weapon. We'd have blood on his clothes. But that's not what happened. Nobody's trying to make square pegs fit in round holes. The evidence is there. It's like a trail. It leads from the house to Mr. Campbell. It's an unequivocal trail, because this man committed the murders."

Mistakes made by killers in leaving evidence, couldn't always be explained, Lind said. "If every crime was committed in a perfect fashion . . . there would never be a prosecution."

Once more, Lind asserted his faith in witnesses like Patty Warner and the Ibisons. They had no reason to lie, and they should be praised for having the courage to testify.

The theory of injuries to the right side of the victims not matching the painful right hand of Campbell didn't make any sense, Lind said. That could be explained in any number of ways.

"Campbell left a mark written in stone at that house, his palm print, and there's nothing to dispute that. Nothing."

Clearly deriding the theory of planted evidence, Lind said, "Attacking the prosecutor, the sheriff's office, and the F.B.I in an effort to deceive does not change that."

His voice starting to grow hoarse, Lind wound down. "I'm sure you've heard enough from me. I'm sure you've heard enough from the evidence. I'm sure you're getting tired.

"Just remember what you're going to be doing. You're going to be bringing the law back to life. You're going to be making it count, count for something that it didn't count for on April 14th of 1982. . . . The evidence is there. I ask you to use it. I ask you to return with verdicts of guilty on aggravated first-degree murder. I ask you to do your job as only you can do it and bring the law back to life. Thank you."

In a deadly silent courtroom, Judge Britt's voice boomed. "The jury will now commence their deliberations. The court will be in recess until such time as the jurors announce they have reached a verdict."

It was three-forty-five P.M. on Friday, November 26, 1982. Weak, milky sunlight filtered through leafless branches outside the windows, and into the courtroom, casting long shadows of the spectators, family members, and court officers as they filed slowly out to wait for the verdict. It might take hours, or it might take the rest of the year.

Twenty-three

As soon as the last of twelve jurors had entered the room in which they would deliberate, and closed the door, one of the members spoke up. "Anybody here think this sonofabitch didn't do it?"

The other five men and six women glanced at him, some with pained expressions, others weary. A young man kept mulling over in his mind the gruesome photographs he'd seen of three women slashed to death. Those images would never leave him. Oddly, he also kept picturing the "humongous" knuckles on Campbell's hands. Were they the hands that had held the bloody knife? A compelling thought racked his brain, about Campbell's slipping out of custody: *If he was able to do it once, what's going to stop him from trying it again?*

Images of Campbell had branded themselves in the mind of a third male juror, who would recall, "He had the most steely look. He stared right through you. Cold. If one word could describe him, it's the word cold. He seemed to be defying us to find him guilty."

The group promptly elected a foreman, the man who'd just called Campbell a sonofabitch.

Outside the jury room, family members and reporters milled around in the halls, wondering if they dared leave. No one can predict how long a jury will deliberate. This day was nearly gone. Late autumn darkness hovered in the east, following the sun's drop beyond the chilling Pacific waters. The jury, they figured, would probably elect a foreman, maybe take a straw vote to see where they stood, then adjourn to the hotel.

Mark Mestel and Anthony Savage had left the courthouse, while Jim Roche and Eric Lind chatted for a few minutes with Lorene Ahlers Iverson, Hilda Ahlers, Don Hendrickson, and various relatives. Steve Eckstrom, of Victim-Witness/Families and Friends, stayed to offer his compassionate support to the nerve-wracked kin of the murder victims. Coffee cooled in half-empty cups, and conversation lagged. How long would it take?

Judge Dennis Britt wondered, too, but chose to stay around the courthouse for a while. It was a sound decision. He received notification at six-fifteen that same evening that the jury had reached a verdict.

Astonished court officers, reporters, and family members hurried back into the courtroom. The hushed gallery fidgeted while a bailiff called the court to order, and Judge Britt settled behind his big desk.

"Ladies and gentlemen, have you reached a verdict?" They had.

After deliberating only two hours and thirty-nine minutes, they had unanimously decided that Charles Rodman Campbell was guilty of three counts of first-degree, aggravated murder.

Campbell's only reaction was an insolent sneer.

Absolutely delighted, Detective Rick Bart would later recall one of the jurors telling him, "I don't know what you guys were worried about. Hell, a blind man could have followed his trail."

Campbell's jurors went back to their hotel, for they would have to reconvene on Monday morning to decide the convict's fate. They could send him to prison for the rest of his life, or to death row in the Walla Walla penitentiary. In Washington, condemned convicts have a choice; lethal injection or being hanged.

On Monday, November 29, Jim Roche once again called family members to the stand to tell the jury why they felt Campbell should die for his crimes.

The defense called no one!

"It was a strategic decision," Mark Mestel said. Some of the testimony prosecutors had planned to present during the guilt phase had been ruled out by the judge. But if defenders called witnesses in the penalty phase, they risked opening the door to potentially damaging testimony the jury hadn't heard. Also, the defenders argued, the prosecution had the constitutional obligation to prove the applicability of the death penalty. Campbell shouldn't be required to beg for leniency.

One of the jurors saw it differently. "They could not produce one single solitary soul . . . not his mother . . . not his family, to get up there and ask the jury not to send this guy to death. Nobody. Not an old boss, not a girlfriend. Nobody. It was just unbelievable."

Another said, "He all but laughed out loud at the verdicts. He scoffed. We were amazed at the way he took it, like he couldn't have cared less. If he had taken the stand and begged for his life and showed some form of remorse, I have grave doubts we would have sentenced him to death. We tried to find something good about him to spare his life. Nobody wanted to do this. (But) it was such a sadistic crime and he planned it." The juror also expressed his fear of Campbell. "He never came out and said anything, but the way he looked (at jurors) was so intimidating. His eyes were very penetrating. If he was to break out of prison, I would be in fear for my life. I'd go out and pick myself up a handgun."

On Tuesday afternoon, the seventeenth day of court appearance for the jurors, the foreman handed in another verdict. Charles Rodman Campbell should face an executioner to suffer the pain of death for his crimes.

The trace of a shadow drifted momentarily across Campbell's face, then he grinned.

Don Hendrickson later said, "The end result is, I'm very pleased with the verdict. It's a happy day for me." Eventually, he would discuss the subject of vengeance. "There's something people are uncomfortable with, and that's the idea of revenge. I don't apologize for wanting revenge. It's a normal human feeling and I think a person would be abnormal if he didn't feel like that." His face reflecting torment, Don continued, refusing to use Campbell's name. "It is offensive to me to have him still breathing with Renae and Shannah and Barbara having died. You go from complete normalcy to a nightmare. In my case it was particularly bad, having found them." He would always remember the bright happy faces of the victims, and their laughter. It would still be a long time, though, before Don Hendrickson could laugh again.

While Campbell's defense attorneys were disappointed, only one person appeared to be truly saddened by the verdict. Ladonna Layton, carrying the infant she and Campbell had brought into the world, held back tears.

Eight days before Christmas, Judge Britt handed down the formal sentence to an impassive Campbell. In the hallway outside the courtroom, a photographer snapped a picture of Campbell being escorted to a vehicle that would take him to prison. He wore a light sport coat, dark slacks, white shirt and checkered tie. His hair, though bushy, had been neatly trimmed. Thirteen people could be seen in the picture, three uniformed guards, conservatively clad attorneys in the background, and curious onlookers. Every person in the photo looked grim, except one. Charles Campbell wore his usual arrogant smirk.

Rick Bart stared angrily at another photo of the convict, several days later. It depicted Campbell arriving at the prison, holding three fingers up in plain view. Streetwise cops and cons knew what his gesture meant; it symbolized Campbell's pride for killing three people. Bart met Joe Ward and Lorene Ahlers Iverson for coffee to mull over the case and the death penalty. Ward said, "We'll never see the day he's executed."

Renae's sister Lorene, and mother Hilda, packed up with their families for the return trip to North Dakota. The trial had been emotionally exhausting, and it was time to go home. Strong, tenacious women, like Renae, they'd tried to control the tears, sometimes successfully, sometimes not. For Hilda, one of the toughest times had been a short time after they arrived in Washington. Rick Arriza, the Clearview grocery store owner, drove her to Cathcart Elementary School where Shannah had attended. They collected the child's meager possessions: crayons, books, an umbrella, glue, and her assorted completed lessons. Hilda's throat ached, and she could no longer hold back the tears.

The school principal, Don Hanson, sympathized with Hilda, and personally felt the tragic loss. His school was scheduled to be remodeled. Upon completion of the overhaul, Hilda and Lorene would receive a letter from Hanson. In it, the principal described a memorial plaque placed beside an oak tree "as a reminder that Shannah will always be remembered."

Officials of the State Parole system launched a damage repair program, trying to stem a growing tide of public unrest following the Campbell trial. "How could a convict who'd violated so many rules be given enough freedom to kill the women who'd testified against him?"

The chairman of the Board of Prison Terms and Paroles, after an internal audit of the records, told reporters that it was "a string of highly improbable circumstances" that led to Campbell's being placed in minimum custody. The answer didn't placate lawyers who represented the victims' families. They went ahead with plans to file lawsuits. The action would bring Renae's family back to Everett for a civil trial in which a jury would award a substantial amount of money to the estate of Renae Wicklund. Barbara Hendrickson's family, too, accepted a settlement by the state to pay her estate approximately the same amount.

Someone else filed a lawsuit, too. Rosalie Campbell felt the state owed her something for allowing her ex-husband to leave custody on Christmas day, and a few days later, when he raped her. Eventually, a settlement was reached out of court. She accepted a one-time payment of $25,000 and $600 a month for life.

Campbell had tapped the taxpayers for much more than that. The trial gouged over one million dollars out of their pockets, not including the costs to house, clothe, and feed him, plus take care of his medical needs. The legal bills related to his case, had just started. Attorneys were already at work preparing appeals to have the verdict and the sentence overturned.

Twenty-four

It's common knowledge that condemned prisoners, across the entire United States, have little to fear during their first few years on death row. Appeals take years. The controversial system of delays and endless court dates is a sore point among death penalty advocates, and a source of hope for opponents of capital punishment. Since the halfway point of the twentieth century, U.S. Supreme Court decisions have been a pendulum swaying from extremely liberal views, in the sixties, to the more conservative actions of the nineties.

When Charles Rodman Campbell received his death sentence in 1982, there were 1,050 condemned prisoners in the United States. In the fourteen years before that, only six had been executed. By 1995, the national death row population would soar to over 3,000 inmates.

Only four states retained laws allowing hanging as a method of execution, and just two of them, Washington and Delaware, contemplated actually using the gallows.

Campbell wouldn't have to concern himself about execution dates for a while, but he planned to fight it all the way.

During that first year in Walla Walla, reporters periodically exhumed the case, looking for a new spin on it, and hoping for a statement from Campbell. He obstinately refused to speak for over sixteen months, but finally granted an interview to the *Seattle Times* in August, 1983. The fundamental gist of his statement was that he didn't give a damn what anyone thought of him. To a reporter's comment that many people seemed to dislike

Campbell, the convict smirked and said, "So what? They can hate me all they want. I'm not concerned with that. What do they know, if anything?"

Asked to explain, Campbell snorted, "When I hate something, I have a reason to hate it. When it comes right down to it, there isn't no confusion in my mind. I hate something . . . I know why I hate it."

His behavior at Walla Walla reflected that attitude. He didn't have as much freedom to seek out trouble as he had at Monroe, but he managed to break rules and behave with his usually hostile and disruptive attitude. Other inmates loathed him. Child killers are low on the peculiar pecking order of convicts, and the newly restrictive rules for work release residents didn't earn Campbell any peer points, either.

As before, one person maintained steadfast loyalty to Campbell. Ladonna Layton moved to Walla Walla, and visited him two or three times each week, usually bringing their baby son.

Spring renews the prairies and pastures surrounding Jamestown, North Dakota, breathing fresh new life into the land and its people. Melted snow fills the reservoirs formed by dams on the James River and Pipestem Creek, new bison calves romp with small herds, and children play in the town's eight parks. On Sundays sweet music flows from twenty-six crowded churches, eight of which are Lutheran.

For Hilda Ahlers, spring contained beauty, but also painful memories and torment: *"I'm in bed sleeping. I hear a tapping at my apartment door. I ask, 'Who is it?'*

"Lorene's soft voice replies, 'It's me.'

"My thoughts go to Jerry, her husband, and the three children. 'Which one did I lose?' I go to the door, and as I turn the knob . . ." Hilda snaps awake, standing at her door. Sleepwalking. She flips the light switch on, and looks at a clock. It's the exact time she had answered the door before dawn on April 15, 1982! The shock and pain tear her heart and soul again.

Hilda's sleepwalking, and answering the door, would continue for years.

During those years, lawyers representing Charles Campbell stood before courts to routinely argue standard appeals for a new trial. In November, 1984, the second anniversary of the trial, the Washington State Supreme Court affirmed the conviction and death sentence, and six months later, the U.S. Supreme Court refused to hear the same issues.

In '86 and '87, a federal district court rejected an appeal based on alleged evidentiary errors and the federal ninth circuit court followed suit.

Based in San Francisco, the ninth circuit court, some conservatives suggested, had a built-in bias against the death penalty. Handling appellate issues in the nine western states, Guam, and the Mariana Islands, the court tilted toward a liberal bent in the 1970s when President Jimmy Carter increased the panel of judges from thirteen to twenty-three with a flurry of new appointments. During the '70s and '80s, not one convict who appealed to the ninth circuit court was put to death. The first trickle of executions carried out after the death penalty was reinstated in the mid-'70s occurred because the condemned individuals chose not to fight for their lives.

The U.S. Supreme Court, as it grew more conservative, became impatient with the ninth circuit members. In 1984 alone, the black-robed jurists in Washington D.C. reversed twenty-eight of the twenty-nine decisions out of the ninth circuit. Top ranking law officials of some of the western states hinted they'd like to escape from the ninth circuit court's jurisdiction.

In Walla Walla, officials issued a scheduled date for Charles Campbell to be executed in 1988. An appellate court heard arguments by Campbell's attorneys, and issued a stay of execution. Prosecutors appealed to the ninth circuit, but on July 10, the court denied the State's request.

Meanwhile, Campbell's case filtered up to U.S. Supreme

Court, which again refused to hear appeals to overturn the conviction. By the end of 1988, the legal process regarding Campbell had revolved around attempts to win a reversal through the standard legal ploys. In 1989, the litigious skirmishes would heat up, leading to all out war.

That year began with a sobering event for Campbell, and occupants of death row across the country. Ted Bundy, Washington's most notorious native son, had confessed to killing eleven young women in his home state, plus nineteen murders in other states, and was suspected of slaying more than one hundred victims. He walked down a short hallway to a gray room in a Florida prison. A wooden chair equipped with leather straps, gruesomely referred to as "Old Sparky," waited for him. At 7:06 A.M., January 24, 1989, two thousand volts of electricity ended his bloody career of murder.

The seven residents of Walla Walla's death row didn't have to worry about the electric chair. They would have to choose between lethal injection and hanging.

Six days after Bundy died, the ninth circuit court surprisingly lifted their stay of execution for Charles Campbell, allowing prosecutors to seek a quick hearing to set a new date.

Anticipating the upcoming hearing in February, Larry McKeeman, Chief Deputy Prosecutor for Snohomish County, wrote to the families of Campbell's victims, and to detectives, soliciting their opinions about the killer, asking them to express their thoughts to the governor's legal counsel for the State Clemency and Pardons Board.

Detective Rick Bart responded by letter to "share some insights" regarding Campbell's case. In his ten years as a homicide detective, he said, he'd seen many senseless killings in which victims were "brutalized, raped, and shown no compassion," but the murders Campbell committed had no equal. Bart detailed the bloody sequence of events in the Wicklund home, then commented, "With Campbell's threat to kill now completed, his revenge satisfied, his own ego bolstered, he walked out of the house."

Fuming anger dripped from Bart's pen. "I submit to you that Charles Rodman Campbell deserves no clemency, no compassion. He is *not* the victim here. He has devastated the lives of two families and all the lives those three touched. Lives that will never be the same, wounds that will never heal." The community had been affected, too, Bart said, and Campbell should have been put to death years ago. "He's been bleeding the court system with his appeals just like he bled his victims."

Concluding, Bart wrote that he had no compassion for Campbell and could never forgive the killer's crimes. Campbell deserved to be put to death. "And I want to personally witness his execution."

Don Hendrickson and his three grown offspring signed a letter of reply that described seven years of pain and sadness since the murders. They dreaded the possibility that Campbell, through legal maneuvering, would eventually be freed to seek more vengeance. "We watched in the courtroom as the defense attorney pointed out the wives of the prosecuting attorneys to his client. We understand that Campbell's life-long pattern has been if you hurt me, I will hurt you more. . . . The murderer clearly has no concern or remorse for this atrocity. We wonder whose wife and children he would seek out to revenge himself upon, perhaps the daughters and granddaughters of Donald Hendrickson?"

Commenting on the typical early release of prisoners who serve only a fraction of their terms, the family said they would live in terror if Campbell manipulated his way into freedom. "We will continue . . . in the hope that the murderer will receive the penalty he so richly deserves."

Three weeks after Bundy's death, Charles Campbell traveled again across Washington back to Everett. Wearing orange coveralls and heavily shackled, he shuffled into a courtroom under the watchful eyes of security officers.

In the gallery, Don Hendrickson watched the ponytailed prisoner and felt anger and frustration boiling up inside him.

A new appeals attorney had been temporarily appointed, just one week earlier, to represent Campbell in opposition to setting an execution date. Al Lyon, thirty-six, a sandy-haired litigator with dark brows, had been a public defender before hanging out his own shingle. The father of a three-year-old son, and a regular jogger, Lyon would be helped by another appointed lawyer, Robert Gombiner. They were the fourth set of attorneys to represent Campbell, the previous ones having either dropped out or been fired by the cantankerous con. Lyon requested Judge Joseph Thibodeau not to set an execution date for his new client, pleading the need for more time to study the voluminous records of the case.

Campbell spoke up several times during the hearing, declaring to the judge, "I do not believe you have the authority to impose this sentence on me . . ." He insisted that an execution date could not be set because the Constitution required him to serve the sentences previously imposed on him prior to the murders. Campbell also complained of cruelty by the State in forcing him to choose between lethal injection and hanging.

The prosecutor countered, "The State is clearly interested in the finality of this matter. The only way to get that finality is to bring about the execution . . . imposed years ago."

Judge Thibodeau concurred and set a date of March 30 for Campbell to die.

Commenting afterward, Don Hendrickson, now sixty, said, "The wound never heals." Since the trial, Hendrickson had joined the Families and Friends of Missing Persons and Crime Victims organization as an active member and leader. Having suffered so deeply, he felt a great sense of reward in helping other victims' survivors, "navigating them through the grieving process." One key element in helping them, Don said, was simply listening. In some cases, he assisted by making referrals to counselors or psychiatrists.

Regarding the complaint by Campbell of being forced to

choose his method of execution, Hendrickson reportedly said, "I'd like to kill the sonofabitch myself."

Something else therapeutic had happened to Don. "It was close to a year before I laughed a real laugh, and it surprised me very much."

As soon as Hilda Ahlers heard a date had been set, she, too, composed a touching letter asking for justice. Stating her belief in the death penalty, Hilda said she hoped and prayed that Campbell would be executed on the date set. "Delays add stress," she wrote, "and the burden continues to accumulate. The earlier pain does not fade away." Perhaps she could finally sort through Renae's and Shannah's things she'd brought home.

Hilda described a life in which she often avoided well-meaning people who asked questions about the case. She looked forward to the day she could simply say the killer had been executed, thus he could take no more lives. Referring to hideous carnage depicted in the crime scene photos of the bodies, Hilda worried that someone in power would be merciful to Campbell, who'd showed absolutely no pity or mercy for his victims.

With reference to the Bible, Hilda said, "Please hear the silent cries of Renae, Shannah, and Barbara . . . and please hear my cries of pain caused by the indescribable horrors that my Renae and Shannah were put through . . ." She closed by asking for justice, and finally peace for herself and her family, which could be accomplished through the execution of Charles R. Campbell, "as soon as possible."

Scrambling to find a convincing appeals argument, Al Lyon prepared for a hearing before the state supreme court. He planned to present the same contention that Campbell had touched upon in Everett, that his client could not be executed until completion of the sentences meted out for earlier crimes. Laymen could see a certain irony in that logic. . . . We can't execute Campbell for killing Renae Wicklund until he serves the full sentence for sexually assaulting her. They scratched their heads.

Always an active participant in his legal maneuvers, Campbell hand printed a petition to the state supreme court. In it, he complained of prison abuses, including limited access to the law library and mistreatment by the guards. In addition, Campbell asked for Al Lyon and Bob Gombiner to be appointed as his representatives in all appeals matters. "The outcome of my life is going to be severely affected by this court's action," he concluded.

On Wednesday, March 8, the state supreme court accepted Campbell's request for the appointment of the two attorneys, and gave them eight days to present matters not previously litigated that might justify the issuance of a stay of execution.

Prosecutors, while waiting for the court to hold the next hearing, filed a brief arguing that Campbell didn't deserve a court appointed attorney. "He's had more than ample time to challenge his conviction and sentence, and now it's time to get on with it. Now he wants the citizens of the state to pay for yet another counsel. . . . We don't believe they should. . . . He has abused the privilege."

Al Lyon submitted his sixty-two-page brief to the supreme court in advance of the hearing. In it, he argued that the state, in requiring Campbell to choose between lethal injection and the gallows, was in effect forcing him to commit suicide. "Mr. Campbell's religious beliefs forbid him from committing the act of suicide." That was a violation of constitutional guarantees of religious freedom, the attorney said. A state attorney general representative couldn't believe it, pointing out that suicide was taking one's own life. An execution was not suicide.

Campbell's attorney brought up another issue that infuriated prosecutors. Campbell, he wrote, had been improperly excluded from court during jury selection. It didn't seem to matter that Campbell himself had insisted on staying in Everett while attorneys and Judge Britt selected jurors in Spokane, or that Britt had given him every opportunity to participate.

The brief also criticized Judge Britt for failing to tell the jury, in the penalty phase, that they shouldn't give any weight to the fact that Campbell had chosen not to testify. And to be sure all bases were tagged, Lyon tacked on the argument that Campbell must complete serving his original sentence, thirty years, before the state could execute him.

Members of the state attorney general's office would argue in front of the justices, but the brief was prepared by Snohomish County Deputy Prosecutor Aaron "Seth" Fine. Answering the suicide issue, the brief stated that the defendant does not have to make a choice. If he fails to, the state will do it for him, and hang him. Regarding the request for a stay, Fine said that Campbell shouldn't be rewarded for "dilatory tactics," meaning that the defendant had deliberately caused long delays. No legitimate issues were raised, the brief said, and certainly no issues were presented that could not have been dealt with much earlier.

While tension built up over the pending court hearing, and possibly the first execution in more than twenty-five years, the *Seattle Times* conducted a poll to see if Washington residents really wanted the death penalty. They contacted 401 people, and learned that seventy-seven percent of them clearly favored capital punishment. The number jumped to eighty-two percent for premeditated first-degree murder.

An Everett newspaper's editorial didn't agree with the majority. "Not even the crimes of Charles Rodman Campbell make the death penalty right," the article said. Calling for the creation of a more decent society, the writer said the people of Washington could still choose to act in a way that looked beyond simple retribution. "The community can aspire to a higher standard of behavior than retributive violence." An execution did not protect life, it asserted.

Readers protested. The paper's editor answered a flood of angry phone calls. "We knew we'd catch some heat for it," he said. "But that's what we're here for. We just decided that in good conscience, we had to say what we believed."

* * *

The Ahlers family, in Jamestown, North Dakota, embarked on the long drive to Washington. If Charles Campbell was going to be executed, they wanted to be there.

In Washington's capital city, Olympia, on Thursday, March 23, the state supreme court justices listened to arguments by Larry McKeeman for the state, and Robert Gombiner for the defense. Gombiner accused the trial defense team, Mark Mestel and Anthony Savage, of malpractice and gross incompetence for failing to insist on Campbell's presence at jury selection. Judge Britt also erred in permitting it, the attorney said.

When the oral presentations ended, the justices conferred, then presented their findings. All nine unanimously rejected the argument that Campbell must serve the previous sentence before he could face execution. Regarding the motion for a stay of execution, only two of the robed jurists thought that the appeal should be approved.

The March 30 date set for Campbell to hang, or to choose lethal injection, would remain in effect.

Campbell's defense attorneys prepared to take their case to the federal level.

Twenty-five

The needle or the noose? A newspaper article summarized the choice Campbell might be facing in just a few days. Two separate teams would prepare for the execution at Walla Walla so that Campbell could wait until the last moment to make his choice. If he remained silent, he would be taken to the gallows.

An administrator at the prison described the difficulty he'd had in finding a qualified hangman, but refused to say who the person was or where they'd located him. The American Civil Liberties Union invoked freedom of information rules to force officials into disclosing the executioner's identity, but prison officials declined to reveal any details or information.

The controversy surrounding Campbell's pending choice had led to a move in the state legislature to abolish hanging and rely solely on lethal injection.

Within twenty-four hours of the supreme court's decision, Federal District Court Judge John Coughenour made ready to hear Campbell's lawyers. He summoned them, along with the attorney general's team, into his chambers to discuss the matter. Al Lyon made it clear that he planned to file an appeal the next Monday, March 27. Not wishing to waste time, Coughenour scheduled an immediate evidentiary hearing, that same day, to tell him in advance what issues would be raised on Monday. Lyon wanted to know if there were any limitations on what he could present. The judge left it wide open. When Lyon had completed laying his cards on the table, Coughenour ordered all parties into court on the 27th.

In the formal court session, Campbell's team presented three issues. Hanging, they said, would deprive their client of his constitutional right against cruel and unusual punishment. Second, they claimed, the state had no one qualified to perform the hanging. And third, they repeated the assertion that forcing Campbell to choose between lethal injection and hanging violated his protection against cruel and unusual punishment and his First Amendment freedom of religion rights. Judge Coughenour ruled that the attorneys offered no evidence to substantiate any of these issues. Campbell threw in his claim that he'd been represented in the trial by ineffective counsel.

Late that afternoon, Coughenour issued his over all ruling. He found no substance in any of the motions, and denied the request for a stay of execution.

Campbell was down to his last three days.

In Clearview, residents watched news reports hourly to see if Charles Campbell would face execution. Grocer Rick Arriza said, "It's time to put it to rest. It's time for Campbell to die and pay for the crimes he committed, and put an end to the story."

Don Hendrickson tried to avoid speaking out about it because it stirred up painful memories. In one of his few comments, he fondly remembered Barbara. "She was a particularly warm and bright woman. Very intelligent. Liked by almost everyone in the area." Asked about Renae, he said, "She was kind of like a daughter to us, and her little girl was like a granddaughter." The pending execution drew a brief remark from Hendrickson. "Campbell needs to die. It would help with closure, I think, for myself and my family. It's not going to change anything, but it would help us."

Gallows or gurney? Thirty-three hours remained before Campbell would be required to let a hangman slip a noose over his neck, or lie on a gurney and wait for a fatal injection.

Al Lyon stayed up all night on Monday night, March 27, working on the text of his motion requesting a stay of execution, and stating his legal reasoning.

A three judge panel of the ninth circuit court of appeals, on Tuesday morning reviewed the motion filed by Al Lyon and Robert Gombiner. Without considering opposing arguments from the state, they granted Charles Campbell a stay of execution pending an appeal! No specific time frame was announced. It could be a year or longer. They held that two key issues hadn't been resolved: the charge of inadequate representation at the trial, and the failure to have Campbell present during jury selection. In three months, they would hear oral arguments from both sides.

Walla Walla penitentiary officials carried the message into the "intensive management unit" which housed problem prisoners, and served as death row for seven inmates. At Campbell's narrow cell, they notified him of his last-minute reprieve. He didn't collapse, he didn't cry, and he didn't say thank you. He laughed. And in his inimitable way, said, "It's about time."

A pall of shock and disappointment spread quickly. The Ahlers and Iverson families, feeling betrayed, departed for Jamestown. The crestfallen Hendrickson family spoke out. One of Barbara's daughters said, "We've been waiting these last seven years to see the justice system work. We're still waiting. The thought of having to go through it yet another time is not something we're looking forward to."

Her brother, too, was disillusioned. "The frivolous arguments they're bringing forth are a waste of time for the court system."

Clerks and telephone operators at the San Francisco headquarters of the ninth circuit court were bombarded with messages expressing outrage.

Comments among Clearview residents ranged from, "It's a travesty," to "I think it's horrible. I'd like to see him executed."

* * *

Well aware that the ninth circuit court had struck down the entire death penalty law in the State of Arizona the previous December, Assistant Attorney General Paul Weisser had good reason to worry. He would present the argument for the state against Campbell on June 27, and he certainly didn't want to be the one who stood before the court while they decided to invalidate Washington's capital punishment law. The same three judges who had made the decision to give Campbell a stay would hear the arguments. Justices Cecil Poole, seventy-four, and Proctor Hug Jr., fifty-eight, were appointees of President Jimmy Carter, and Cynthia Holcomb Hall, sixty, had been appointed by President Ronald Reagan. Hug was on the bench with eleven of his colleagues when they struck down the Arizona law, and had voted with the majority.

The hearing took less than two hours on Wednesday, June 27. If Paul Weisser or Al Lyon expected a quick decision, they would be quite disappointed. It took the court twenty months, until February, 1991, just to decide to issue another delaying action. Campbell showed his gratitude to his two attorneys, Lyon and Gombiner, by asking the ninth circuit court to fire them because of "irreconcilable differences." Campbell claimed that the lawyers were motivated only by their self-interests. "They are detrimental to this appeal," he said. The court also delayed that decision.

The seven man population of death row at Walla Walla grew during the twenty months while the ninth circuit court delayed and ruminated. Michael Furman, age nineteen, became the eighth man, in March, sentenced to die for raping and beating to death an eighty-five-year-old woman. Gary Benn, forty-five, who'd shot his half brother and another man in a dispute over sharing insurance money after an arson and burglary, joined the group in June. And one month after the ninth circuit court's June 27 hearing, a pedophile truck driver became the tenth man on death row. Westley Allan Dodd, twenty-nine, who had been sexually attracted to young boys in Richland, not far from Walla Walla, had once promised, "I'm done hurting kids that way." But he hadn't been able to resist the compelling urge to fellate very young boys.

Dodd was arrested on November 13, 1989 in Camus, Washington, after accosting a six-year-old boy in a theater bathroom, and trying to carry him away. A friend of the child's family came to the rescue, chased Dodd down, subdued him, and turned him over to the police.

Two brothers, William Neer, age ten, and Cole, eleven, had been abducted, bound, and stabbed to death in a forest park on Labor Day, September 4, 1989, in Vancouver, Washington. Less than two months later, a four-year-old boy, Lee Iseli, was abducted from a Portland, Oregon, playground and murdered.

Only after his arrest did Dodd become a suspect in the murders. The whole Pacific Northwest recoiled in horror when his crimes became public. He had grabbed the two brothers, taken them into the woods, and forced each to watch as he performed fellatio on the other. Then he'd bound them and stabbed them to death. Little Lee Iseli had lasted longer. Dodd kept him overnight, slowly strangled him, revived him from unconsciousness, and strangled him again, during a perverted twenty-four-hour period of sexual abuse. To horrified investigators, Dodd confessed to hanging the child by the neck in a closet, then having postmortem anal sex with the corpse.

Westley Allan Dodd received the death penalty, and became the tenth resident of death row on July 26, 1990.

In his cell at Walla Walla, Charles Campbell regarded himself as his own attorney. He laboriously hand printed a forty-two-page motion to the Washington Supreme Court, using correct legal language and a comprehensive argument. For someone who had dropped out after junior high school, the document reflected remarkable lucidity and intelligence. Perhaps he had assistance from a jailhouse lawyer. Certainly, he had access to volumes from an extensive law library.

Campbell sought a new penalty hearing. One of the interesting aspects of the plea involved his protest of the prosecutor's closing arguments to the jury, in which Eric Lind had attempted to "invoke the jurors' passion and prejudice by repeated reference to the brutal and savage nature of the crimes and emotional effect on the victims."

Campbell quoted Lind's comments:

"We don't know how long she (Renae Wicklund) lingered. We don't know how long she suffered, but it was very severe."

"She (Shannah) was almost beheaded. A very, very savage attack on an eight-year-old girl. Why? Was it because he killed her in front of her mother?"

"There is undisputable evidence that they (Shannah and Barbara) were dragged down that hallway and forced to look at Renae Wicklund. I think that it is impossible for us to imagine the terror that those people felt while Mr. Campbell was there. I don't think we could even imagine the terror and pain, the horror of it all."

"There are very few crimes that are more revolting and more humiliating to a victim than the crime of sodomy."

Noting that the defense had objected to this type of argument, Campbell complained that the court refused to restrict the penalty phase argument in any manner. Similar arguments, Campbell wrote, were used in the guilt phase. He added more quotes:

"The pleas for mercy, the screams of horror, the begging for the sparing of life . . ."

"And what about the beautiful eight-year-old child? The child who won't grow up . . . because her life was stolen by Charles Campbell?"

"He drug (sic) her (Shannah) after he'd subdued her, into the back bedroom where her mother was, so she could see the maniacal attack that he had inflicted on her mother. The horror that this child must have felt shortly before death is unspeakable. Not only being killed in a savage fashion herself—she was nearly decapitated—but having to see her mother in that condition . . . the mother that she loved, the mother who loved her."

"These arguments are clearly improper," Campbell wrote, "as they are blatant attempts by the prosecution to invoke the jurors' passion and prejudice by repeated reference to the brutal and savage nature of the crime . . . and had nothing to do with the establishment of guilt . . ."

Anyone reading the document might wonder if Campbell was bragging or complaining.

Time was the ally of Charles Campbell, and the court system seemed to have an abundant supply, with which they were infinitely generous. After nearly two years, in February, 1991, the ninth circuit court ordered withdrawal of Campbell's latest appeal until attorneys could provide the court with assurance that all legal avenues in Washington State Courts had been exhausted.

Don Hendrickson expressed his thoughts about the interminable delays. "The possibility that the guy (Campbell) could outlive me really offends me. I'm offended by the fact that he's still breathing the same air law abiding citizens are."

So far, none of the issues weighed in the courts had anything to do with Campell's guilt or innocence. They revolved around so-called constitutional protection issues. To the general public, even those seemed stretched to ridiculous extremes. Where did it say in the Constitution that Campbell should have been forced to go to Spokane and observe jury selection when he specifically, of his own free will, chose not to go? And what about the attack on his trial attorneys' qualifications? Both men enjoyed exceptional respect in the state and by peers, were members of the bar, and had pushed hard to neutralize evidence against Campbell. One of the hardest of Campbell's arguments to swallow was his plea that forcing him to choose between lethal injection and hanging violated his religious freedom. Where was his religion when he brutally slaughtered three innocent people? Where was the protection for their religious choices? And the protracted wait of months and years it took to navigate the legal labyrinth. Would it never end?

The state attorney general's lawyers did their best to shorten time intervals. Just eleven days after the ninth circuit's order, the attorneys presented a thick stack of documents showing Campbell had exhausted all available remedies in state courts. But while the jurists digested that material, Al Lyon informed the state supreme court that Campbell would be filing yet another appeal, adding a third one to the two still unresolved. It would be like a street-corner juggler, tossing and spinning three separate plates in the air simultaneously. If one fell and broke, he'd still have two with which to entertain passersby.

The new appeal gave the ninth circuit court a rationale for more delays. In August, 1991, they announced that rulings on all other issues would be delayed pending review of the latest appeal, which still hadn't been officially filed by the attorneys. They did make one decision, though. They approved Campbell's request to fire Al Lyon and Bob Gombiner.

Growing impatient with the ninth circuit's inertia, the state attorney general decided to bypass them, and go directly to the U.S. Supreme Court. In October, the A.G. asked the high court to compel the slow-moving ninth circuit to resolve at least two of the appeals being juggled. The most recent appeal hadn't even been read yet.

Snohomish County Deputy Prosecutor Seth Fine assembled supporting affidavits and attached them to the state's request. He included statements from Lorene Ahlers Iverson and Hilda Ahlers.

Lorene wrote in succinct paragraphs, "It will be ten years in

April of 1992 that my sister and niece were murdered by Charles Rodman Campbell. I live in fear that one day he will either escape prison or the judicial system and take revenge on myself or my family. I know in detail what this man is capable of doing to a human life. The longer the system delays Charles Campbell's execution, the more intense my fear becomes of him being released or escaping into society. I don't want Charles Campbell executed for revenge. I need to positively know that he will never physically harm any human being again. Every day that he is allowed to live is another day that I live in fear of my life and that of my family."

Her mother, Hilda, wrote, "Although I never saw the murder scene, I can still see it and hear screams in my mind. Life will never be the same again. We cannot bring our loved ones back, but our good memories will keep them alive for me. I can have these good memories only if I am healing. Healing will come only after the execution. For a long time, I blamed the delays in this case on Campbell and thought that he was still victimizing us. Now, I believe that it is no longer Campbell who is doing this to us, it is the criminal justice system that is allowing him to do it. I thank God for giving me the strength to stand under this terrible shock and continued stress. I pray that soon justice will be accomplished, so that I may start healing and go on with my life and fight for victims' rights so that I may help others to survive such tragedies."

The desire Hilda expressed to fight for victims' rights were not empty words. She launched a personal crusade in which she helped establish victim and witness advocacy programs in Stutsman County, in which Jamestown was located, and in Grand Forks County, North Dakota. Hilda made monetary donations that matched federal grants to the victim-witness program. In 1988 she contributed money to the Stutsman County State Attorney's office to begin full time victim-witness activities. In addition, she participated in establishing the North Dakota Families and Friends of Murder Victims support group, in tribute to the people in the Seattle organization who'd provided the desperately needed help for her and Lorene. The North Dakota attorney general recognized Hilda's outstanding work in his 1991 selection of her as one of three recipients of the first annual Outstanding Victim Advocacy award. In his speech, the attorney general recalled the murders in Washington, and said that Hilda, "turned a tragic event into a positive commitment to help others avoid the grief and suffering she experienced from the crime."

A Spokane newspaper quoted the state's governor, Boothe Gardner, who'd refused to commute Campbell's death sentence, saying "We have to wait until the legal system finishes its work." The paper's columnist wrote, "When the ninth circuit court of appeals is involved, the legal system *never* finishes its work—at least in death penalty cases." He noted that the U.S. Supreme Court had commented that the ninth circuit's foot-dragging in Campbell's case "has prevented Washington from exercising its sovereign power to enforce the criminal law."

But the U.S. Supreme Court didn't exactly deliver a swift kick to the ninth circuit. They considered Washington's petition to compel the ninth circuit court to rule on Campbell's appeal. After three months, they denied the request. In the high jurists' comments, they encouraged the state to resubmit the motion "if unnecessary delays or unwarranted stays" occurred in the Campbell case.

Even the president of the United States had expressed impatience with the cold molasses rate of movements in the court system, and had urged Congress to put reasonable limits on appeals.

One of the spinning plates of Campbell's three-pronged litigation fell to the pavement in April, 1992, when the ninth circuit affirmed a lower court's dismissal of an appeal. Now, only two plates remained, but they contained the key issues relating to the constitutionality of the death penalty, the pressure on Campbell to select the method of his execution, and his absence at the jury selection. Within days after that action, the state attorney general asked the ninth circuit to conduct an expedited review of the remaining appeals and allow Campbell's execution and to move forward. The court rejected both requests.

After a series of volleys, the ninth circuit opened 1993 by granting a rehearing for the appeal they'd virtually ended the previous April! Now three plates whirled through the air again in the jurisprudence juggling act. The court threw another bit into the show with an order for Campbell's attorneys and the state to submit written arguments on whether hanging is cruel and unusual punishment.

A grumbling public and the disillusioned members of the victims' families began to wonder just when Campbell would finally beat the system, walk out of prison, and seek more savage vengeance.

Twenty-six

A far more dramatic event occurred on the fourth day of January, 1993, relegating court hearings and decisions to the back pages of newspapers.

Westley Allan Dodd, the tenth addition to Walla Walla penitentiary's death row, had chosen not to struggle through the tortured maze of the judicial system. He just wanted to get it over with. No one had been executed in Washington for thirty years, since Chester Self was hanged in 1963 for the fatal shooting of a taxi driver during a Seattle robbery.

Like Self, Dodd chose to go to the gallows. "I don't believe I deserve anything better than those kids got," he said. "Those kids didn't get a nice, neat painless easy death. Why should I? In my case, I knew I could get the death penalty if I was ever caught, but I didn't care. A lot of people won't believe me when I say that I am sorry for the things I've done, but that's something that I need to say." He hoped to go to heaven since he'd confessed all his sins. ". . . I'd really like to . . . be able to go up to the three little boys and give them a hug and tell them how sorry I was. . . . I know they're there already."

With snow softly falling in the serene countryside of Walla Walla County, making the world look pure and white, harsh lights reflected outside the prison. Demonstrators marched, waving their anti-death-penalty signs.

Inside, Dodd had finished his last meal of salmon, scalloped potatoes, and lemonade. Wearing a white T-shirt, gray prison shirt, jeans, and sneakers, he left his holding cell a few seconds after midnight, and followed escorts into the upper level of the gallows chamber. He stood in front of a window, where witnesses could see through from the other side. Among the silent group sat the mother of one little victim and the father of the other two. Media representatives along with law enforcement personnel filled the remaining chairs.

Dodd had a last statement to make. "I was once asked by somebody, I don't remember who, if there was any way sex offenders could be stopped. I said no. I was wrong. I was wrong when I said there was no hope, no peace. There is hope. There is peace. I found both in the Lord, Jesus Christ. Look to the Lord and you will find peace."

A translucent screen then covered the window, and a back light switched on to silhouette Dodd for the witnesses as he stepped onto the trapdoor. Executioners covered Dodd's head with a black hood, bound his ankles, tied his hands in front of him, and slipped the noose over his head. A wooden board, to which the condemned man could be strapped so that he wouldn't collapse, stood unused.

Within seconds, the trapdoor dropped, and Dodd fell seven feet. Some jerking of the hands, abdomen, and legs could be seen momentarily before he went limp. At 12:09 A.M. a doctor pronounced him dead.

There is no record of how Charles Rodman Campbell reacted to the news of Dodd's hanging. Since he seemed certain that he would never be executed, he probably smirked.

A female reporter for a television network tabloid show requested an interview with Campbell. She later revealed that he told her if she tried to do a show on him, she was a dead woman.

Campbell's newly appointed lawyer, James Lobsenz, worked periodically through the entire year of 1993, dealing mostly with the legal battles over the question of whether hanging was cruel and unusual punishment. The issue bounced from federal court to the ninth circuit court, to the supreme court, and back again.

In May, the Washington Attorney General Christine Gregoire again asked the U.S. Supreme Court to apply some leverage to the ninth circuit so the case could move ahead. "I believe the public is sick and tired of needless delays and the manipulation of the judicial system by Charles Campbell," she said. "This case has been stalled in the appeals court for more than four years. Now, fifteen months after the Supreme Court ruled the case should be decided expeditiously, the attorney general's office and the taxpayers are faced with yet another hearing on an issue that could have been raised four years ago, but wasn't."

Gregoire pointed out that in the ninth circuit's most recent ruling, two of the justices had dissented, saying that the court was doing nothing more than giving Campbell a second chance to prove claims he had failed to prove before.

Supreme Court Justice Sandra Day O'Connor fielded the request from the state. O'Connor cited the "glacial progress" of the ninth circuit, but bounced the issue back downstairs.

Midway through the year, Snohomish County Sheriff James I. Scharf singled out one of his subordinates for special recognition. Detective Joe Ward received the Meritorious Service Medal for "sustained superior performance as a major crimes investigator since 1978." Scharf noted that "Detective Ward has investigated many of this county's most serious high-profile cases," and lauded him for personal sacrifice.

It took the ninth circuit the rest of 1993 to make a decision. As they struggled with the controversial issue of hanging, one of the justices, Stephen Reinhardt, characterized it as a "savage and barbaric method of terminating human life." The rest of the civilized world, he said, had abolished it. Other jurists found reference material saying that when proper procedures were followed, hanging caused "rapid unconsciousness and death . . . within a matter of a few seconds."

The second thorny problem was Campbell's absence at jury selection. The justices examined the convict's own words prior to the departure of the judge and lawyers to Spokane. "I have a lot of confidence in Mr. Mestel and Mr. Savage going over there. They do that for a living. I am trying to prepare myself for my part in the trial and I'm trying to relax and get my head together. . . . I feel like going to Spokane will be a real inconvenience . . . my time will be limited and I will not be able to prepare things I am working on right now. It is my decision to stay here in Snohomish County so that I can accomplish that."

The words Campbell spoke were supplemented by his written waiver. "The defendant being advised that he has an absolute right to travel to Spokane and be present during selection of the jury to sit in the guilt and penalty phases of this cause of action and mindful that by not attending the jury selection proceedings he will be forever precluded from challenging those persons impaneled by his counsel or from contesting its composition, knowingly, intelligently and voluntarily waives his right to be present to allow him to remain in Snohomish County to continue his preparation for trial."

The public would wonder just what the hell these learned justices had found controversial about Campbell not attending the jury selection, and in view of the defendant's own statements, how they could, in good conscience, even consider allowing the issue to be litigated.

At long last, on February 8, 1994, with a narrow six to five margin, the court ruled that hanging did *not* constitute cruel and unusual punishment. They also concluded that to choose death by lethal injection or face death by hanging did *not* violate Campbell's constitutional rights. The issue of his absence at jury selection did *not* warrant a new trial. The ruling stated that the stay of execution would be lifted and the mandate ordering the execution would be issued in twenty-one judicial days, pending arrival of a motion by the state.

All three of the spinning plates whirled out of control and crashed to the ground.

Christine Gregoire, Washington's A.G., promptly filed the obligatory motion with the ninth circuit to lift Campbell's stay of execution. Jim Lobsenz, for Campbell, scrambled to find rationale for fresh requests to renew the stay of execution and to reconsider the February ruling.

After waiting for more than a month for the ninth circuit to act on her motion, Gregoire faxed the U.S. Supreme Court asking them to remove the stay of execution. Justice Sandra Day O'Connor refused the request.

While everyone anxiously awaited the outcome of court decisions, Campbell and his lawyer reviewed other possible routes of escape from the gallows. One possibility lay with the Governor of Washington, Mike Lowry. In his election campaign, Lowry had made no firm promises about his stance on the death penalty, which he personally opposed, but said that each case must be weighed on its own merits. Now, he might be faced with the tough decision to either allow an execution to proceed (Dodd had not fought his) or commute Campbell to life in prison.

The state Clemency and Pardons Board scheduled a hearing on Campbell's case for Wednesday, March 23. The board would then make a nonbinding recommendation to the governor. Although many members of the board hadn't been there in 1982, some people recalled that it was the board who had approved Campbell's placement into minimum custody.

Relatives of Renae Wicklund were determined that Campbell would not receive lenient treatment again. They journeyed once more to Washington with the intent of a face-to-face meeting with Governor Lowry.

Charles Campbell had already asked for a personal meeting with the governor. He wrote an eighteen-page letter to Lowry complaining that it would be difficult for him to submit a petition to the pardons board in time for the March 23 meeting. So, he demanded the opportunity to personally address the board, which, he said, would enable him to question members as to possible bias. Campbell also wished to take depositions from Attorney General Christine Gregoire and her staff, as well as meet with the governor. Such a meeting, he wrote, would "allow the governor the opportunity to view my sincerity, candor, and demeanor."

Governor Lowry did not meet with Charles Campbell. He did, however, extend an invitation to host a discussion with the victims' families.

Lorene Ahlers Iverson, her husband Jerry, and her mother, Hilda Ahlers, met with the chief executive on Friday, March 18. Impressed with his warm kindness, they voiced their concerns about possible commutation of Campbell's death sentence. To provide details to Lowry, they handed him a four-page typed letter jointly composed by all three of them. It contained an eloquently written statement of their fears, beliefs, and desires:

"With all our hearts and souls, we have come before you to plead for our very lives . . . with the deep conviction that we are representing millions of other citizens in our country and the state of Washington." Their purpose was not revenge, they wrote, but a desire to live in safety from Campbell's vengeance. Campbell should be put to death because the state had already shown failure to protect his victims. In bold capital letters, they stated, "BEING SENTENCED TO LIFE IMPRISONMENT DOES NOT MEAN A MURDERER WILL SPEND HIS WHOLE LIFE IN PRISON. (THEY) CAN COME OUT, AND DO COME OUT, TO KILL AGAIN."

Reminding Lowry of the case details, the letter continued, "It is hard for us to think that (Renae's) home, which should have been a place of security, love, and laughter has become a place of rape, revenge, and murder."

The next paragraph may have been an uncomfortable reminder for the governor, but it had to be said. "After the state of Washington had to accept responsibility in court for its failure to keep proper custody of a criminal, thus in some measure becoming an accessory to the crime, it would be a supreme irony of injustice were Campbell now to have his death sentence commuted by the chief executive of this state." The paradox would be that "the state, which in part had caused the crime, now exonerates the criminal."

Citing President Bill Clinton's call for "three strikes" legislation, the trio wrote, "For twelve years we have lived in the dark shadow of death and fear caused by failure within the criminal justice system. There are no words to describe our anguish over this eternity of years. Our grief has seemed too great to be shared; our tears have flowed like rivers and our fears are beyond the understanding of our friends."

In the concluding lines, they complimented the man who had been an emotional pillar for them during the trial, Steve Eckstrom, for his work in crime victims advocacy. They asked the governor to "allow a course of action to go forward that will enable us to secure a future for ourselves, our children and our grandchildren." All three of the still-grieving family members signed the letter.

Two of Barbara Hendrickson's grown children also had a private audience with the governor, in which they expressed hope that Campbell wouldn't get away with his crimes by escaping the death penalty.

The next day, Renae's family met with the press in the north Seattle quarters of Families and Friends of Missing Persons and Violent Crime Victims. A walnut-paneled wall behind the family displayed heart-rending photographs: glowing, smiling images of boys, girls, men, women, all victims of brutal killers. Barbara Hendrickson, pictured in a ruffly white blouse, looked radiant. Shannah, wearing a cranberry velveteen blouse with a white embroidered yoke smiled shyly from beneath shiny brown bangs. And Renae looked cheerfully into the bright, happy future from her black and white graduation picture.

Family members spoke of their gratitude to Governor Lowry for hearing them. Lorene, wearing a jacket of geometric-patterned fall colors over a magenta blouse, dangling earrings, and chestnut hair styled short at the neck with a tousled top, had many of the same beautifully delicate facial features of her late sister. Her three-year-old daughter, Shaulee, sat beside her in Jerry's lap as Lorene read from a prepared statement: "We are unable to put these murders behind us and get on with our lives because we fear that given the chance, Charles Campbell will murder again." Summarizing contents of the letter given to Lowry, she ended by saying, "If Charles Campbell's sentence is changed to life imprisonment, we, too, shall be sentenced for life, but our prison will be the prison of fear."

Hilda Ahlers, elegant and dignified with gray hair styled like her daughter's, wearing eyeglasses, and a conservatively tailored dark suit, white blouse, and large pendant, read a portion of the letter aloud. ". . . I, Renae's mother, know how long murder leaves horrible images of pain, suffering, abuse, and terror as I think of how our loved ones fought for their lives. We hear their screams. We wonder—what were the thoughts of Renae, Barbara and Shannah in the last moments of their lives? For their sake I have endured the suffering of sitting day after day, week after week in courts where the chief concern has been to see that a murderer's rights have been protected. Nearly twelve years I have watched and waited, wondered and worried, and feared what might happen. Sadly, I feel that the criminal justice system is just what it says—a system only of justice for the criminal. Through the ongoing appeals, delays, stays and every sort of legal maneuver for those twelve years, we the family have become confused, bewildered and evermore insecure. I ask, what is justice? Murder has no justice. Murder knows no end."

Courageously avoiding tears, Hilda told the assembly that only after the punishment of execution had been administered to Charles Campbell, ". . . will I be able to lay my loved ones to rest and know that those who live are secure. Only then will I be able to try to live beyond murder."

It had been five years and eighteen days since the ninth circuit court of appeals imposed the stay of execution. And it had been twelve years and one day since the murders. At last, on April 15, 1994, the court lifted the stay, dissolving the legal obstacle between Charles Campbell and the gallows.

Twenty-seven

"This should be the major breakthrough we've been waiting for," said Seth Dawson, prosecuting attorney for Snohomish County. He predicted that Campbell might go to the gallows by the end of May.

Campbell's attorney, James Lobsenz, recognized the major setback, but vowed to take the case once again to the U.S. Supreme Court.

Attorney General Christine Gregoire declared that the ninth circuit court had ruled correctly, but realized that anything was possible in the world of jurisprudence. "We expect Mr. Campbell and his attorneys to use any and all tactics to further delay his execution," she said, but pledged that her office was ready to meet those tactics. More importantly, she added, "now is the time for the victims' families to get on with the rest of their lives and Washington state citizens to finally see justice carried out." The frustrated public, at least the majority in favor of capital punishment, began to hope that it might actually happen.

Renae's family, who had returned to North Dakota, heard the news of the court's decision, and began planning another trip. Hilda told a reporter, on the telephone, that she and her family wanted to witness the death of the man who killed her daughter and granddaughter. "I hope we can be there for the execution. It's wonderful news . . . I'm just ecstatic about it. This should have happened a long time ago." Her voice broke as she said, "I'm too excited to talk," then hung up.

Lorene had long ago known that she must witness the execution of Charles Campbell. She explained, "I need to see the last chapter completed." But she also knew that it would be an uphill battle. She had traveled with her family to Washington in March, 1989, when Campbell dodged the noose by only thirty-three hours. The governor at that time had informed her that no family members would be allowed to watch. His statement outraged her. If anyone deserved the option of witnessing the event, it should be the relatives. The current 1994 law allowed a total of seventeen people in the witness chamber. Applications from judicial officers (the judge, prosecutor, and defense attorney), media representatives, victim's families, and inmate's family, would be screened by the prison superintendent, who had final approval authority. The policy seemed to favor news reporters since twelve seats had been allotted for them. Lorene felt strongly that fewer reporters should be allowed, making room for more family members and for investigating officers, such as Rick Bart, for whom no chair would be available. Not an easy woman to discourage, Lorene had taken on the state before, and would do it again if necessary.

If the execution took place, Charles Campbell could have one of his relatives present. The Department of Corrections Superintendent sent him a letter on April 22. "In accordance with the law, you are authorized to designate one family member to serve as a witness to your execution currently scheduled for May 27, 1994." The convict not only refused to select anyone, he turned the selection process into a new issue to appeal!

The presence of certain reporters and members of the victims' families, Campbell said in his written motion, would "cause me unnecessary pain and suffering." He complained that some of the reporters who might attend have reputations for unethical conduct. And the motion specifically asked that Lorene Ahlers Iverson, Don Hendrickson, and Snohomish County Prosecutor Seth Dawson be prohibited from watching.

Dawson's deputy prosecutor, Seth Fine, worked with A.G. attorney Paul Weisser to counter attack. "In an attempt to postpone justice," they wrote, "Mr. Campbell has now filed claims relating to the process by which witnesses are selected to view an execution, hoping this court will issue some type of order further delaying the process." The frivolous motion should be tossed out, they said. Another thrust by Campbell's attorney had been expected by the A.G.'s office, and James Lobsenz didn't keep them in suspense very long. He appealed directly to Governor Lowry to halt the killing of his client. The governor, wrestling with his own personal view which conflicted with the outcry to execute Campbell, decided to wait for the recommendation of the Parole and Pardons Board.

Most people agreed that the main reason for the extreme hostility against Campbell stemmed from the savagery of the killings. Rick Bart, the detective (now lieutenant) who inherited the case the first night, agreed, but said there was more. "There is another reason for the strong feelings against Campbell," commented Bart, "and the reason is Campbell. It's his attitude. It is the way he has come off to the public, so completely uncaring. It's like he looks at the world and asks, 'Hey, why are you guys mad at me?' " Privately, Bart's language was a little stronger. "I hate Charles Campbell. I'd kill him if I could do it. And he knows it. He doesn't deserve to live."

Not everyone felt that way. Four Catholic Bishops, who said they represented 500,000 faithful throughout the state, said, through their spokesman John McCoy, that the execution should be called off because it only perpetuated violence. Another group, the Washington Association to Abolish the Death Penalty, said that capital punishment was morally wrong, discriminatory, costly, and failed to deter crime. A religious leader argued, "We do not rape the rapist or abuse the perpetrators of domestic violence with physical punishment. When we sentence people to death, we lower ourselves to the same level as the murderer."

One surprising dissent came from a woman, vice chairperson of Murder Victim's Families for Reconciliation, whose own brother was a homicide victim the year after Campbell's savage killing spree. If we are serious about executing Campbell, she said, "we are about to create another family of murder victims."

Other groups decrying the penalty on grounds of morality, religious beliefs, or philosophical terms voiced opinions and announced plans to demonstrate in efforts to save Campbell's life.

Campbell's motion to delay the execution based on witness selection procedures died a quick death. Witnesses would be selected according to existing law. People eligible to fill the seventeen seats available confirmed their intentions. Media representatives filed requests to fill the twelve seats allocated for them. Snohomish County Prosecutor Seth Dawson said he would attend for several reasons. He felt the importance of witnessing the event as a representative of the community and he needed to understand it in other than abstract or rhetorical terms. Peggie Hendrickson, Don and Barbara's daughter, told reporters that her father and brother would attend. Don chose not to discuss it until the execution was over. Peggie, in discussing the matter, refused to use Campbell's name, and explained why. "I don't think his name should ever be uttered again. My mother, in news accounts, is always referred to as 'the neighbor.' We hear his name again and again. We lose track of the fact she was a real person who meant a great deal to her family." Peggie said she intended to wait outside the penitentiary for her father and brother. During her father's testimony in the trial, she said, Campbell refused to look Don Hendrickson in the eyes. Now, Peggie added, her father wanted the last thing "the defendant" saw on this earth to be the face of Don Hendrickson.

In North Dakota, Lorene Ahlers Iverson, didn't begrudge the two seats assigned to the Henderson family, but felt strongly that more of her own relatives should be admitted. Lorene knew that her husband, children, and her mother felt deep concern about the possible effect on Lorene of watching a man die. They all agreed that it was wrong not to allow someone to go in with her. "But I'm pretty independent, just like Renae," Lorene said. It just didn't seem fair to allot so many seats to the media, and exclude the family. Couldn't fewer news people report it, and share with the other media representatives, so Lorene wouldn't have to sit by herself? She admitted that watching the hanging would be the second hardest day of her whole life.

Her other concern came from so many previous postponements. It wouldn't surprise Lorene at all if she and her family made the long trip to Walla Walla again, only to be turned back by a last-second reprieve again.

The jurors in Spokane who had convicted Campbell and sent him to death row anxiously watched news reports on the case. One of them, who now refueled jet airliners at the Spokane airport, hoped the execution wouldn't be postponed again. Nearly twelve years after the trial, he still couldn't shake the mental images of the murdered women, and especially the little girl. The ex-juror had no children then, but now had a son, age eleven. What if Campbell slipped through the cracks of the system? Would he seek vengeance on jurors and their families?

Another member of the panel, a bearded repair technician for U.S. West Airlines, didn't put much faith in the execution taking place on May 27 as scheduled, only one week away. "I've heard that before," he scoffed. "He's had lots of execution dates. . . . He's still sitting there and we're still paying to feed and clothe him. To me, it doesn't say much about the system."

One of the six women had been through counseling sessions after the trial, suffering post traumatic stress disorder like a combat veteran. She recalled yet another woman who had burst into tears during the short deliberation period, and was consoled by fellow female jurors while the men huddled in an adjacent room.

A retired immigration officer, one of the twelve, had once predicted that many of the jurors would die before Campbell did. In one case, he was right. A female member of the group had passed away. The rest of them hoped the sad prophecy had run its course.

It didn't seem possible, but children who had been classmates of Shannah Wicklund were now grown up. Her contemporaries were adults, twenty years old. One female friend recalled Shannah's last birthday party, August 20, 1973, and games the two friends had played. She felt like the murders had changed her perspective on life forever. Two young brothers, twelve and thirteen at the time, flashed back to one of their birthdays, and a trip home from purchasing ice cream. A fire truck and police cars flashed red lights in Shannah's driveway. The boys waited at home while their parents went to a neighbor's house to inquire about the emergency. They recalled cowering down with their .22 rifles held tightly in their arms while they waited.

Another young woman, who said she was Shannah's best friend, hoped Campbell would finally die for his crimes. The day Shannah died, the girl had invited her to play after school. But Shannah couldn't. Her mother was at home, sick with a sore throat, and Shannah wanted to get home and make some Jell-O for her mom.

With forty-eight hours left before the execution, scheduled for the first few minutes of Friday morning, May 27, lawyer James Lobsenz worked frantically. For years, litigation had moved at the same speed as the glaciers on Mt. Rainier. To Lobsenz, discouraging court decisions now cascaded down like an avalanche.

Some hope remained in a motion for delay, based on the cruelty of hanging and its potential to cause decapitation, which had reached the top of the stack in the U.S. Supreme Court. Lobsenz also filed a motion with the state supreme court, hand printed by Campbell, arguing that the murders did not warrant a death sentence since the state had no scale for comparing crimes to determine which ones deserved capital punishment. And there might still be a chance, Lobsenz hoped, that the Pardons Board would recommend clemency to Lowry, or that Lowry might exert his own personal principles regarding the death penalty. An additional glimmer of chance popped through the gathering clouds when attorneys for another inmate on death row announced they would ask a federal court to allow videotaping of the execution, if the state elected to hang Campbell, to prove that decapitation was a possibility. Any motion seriously considered by a court, at all levels, might result in a delay.

Lobsenz spoke of the possibility of clemency from the Pardons Board or Governor Lowry. He would present to them a plea for mercy based on Campbell's rocky childhood and teen years. "Society failed him," Lobsenz said, suggesting that Campbell had fallen into a pattern of drug abuse and criminal behavior because he'd been mistreated and neglected. The issue had never been made public before, according to Lobsenz, because Campbell had instructed his attorneys not to bring it up. He didn't want his family humiliated. Furthermore, Campbell now had his own nuclear family. Did the state really want to leave the little son without a father?

The dedicated lawyer felt it his duty to try every legitimate path that might lead to commutation for Campbell to life in prison instead of execution.

On Tuesday, the Pardons Board voted 4-0 against recommending a commutation to life without parole. One member abstained. Now it would rest in Lowry's hands.

The videotaping motion floundered and died.

On Wednesday, the state supreme court rejected Campbell's hand printed motion for a delay, calling it "frivolous."

And the U.S. Supreme Court refused to intervene.

Charles Rodman Campbell faced a date with the gallows, or a choice of lethal injection, in thirty-six hours unless Governor Lowry halted the slow walk to death.

Twenty-eight

Ten men sitting on death row at Walla Walla prison, including Charles Campbell, waited in agonizing suspense for a decision from Governor Mike Lowry.

During his campaign for election, Lowry had successfully skirted the issue of capital punishment, saying he would judge each condemned convict on the individual merits of the case. The electorate knew of his personal opposition to the death penalty, but accepted Lowry's commitment to fairly review each case. Now he faced a difficult decision.

Charles Campbell arrogantly ignored another kind of decision facing him, still refusing to choose between lethal injection or hanging. So executioners at the penitentiary continued to prepare for both methods.

If legal appeals failed, and the execution actually took place, many people figured that Campbell would opt for injection. Surely, it would be the easier way to die. He would lie strapped on a gurney, with a catheter in his arm. Three chemicals would then be delivered into his bloodstream: thiopental sodium, a sleep-inducing barbiturate, pancurium bromide to paralyze the muscles, and potassium chloride, which stops the heart.

The gallows, to be used if Campbell refused to make a choice, stood in place. It had only been seventeen months since Westley Allan Dodd plunged through the trapdoor.

* * *

Lorene Ahlers Iverson had been officially advised by a letter from the Washington Department of Corrections that only one person from her family would be allowed to witness the execution. She'd have to settle for that, for now. Knowing full well that Governor Lowry still could decide to commute the sentence, Lorene, Hilda, and the family traveled again to Walla Walla. They checked into a small hotel a few miles from the gray buttressed stone walls of the prison.

Detective Rick Bart, too, drove to Walla Walla. He hadn't been allotted a witness seat, but wanted to be nearby for the final act.

On Thursday morning, with sixteen hours remaining, barring intervention by Lowry, Ladonna Layton brought Campbell's twelve-year-old son for a visit. They stayed for two hours, during which Campbell gave her his old Ford Torino and fifty dollars in cash. He also asked Ladonna to take care of the burial of his body if the execution took place. She said she would.

Governor Mike Lowry struggled with the heavy decision. Not only had he met with the victims' families, he listened to death penalty opponents, and to Prosecutor Seth Dawson. By midday Thursday, he at long last issued a written statement through an aide. His spokesperson, Anne Fennesy, said that Lowry had completed a "very thorough and exhaustive review."

In Lowry's words, "The legal appeals and judicial reviews of this tragic case have spanned three governors and I am satisfied the process has been comprehensive. I have completed my review and have decided that in accordance with my responsibilities as governor, I should not intervene to stop the execution of Charles Campbell."

The final barrier had fallen.

* * *

In a quiet church outside the prison walls, on a warm Thursday evening, May 26, 1994, the victims' families gathered. Lorene took a pew seat and tried to organize her thoughts. She'd been to Walla Walla before, and had seen the demonstrators, both for and against the death penalty, and wished that such spectacles weren't part of the proceedings. All Lorene wanted was the closure and assurance that Campbell would never kill again. Her thoughts flashed back to the endless days of fear. "There was probably never a day," she would recall, "when I'd walk into my garage, or open my car door, or open the door to my house, and not fear being attacked like Renae was, and Shannah, or Barbara."

Coming to terms with her reasons for wanting to witness Campbell's death hadn't been easy for Lorene. Watching a man die held no attraction for her. And in her heart, Lorene didn't think she wanted revenge. "I just needed to know that he would never harm anyone else." She had seen the grisly crime scene photos depicting the savage cruelty Campbell had inflicted. They'd branded on Lorene's mind exactly what he was capable of doing. He should never, never, have the opportunity to exercise that capability again. Campbell's death would be the only absolute guarantee that she could put the fears to a final rest for herself, and for her family.

A separate concern crept into Lorene's thoughts. She could hear again the stern voice of Judge Britt cautioning everyone in the gallery that he would allow no display of emotions by anyone in the courtroom. If gallery observers felt the need to cry, groan, or express anger, they must step out into the hallway. Lorene and Hilda had forced themselves to bottle up the fury, tears, and sadness, and to conceal the hurt. Through endless subsequent appeals by Campbell, they'd heard him complain about his problems and treatment, and they'd kept the masks of impassiveness, hiding the turmoil inside. Now, just one more time, Lorene would wear the mask.

Sitting in the little church, Lorene heard voices offering reassurance, worrying about her strength to withstand this ordeal, and giving advice. One voice made a suggestion that seemed to make a lot of sense. Try to focus on something.

A driver announced that the van taking witnesses into the prison would leave in about two minutes. Startled, Lorene felt the first sensations of panic. *I need to focus. What am I going to focus on?* Maybe pictures of Renae and Shannah would help. She could just hold onto them, something just to feel in her hands, and to focus on. Lorene carried an assortment of photos in her purse, but had been told that she could take nothing into the witness gallery, not even a purse. If she could just hold a couple of photos, no one would notice. She began to rummage through her purse, hands shaking, trying to hurry, and withdrew an old snapshot of Renae and her father back on the farm. But she couldn't find one of Shannah. Her anxiety tautened.

From out of the mental fog that surrounded her, Lorene heard a warm, familiar voice. Rick Bart asked, "What are you looking for?"

"I need some pictures to focus on—" Lorene's voice faltered, and sounded higher than usual. "—photos of Daddy—and Shannah, and Renae."

Gentle and comforting, Bart said, "You need pictures? I've got pictures." With a reassuring smile, he reached for his billfold, flipped through it, and pulled out a photo of himself and his two young daughters. He placed the little picture in her hand, and with it, the gift of his strength and dignity. As she stood Bart gave her a little hug and said, "Go in there for me, too."

Lorene would later say, with a shaking voice and moist eyes, "He probably doesn't realize what that meant to me or how important that statement was."

She rushed to the van, and during the ride in, looked at the photos she held. *These are the ones I have to focus on. These are my strength.* A revelation settled into her mind, like a soothing warm spring breeze. "Yes, I need to be there for myself, but I also need to be there for many others." She needed to be there for all the people who had worked on the case, the detectives, the lawyers, and the jurors, because without them, justice would never have been realized. She needed to be there for the friends and families of the three victims, and the courageous witnesses who had overcome fear to testify. And she needed to be there for thousands of people had been affected by Campbell's crimes, both directly, like the families, and indirectly, like the people who became frightened and mistrustful after they learned of the murders.

The rush of enlightenment gave Lorene a sense of comfort and strength. Any doubts about her ability to maintain composure faded away. She would be just fine.

A few minutes before midnight, the group of witnesses filed into a silent, dimly lit room and filled the seventeen chairs. Prosecutor Seth Dawson sat as if at attention, while defender James Lobsenz slumped forward, his forehead cradled despairingly in his hands. Don Hendrickson and his son, Daniel, sat close to Lorene. Each of the trio wore a white carnation with three ribbons extending down, bearing the names Renae, Shannah, and Barbara. Representatives of the Associated Press, the *Seattle Times,* the *Seattle Post-Intelligencer,* KIRO-TV, the *Spokesman Review of Spokane,* the *Walla Walla Union Bulletin,* and other reporters from across the state filled the remaining twelve seats.

The only discomfort Lorene felt came from the stares of reporters. She wondered if they wanted to view the execution or to write about the family members. She didn't want to be part of a public spectacle.

Outside the prison walls, at the floodlit chain link fence gate, the usual small groups of demonstrators lined up for admittance into the perimeter. Security officers maintained a close watch. They methodically searched everyone who came through the gates, including a nun. An elderly man marched, holding up a black sign, one yard square, lettered in white. "IF YOU WERE TO BE THIS KILLER'S NEXT VICTIM, WOULD YOU LET

THIS KILLER LIVE, SO THAT HE COULD KILL YOU?" He told reporters, "I'm definitely for the death penalty. I think this man deserves to die."

Four out of five of the crowd, about 250 people, agreed with him. One group of young men chanted, "Hang him high."

The dissenters carried candles and shed tears. A young woman cried, saying, "I feel helpless. I can't believe we're here to stand outside a prison waiting for someone to die."

Earlier that day, Charles Campbell had been granted "double yard time," that is two hours of time out of his cell to exercise or relax. He chose to use all of it on the telephone with his attorney. Back in his tiny gray cell on death row corridor, Campbell spent some time talking with a chaplain, paced, then dozed fitfully for a few minutes. He declined to order anything special for his last meal, so guards brought him the fare served everyone else that day: fish sticks, green salad, scalloped potatoes, and a cherry desert. It sat untouched on the tray.

Campbell had stubbornly refused to make a choice of execution methods, so the state chose for him. Campbell would hang.

When it came time to move the condemned man to a holding cell near the gallows, about three P.M., he didn't cooperate. A spokesman said the prisoner was "unresponsive to a command to cuff up." Instead, Campbell slumped to the floor, curled into a fetal position, and refused to move. After repeated warnings to stand up and submit to handcuffing or the guards would use pepper spray on him, Campbell remained on the floor. The guards entered the cell, holding containers of the stinging mist, and Campbell finally cooperated. An assistant to the prison superintendent, Mary Christensen, explained, "He did not respond. It (the pepper spray) is a protection for the staff, because if they just walked in there he could just rise up and attack them."

The reason for Campbell's fractious behavior became apparent when guards searched him and his cell. They discovered a four-inch piece of metal apparently being honed into a blade, a four-inch lag bolt, with threads tapering to a sharp point, a two-inch nail, a two-inch screw, and a spring from a ballpoint pen. Some of the contraband had been concealed in the metal work of his bunk, and some of it they found in his body cavities. They didn't say which items were found where. The cell had been searched the previous day, and nothing was found. No one ever explained how he obtained the potential weapons, or tools for suicide.

A few minutes before midnight, guards opened the holding cell to walk Campbell to the gallows. The prisoner, wearing only a bright orange jumpsuit, and slippers with no socks, passively resisted again. A spokesperson later said that Campbell's legs were shaky and he had trouble staying on his feet, but Mary Christensen corrected that "misunderstanding." She said Campbell was conscious but passive. The guards strapped him to a board designed to keep his body rigid, and carried him to the gallows.

Before lifting him to the trapdoor, a guard reached for Campbell's head, to cover the bushy, shoulder-length hair and the face with a black hood. Campbell turned his head to the left, requiring a second effort by the guard to place the hood on him.

During the whole process, Charles Campbell hadn't spoken a word.

In the witness chamber, seventeen people could at first see only the silhouette of a noose through a backlit translucent muslin curtain. The screen covered an upper window, but through a lower window, more details could be viewed below the gallows. At five minutes after midnight, they heard a scraping sound and a human shadow came into view. A voice announced, "Mr. Campbell has declined to give any last words." Reporters understood that the muslin curtain would have opened if Campbell had chosen to speak, but his silence kept the translucent screen in place. Three shadows moved to center stage, over the trapdoor. The slow moving figures resembled the silhouetted puppet shows popular in Thailand.

The placing of the hood confused some of the witnesses. They could easily identify Campbell when they saw the long, bushy hair—the same characteristic that witnesses remembered twelve years ago, and helped Renae identify him in 1976. When Campbell's head moved, forcing the guard into a second effort to slip the hood on, some viewers thought it a feeble resistance by Campbell.

Absolute silence gripped all seventeen witnesses as the noose was slipped over Campbell's head. The only sound was feet shuffling behind the screen. The next sound seemed extraordinarily loud, like a huge fist hitting a leather bag, as the trapdoor opened. Campbell's body plunged into view in the lower window, then abruptly halted, with a slight bounce, at the end of the rope's length.

No sound.

No moans, or screams, or blood.

No gory wounds of sliced flesh and bone.

Only an orange-clad, hooded, sockless body turning in a gentle clockwise motion. In fewer than sixty seconds, someone closed a curtain behind the lower window, sealing off the view.

Don Hendrickson and his son both turned to Lorene, seated behind them, and gently touched her hand.

A red light blinked on a wall phone. Quickly grabbing the handset, an official listened for a moment, then turned to the still-silent seventeen, and said, "The execution of Charles Rodman Campbell by hanging has been completed. The doctor pronounced death at 12:14 A.M."

It was over. For some. For others, it would never end.

Epilogue

Another convict paid for his crimes by hanging on January 25, 1996; this one in Delaware. Billy Bailey shotgunned an elderly couple to death in 1979. Not long after his trial, he scoffed, "I just hope they bought a strong enough rope."

Courage is the keyword in characterizing and remembering Renae Wicklund. John Segelbaum, who prosecuted Campbell in 1976, said, "It moved me, her courage in confronting this guy." Her family also emphasizes her bravery and tenacity when they speak of Renae. Shannah will always be remembered for her innocence and sweetness.

Barbara is revered in memory for her generosity, friendliness, and love of her family. Her daughter, Peggie Hendrickson, expressed the belief that her mother watched the execution in spirit. "I hope this will finally allow her to rest in peace."

Renae Wicklund's home sat empty for several months. It has since been sold and completely remodeled, unrecognizable from the original.

* * *

The old house in which Everett Work Release residents lived has been demolished.

Congress recently considered a proposal to break up the Ninth Circuit Court of Appeal's territory. If it ever happens the state of Washington would no longer fall under their jurisdiction.

Partly because of the Wicklund-Hendrickson murders, the Washington legislature enacted a law requiring the notification of sexual assault victims when the perpetrator is released from prison.

In January, 1995, Lorene Ahlers Iverson spoke to the Washington Legislature in an appeal to limit to five the number of news media representatives allowed to witness an execution, thus making room for more victim's family members and investigating officers. House Bill 1276 is still under consideration. Lorene lives in Jamestown North Dakota, with her husband Jerry Iverson, and four children, not far from her mother, Hilda Ahlers.

Charles Campbell's mother, Betty Lou Campbell, predeceased him, sparing her the pain of seeing her son executed for murder. Oliver Campbell has since avoided publicity.

Don Hendrickson, too, prefers anonymity. He worked for several years with Families and Friends of Missing Persons and Violent Crimes Victims, then retired and moved to another state. That benevolent organization recently celebrated their 20th year. Housed in small north Seattle offices, they continue to provide sorely needed help for bereaved relatives of murder victims or missing persons. Only partially supported by government grants, they need financial contributions. For information, telephone (206) 362-1081.

Lawyers Jim Roche and Eric Lind have left the Snohomish County Prosecutor's Office to practice the legal profession elsewhere.

Detective Joe Ward and Tom Psonka, now a sergeant, continue investigating major crimes for the Snohomish Sheriff's Office.

Robert "Rick" Bart hoped until the last minute that Campbell would explain exactly what happened on that tragic day, April 14, 1982, and why it happened. Bart still regards the Clearview murders as the worst case he's ever handled. After his encounter with a sergeant over premature release of information about the case, he mused about running for sheriff someday. On November 7, 1995, Rick Bart was elected Sheriff of Snohomish County, by an overwhelming majority of seventy-two percent of the voters.

Acknowledgments

Every true crime writer owes a debt of gratitude to scores of people. Without them, the research would be virtually impossible.

Robert "Rick" Bart, Joe Ward, and Joe Belinc generously sat for interviews and shared investigative and emotional insights. Deputy Prosecutor Aaron "Seth" Fine, and his staff, provided indispensable assistance in researching mountains of documents, with infinite patience and courtesy.

Bobby Costa, Executive Director of Families and Friends of Missing Persons and Violent Crime Victims, shared heartbreaking stories. She and her organization extended their hands to Don Hendrickson, Hilda Ahlers, Lorene Ahlers Iverson, and many others who loved Renae, Shannah, and Barbara, and rescued them from the maelstrom of pain.

Lorene Ahlers Iverson unselfishly gave of her time and resources, reopening emotional wounds, to share her memories, and those of her mother, Hilda Ahlers. We cannot adequately express our gratitude to them.

Susan Crawford, of the Crawford Literary Agency, pulled the project together. Paul Dinas, Editor in Chief of Kensington Publishing Corporation, encouraged the completion of it, and Karen Haas, Consulting Editor, sorted out the text.

Savage Vengeance is a true story. There are no fictional characters or events. Dialogue is recreated from court documents, police records, interviews, and testimony. Some names have been changed to protect the privacy of the individuals involved.

INFORMATIVE—
COMPELLING—
SCINTILLATING—
NON-FICTION FROM PINNACLE TELLS THE TRUTH:

BORN TOO SOON (751, $4.50)
by Elizabeth Mehren
This is the poignant story of Elizabeth's daughter Emily's premature birth. As the parents of one of the 275,000 babies born prematurely each year in this country, she and her husband were plunged into the world of the Neonatal Intensive Care unit. With stunning candor, Elizabeth Mehren relates her gripping story of unshakable faith and hope—and of courage that comes in tiny little packages.

THE PROSTATE PROBLEM (745, $4.50)
by Chet Cunningham
An essential, easy-to-use guide to the treatment and prevention of the illness that's in the headlines. This book explains in clear, practical terms all the facts. Complete with a glossary of medical terms, and a comprehensive list of health organizations and support groups, this illustrated handbook will help men combat prostate disorder and lead longer, healthier lives.

THE ACADEMY AWARDS HANDBOOK (887, $4.50)
An interesting and easy-to-use guide for movie fans everywhere, the book features a year-to-year listing of all the Oscar nominations in every category, all the winners, an expert analysis of who wins and why, a complete index to get information quickly, and even a 99% foolproof method to pick this year's winners!

WHAT WAS HOT (894, $4.50)
by Julian Biddle
Journey through 40 years of the trends and fads, famous and infamous figures, and momentous milestones in American history. From hoola hoops to rap music, greasers to yuppies, Elvis to Madonna—it's all here, trivia for all ages. An entertaining and evocative overview of the milestones in America from the 1950's to the 1990's!

Available wherever paperbacks are sold, or order direct from the Publisher. Send cover price plus 50¢ per copy for mailing and handling to Penguin USA, P.O. Box 999, c/o Dept. 17109, Bergenfield, NJ 07621. Residents of New York and Tennessee must include sales tax. DO NOT SEND CASH.